Connexions

Connexions

Histories of Race and Sex
in North America

Edited by
**JENNIFER BRIER, JIM DOWNS,
AND JENNIFER L. MORGAN**

UNIVERSITY OF ILLINOIS PRESS
Urbana, Chicago, and Springfield

Cataloging data available from the Library of Congress
ISBN 978-0-252-04039-9 (hardcover)
ISBN 978-0-252-08187-3 (paperback)
ISBN 978-0-252-09881-9 (e-book)

For Stephanie M. H. Camp, 1967–2014
Colleague, Mentor, and Friend

Contents

Connexions

Introduction

JENNIFER BRIER, JIM DOWNS, AND JENNIFER L. MORGAN

Beginning in the late eighteenth century, the spelling of the word *connection* with an *x* instead of *ct* indicated that the subject at hand was illicit sex. In his 1791 biography of the famous literary figure, Samuel Johnson, James Boswell wrote, "The Earl Rivers, on account of a criminal connexion with whom, Lady Macclesfield is said to have been divorced from her husband." In this case, connexion implies a "sexual relation or intercourse; a liaison."[1] The term's negative connotation also found use in medical accounts of sex. John Abernethy, an English surgeon, employed *connexion* twice in his medical writings. His first reference appeared in 1804 in "Surgical Observations, Containing a Classification of Tumours," when he wrote, "He had had no connexion with any other woman." The second reference appeared in 1810 in his published writings on diseases resembling syphilis: "A gentleman was connected with a female . . . and derived from such connexion several . . . sores."[2]

In nineteenth-century legal discourse, petitioners filing for a divorce often used the term *connexion* in order to describe their spouse's infidelity. Connexions did not mean just adultery, however; it also connoted illicit racial liaisons, namely, intercourse between whites and enslaved people. In West Baton Rouge, Louisiana, in 1826, Margaret Constance Richard sought a divorce from her husband on the grounds that he had tried to kill her and then defamed her character, accusing her of having sex with enslaved men. According to the court transcript, he called her a "damned bitch" and a whore, and accused "her of sleeping with negroes, meaning thereby that [the] petitioner had been guilty of having criminal connexion with negroes."[3] Almost twenty years later, in Sumter, Alabama, Catherine Underwood sought a divorce from her husband because he had "commenced an 'adulterous connexion' with a female slave he had purchased."[4] Additionally, during the Civil War, a surgeon for the Union Army described having to treat a military captain for "venereal warts" because of his "licentious" behavior and "his connexions with abandoned women."[5] The unspoken interplay between race and sexuality embedded in the term evoked something out of bounds, something that gestured toward the spaces where various forms of behavior were rendered illicit.

While the term *connexion* fell out of parlance during the twentieth century, it remerged in 2003, when Tim Gill, a gay rights activist and computer scientist, founded Connexion.org as a forum to promote gay activism. Despite Gill's political intentions, gay men were more taken by the *x* at the word's center and used the site as a place to post shirtless photographs and rank each other based on their sexual appeal, resurrecting the sexual meaning of the term *connexion*, this time with an unknown racial politics.[6] The response to the site suggested that the *x* again indicated the presence of multiplicities—of desire, of the illicit, and of complex interactions.

When we found the word *connexion*, it resonated for us etymologically and because we had come to our own work deeply engaged with intersectionality, both theoretically and spatially. The *x* immediately functioned as a metonym for both sex and its intersection (think *x* marks the spot) with race. While it would be impossible to fully detail the long and complicated history of intersectional feminist analysis here, we want to call attention to some of the most important intellectual and political changes taking place in the fields of women's and gender history, as well as to gesture toward the more interdisciplinary formations of critical ethnic, gender, and sexuality studies that drove our desire to collectively imagine how attention to connexion could help us do the kind of work we wanted to do.

The rhetorical effort to situate race and sexuality can be traced to the groundbreaking writing in the 1970s and 1980s by women of color, who conceptualized theoretical and political frameworks to bring race, sexuality, and gender together. Classic anthologies such as *This Bridge Called My Back* and *All the Women Are White, All the Men Are Black, but Some of Us Are Brave* articulated how sexism, racism, homophobia, classism, and other forms of discrimination coalesced and oppressed women and lesbians of color.[7] Women of color could not find refuge in patriarchy as men of color allegedly could, nor could they find shelter in whiteness in ways that white feminists could. Instead, they revealed the suffocating oppression that results from being marginalized within the marginalized and the way that structural inequalities magnify one another. The articulation of those claims, in documents like the Combahee River Collective Statement, centered the writers as racialized, gendered, and sexual subjects. By telling their personal stories, disclosing their experiences, and expressing their politics, they embodied the connexion between race and sexuality.[8]

Thirty years after the publication of *Borderlands/La Frontera* and *Sister Outsider*, we continue to embrace the political imperatives of these manifestos but feel a need to examine the deep history of how racial subjugation feeds sexual normativity as well as how sexual and racial subjects enact liberating claims that can fall short of liberation even as they bring into being imaginative ideas about social, political, and cultural change. In conversations that span historical periods and subject matters, we see the potential for our own collective intervention to offer historical grounding to work that has more often *theorized* the intersection between race and sexuality. Further, while we are cognizant of the significant inroads made in the histories of race and sex in particular historical moments, we believe that *Connexions* offers one attempt to begin reimagining the larger arc of American history by making race and sexuality the focus.

It was in this generative intellectual and interdisciplinary context that we began to imagine what three historians, Jennifer Brier, Michele Mitchell, and Jennifer L. Morgan, working in three different time periods, could do together. Our collaboration began at the Berkshire Conference of Women Historians in 2004–5, where our conversations returned again and again to the state of the fields of gender history, history of sexuality, and the history of race and slavery. This not only helped us frame the topic at the intersection of our historical research but also helped us articulate why we needed to span such a long time frame, attending to change over time from colonial America to the turn of the twentieth and twenty-first centuries.

The volume started to come into form through a conference organized by Brier, Mitchell, and Morgan held at New York University in November 2008. This conference was conceived as a way to formalize conversations that bridged histories of race and sex in the United States over three hundred years, for we knew that bringing together scholars from a range of historical periods would highlight our conviction that broad histories of race and sexuality might offer unique theoretical insights and collective conclusions. It was also at this conference that Jim Downs came to play an integral role in the project: first as a contributor to the volume, then as an editor who refused to let us scrap the project when our lives intervened, making it too difficult for the three original conveners to complete the project. *Connexions*, as it now appears, evokes both the historically grounded sexual connotation of the term *connexion* and pushes on its historical etymology to insist that racial and sexual practices, economies, and ideologies are always and already deeply connected even as they change over time. It asks what the American past looks like when race and sexuality become the animating questions that dictate our course of study? *Connexions* seeks to investigate the ways that race and sex intersect, overlap, and inform each other throughout U.S. history, paying particular attention to how these developments unfolded over three centuries.

The work collected here is engaged in an explicit and implicit conversation with the fields of histories of feminism and of women of color, particularly Chicanas and

African American women, all of which have grown exponentially in the last several decades. We have been inspired by revisions to the "wave" model of the history of feminism that have insisted that we replace the image of feminist tidal waves with ones that center radio waves that have, according to historian Nancy Hewitt, "different lengths and frequencies."[9] This new model for understanding feminist history centers race, class, and sexuality in the narrative and as such exemplifies how we have tried to move forward here. It also fundamentally changes what periodization looks like, extending historical paths back in time at the same time that it widens the entry points to mark the scope of social and political movements.[10]

Because we understand our work as moving beyond the discipline of history, we have also benefited from engagement with queer studies, as a field, especially as it has witnessed the growth of queer-of-color critique since the turn of the twenty-first century. That incredibly perceptive and powerful work has forcefully made the case for how queer studies, like women's and gender studies before it, has been structured around whiteness and why attention to white supremacy must be at the center of investigations into heteropatriarchy. By focusing on the seemingly concomitant evolution of sexualized race and racialized sexuality, scholars such as Rod Ferguson, E. Patrick Johnson, Juana María Rodríguez, and the late José Muñoz, to name a few, have provided historians with new models to understand the archive and its productions. Whether in the form of Johnson's coining the term "Quare Studies" to mark his grandmother's North Carolina dialect as naming a kind of black queer identity, or Muñoz's notion of disidentification that uses performance theory to understand complicated cultural practices by queers of color, we found theoretical frameworks here that advanced our historical efforts.[11]

Unfortunately, in the eyes of more traditionally trained historians, engagement with literature that seems outside the bounds of U.S. social and political history has positioned us on the outskirts of our fields. Our interdisciplinary openness can sometimes be used against us, even as many of us have attended to some of the most traditional forms of archival research and social history methodology in constructing our work. When emerging historians use theory to engage race and sexuality as critical subjects of inquiry, some traditional historians question how critical theory can be incorporated within historical methodology. Leaving aside the fact that part of what these critically minded, often theoretically orientated, historians seek to do is to question the very construction and meaning of the archive, a larger problem develops, namely, that anyone who does not subscribe to a mid-twentieth-century notion of social history practice is better situated in an interdisciplinary field. The mainstream historical profession's disavowal of new theoretical approaches that race and sexuality historians posit implicitly belies the tradition in which social history emerged almost a century ago. The Annalists pioneered the basic tenants of social history in the early part of the twentieth century, and the discipline unfolded in tandem with a discussion of historical practice.[12] Unfortunately, with few exceptions, the dialogue between the practice and the theory of social history has ceased within the broader field of U.S. history.

Cultural and literary scholars have also been susceptible to these critiques; yet these stigmas and devaluations have seriously undermined the work of intersectional historians working on race, gender, class, and sexuality. Despite the proliferation of books on race and sexuality, graduate faculty increasingly view this scholarship at best as tangential to the traditional historiography or at worse as alchemy.

New analytic frameworks abound, but they appear to do more to situate race and sexuality as a concern mired in identitarian politics rather than as a strategy for reading the archives of the past. While transnationalism has emerged as a new approach, for example, it is often evoked in the form of truism rather than as a radical intervention. Atlantic history carried with it a promise of treating European, African, and American peoples with analytic equivalence, and yet it continues to skew in the direction of the North Atlantic world most narrowly defined.[13] In studies of the seventeenth and eighteenth century, the neo-imperial turn has moved the field away from the social historical and has increasingly emphasized narrowly defined political and economic history.[14] New work on the histories of slavery and capitalism too have emphasized structures over the lived experiences of the enslaved.[15] The emphasis on capitalism, for example, has unwittingly erased the intervention that women and gender historians have made over the last twenty-five years; emphasizing capitalism as the leading framework to study slavery overlooks the scholarship that many historians of women and gender engaged to show how slavery could not be defined monolithically and how it produced gendered asymmetries, making the lived and labored experience of men and women quite different. The capitalist framework also elides the scholarly efforts of women and gender historians who have emphasized the nuances and details of enslaved people that are often lost in the efforts by historians to chronicle the larger forces shaping the institution of slavery. We find ourselves increasingly concerned that the inroads made in the 1960s and 1970s have left our efforts and interventions fragmented rather than conne"x"ed.

Our concerns involve not just our scholarship but also our institutional locations. The growth of ethnic and gender studies programs and departments that followed in the wake of social justice movements of the post-1960s era have often suffered deeply from institutional neglect. Deprived of the financial and intellectual support required to maintain vibrant intellectual and pedagogical programs during the onslaught of neoliberal institutional politics, these spaces have suffered. Yet many of these interdisciplinary departments are neither the solution nor the intellectual utopia that some may have imagined. Women's studies and gender studies remain segregated from African American, Africana, and ethnic studies programs. When there is an intellectual crossover between these fields, scholars of race and ethnicity are marginal in women's studies programs, and race tends to trump gender in African American studies programs. While these programs share similar ideological commitments, intellectual divisions and university debates have been tearing them apart internally. Further compounding these challenges, African Americanists struggle to more fully connect to all parts of the diaspora and have been over the last few decades working assiduously with Latin Americanists and Africanists to broaden their intellectual reach. Meanwhile, within many traditionally defined women's studies programs, there remains the unresolved debate between gender history and women's history, which has left the history of sexuality straddling this divide. Furthermore, historians of sexuality wage their own wars within their fields—splits have developed between queer theorists and queer historians, between gay and lesbian history and the emerging field of trans-history. For many of the contributors to this volume, these issues represent real concerns as some are in traditional history departments, others are in gender studies programs, and a few are in places where cross-interdisciplinary collaboration between race and sexuality studies are encouraged. Evidence of these diverse and competing scholarly influences can be found in the notes accompanying the essays collected in this book.

Historians of sexuality and race can help all historians think more carefully about the meaning and definition of evidence as well as the political forces that led to the construction of the archive. Since these historians investigate the ellipses in sources, the utterances in the public record, and the silences within documents, their scholarship represents a meditation on the very meaning of evidence as well as a vital interrogation of historical practice. Additionally, due to both the political forces that inspire their work and the need to draw on other disciplinary methods, their scholarship also exemplifies the objectives of interdisciplinarity. Over the last two decades, for example, historians of race and sexuality have benefited enormously from the scholarship produced by anthropologists, sociologists, economists, and literary and legal scholars.[16]

Historians are only beginning to attend to the intersections of race and sexuality.[17] Historical studies continue to be organized primarily on one or another identitarian concern, despite the widespread understanding of the role of intersectional subject positions. In *Connexions*, we offer ruminations on particular historical moments in order both to understand our inspirational texts of the 1970s and 1980s and to emphasize the importance of thinking historically about race and sexuality as constitutive forces that have critically informed the United States since its founding.

Connexions opens with essays that ask us to consider broadly how race and sex frame historical inquiries. It then moves to essays that explore questions of beauty and desire and of subjectivities in specific times and spaces. We cast a wide temporal net in order to reveal the connexions between race and sex that emanate across time and space. The essays, in turn, push at the very boundaries of American historiography and challenge the traditional meaning of evidence, methodology, and historical practice. The authors of the following essays use their scholarship both to introduce neglected subjects into the lexicon of American historiography and to rethink the historian's craft. In particular, scholars in this volume raise a number of questions from the construction of the archive to the use of critical theory. That said, the spirit of this volume aims more to raise questions and to initiate a broader discussion across the discipline than to assert final conclusions. The value of an edited anthology is that it allows for a wide array of voices, from scholars whose work is at different stages, to come together under a single title. We have taken full advantage of that implicit license. Some of the essays grew out of forthcoming manuscripts; some developed from the "Connexions" symposium hosted at New York University in 2008; a handful have been solicited to fill in the temporal parameters of the volume; and, last, a few are republished from academic journals but had their start at the NYU conference.

We have arranged *Connexions* thematically in order to best capture the themes that unite the various essays. In our first section, "Deep Connections," the authors probe the implications of examining race and sexuality together, both in terms of constructing a narrative about the past as well as evaluating the tools of historical practice. Jim Downs investigates the question of same-sex desire, intimacy, and violence among enslaved men in the eighteenth and nineteenth centuries and rethinks the definition and meaning of evidence. Julian B. Carter interrogates how "whiteness" shaped the ways in which the early chroniclers of gay and lesbian history considered the relationship between race and sex. He argues that many of these early historians examined the experiences of people of color but often failed to see how their "whiteness" shaped their investigation of the past. In keeping with the broader methodological questions that this volume raises, Carter also traces the decline of experimental models of historical analysis that the first generation of queer historians developed as well as the loss of a particular revolutionary fervor that defined the field.

Similar to Carter's efforts to consider the ways in which race influenced the writing of the first generation of queer historiography, Marc Stein questions how race influenced the Supreme Court's decisions on cases that pertain to sex, marriage, and reproduction during the height of the sexual revolution. He conversely asks what the effect would be of making sex and reproduction more central to cases that deal with race. His essay fleshes out one of the major themes of the volume, namely, what happens when race and sexuality become the organizing principles in our investigation of the twentieth century.

The next section of the volume turns to the questions of "Beauty and Desire." Within the historiography, the intersection of race and sexuality often produces scholarly assessments of violence, degradation, and oppression. While we recognize those conclusions as critical and useful analyses, the historians in this section uncover new evidence that reveal an interpretation about beauty and desire that animated the nexus of race and sexuality. Sharon Block investigates how physical descriptions of bodies shaped understandings of race and sexuality in the eighteenth century. Moving beyond the literary and rhetorical representation of bodies, Block analyzes over one thousand newspaper advertisements of runaway slaves and servants and soldiers, published between 1750 and 1775, to map how colonial perceptions of bodies imbued historical meanings of sexuality and how colonialists daily constructed and created bodies around them.

Moving into the nineteenth-century, Stephanie M. H. Camp furthers Block's focus on the body by investigating how an aesthetic of sexualized bodies contributed to ideas of racial formation. Camp charts how the emergence of race as a category of analysis remained tethered to questions about beauty and sexuality. Focusing primarily on the nascent field of nineteenth-century racial science, Camp explains how aesthetics formed crucial markers in articulations of racial difference. Ernesto Chávez's essay shifts this discussion into the twentieth century by focusing on the life of the Mexican film star Ramón Novarro; Chavez interrogates how Novarro used his racial identity to mask his homosexuality throughout his forty-year career. By excavating images of and articles about Novarro in print culture, Chávez discovers how Novarro self-fashioned a narrative that obfuscated his sexual orientation and at times coded his sexuality through a complex narrative of self-presentation. His essay highlights many of the integral themes of *Connexions*, namely, the interplay between beauty and desire as well as the tension between subjectivity and the archive.

The final section of the book explores the meaning of subjectivity within the context of race and sexuality, turning to how various historical actors over the course of four centuries navigated this terrain. In an effort to uncover these histories, this section also explores the politics surrounding the construction of the archive and the meaning of historical practice. Marisa J. Fuentes tells the story of Rachael Pringle Polgreen, a freedwoman in Barbados who owned a brothel in the late eighteenth century, but whose life can be pieced together only through scraps of evidence; she argues that Polgreen's experiences represent a larger problem of how archives systematically prevent the experiences of African women from being uncovered.

Building on Fuentes's historical analysis of the problems of the archive, Brian Connolly turns his attention to the ways in which nineteenth-century Americans retold the biblical story of the "curse of Ham" as a fantasy to promote the notion of racial purity, which contradicted the social reality of interracial reproductive sex that prevailed throughout slavery. Connolly argues that nineteenth-century Americans clung to the so-called curse of Ham or curse of Canaan as a religious fantasy that attempted to negate interracial sex as foundational to the origins of race and instead propagated a fantasy about racial purity.

Similar to Connolly, who examines a canonical story and how it produced racial and sexual meaning, Wanda S. Pillow raises the question of what becomes visible when we center gender, race, colonialism, and sex as the animating forces in the telling of Lewis and Clark's famous expedition. Pillow narrates the fateful journey from the perspective of Sacajawea, the Indian woman, and York, the enslaved man. In taking this approach, she also scrutinizes the construction of the archive, considering how the representation of York and Sacajawea in the sources illustrates a case of both invisibility and hypervisibility.

In the twentieth century, the motif of invisibility and hypervisibility continues to haunt the archive. In an essay that forecasts the rise of civil rights activism in the mid–twentieth century, Susan K. Cahn examines how the discourse of democracy led female students at black, white, co-ed, and single-sex colleges to agitate against rules and regulations that solidified heterosexual norms. She uncovers a moment in the early twentieth century when female students engaged in faux marriage ceremonies, in which women played the roles of groom, bride, bridesmaids, and presiding minister in full drag. Cahn charts how these traditions faded in the postwar period, but she perceptively argues that in this transition, openings emerged to define new racial and sexual relations. Heterosexuality became a concerted, deliberate choice that did not naturally grow from various southern traditions. This transition, according to Cahn, also paved the way for increased women's activism in the South.

Shifting gears from actions to images, Leisa D. Meyer turns to representations of women's sexuality in twentieth-century black print culture. Like many of the scholars in this anthology, Meyer raises questions about how black women's subjectivity can be excavated from the archive. Her essay exemplifies both an effort to chart mid-twentieth-century representations of race and sex as well as a to reflect on the challenges of uncovering subjectivity in the public record, even when the archive seems to be replete with bountiful evidence.

In the final essay in the volume, Deborah Gray White investigates how the gay community marginalized black people and then how the black community marginalized gay people of color. White turns her attention to the Million Man (1995) and Million Woman (1997) marches and the 1993 and 2000 LGBTQ marches and examines how people whose lives straddle both these intersections have sought community and comfort. White's analysis of their search for both community and political recognition reveals many of the key tensions of this book; her actors embody the intersections of race and sex that inform the analytical work found in this volume. While the book begins with Downs's essay on the questionable subjectivity of race and sex among enslaved people in the eighteenth and nineteenth centuries, White's essay probes the political implications of this subjectivity in the late twentieth century.

Connexions ultimately aims to raise more questions than answers about the intersection of race and sexuality. It seeks to contribute to a scholarly discussion that centers race and sexuality as driving forces of historical research that can ultimately lead to new interpretations of the past as well as more-rigorous evaluations of historical practice. Finally, it serves as an invitation and a provocation to mobilize connexions in our work across the various time periods of the American past. Those connexions will serve us well as we continue to engage the archive and work to construct a complicated understanding of the past and its reach into our present.

Notes

1. *Oxford English Dictionary*, 2nd ed., 20 vols. (Oxford: Oxford University Press, 1989).
2. *Oxford English Dictionary*.
3. Petition 20882632, Race and Slavery Petitions Project, https://library.uncg.edu/slavery/petitions/details.aspx?pid=7421 (accessed January 21, 2016).
4. Petition 20184306, Race and Slavery Petitions Project, https://library.uncg.edu/slavery/petitions/details.aspx?pid=3097 (accessed January 21, 2016).
5. William Mervale Smith and Thomas P. Lowry, *Swamp Doctor: The Diary of a Union Surgeon in the Virginia and North Carolina Marshes* (Mechanicsburg, Penn.: Stackpole Books, 2001).
6. In 2011, the site closed due in part to the explosion of gay social media and the creation a number of other competing sites.
7. The most widely read anthologies are Cherríe Moraga and Gloria Anzaldúa, eds., *This Bridge Called My Back: Writings by Radical Women of Color* (New York: Kitchen Table, Women of Color Press, 1983); Gloria T. Hull, Patricia Bell-Scott, and Barbara Smith, eds., *All the Women Are White, All the Blacks Are Men, but Some of Us Are Brave: Black Women's Studies* (Old Westbury, N.Y.: Feminist Press, 1982); Barbara Smith, ed., *Home Girls: A Black Feminist Anthology* (New Brunswick, N.J.: Rutgers University Press, 2000); and Gloria Anzaldúa, ed., *Making Face, Making Soul/Haciendos Caras: Creative and Critical Perspectives by Feminists of Color* (San Francisco: Aunt Lute, 1990). The work of Gloria Anzaldúa, Audre Lorde, and Barbara Smith served as particular inspiration, most notably Anzaldúa's *Borderlands/La Frontera: The New Mestiza* (San Francisco: Aunt Lute, 1987); Lorde's *Sister Outsider: Essays*

and Speeches (Berkeley, Calif.: Crossing Press, 1984); and the anthology of Smith's writing, Alethia Jones and Virginia Eubanks, eds., *Ain't Gonna Let Nobody Turn Me Around: Forty Years of Movement Building with Barbara Smith* (Albany: State University of New York Press, 2014). Beyond these publications that collected poetry, prose, fiction, and nonfiction, scholarly collections that centered feminists of color also found circulation by the early 1990s: again the list is too long, but we want to note the influence of Chandra Talpade Mohanty, Ann Russo, and Lourdes Torres, eds., *Third World Women and the Politics of Feminism* (Bloomington: Indiana University Press, 1991).

8. The Combahee River Collective Statement has been reprinted in various locations. See Estelle B. Freedman, ed., *The Essential Feminist Reader* (New York: Modern Library, 2007). For a historical account of black feminism in the postwar era, see Kimberly Springer, *Living for the Revolution: Black Feminist Organizations, 1968–1990* (Durham, N.C.: Duke University Press, 2005); and Jones and Eubanks, eds., *Ain't Gonna Let Nobody Turn Me Around*.

9. Nancy A. Hewitt, "Introduction," in *No Permanent Waves: Recasting Histories of U.S. Feminism*, ed. Nancy Hewitt (New Brunswick, N.J.: Rutgers University Press, 2010), 8.

10. For examples beyond the Hewitt anthology, which has collected a wide range of insightful essays, see Benita Roth, *Separate Roads to Feminism: Black, Chicana, and White Feminist Movements in America's Second Wave* (New York: Cambridge University Press, 2003); Marcia M. Gallo, *Different Daughters: A History of the Daughters of Bilitis and the Rise of the Lesbian Rights Movement* (New York: Carrol and Graf, 2006); Springer, *Living for the Revolution*.

11. Queer-of-color critique has grown significantly in the last decade and a half. For work that focuses on the U.S. racial and sexual formations, see, for example, Roderick A. Ferguson, *Aberrations in Black: Toward a Queer of Color Critique* (Minneapolis: University of Minnesota Press, 2004); E. Patrick Johnson and Mae G. Henderson, eds., *Black Queer Studies: A Critical Anthology* (Durham, N.C.: Duke University Press, 2005); José Esteban Muñoz, *Disidentifications: Queers of Color and Performance Politics* (Minneapolis: University of Minnesota Press, 1999); Muñoz, *Cruising Utopia: The Then and There of Queer Futurity* (New York: New York University Press, 2009); Juana María Rodríguez, *Queer Latinidad: Identity Practices, Discursive Spaces* (New York: New York University Press, 2003); Rodríguez *Sexual Futures, Queer Gestures, and Other Latina Longings* (New York: New York University Press, 2014); Kwame Holmes, "What's the Tea: Gossip and the Production of Black Gay Social History," *Radical History Review*, no. 122 (May 2015): 55–69.

12. French historian Marc Bloch, one of the leading architects of the Annales School, penned *The Historian's Craft* (New York: Knopf, 1953), which ruminated on these issues. His book was followed by other well-read meditations such as British historian E. H. Carr's *What Is History?* (New York: Random House, 1961).

13. Alison Games, "Atlantic History: Definitions, Challenges, and Opportunities," *American Historical Review* 111, no. 3 (2006): 741–57.

14. James Sidbury and Jorge Cañizares-Esguerra, "Mapping Ethnogenesis in the Early Modern Atlantic," *William and Mary Quarterly* 68, no. 2 (2011): 181–208.

15. Walter Johnson, *River of Dark Dreams: Slavery and Empire in the Cotton Kingdom* (Cambridge, Mass.: Harvard University Press, 2013); Joshua Rothman, *Flush Times and Fevered*

Dreams: A Story of Capitalism and Slavery in the Age of Jackson (Athens: University of Georgia Press, 2014); Edward Baptist, *The Half Has Never Been Told: Slavery and the Making of American Capitalism* (New York: Basic Books, 2014).

16. Historians of the colonial period in the Atlantic world, for example, have most effectively revealed how the investigation of the past has also led to a simultaneous meditation on the definition of evidence and the meaning of the archive. Saidiya Hartman, "Venus in Two Acts," *Small Axe* 12, no. 2 (June 2008): 1–14; Jennifer L. Morgan, "Why I Write," in *Why We Write: The Politics and Practice of Writing for Social Change*, ed. Jim Downs, 39–48 (New York: Routledge, 2006); Stephanie Smallwood, *Saltwater Slavery: A Middle Passage from Africa to American Diaspora* (Cambridge, Mass.: Harvard University Press, 2007).

17. For some historians and historical thinkers who engage the intersection of race and sexuality, see Anne McClintock, *Imperial Leather: Race, Gender and Sexuality in the Colonial Contest* (New York: Routledge, 1995); Kevin Mumford, *Interzones: Black/White Sex Districts in Chicago and New York in the Early Twentieth Century* (New York: Columbia University Press, 1997); Martha Hodes, *White Women, Black Men: Illicit Sex in the 19th Century South* (New Haven: Yale University Press, 1999); Siobhan Somerville, *Queering the Color Line: Race and the Invention of Homosexuality in American Culture* (Durham, N.C.: Duke University Press, 2000); Laura Briggs, *Reproducing Empire: Race, Sex, Science, and U.S. Imperialism in Puerto Rico* (Berkeley: University of California Press, 2002); Joanne Nagel, *Race, Ethnicity and Sexuality: Intimate Intersections, Forbidden Frontiers* (New York: Oxford, 2003); Joshua Rothman, *Notorious in the Neighborhood: Sex and Family across the Color Line in Virginia, 1787–1861* (Chapel Hill: University of North Carolina Press, 2003); Alecia P. Long, *The Great Southern Babylon: Sex, Race, and Respectability in New Orleans, 1865–1920* (Baton Rouge: Louisiana State University Press, 2004); Chad Heap, *Slumming: Sexual and Racial Encounter in American Nightlife, 1885–1940* (Chicago: University of Chicago Press, 2009); Jennifer Spear, *Race, Sex, and Social Order in Early New Orleans* (Baltimore: Johns Hopkins University Press, 2009); Pablo Mitchell, *West of Sex: Making Mexican America, 1900–1930* (Chicago: University of Chicago Press, 2012); Nayan Shah, *Stranger Intimacy: Contesting Race, Sexuality, and the Law in the North American West* (Berkeley: University of California Press, 2012).

PART 1

Deep Connections

CHAPTER 1

With Only a Trace

Same-Sex Sexual Desire and Violence on Slave Plantations, 1607–1865

JIM DOWNS

They say, "Love comes when you least expect it." And that's when I found him. He was in a hospital bed in Alexandria, Virginia, a few miles away from the nation's capital. It was October 1865. The American Civil War had been over for about six months, and most of Virginia remained in a state of utter chaos. Schools had been turned into hospitals, empty plots of land converted into burial grounds, and the famous slave auction houses of the 1850s, known as slave pens, became the final destination for newly freed people hoping to make it to the North.

Once enslaved, he became free when he donned a Union uniform and marched through the rubble of the Virginia battlefields.[1] What brought him to the "colored hospital" was neither injury inflicted from battle nor a sickness contracted from the unhealthy climes of the Union camps but rather "a sickness" that he caught from waiting for "an officer in the navy."

His story of waiting for an officer made its way into the pages of the northern benevolent society newspaper the *Freedmen's Record*.[2] A representative from the New England Freedmen's Aid Society traveled to the South to inspect and report on the status of rebuilding the South. Since the start of the war, abolitionists donated money, clothes, and food to support freed slaves. Their efforts led to the construction of schools, hospitals, and shelters for newly freed people, and periodically members of these organizations visited the South in order to highlight the progress of emancipation. In their evaluations of the former bondspeople, they often wrote glowing reports of the desire of formerly enslaved people to learn to read, to earn a fair wage, and to own a plot of land.

What is so striking about the story of the black Union solider waiting for the naval officer is that it departs from the uplifting portrayal of ex-slaves that typically appeared in the pages of the *Freedmen's Record*. The writer describes the Union solider as a "poor, stupid, and almost loathsome-looking youth . . . He appeared to be a revolting mass of disease." This description conforms to representations of black people that appeared in Confederate and southern periodicals like *DeBow's Review*, not in a northern publication that prided itself on the progress and promise of emancipation. More importantly, erstwhile abolitionists often sympathized with the plight of formerly enslaved people who were stuck in unsanitary hospitals, overcrowded refugee camps, and former slave pens; former abolitionists did not criticize them for inhabiting these places but instead blamed the federal government for not providing them with adequate shelter. Therefore, casting the black solider as "loathsome" contradicts the mission of this particular publication.

Nineteenth-century Americans used the term *loathsome* to refer to acts that were considered "hateful, distasteful, odious, repulsive, and shocking."[3] People in the nineteenth century also used the term *loathsome* when describing ghastly health conditions, which does accord with the writer's description that the man appeared as a "revolting mass of disease."

Why would a northern writer and reformer committed to the progress of black people employ such disdainful language? Simply because the soldier got sick? Rather, it seems that the writer senses a relationship between the two men that he considers "loathsome." According to the journalist in the *Freedmen's Record*, the black youth became sick because he waited for the officer. In the context of war, male companionship was paramount to the success of the military campaign and common throughout the period. Yet the writer does not portray the sick soldier as waiting for a friend or compatriot but rather indicts the man for his decision to wait for the sailor to arrive on the dock. The tone of the description is distain, not praise or even sympathy for the men who had served in the Union Army.

A closer examination of the term *loathsome* reveals that nineteenth-century Americans often employed it as a code word that signaled aberrant sexual behavior. During the nineteenth century, many people used coded rhetoric or concealed idioms to talk about sex; sexual experiences were not directly stated but often alluded to. Given this cultural practice, many nineteenth-century Americans—both black and white—drew on a widely accepted nomenclature. For example, Harriet Jacobs, author of the famous slave narrative *Incidents in the Life of a Slave Girl*, never directly uses the term *rape* throughout her autobiography despite the fact that the entire objective of the book was to alert northern women readers about the sexual abuses committed against enslaved women in the plantation South. She instead writes, "No pen can give an adequate description of the all-pervading corruption produced by slavery. The slave girl is reared in an atmosphere of licentiousness and fear. The lash and the foul talk of her master and his sons are her teachers. When she is fourteen or fifteen, her owner, or his sons, or the overseer, or perhaps all of them, begin to bribe her with presents. If these fail to accomplish their purpose, she is whipped or starved into submission to their will."[4]

By not directly stating the word *rape* but alluding to it, Jacobs's book reveals two important rhetorical strategies of nineteenth-century America that help to uncover the hidden history of sexuality. First, she reveals the rhetorical convention that many did not speak or write about sex in direct, clear language. Second, her writing reveals how the use of adjectives often became the way in which many during the nineteenth century coded sexual activity. She describes the plantation as an "atmosphere of licentiousness" and describes the language of her master as "foul talk." Therefore, the process of uncovering the history of sexuality among enslaved people in the antebellum period may not lie in the direct excavation of incidents that illustrate sex but may be found in coded adjectives, modifiers, and phrases employed by those during the period who spelled out sex through the usage of a multilayered parlance.

The adjective *loathsome* seems to exemplify this rhetorical practice. In the preface to Jacobs's autobiography, for instance, Lydia Marie Child, a leading abolitionist, underscores the theme of sexual abuse in Jacobs's book by using the term *loathsome*. Child writes, "No fugitive from slavery shall ever be sent to suffer in that loathsome den of corruption and cruelty."[5] By using the term *loathsome* in the preface, Child telegraphs to antebellum readers the sexual nature of the pages that follow.

Child is not alone in using the term *loathsome* to connote sexual behavior. In the early eighteenth century, John Lawson in his account of his travels to "Carolina" directly articulated the relationship between the term *loathsome* and sexuality when he wrote about Indian sexual practices. He stated, "Although these People are call'd Savages, yet Sodomy is never heard of amongst them, and they are so far from the Practice of that beastly and loathsome Sin, that they have no Name for it in all their Language."[6] Here, Lawson directly draws on the term *loathsome* to describe sodomy, illustrating the ways in which the term was often used in conjunction with aberrant sexual behavior.

Like Lawson, many writers in the eighteenth and nineteenth centuries followed literary conventions of the time that used the term *loathsome* to evoke sexual behavior, practices, or desires that they found to be aberrant. In one of the most widely read fictional slave narratives of the nineteenth century, *Autobiography of a Female Slave*, Martha Griffith Browne, like Child, used the term *loathsome* to describe a master sexually threatening the female protagonist. Browne writes,

> "You is a bright-colored mulatto. I must have you."
> "Heavens! I hope not," was my half-uttered expression, as I turned away, for I had caught the meaning of that lascivious eye, and shrank from the threatened danger.

> Though I had been cruelly treated, yet had I been allowed to retain my person invio-
> late; and I would rather, a thousand-fold, have endured the brutality of Mr. Peterkin,
> than those loathsome looks which I felt betokened ruin.[7]

Describing the threat of sexual violence, Browne uses the term *loathsome* in an effort to signal to the reader that the protagonist could be raped. More to the point,
Browne, similar to the author of the *Freedmen's Record* article, describes the assail-
ant's appearance as "loathsome," indicating how nineteenth-century Americans
relied on code words about appearance to connote sexual desire and behavior.

The idea that the term *loathsome* functioned as a code word that conveyed to
eighteenth- and nineteenth-century American readers aberrant sexual violence
and behavior can also be found in Frederick Douglass's classic slave narrative, *My
Bondage, My Freedom*. In the following scene, Douglass employs *loathsome* in what
could be interpreted as a moment when slaveholders sexually abused enslaved
men. Douglass writes that slaveholders resorted to "cunning tricks" and got enslaved men "deplorably drunk." According to Douglass, slaveholders would make
bets on which slave could "drink more whisky than any other." While this event
could easily be interpreted as yet another example in a long list of atrocities and
violence committed against bondspeople, it is crucial to pay attention to Douglass's choice of words. "The scenes, brought about in this way," Douglass writes,
"were often scandalous and loathsome in the extreme. Whole multitudes might
be stretched out in brutal drunkenness, at once helpless and disgusting."[8]

For Douglass to use the term *disgusting* in relation to his fellow enslaved brethren immediately signals an alarm. In his *Autobiography*, Douglass evinces strong
feelings of camaraderie and love for other enslaved men. "I loved them with a love
stronger than any thing I have ever experienced since," Douglass writes. He further
states, "It is sometimes said that we slaves do not love and confide in each other.
In answer to this assertion, I can say, I never loved any or confided in any people
more than my fellow—slaves."[9] Given this assertion, why would Douglass not feel
sympathy for his brethren who had been tricked and exploited by their master?
Why would he describe them as simultaneously "helpless and disgusting?" What
occurred between those two words? For Douglass not to feel complete empathy for
his fellow slaves but instead to refer to them as "disgusting" suggests that something else was happening.

Clearly, Douglass could be simply referring to the slave master's "cunning tricks"
as disgusting, but his tone sharply shifts in the matter of a few words. He refers to
the enslaved men as "helpless and disgusting." The drunken condition certainly
made the bondsmen "helpless," but what made them "disgusting" as well as "scandalous and loathsome in the extreme?" Indeed, Douglass may have been concerned
with offending the temperance sensibilities of his northern reformer audiences and

therefore referred to their drunkenness as "disgusting." But using *disgusting* along-side *loathsome* and the description of the "multitudes" of men's bodies "stretched out" suggests that this episode might have also portended a chance for slaveholders to sexually abuse enslaved men or, at the very least, pruriently observe their bodies.[10]

Within the historiography, scholars have documented the sexual abuse and rape committed against enslaved women by white men, but few have examined how enslaved men also suffered from sexual violence.[11] In another episode in her autobiography, Harriet Jacobs tells the poignant story of an enslaved man named Luke, whose master kept "a cowhide beside him, and, for the most trivial occurrence, he would order his attendant to bare his back, and kneel beside the couch, while he whipped him until his strength was exhausted. Some days he was not allowed to wear any thing but his shirt, in order to be in readiness to be flogged."[12] Jacobs further describes how the master was entirely dependent on Luke's care, but instead of showing compassion to Luke, the master only increased his demands. Jacobs writes, "As he [the master] lay there on his bed, a mere degraded wreck of manhood, he took into his head the strangest freaks of despotism' and if Luke hesitated to submit to his orders, the constable was immediately sent for. Some of these freaks were of a nature too filthy to be repeated. When I fled from the house of bondage, I left poor Luke still chained to the bedside of this cruel and disgusting wretch."[13]

By using the term *disgusting*, Jacobs, like Douglas, evokes a sexual relationship between the two men. That she writes, "Some of these freaks were of a nature too filthy to be repeated," conforms with the narrative representation of sexuality throughout her autobiography as well as nineteenth-century understandings of same-sex male sexual activity as aberrant, repulsive, and, in this case, violent. Throughout *Incidents*, as many literary scholars have pointed out, Jacobs does not explicitly detail or describe the sexual violence committed by white slaveholders toward enslaved women. Instead, she suggests to her readers that such atrocities were committed, but that she cannot break the antebellum literary conventions and explicitly define or describe these acts. Similarly, in her recounting of Luke and his master, Jacobs employs narrative devices that signal to antebellum readers (and to literary critics today) that Luke was, in fact, raped or that, at the very least, a sexual relation between the two men existed. Jacobs's use of the terms *freaks* and *filthy*, combined with her descriptions of Luke's naked body, further corroborates such a claim, suggesting that the master, who was totally incapacitated, still maintained power over Luke and could force him to execute certain sexual acts.

In Jacobs's narrative as well as in the many aforementioned episodes, each observer perceived male sexual relations as "disgusting" and "loathsome." For Jacobs, the use of this language marks the aberrant and ghastly violence that unfolded between Luke and the master, whereas, for the writer of the *Freedmen's Record*, the Union soldier was considered "loathsome" due to his desire to wait on the dock for another man. Therefore, the use of the terms *loathsome, disgusting,* and even *filthy* can be seen as a way eighteenth- and nineteenth-century Americans marked relations between men who engaged in sexual relations with other men—even when those relations were strikingly different. Jacobs tells of violence and rape, whereas, the story in the *Freedmen's Record* hints at desire, longing, and intimacy.

The writer of the *Freedmen's Record* believes that he knows something about the man and his relationship to the officer in the navy, not because he witnessed the two men interact, but because he evaluated the soldier's appearance. Attempting to draw a conclusion about the soldier's behavior based on his appearance accords with how nineteenth-century Americans attempted to understand one another. In other words, outward appearances often became the signifier of the internal moral character and integrity of a particular individual. For example, when one became ill in the nineteenth century, physicians understood the ailment in terms of how one appeared. Medical diagnoses often followed along class lines, and class status could be read based on particular clothing or behavior. People of the lower classes and those who were perceived as immoral risked a great chance of being perceived as diseased. This logic seems to follow in this case. According to the writer for the *Freedmen's Record*, the man is ill because he did something to cause the illness. That would then explain why the writer also refers to him as "stupid."

Yet the writer nonetheless is perturbed by the Union soldier's sickness because of what he senses about the young black man, and more importantly, what he does not write about him. That is, beyond a medical discourse, the writer makes a claim about the nature of the soldier's relationship simply by looking at him. Within the context of the army, an all-male regime, such evaluations of bodily expression and countenance may have in fact been a way that some nineteenth-century American military men defined masculinity and its discontents. Take, for example, the case of Billy Yank, a Union military official, who described a newly freed slave who joined the ranks of the army as "filthy and lazy." The officer also noted, "He never looks at you when talking but shifts uneasily from one leg to the other and turns his head from side to side, rolling his eyes and grunting queer laughs. We make all kinds of sport of him."[14]

In this case, Yank makes innuendos and claims about the freedman simply by judging his outer appearance. By narrating the former bondsman's gesticulations, the Union official attempts to make a claim about the soldier simply by interrogating his bodily motions. Similar to the story in the *Freedmen's Record*, the writer suspects aberrant or questionable behavior simply by observing the individual; the officer also uses the term *filthy*, like *loathsome*, to indict this man. Here, the black soldier is referred to first as "filthy," then as delivering "queer laughs." Certainly, the meaning of "queer," could mean odd or strange, as it was often used during the nineteenth century, but given the context of this quotation and its connection to the term *filthy*, it seems to only buttress the theory that to be marked as "filthy" connoted sexual behavior between men.

Therefore, uncovering the history of sexuality among enslaved men during the eighteenth and nineteenth centuries may not produce in-depth biographical portraits and it may not even tell us their names. Instead, what we are left with are clues: scattered pieces of evidence, idioms, and adjectives that could point to same-sex behavior and desire. In a letter to the editor of the *National Gazette* in Philadelphia in 1828, for example, a reader listed "sodomy" alongside "lust" under the heading "specimens of filthiness and obscenity."[15] According to historian Kathleen M. Brown, the term *foul* held connotations that often signaled sexual aberrance, abhorrence, and wrongdoing to early Americans.[16] While the term *foul* is clearly different from the adjective *filthy*, Brown's study can help us excavate how early Americans employed various adjectives to convey dissatisfaction, intolerance, and even awareness about sexual behavior. In 1837, a Virginia slaveholder, for example, attempted to sell an enslaved man named Beverly because Beverly was a burden to the slaveholder. According to the slaveholder, Beverly was "addicted to running away, to Drunkenness, and a habit of life and vices which bring upon him loathsome and deadly diseases, which and on this account he is a frequent and fruitful source of expense to your orator's estate, for it has not been very long since he had the venereal disease, which rendered him useless for a whole year besides the large costs for a cure."[17]

On one level, the use of the term *loathsome* accords with the antebellum meaning of disease, but the writer of the document makes a distinction between a deadly disease and venereal disease within the span of a single sentence. The reference to a venereal disease illustrates the sexual connotation of the term *loathsome*. That Beverly runs away and has "a habit of life and vices," however, suggests the possibility that loathsome could relate to some type of same-sex intimacy or act. Within the historiography, when historians describe sex, romance, and love as the impetus for truancy in the plantation South, they often define these acts as women seeking men or vice versa, but what about men seeking men or women seeking women?[18] How can we begin to read the cases of truancy and running away as moments within the historical record that could have portended the chance for same-sex love, desire, and intimacy? That Beverly's desires to often run away resulted from his "habit of life and vices" combined with the sexually charged notion of "loathsome" disease indicates the possibility that he may have been running toward another man.

The subtle use of adjectives to uncover the history of same-sex desire, practice, and intimacy among enslaved men follows similar rhetorical practices employed within the broader historical context of the eighteenth and nineteenth centuries.

Throughout these periods, there were large populations of mixed-race people often born out of violent sexual acts committed by white men against enslaved women, yet this social phenomenon remained largely absent from the historical record.[19] The proof of the high rate of rape appears, in part, in the use of adjectives. References of enslaved people as "mulattoes" or descriptions of their skin in terms of its color in plantation records, census reports, and other sources illustrate this violence. In her autobiography, Harriet Jacobs refers to this phenomenon and illustrates this rhetorical practice. "The young wife soon learns that the husband in whose hands she has placed her happiness pays no regard to his marriage vows. Children of every shade of complexion play with her own fair babies, and too well she knows that they are born unto him of his own household."[20] As Jacobs shows, adjectives and evocative language became the way that Americans from the antebellum era reported on and discussed sexuality in public discourse. Just as terms relating to racial classification indirectly point to rape throughout the period, then the history of same-sex desire as well as the broader history of sexuality depend on the excavation and interrogation of multilayered adjectives and subtle turns of phrase.

Since adjectives might be used to uncover the history of sexuality, we also must consider the meaning of various nouns within the historical record. For example, when used alone as a noun the word "Negro" refers to a male, not a female.[21] When antebellum Anglo-Americans used the term "my Negro" or "a Negro," they were often referring to a man, not a woman; when they wanted to refer to a woman as "a Negro," they would often add her name or the word *woman* to the description. When slaveholder's wives, for example, petitioned for divorce from their philandering husbands, they referred to enslaved women as "Negro women," not simply as slaves, distinguishing the enslaved person as a female.[22] In 1846, for instance, Eliza H. Glover claimed that her husband had left her in order to pursue a sexual relationship with "a Negro woman." Glover alleges that her husband "was at the time he left, and had been for some time previous, in habits of illicit intercourse with said negro woman, and as your Oratrix believes still keeps the said woman for the purpose of sexual intercourse."[23]

Additionally, Catherine Awtry petitioned to divorce her husband a few months after marrying him because of his sexual transgressions, and like Eliza H. Glover, Awtry referred to the enslaved person as a "negro woman." She posited that he engaged in "criminal intercourse and Sexual connection with his own Negro woman Slave in his own house and had a child by her the offspring of his illicit connection." By adding the qualifier *woman* to the term *negro*, Awtry illustrates how "negro" often meant male in popular southern nomenclature and thereby required the use of the term *woman* to distinguish her husband's sexual relation with a female.[24]

Throughout a number of petitions filed in the nineteenth-century courts for divorce, southern white women also included the names of the enslaved women who had sexual relations with their husbands and did not simply refer to the en-slaved woman as a "Negro." In 1845 in Dallas, Alabama, Jane M. Porter filed for divorce because her husband "was keeping up a criminal connection" with "a negro woman of light complexion named Mary."[25]

Further, the stand-alone description of an enslaved person as a "Negro" with-out a name or a reference to gender means a man. Take, for example, the case of Thomas Cain, who petitioned for divorce from his wife because of "of an adulterous intercourse with a negro."[26] Unlike the slaveholders' wives, who refer to enslaved women either as "Negro women" or by their names, Cain simply refers to the en-slaved man who had adulterous sexual intercourse with his wife as "a Negro." In another case, Nancy Graves sought a divorce from her husband based on the fact that he assaulted her and treated her poorly; Graves also notes that he accused her of "having connection with negroes, and other indignities," condemning her for having sex with enslaved men.[27]

Drawing on this usage that "Negro" means male, the reference to slavehold-ers having sexual relations with their "Negroes" could indicate sex with men, not women. In Randolph, North Carolina, in 1849, Nancy Jane Brooks sought a divorce from her husband on the grounds that he "kept shameless adulterous intercourse with divers negroes."[28]

Similarly, throughout the petitions, many slaveholders' wives appealed for divorce because their husbands had sex with their "slaves." Not referring to the said enslaved person either by a female name or by the noun *woman* but simply as "slaves" forges the interpretive space to imagine that these white men may have engaged in same-sex sexual relations. In South Carolina in 1845, Sarah Ann Simp-son stated that she had to contend "with the pollution of her bed, [perpetrated] in a manner the most offensive to the feelings of the wife—the disgusting intercourse of her said husband, with his own slave."[29] The descriptor *disgusting* could have been a way for Simpson to amplify her abhorrence of her husband's adultery, but given the ways in which *slave* as a stand-alone noun often meant male, it could also signal same-sex relations.

Further, as historian Jennifer Manion incisively asserts, "Most scholars presume that historical actors are heterosexual, that sexual acts and desires are aimed at members of the opposite sex, and that the incidence of same-sex desire or inti-macy has no bearing on the meaning of heterosexuality."[30] Considering Manion's first claim, we should not simply assume that all historical actors are, in fact, het-erosexual; therefore, the noun *slave* could mean male, and in the context of *Negro* meaning male, it seems to have a similar rhetorical connotation. Manion's second claim, that same-sex desire, intimacy, and rape have an effect on heterosexuality, suggests why and how someone like Sarah Ann Simpson filed for a divorce and did so with such vehement indignation. Certainly the mere practice of her husband having an adulterous relationship with an enslaved woman would incite similar feelings, but Simpson's vitriolic references to the affair as "disgusting" and polluting her bed combined with the fact that she is filing for a divorce suggests how a same-sex act might have impelled slaveholding women to march into courts, make public their husband's sexual transgression, and risk social marginalization and even economic instability. A same-sex act could, as Manion suggests, affect heterosexuality in such a crippling way that it might inspire such drastic legal measures of divorce.

In crafting the divorce petition, southern wives needed to, as historian Laura Edwards perceptively notes, "force the unruly details of their lives into the required formula."[31] As Edwards explains, southern women knew enough to posit the legal causes for divorce and in the process cast themselves as "hapless innocents in conflicts beyond their control."[32] The challenge came, as Edwards suggests, in turning the "unruly details into the required formula." There was little rhetorical space for these women to expand on the fact that their husbands engaged in same-sex sexual relations, so as a result they spoke in a lexicon that was legible to the courts and that did not directly insult the foundations of southern society and etiquette. Claiming that their husbands had sex with "the slaves" accomplished this objective in two ways. First, in making such a claim, the wives could portray themselves as "hapless innocents in conflicts beyond their control." Second, they could translate the graphic, messy details of potential same-sex sexual relations into a digestible idiom that the courts could understand as aberrant.[33]

A year after the start of the American Civil War in Franklin, Virginia, for example, Elizabeth Wade also requested a divorce from her husband because he engaged in "criminal intercourse with his own slaves."[34] From a contemporary perspective, it is easy to gloss over this seemingly innocuous phrase and simply assume that Wade divorced her husband because he engaged in sexual relations with enslaved women on his plantation. Considering this phrase in the context of both Manion's and Edward's analyses, however, suggests that all acts of intercourse reported in the archival record do not mean heterosexuality; also, the drafting of the petition followed particular nineteenth-century rhetorical conventions that elided the possibility to be direct about sexual intercourse and instead prompted many early Americans to sublimate meaning in ways that were legible to those who lived during the era.

Structures

Peeling away the scaffolding in the divorce petitions or dissecting the meaning of the term *loathsome* offers a semantic way to investigate the hidden history of same-sexual relations; another possibility is to move away from poststructuralism and move toward the actual structures of the eighteenth and nineteenth centuries to explore how the very institutions that facilitated the development of slavery were complicit in both promoting same-sex sexual violence, desire, and intimacy, and concealing it. Throughout the antebellum period, the domestic slave trade served as one of the most powerful engines fueling the institution of slavery; it was responsible for the buying and selling of enslaved people from the Upper South to the Lower South and the Mississippi Valley in the decades before the outbreak of the Civil War. Some scholars have argued that men could unleash their sexual desires onto the bodies of enslaved women openly, publicly, and often without punishment. Despite the fact that the rape of enslaved women often transpired in hidden and closed-off settings, southern white men in power turned the institution of the domestic slave trade into a public theater for their sexual desires. As historian Walter Johnson explains, "The bodies of light-skinned women and little girls embodied sexual desire and the luxury of being able to pay for its fulfillment" for slave buyers and slave masters.[35] While this is certainly an important and insightful moment, it nonetheless propagates a heteronormative logic that sexual desire flowed only from white masters to enslaved women, not considering that many enslaved men, standing on the auction block, having their bodies similarly inspected, groped, and measured, embodied "sexual desire and luxury" to some white slaveholders as well.

Thus the domestic slave trade must be viewed as one of the possible arenas where southern white men in power could act out their desire toward male bodies in a public and open setting that was sanctioned by the state. As Johnson argues, the success of antebellum slavery rested on the domestic slave trade; given that assertion, it is critical to recognize that this landmark of the antebellum southern landscape could have also been the harbinger of sexual violence and assault against enslaved men. Therefore, the buying and selling of enslaved men transported to the Deep South was not just about forming a labor force in the Mississippi Valley, but it also was about encapsulating desire, lust, and sexual violence into a market that fueled a regional institution that built a national economy.

Recognizing the ways in which sexual desire participated in the making of slavery in the South also reinforces legal scholar Adrienne Davis's claim that slavery was a sexual economy. As Davis notes, "Pleasure, punishment, politics, and profit: once laws of rape authorized elite white male legal and economic control over enslaved women's sexuality, their sexuality could be manipulated to serve any number of interests."[36] Davis's formulation reveals the structural ways in which sexual violence and lust toward enslaved men could be justified and even codified as part of the making of American slavery. The economy that grew out of the slave trade combined with the legal, social, and economic institution of slavery created both the space and the opportunity for white men to use enslaved men as sexual objects in ways that would remain concealed and separated from their families and the propriety of southern life. Unlike the plantation South, which risked slaveholders being caught by their wives and filing for divorce, the domestic slave trade provided the space for such sexual acts to take place and permitted slaveholders to engage in such acts with little consequence; it empowered white men with the ability to use enslaved men's bodies, in the words of Adrienne Davis, for "pleasure, punishment, politics, and profit."

The domestic slave trade, the petitions, and even the poststructuralist unpacking of the word *loathsome* suggest ways to uncover the history of same-sex sexual relations. Yet the common denominator in all these scenarios is violence: violence, rape, and sexual assault only made these episodes of sexual interaction visible. These vignettes, while helpful in broadening the narrative of subjugation and brutalization against enslaved men, tell us only about an interaction between white men and enslaved men, not of the intimacy, desire, and even love that may have existed among enslaved men for each other.

That said, the violent and horrific spaces that produced sexual violence, rendering same-sex desire, love, and intimacy among enslaved men virtually invisible may, in fact, produce the social geography that makes such desire, love, and intimacy visible. Building on historian Evelynn Hammonds's brilliant theory of "black (w)holes," invisibility does not mean inaction or lack of discourse. Within the context of science, particularly astrophysics, Hammonds contends, that invisibility is actually "a black hole" that is not empty—it just cannot be readily seen. In an effort to observe a black hole, astrophysicists must examine what is on its margins, what can concretely be seen around the circumference of the black hole that forms it. In that case, the domestic slave trade, the use of language, and the divorce petitions form the concrete, observable circumference in which sexuality can be observed. The black hole, which is intimacy, desire, and love among enslaved men, cannot be readily visible, but it is not invisible; its existence lies in the construction of concrete markers that surround it. Acts of sexual violence against enslaved men (as well as heterosexual sex) provide the markers that at first glance may seem to render same-sex desire invisible but actually establish the coordinates to map the black (w)hole in which same-sex desire among enslaved men exists. In order to see enslaved men's same-sex desires and intimacy, we must, therefore, follow Hammonds's theory and "develop reading strategies that allow us to make visible the distorting and productive effects these sexualities produce in relation to more visible sexualities."[37]

Violence and even heterosexual practices can shape the contours of an intimacy among enslaved men that is not invisible but rather unfolds within a black hole. Heteronormativity, the crisis surrounding black emasculation, the brutalities of slavery, among other forms of degradation have purposely conspired in the construction of various representations of black manhood that have made their sexuality not invisible but rather part of a black hole that must be carefully interrogated. The margins of that black hole, its circumference and edges, point to the possibility of an experience that if left unarticulated would be seen only as nonexistent. Hammonds's formulation of a black hole and her insistence on using geometry to detect the parameters of an experience not literally recorded in the archive offers a method to theorize about a form of sexual desire, intimacy, and love among enslaved men that is not invisible or empty but rather just cannot be readily seen.

While this may sound like mumbo jumbo, my point is to consider another route into the archive—a circuitous if subversive strategy to map the existence of intimacy, love, and desire among one of the most dispossessed populations of people in North American history. Without ample archival evidence, how might we write a history of sexuality among enslaved men? Hammonds's formulation justifies the need to theorize about a form of subjectivity that otherwise remains invisible; it offers an explanation for the lack of subjectivity within the record beyond the mere assertion that it does not exist. It also helps to untangle the various forces that have conspired against the telling of enslaved men's sexuality; instead of retreating from the prohibitions around sexuality, it suggests using them to detect the possibility of intimacy, love, and desire.

This theoretical move also attempts to circumvent the epistemic violence that otherwise informs the representations of enslaved men who have engaged in same-sex sexual relations in both the archives and historiography. Developing a theory that attends to their intimacy, love, and desire seeks to bypass these tropes. Often narrated through cases of buggery or sodomy or other discourses of criminalization, enslaved men's sexuality appears in the historical record only as aberrant. The history of same sex-relations among enslaved men only becomes visible due to illegality and violence associated with the act. In colonial Pennsylvania, for example, the legal prohibition of buggery made sexual relations among enslaved men visible; according to the logic of the archive, only through acts deemed criminal can same-sex sexual experience among enslaved men be fully excavated. Furthermore, the Pennsylvania law identified "buggery" as the "most heinous crime" that enslaved men could commit, and the court consequently enacted ghastly punishment on anyone charged with the offense.[38]

Throughout early America, colonial governments often murdered enslaved men who committed these sexual acts and made their torture a public event. In New Netherland in 1646, the state executed one Jan Creoli for committing sodomy a second time. As the court record notes, Creoli was to be "conveyed to the place of public execution, and there choked to death, and then burnt to ashes." Yet the state did not stop there. It then went after one Manuel Congo, "a lad ten years old, on whom the above abominable crime was committed." In a symbolic and quite eerie gesture, the state ordered Congo to be brought to the place where Creoli was executed. After being forced to witness the execution of the man with whom he had sex, Congo was "to be flogged" for "justice sake."[39]

The next known example of a black man being sentenced for death for buggery happened half a century later in Charlestown, Massachusetts. In 1712, an enslaved man owned by Wait Winthrop entered the historical record as "Mingo," alias "Cocke Negro," accused of "forcible buggery."[40] Given the pernicious ways in which slaveholders often named their slaves, the fact that "Mingo" enters the historical record with an alias of "Cocke" for a sexual offense should not be go unnoticed. That said, Mingo enters the archive not through his own testimony or words but rather through the pen of one Samuel Sewall, who recorded scant details about Mingo's trial in his diary. As a result, we know very little about said "Mingo." Why did he earn the nickname "Cocke?" Was the act of "forcible buggery" an act of violence and rape? We know that one of his victims was a thirteen- to fourteen-year-old girl named Abigail Dowse, but who was the other person with whom he was charged with committing sodomy? Was it a woman or a man?

The problem is that we may never know. Yet for some historians, "Mingo" prominently appears in the historiography as the first case in the history of sodomy laws in the United States and as part of the genealogy that forms the history of homosexuality.[41]

Yet, what is at stake in picking out the rare examples of men being choked and burned to death as the foundation for queer historiography, especially when we are unsure of their motivations or whether they even had sex with men? What is at stake in uncovering the history of same-sex sexual relations only to uncover more evidence of violence committed against enslaved men? What is the social and cultural repercussion of enslaved men's sexuality becoming visible only in the criminal nomenclature of sodomy and buggery? Why is sodomy an origin narrative for the history homosexuality? More to the point, what is at stake in defining that an enslaved man committed the first act of sodomy in the United States? How does this perpetuate the myths of hypersexuality surrounding people of African descent that black feminists have been attempting to dismantle for generations?[42]

In addition to the fact that enslaved men who engaged in such acts appear as criminals in the record, uncovering this history also decrees an act of epistemic violence. As theorist Gayatri Spivak explains, epistemic violence refers to acts of violence committed against individuals through discourse.[43] In the cases of sodomy, there is the violence inflicted on the enslaved men who committed these crimes in the past as well as the violence committed against them in the present when those cases are retold and propped up as part of the genealogy of homosexuality.

I have purposely concluded with the history of sodomy instead of beginning with it because I wanted to imagine another way to uncover the history of sexuality: to move beyond the genealogy of homosexuality in the United States as simply a story of aberration.[44] I did not want to engage in another act of epistemic violence committed against both the subjects whom I describe and the audiences for whom I write. I began with a story of longing, of intimacy, of beloved friends or lovers, because I wanted to reconstruct a history of same-sex desire that may have interpolated an archival record that refused to name their intimacy or say their name. I pushed for a theoretical interpretation of how to read clues in divorce petitions and to unpack the meaning of the term *loathsome* because I wanted to see where other details about same-sex sexuality might be hiding beyond the discourses of criminality and violence; I wanted instead to consider how the ordinary, everyday iterations of a particular period may have dropped clues about the lives, intimacies, and desires that happened offstage, away from the traditional specter of archival accounting. I also wanted to examine closely the language that those in the past spoke to examine the multilayered meaning of their words that may have subversively, if opaquely, connoted sexuality.

On Evidence

This exercise thus raises a larger question beyond the scope of enslaved men's sexuality: can theory take the place of evidence? Raising that question, which has animated polemical debates across the scholarly profession in a number of fields, leads to an interrogation of historical practice. Too often historians fail to see how their very methods, practices, and definitions have a distinct history similar to the subjects that they study. The very notion that evidence, as a form of proof, buttressed by empiricism, becomes the leading marker of historical scholarship is a relatively new phenomenon within the profession. As historian Michael Zuckerman once said, "Major American historians used to lie about the past." Historians used to lie in the special way that writers lie "in order to unveil larger and more potent truths. Their service was always immense, and essential," Zuckerman tells us. "Out of fables as much as from facts, they shaped vast visions and fashioned faith for a people. Out of imagination as much as by scrupulous empirical investigation, they instructed a democracy."[45]

Zuckerman reveals the extent to which the empirical writing of history has produced renderings of the past that cannot often be located within the archives or qualified by exacting historical data. He challenges the historical profession's obsession with evidence—a concept that since the early twentieth century has actually remained in flux. Too often, contemporary historians do not actually think about the meaning or the definition of evidence but burrow themselves in the archives, year after year, month after month, attempting to find the "smoking gun" that will finally settle their research query without every seriously thinking about what constitutes evidence or how the category of evidence, just like any other analytical tool or artifact, reflects its own social and political context.[46]

Unlike today, at the turn of the twentieth century, a number of historians questioned and explored the meaning of history. French historian Marc Bloch understood the problematic nature of evidence when he wrote, "Documents do not suddenly materialize, in one place or another, as if by some mysterious decree of the gods. Their presence or absence in the depths of the archive or that library are due to human causes which by no means elude analysis."[47] By midcentury, the Annales School had begun to lay the groundwork for the writing of social history, but the idea of how documents enter the archives has been often overlooked in current historical practice, and instead historians of sexuality have been held to the same standards as historians in economics, law, and religion, who have access to significantly more material. Bloch, however, understood the social forces that would result in one specialty having more documents than another.

With the exception of historian Bonnie Smith's *Gender of History* and the work of a few other historians of gender and women's studies, Bloch's warning has been virtually ignored by those who practice social history.[48] Bloch understood that the archival material and the notion of evidence were politically and socially biased and that certain questions could not be fully answered by the most sophisticated search aids. He also brilliantly pointed out that "it would not be wise to rely entirely upon academic bodies for these instruments, for their methods of recruiting, favoring seniority and orthodox scholarship, do not particularly incline them to the spirit of enterprise."[49] Some historians of sexuality have unwittingly heeded Bloch's advice and have turned to linguistic and theoretical models as a way to engage issues in which the archives are silent. In discussing the theoretical frame of her study on the intersections of race and homosexuality, Siobhan Somerville explains that the fields of literary and cultural studies "have historically been receptive to some degree of ambiguity and connotation" in defining evidence.[50]

The greatest contribution of the Annales, in turn, has been in their expansive and inclusive definition of what constitutes evidence.[51] Bloch's idea is that "the variety of historical evidence is nearly infinite. Everything that man says or writes, everything that he makes, everything that he touches can and ought to teach us about him."[52] This expansive definition of evidence ignited an explosion among historians of the last forty years or so and has guided social historians in their investigations of those who have often left little archival trace. Yet this history of the bottom up has in many respects failed to progress theoretically. Instead, definitions of evidence seem almost impenetrable and obdurate.

Therefore, in thinking about the history of sexuality, in general, and the question of same-sex relations among enslaved men, in particular, I suggest—in addition to Hammonds's theory of the black (w)hole—that we refashion a definition of evidence in order to better understand the past. As such, I would like to rely on the theoretical work of queer theorist Lynda Hart.[53] Hart's work, in particular, posits a theoretical language that manipulates the very act of constructing the past. She writes, "The tense is the future anterior—the past that will have been. Still I cannot get this right. I want so much to write in the subjunctive—the past that would have been—the mood/mode of subordination."[54] Hart's theoretical intervention unleashes a reconfiguration of how the past could be constructed; possibility, for Hart, lies in the mere variations of the verb tense. More than just a play on grammar, Hart's project suggests a way to rethink the past by rethinking the verb. Changing the tense, in turn, reorders the subject of the sentence and the actions in which they could be executed. The outcome, therefore, disavows a strict application of empiricism and archival recounting and instead imagines the possible. While the possible could potentially range from mere fabrication and fable, to borrow Zuckerman's position, it, nevertheless would adhere to, at the very least, a context in which the often-undocumented issues of sexuality—power, lust, and eroticism—could enter a discussion without the burden of lengthy footnotes. How might imagining "a past that would have been" offer a theoretical strategy to inform the black (w)holes in which enslaved men sexuality exists?

In order to put this to test, I want to return to the story of the youth waiting for the naval officer. There is something that I have not told you about that episode. He spoke. He said something to the writer for the *Freedmen's Record*. He told him how he felt, but the writer heard only what he wanted.[55]

> His poor parched lips whispered his love for Jesus, and a little gleam of light spread over his swollen features when one spoke to him of this precious Friend of the friendless, and he said, in a broken accents, "I tinks of Him often,—He all de comfort I got."[56]

The writer goes on to explain that a few of the men in the hospital had learned how "to read since their emancipation," which was intended to inform readers of the *Freedmen's Record* how newly freed people had read the Bible and developed a closer and more intimate relationship with God. The writer also notes how the formerly enslaved people found comfort in God's love. When the writer heard the Union soldier speak of "Him often," he assumed that the man meant Jesus. The former enslaved man, however, may have been referring not to Jesus but to the sailor. When the writer witnessed the man opening his "parched lips" and heard him whisper love for God, the soldier could have been expressing his love for the man in the navy. When the writer heard the soldier say that he "tinks of him often," the ex-slave could have been referring not to Jesus but to the man whom he waited for on the dock in the rain and cold for days. When the writer documents that the Union soldier stated, "He all de comfort I got," the solider—lying alone in a crowded hospital on the verge of death—may have been referring not to Jesus but to the man whom the war separated him from; the man who gave him comfort, who allowed a "gleam of light to spread over his swollen features"; the man whose name could never be spoken but was referred to only as "him."

According to the writer for the *Freedmen's Record,* the sick man's testimony about intimacy, love, and desire must have been about Jesus. As a reformer sent to the South from the North, hoping to spread Christianity to the formerly enslaved, the writer interpreted the man's words as religious. According to the writer, religion gave the Union solider access to a language that would enable him to speak of his adoration and feelings for another man; religion and God fit into the cultural narratives that many dying men espoused to those who would listen at their bedside.[57]

The sick soldier may have been speaking about Jesus, but I suspect that he was speaking about the sailor he was waiting for on the dock.[58] I want so badly to tell this story as a romantic narrative, to rescue the Union soldier from the archives and to acknowledge his love, his adoration, and his comfort in the face of an overwhelmingly vast historiography that cannot imagine his existence. If nothing else, I want to pay homage to his relationship and to reunite him with his lost love if only on the pages of an academic book a century and half later. But I realize this is more about me, and less about him. I said that I wasn't looking for love, but I lied. What if I am wrong and religion did form the subject of his statements, and I am propping him up to ventriloquize a past that could have been for me, not for him?

All historical scholarship, however, rests on interpretation—all depends on speculation, doubt, and uncertainty; the history of sexuality has just carried this burden more publically. More cogent evidence has not materialized in the archive, as Marc Bloch suggests, for a reason. Historians of slavery in the United States have often told us that the institution of slavery eradicated any chance for enslaved people to articulate their desires, their voices, and their wishes.

The absences and silences are produced by the mere construction of the archives.[59] While the archives on slavery have produced important detail about the economic, labor, social, political, and even gendered lives of bondspeople, the archives have been purposely quiet on the subject of enslaved people's intimate lives. By their very nature, the archives have been constructed to capture records that dealt with labor, politics, economy, and the law. What happened offstage—away from the mechanizing forces that recorded public behavior—has historically been an issue that has fallen outside the purview of archival documentation and thus is difficult for historians of sexuality to uncover. Additionally, given the fact that most of the extant evidence about slavery comes from the pens of white people, it is even that much more difficult to find first-person testimonies of bondspeople from the eighteenth and nineteenth centuries—which is further complicated by the fact that those in power in the South deemed enslaved people who learned to read and write as criminals.[60] As a result, we must carefully consider this sick soldier's statement within the context of these historical forces in order to detect "the black (w)hole" surrounding his sexuality. His sexuality will not be fully disclosed like a parable in a sermon or an accounting figure in a ledger book; his sexuality can only be detected and made visible by the cultural markers that surround it. That he was called "loathsome" and "loving Jesus" in the same passage offers useful context clues to detect his intimacy, desire, and love; further applying Hart's formulation of "the past that will have been" directs the historian away from a strict accounting of "what happened" to focusing on the mood of the sick soldier's statement, to imagine his future anterior—the tomorrow when the sailor would have arrived or when he would have been able to live in a world where his intimacy, desire, and love would have a name.

The toll of enslavement in the United States has had many effects on the history of the nation; so much of the work of historians over the last sixty years or more has been to demonstrate the existence of the system and to detail the violence, degradation, and exploitation that slavery inflicted. But the other equally violent outcome has been the burden of the historian to prove with herculean might that enslaved people experienced the full range of human emotion and desires despite their enslavement. The call for uncovering more evidence about their intimacies and desires from a hollow archive is to only reinscribe the violence committed against them: to negate their lives with one more lash of the whip.

Enslaved men experienced the range of human emotion and connection that people have felt throughout history, but because of their enslavement it has been almost impossible to imagine, let alone document. Fortunately, bits and pieces of their experience have survived, offering an outline of their intimacies and desires. With only a trace, we may be able to recover only part of their story, but this scant evidence should not deter it us; it should instead compel us to rethink how we write history and how we define evidence.

Notes

1. On postwar conditions, see Jim Downs, *Sick from Freedom: African-American Illness and Suffering* (New York: Oxford University Press, 2012).

2. *Freedmen's Record* 1, no. 10 (October 1865), 160.

3. "Loathsome, adj.," OED Online, March 2015, Oxford University Press, http://www.oed.com/view/Entry/109476?redirectedFrom=loathsome (accessed April 21, 2015).

4. Harriet Jacobs, *Incidents in the Life of a Slave Girl*, ed. Jean Fagan Yellin (Cambridge, Mass.: Harvard University Press, 1987), 79.

5. Lydia Marie Child and Amy Post's comments not only appeared in the "Preface of Incidents" but were also simultaneously published in the abolitionist press. See *National Anti-Slavery Standard*, February 23, 1861.

6. John Lawson, *A New Voyage to Carolina; Containing the Exact Description and Natural History of That Country: Together with the Present State Thereof. And a Journal of a Thousand Miles,*

Travel'd thro' Several Nations of Indians. Giving a Particular Account of Their Customs, Manners, &c. (London, 1709), 186.

7. Martha Griffith Browne was a white woman who posed as an enslaved woman. See Martha Griffith Browne, *Autobiography of a Female Slave* (New York: Redfield, 1857), 170; Throughout this book, Browne uses the term *loathsome* in relation to sexual threats. See also Browne, *Autobiography of a Female Slave*, 288, 384.

8. Frederick Douglass, *My Bondage, My Freedom* (1855; repr., New York: Penguin, 2003), 187.

9. Frederick Douglass, *Narrative of a Life of Frederick Douglass, an American Slave, Written by Himself* (1845, repr., Cambridge, Mass.: Harvard University Press, 2009), 86.

10. There is a cultural memory of "buck breaking," which describes how masters publicly sodomized unruly enslaved men, often in front of their families, especially in front of their sons to warn them of misbehaving. I have not found any references to this practice in the many primary sources that I have examined. According to popular memory, however, these public acts of discipline became a way for white men interested in having sex with enslaved men to tour the South in search of these public acts of punishment. The scene that Douglass describes here seems to evoke similar moments of sexual exploitation or, at the very least, illustrate how white men had power over enslaved men and could do what they wanted to their bodies sexually. See http://diaryofanegress.com/2012/10/17/buck-breaking/ (accessed January 21, 2016). See also http://tinyurl.com/zn2ca3h (accessed January 21, 2016).

11. Thomas Foster has recently addressed the issue of sexual violence against enslaved men. Drawing on the only existing scholarly literature on this topic, Foster astutely defines sexual violence as covering a range of issues from forced breeding to assaults made by white women on enslaved men to the threat of rape. Thomas A. Foster, "The Sexual Abuse of Black Men under American Slavery," in "Intersections of Race and Sexuality," special issue, *Journal of the History of Sexuality* 20, no. 3 (September 2011): 445–64. Furthermore, Darieck Scott brilliantly argues that sexual exploitation among enslaved men rarely appears in the archives, and consequently historians must rely on "logical deduction" and "oblique digressive references in slave narratives or little-known mentions that may appear in the records of the odd legal adjudication." Scott also explains that while few references to sexual exploitation appear among enslaved men in the English archives, there are more references in the Portuguese records. Scott cites, for example, Harold Johnson and Francis A. Dutra, eds., *Pelo Vaso Traseiro: Sodomy and Sodomites in Luso-Brazilian History* (Tucson, Ariz.: Fenestra Books, 2007). See Darieck Scott, *Extravagant Abjection: Blackness, Power, and Sexuality in the African American Literary Imagination* (New York: New York University Press, 2010), 289n20.

12. Jacobs, *Incidents*, 192.

13. Jacobs, *Incidents*, 192.

14. Wiley, *Life of Billy Yank*, as quoted in Leon Litwack, *Been in the Storm So Long* (New York: Vintage, 1980).

15. *National Gazette*, May 24, 1828.

16. Kathleen M. Brown, *Foul Bodies: Cleanliness in Early America* (New Haven, Conn.: Yale University Press, 2009), 58–59.

17. Petition 21683702, April 3, 1837, Race and Slavery Petitions Project, hereinafter cited by only the petition number, PAR, http://library.uncg.edu/slavery/petitions/details .aspx?pid=15070 (accessed January 21, 2016).

18. For an excellent analysis of the relationship between truancy, gender, and sexuality, see Stephanie M. H. Camp, *Closer to Freedom: Enslaved Women and Everyday Resistance in the Plantation South* (Chapel Hill: University of North Carolina Press, 2004).

19. Many historians have carefully mined the archival record to find empirical evidence of rape, but even these herculean efforts do not fully account for the large number of rapes that occurred throughout the eighteenth and nineteenth centuries. See Thelma Jennings, "'Us Colored Women Had to Go through a Plenty': Sexual Exploitation of African-American Slave Women," *Journal of Women's History* 1, no. 3 (Winter 1990): 45–68; Nell Irvin Painter, "Soul Murder and Slavery: Toward a Fully Loaded Cost Accounting," in *U.S. History as Women's History*, ed. Linda K. Kerber, Alice Kessler-Harris, and Kathryn Kish Sklar (Chapel Hill: University of North Carolina Press, 1995), 125–46; Deborah Gray White, *Ar'n't I a Woman: Female Slaves in the Antebellum South* (repr., New York: Norton, 1999).

20. Jacobs, *Incidents*, 57.

21. Ubiquitous throughout the plantation records, "Negro" is also used as an adjective, such as "Negro people" or even as a plural noun, "the Negroes."

22. See, for example, PAR number 21284004, PAR number 20684310, PAR number 21284303, PAR number 21685327.

23. PAR number 20184629.

24. PAR number 20184612.

25. PAR number 20185212.

26. PAR number 11684104.

27. PAR number 21285608.

28. PAR number 21286114.

29. PAR number 21384547.

30. Jennifer Manion, "Historic Heteroessentialism and Other Orderings in Early America," *Signs: Journal of Women in Culture and Society* 34, no. 4:1000.

31. Laura Edwards, *The People and Their Peace: Legal Culture and the Transformation of Inequality in the Post-Revolutionary South* (Chapel Hill: University of North Carolina Press, 2009), 169.

32. Edwards, *People and Their Peace*, 169.

33. Edwards, *People and Their Peace*, 169.

34. PAR number 21686214.

35. Walter Johnson, *Soul by Soul: Life inside the Antebellum Slave Market* (Cambridge, Mass.: Harvard University Press, 2000), 155.

36. Adrienne Davis, "'Bother Yo' Principle': The Sexual Economy of American Slavery," in *Sister Circle: Black Women and Work*, ed. Sharon Harley and the Black Women and Work Collective (New Brunswick, N.J.: Rutgers University Press, 2002), 117.

37. Evelynn Hammonds, "Black (W)holes and the Geometry of Black Female Sexuality," *differences: A Journal of Feminist Cultural Studies* 6, no. 2–3 (Summer-Fall 1994): 138–39.

38. Paul Crawford, "A Footnote on Courts for Trial of Negroes in Colonial Pennsylvania," *Journal of Black Studies* 5, no. 2 (December 1974): 167–74. Authorities in colonial

Mexico enacted similar legislation that defined sodomy among slaves as a crime. Peter Boyd-Bowman, "Negro Slaves in Early Colonial Mexico," *Americas* 26, no. 2 (October 1969): 134–51. Interestingly, Boyd-Bowman argues with regard to enslaved men who were charged with this crime that it resulted from the fact that an enslaved man could not lead a "normal sex life."

39. See Jonathan Ned Katz, *Gay/Lesbian Almanac* (New York: Harper and Row, 1983), 90, citing Edmund B. O'Callaghan, ed., *Calendar of Historical Manuscripts in the Office of the Secretary of State, Albany, N.Y.* (Albany, N.Y.: Weed, Parsons, 1865); reprinted as *Calendar of Dutch Historical Manuscripts* (Ridgewood, N.J.: Gregg Press, 1968), 103; Jonathan Katz, *Gay American History: Lesbians and Gay Men in the U.S.A.* (New York: Crowell, 1976), 22–23, 570n23.

40. Katz, *Gay/Lesbian Almanac*, 127–28, citing Samuel Sewall, *The Diary of…1674–1729; Newly Edited from the Manuscript at the Massachusetts Historical Society by M. Halsey Thomas*, 2 vols. (New York: Farrar, Straus and Giroux, 1973), 2:677, 678. For additional references to Mingo, see 1:388, 446; 2:617. For a reference to the Massachusetts "buggery" law of 1697, see 1:380. Jonathan Ned Katz thanks Robert Joyce Jr. for informing him of this document.

41. William N. Eskridge, *Dishonorable Passions: Sodomy Laws in America, 1861–2003* (New York: Viking, 2008); Katz, *Gay/Lesbian Almanac*.

42. In history, see White, *Ar'n't I a Woman?*; in feminist discourse, see bell hooks, *Ain't I a Woman: Black Women and Feminism* (repr., 1981: New York: Routledge, 2014).

43. Gayatri Chakravorty Spivak, "Can the Subaltern Speak?," in *Marxism and the Interpretation of Culture*, ed. Cary Nelson and Lawrence Grossberg, 271–313. (Urbana: University of Illinois Press, 1988).

44. Even in George Chauncey's brilliant landmark study of gay life in New York City at the turn of the twentieth century, which reveals "a golden age" of gay community decades before gay liberation in the 1970s, the experiences, names, and people whom Chauncey documents become legible only in court records because they were arrested or suffered from some other economic or social disruption. George Chauncey, *Gay New York: Gender, Urban Culture, and the Making of the Gay Male World, 1890–1940* (New York: Basic Books, 1995).

45. Michael Zuckerman, "Myth and Method: The Current Crises in American History Writing," *History Teacher* 17, no. 2 (February 1984): 219–45.

46. See, for example, Jim Downs, "'Do You See What I See?': The Debate over Black Confederates," *Huffington Post*, January 23, 2015.

47. Marc Bloch, *The Historian's Craft* (New York: Knopf, 1953), 71.

48. Bonnie Smith, *The Gender of History: Men, Women, and Historical Practice* (Cambridge, Mass.: Harvard University Press, 2000). See also Carolyn Kay Steedman, *Dust: The Archive and Cultural History* (New Brunswick, N.J.: Rutgers University Press, 2002); Ann Laura Stoler, *Along the Archival Grain: Epistemic Anxieties and Colonial Common Sense* (Princeton, N.J.: Princeton University Press, 2010).

49. Bloch, *Historian's Craft*, 70.

50. Siobhan Somerville, *Queering the Color Line: Race and the Invention of Homosexuality in American Culture* (Durham, N.C.: Duke University Press, 2000), 6.

51. For Fernand Braudel, a leading historian of the Annales School, this meant writing a two-volume history of the Mediterranean, which examined environmental issues, the

arts, and social groups. When Braudel went to chart the history of the sea, he could not use the archives and tools employed by historians of his day, who narrowly focused on the history of diplomats and the political elite and whose research was limited to manuscript collections. Before the creation of environmental history or even the environmental movement, Braudel instead needed to reconfigure the category of evidence in order to tell the history of the Mediterranean. As such, as one scholar has noted, Braudel "accomplished a feat of historical imagination based on detailed knowledge of the habits and techniques of the ploughman, the shepherd, the potter, and the weaver, the skills of the vintage and the olive press, the milling of corn, the keeping of records of bills of lading, tides and winds. It began to seem as important for a historian to be able to ride a horse or sail a ship as to sit in a library." Quoted from http://tinyurl.com/zl6n485 (accessed January 21, 2016).

52. Bloch, *Historian's Craft*, 54–55.

53. The idea of doing a cross-cultural and temporal analysis of sexuality is not that uncommon among practitioners of the history of sexuality, who also confront a paucity of evidence. Scholar David Cohen has used sources from various geographic places and periods to understand law, sexuality, and society in classical Athens, for example. Cohen, *Law, Sexuality, and Society: The Enforcement of Morals in Classical Athens* (Cambridge: Cambridge University Press, 1991), esp. 150–62.

54. Lynda Hart, *Between the Body and the Flesh: Performing Sadomasochism* (New York: Columbia University Press, 1998), 205.

55. According to some historians of early America, some white men often talked about their love, admiration, and dedication to Jesus. Religion functioned as a way for men to describe what we would define as same-sex intimacy. Richard Godbeer broadens this discussion by providing the male version of Carroll Smith-Rosenberg's "female world of love and ritual" in his book *The Overflowing of Friendship*, in which he reveals how some white men of the early Republic created a world of male romantic friendship. Godbeer, *The Overflowing of Friendship: Love Between Men and the Creation of the American Republic* (Baltimore: Johns Hopkins University Press, 2009).

56. *Freedmen's Record* 1, no. 10 (October 1865), 160.

57. For more on cultural rituals surrounding death during this period, see Drew Gilpin Faust, *This Republic of Suffering: Death and the American Civil War* (New York: Vintage, 2009).

58. It is unknown if the man whom the Union soldier waited for was black or white.

59. For an evocative meditation on the construction and nature of the archives in relation to the experience of enslaved people, see Jennifer L. Morgan, "Why I Write," in *Why We Write: The Politics and Practice of Writing for Social Change*, ed. Jim Downs (New York: Routledge, 2006), 39–45.

60. So much of the historical recovery of queer lives has depended on uncovering the subversive and hidden meaning of published writers from the past; this luxury does not exist when working with a community of people in which literacy was prohibited. For an excellent example of unearthing the history of sexuality through an extensive analysis of literary texts, see D. S. Neff, "Bitches, Mollies, and Tommies: Byron, Masculinity and the History of Sexualities," *Journal of the History of Sexuality* 11, no. 3 (July 2002), 395–438.

CHAPTER 2

Historical Methods and Racial Identification in U.S. Lesbian and Gay History

JULIAN B. CARTER

Political consciousness set U.S. gay and lesbian historical research in motion. The first book in the field—Jonathan Ned Katz's 1976 *Gay American History*—opens with a meditation on the way that participating in the Gay Liberation movement inspired historical practice:

> Those of us affected by this movement have experienced a basic change in our sense of self. . . . From a sense of our homosexuality as a personal and devastating fate, a private, secret shame, we moved with often dizzying speed to the consciousness of ourselves as members of an oppressed social group. . . . Starting with a sense of ourselves as characters in a closet drama, the passive victims of a family tragedy, we experienced ourselves as initiators and assertive actors in a movement for social change. We experienced the present as history, ourselves as historymakers. In our lives and in our hearts, we experienced the change from one historical form of homosexuality to another. We experienced homosexuality as historical.[1]

Many gay liberationists attributed this shift in consciousness to the influence and example of race-based social justice movements. As early as 1970, a contributor to the San Francisco Free Press argued that "Blacks provided the concept of an oppressed minority getting their thing together, threw out notions of cooperation with the oppressors and developed concepts of group consciousness and self-pride." A year later, the activist Jack Onge framed his participant-historian's rendering of gay liberation by explaining that "the launching of the various civil rights movements among . . . Blacks, Chicanos and Indians . . . helped raise the consciousness of Gay people. . . . Homosexuals realized, as Blacks had before them, that acceptance and respect were not obtained by winning legal equality."[2] These examples could be multiplied. Many print representations of gay liberation produced in the ferment of its first few years situate its emergence in relation to a history of activism by people of color, acknowledging the extent to which gay liberation relied on analyses, philosophies, and strategies developed in the context of racial liberation struggles.

For most interested activists and academics in the 1970s, paying attention to "race" meant learning from and about the experiences of people of color. Paying attention to "sexuality" in the lives of white gay men and lesbian women did not mandate a simultaneous investigation of how their racial positioning influenced their identities and politics. The experience of historicity therefore did not push all white lesbians and gay men to accept gay liberation's intimate and necessary connection to racial liberation movements, but a core group of influential early historical researchers working outside the academy—among them Allan Bérubé, Eric Garber, Amber Hollibaugh, Jonathan Ned Katz, and Joan Nestle—rejected "single-issue" organizing around sexuality in order to pursue a vision of progressive, socially relevant knowledge production in which race and class sensitivity, inclusivity, and equality were central values.[3] The few U.S. academics in the field—Martin Duberman, Estelle Freedman, and John D'Emilio—published work that suggests they too viewed their research as an expression of participation in a broad-based, coalitional movement for social justice that necessarily included attention to race.[4] Together, the conceptual legacy of race-based civil rights and liberation movements and the political convictions of many members of the field's first generation imply that attention to race has been an important part of lesbian and gay history since its founding. How then might we understand the disjuncture between the racially engaged political commitments that spurred the emergence of lesbian and gay history and the fact that LGBTQ history has only recently begun to generate and sustain a sophisticated racial analysis of its own frequently white specificity?

This essay approaches that question by looking at several core features of the U.S. gay and lesbian past as it was constructed in historical writing between 1976, when the first book in the field came out, and 1989, when the first anthology was released. These publications mark the period of the field's initial formation and thus frame inquiry into basic assumptions and strategies that shaped the field at that important moment. My intention is to open the intersection of race and sexuality to historiographical as well as historical interpretation. Because whiteness usually goes unnamed in these sources, comprehensive review of the literature for mentions of "race" is not especially helpful for this project. Therefore, I have chosen to combine conventional historical methods, including oral interviews and archival research, with close textual interpretation of selected passages from widely read published works in the field. These methods reveal two major trends in early works of lesbian and gay history, trends whose juncture constrained the young field's racial analytics during the period of the field's formation. The first trend was the gradual decline of methodological experimentalism and the eventual institutionalization of some historical methods as more legitimate than others. The second trend involved a particular vision of history as a form of revolutionary political practice, and the forms of racial identification that this vision supported.

On the Racial Ramifications of Historical Method

Developing workable methods was a central concern for early lesbian and gay historical researchers, who had no authoritative research base or interpretative tradition on which to draw even for such basic, but hotly contested, issues as defining the object of study.[5] Researching the lesbian and gay past required generating original strategies for identifying and locating relevant sources, interpreting them, and sharing them with others. By the middle of the 1980s, people working outside the academy had developed several major approaches to researching and writing about the LG[BTQ] past.[6] Two of the most important were those I call "archive building" and "critical mythography." This section outlines the emergence of these methods and contrasts them in order to show how they helped construct a historical vision of the gay past as a white past.

Archive builders addressed themselves to generating and accumulating paper sources that contained evidence about past lesbians and gay men, a practice that was certainly broad enough to include research on racialized subjects but that was not particularly finely attuned to the white dominance of the existing documentary record. In contrast, critical mythographers focused on reclaiming agency by evoking a sense of intersubjective connection across time and space. This method granted more evidentiary authority to oral tradition, memory, and community knowledge, and as such offered researchers access to the past experiences of people of color and poor people that were rarely recorded in documentary form. Though elements of the two approaches routinely overlapped in individual historians' work, they can be distinguished by the extent and nature of reliance on written records.

Archive builders generated evidence about the GL[BTQ] past in several ways. Beginning in the mid-1970s, local history projects in Boston, San Francisco, and Buffalo, New York, conducted oral history interviews, which they contextualized with secondary research to construct a written record of past gay and lesbian experiences; archives in Brooklyn, Los Angeles, Toronto, and elsewhere provided repositories for these interviews, alongside collections of primary and secondary materials of all kinds.[7] Frequently both history projects and the creation of archival repositories were undertaken by people with no formal training in historical research or archival technique. Their organizational visions were varied and idio-syncratic, as were the communities that grew up around identity-based historical research. Still it is safe to say that archive builders in general were acting on the desire to redress the exclusion of GL[BTQ] experience from the historical record. Further, they shared the same overarching strategy: all were committed to identi-fying, creating, preserving, and disseminating documentary evidence pertaining to homosexuality.[8]

Archive builders were activists more than antiquarians. They valued the pri-mary-source base that they were helping to create because it provided an eviden-tiary anchor for claims about the past that simultaneously documented the reality of oppression and reflected the experience and perspectives of the oppressed. The political dimension of archival practice was articulated by Joan Nestle, who co-founded the Lesbian Herstory Archives, with the slogan "Our will to remember is our will to change the world."[9] For Nestle, as for many of her contemporaries, the political drive toward social transformation was indistinguishable from identifica-tion with community, an identification registered in the invocation of "our" collec-tive will and imagined as extending across time. Local history projects frequently returned the fruits of their research to the communities that supported them by staging public presentations putting current events into historical context. For instance, in May and June 1979 the gay community in San Francisco staged a series of demonstrations against police violence; the San Francisco Lesbian and Gay History Project responded by staging a forum in which scholar-activists de-scribed and analyzed similar conflicts over the previous twenty years.[10] History felt pertinent. Lesbian, gay, and feminist papers and newsletters often reported on archival activism in terms that suggest enthusiastic reception from local com-munities.[11] For a time in San Francisco, historical presentations were even popular enough to win a regular place in the schedule of events at a local cabaret.[12]

But archive building wasn't the only queer historical game in town. Despite the widely shared perception that history was a meaningful form of cultural produc-tion, many researchers were skeptical about the value of the documentary record as a resource for a politically usable past or a cohesive community in the present. Women of color, joined by a few working-class white lesbians, articulated con-siderable skepticism about the bias inherent in the documentary record. Because such women were marginalized, ignored, or misrepresented not only in hegemonic histories of white men but also in white women's history and black, Latino/a, Asian American, and Native American studies, they concluded that conventional histori-cal sources and methods were too saturated by their oppressors' agendas to yield a reasonably accurate account of the experience of the subjugated. They therefore developed alternative historical strategies. Arguably the most beautiful and evoca-tive was the one I call "critical mythography."

Mythography is a generic term I am using to capture the commonalities among a range of methods and practices that nonetheless shared a common critical goal. Aurora Levins Morales, a poet and activist who took part in developing alternative historical methods in the 1980s, described that goal as being "not so much to document the past as to restore to the dehistoricized a sense of identity and possibility. Such . . . histories seek to re-establish the connection between peoples and their histories, to reveal the mechanisms of power, the steps by which their current condition of oppression was achieved through a series of decisions made by real people to dispossess them; but also to reveal the multiplicity, creativity and persistence among the oppressed."[13] Levins Morales calls the resulting writing "medicinal history" in order to underscore its curative properties. Theorist and poet Gloria Anzaldúa offered the neologism "*autohistoria*" to describe work that "depicts both the soul of the artist and the soul of the *pueblo*. It deals with who tells the stories and what stories and histories are told."[14] I refer to this historical method as "critical mythography" in order to emphasize its incisive critique of conventional standards for measuring the truth of stories about the past. The term quotes poet and essayist Audre Lorde's description of her important 1982 work *Zami* as "biomythography," and so acknowledges the pioneering role that women of color played in originating and developing a genre that intentionally and productively blurs conventional boundaries between literature, history, and critical theory.

The goal of this blurring is to produce a history reflecting the perspectives of the oppressed. Critical mythographies of the 1980s share a commitment to identifying, examining, and exploding hostile legends that had long substituted for historical accounts of the lives of women (and, less often, men) of color and of poor whites. Mythographic recovery projects were based on the principle that much of the available documentary record about any nonheteronormative sexual expression among people of color is—in the words of Maurice Kenny, a gay Mohawk Indian who was active in the Gay American Indian History Project—"distortion," "nonsense," and "sheer insanity."[15] Having "put history through a sieve" to "[winnow] out the lies," many people of color found that there was not much data left with which to build a queer history.[16] Some responded by presenting and interpreting material about the past drawn from oral tradition(s), imagination, memory, identification, and the phenomenological knowledge generated by each researcher's embeddedness in the culture(s) about which she/he wrote.[17]

In short, critical mythographies began with the recognition that it was not necessarily possible to document the history of oppressed people from their own point of view, combined with the refusal to accept that impossibility as the end of historical inquiry.[18] The resulting texts are intentionally metafactual ways of narrating things known as true on an embodied level. Though they often incorporate significant research, they are anchored to the material real less by a paper trail than by attending to the socioeconomic and discursive structures of everyday life. Mythography's medicinal potential—its critical dimension—depends on the mythographer's ability to reflect on those structures in a way that generates a vision of possibilities for other ways of living in relation to them.

Such reflection gains its effectiveness by generating and exploring the affective and intuitive connections that allows researchers (and readers) to make sense of whatever historical legacies are palpable in the present. This is one reason that many mythographies blend fairly straightforward historical narrative with poetry, reminiscence, family stories, theoretical exegesis, and political commentary.[19] A multiplicitous approach reflects people of color's critical analysis of their complex and often contradictory identifications and social situations. In 1986 gay novelist and cultural critic Samuel R. Delany described his resistance to universalizing gay histories, saying, "I have any number of visions, many of them quite contradictory. I distrust people with only one—especially if it's too complete, and they want to thrust everyone into it."[20] Perhaps the most famous articulation of the need for analytic multiplicity to capture the lived reality of people of color is Gloria Anzaldúa's 1987 assessment of "*mestiza* consciousness" as characterized by "tolerance (and intolerance) of ambiguity."[21] Thus the complexity of many mythographic texts is a necessary part of the critical work they do. Part of that work involves inviting readers into the text through a multitude of affectively charged channels. The populist implications of this approach record mythography's emergence from 1970s liberationist culture: it is less attached to interpretative dominance—telling the definitive story, laying claim to Truth—than to offering readers materials and conceptual tools with which to develop their own active understandings of the past.[22]

Mythography diverged from archive building in that its primary focus was on nurturing affective relationships between the past and the present. For this reason it may be easier for twenty-first-century scholars to understand as a creative literary genre than as a form of historical writing. Through the 1980s, however, mythography had a prominent place in gay and lesbian historical practice. That place reflects the community context for research, presentation, and publication by and about sexual minorities throughout the decade. Neither researchers nor readers were necessarily interested in disciplinary integrity or maintaining clear boundaries between different modes of apprehending the past; community standards of authenticity and authority for gay and lesbian historical work did not always require a verifiable documentary base. Affective connection was equally important.

In this context it makes sense that the first anthology of lesbian and gay historical essays, *Hidden from History* (1989), included an excerpt from Paula Gunn Allen's mythographic *The Sacred Hoop* under the title "Lesbians in American Indian Cultures."[23] At the end of the 1980s, mythography was still complementary to more conventionally scholarly, text-based lesbian and gay histories. But complementarity is not centrality. Even a superficial quantitative accounting of *Hidden from History*'s selections suggests that the young field was solidifying around a preference for documentary evidence. In addition to its single mythographic offering, the volume includes one essay rooted in feminist cultural criticism, four that originated in community history projects (three contextualize oral interviews with documentary research), and thirty-two that draw exclusively on print sources in libraries and archives.

In succeeding years mythography lost traction as a historical method, while archive building became increasingly central to gay and lesbian, and later to queer, history. Since the early 1990s, the bulk of the scholarly monographs in the field have rested on oral interviews contextualized by archival research.[24] One reason for this shift is that, as the field professionalized in the late 1980s and 1990s, oral histories served to bridge some of the gap between community and scholarly expectations for what lesbian/gay/queer historical research ought to be and do. Face-to-face interviews honor individual experience and memory as legitimate vectors of historical knowledge, while researchers processing those interviews put them into conversation with existing records in a way that certifies community-generated knowledge as trustworthy. In contrast, critical mythography proved extremely difficult to assimilate into the increasingly professionalized field. Its commitment to embodied, socially relevant, curative history does not consistently produce trustworthy empirical knowledge according to professional standards.[25] Furthermore, its deliberately ecumenical approach can easily appear simply undisciplined to academics, who are trained to value adherence to professional norms over a work's ability to engage nonacademic readers on emotional, intuitive, and political levels.[26] Thus the major historical method developed to capture the experience and perspectives of queer people of color became increasingly marginal as lesbian and gay history professionalized in the late 1980s and 1990s.

The rise of oral history did not cause the demotion of mythography and, with it, important critical perspectives on the political purposes of history and the racialized implications for how we think about historical truth. Oral history's eventual dominance may nonetheless have contributed to gay and lesbian history's persistent lack of critical engagement with white racial positioning, for reasons stemming from the basic techniques of oral history: direct interviewing, balanced by documentary research to compensate for narrators' faulty memories and perspectival limitations. Few white people in the twentieth-century United States were able to articulate their whiteness as a meaningful form of racial experience, with the result that oral interviews were extremely unlikely to yield substantive reflections on its meaning and impact on narrators' lives.[27] The practice of contextualizing oral interviews with archival research could do little to compensate for lack of racial cognizance, as the existing documentary record is not especially rich in sources likely to push white researchers to question the invisibility of whiteness to their narrators. Thus the increasing centrality of archive building, combined with the marginalization of critical mythography as a legitimate historical method, helped to limit the young field's consideration of race as an important determinant of white sexual minority experience.

Racial Identifications and the Politics of History

The second trend in early lesbian and gay history that helped to shape its racial analyses was a pattern of racial identifications that reflects gay movement activism's intimacy with social movements for racial justice. As John D'Emilio has shown, the political analyses and rhetoric of black civil rights leaders had a significant influence on homophile activism in the late 1950s.[28] In 1965 SNCC leader Stokely Carmichael coined the term "Black Power" to describe a new revolutionary racial agenda. The black power movement distinguished itself from earlier race-betterment approaches by focusing its analysis on systems of power rather than on acts of individual prejudice, and it directed its energies toward economic, political, and cultural self-determination rather than toward integration into a system it diagnosed as fundamentally unjust.[29] By 1969, when gay liberation got under way, these revolutionary analyses and goals were broadly familiar to people active in the antiwar, student, and women's movements, in part because radical people of color were involved in all these movements, in part because these analyses had terrific explanatory and motivational force, and in part because activists in a range of movements gained moral legitimacy by adopting the language of racial justice for their own causes. Thus in 1971 a white gay liberationist could dismiss an earlier generation of white homophile activists as "the NAACP of our movement"—a dismissal that implicitly aligned liberationists with the militancy of black power.[30]

Such offhand substitution of the language of race for the language of sexuality suggests widespread recognition that strategies developed in struggles for racial justice had helped to form the political vision of activists focusing on other axes of oppression. It simultaneously suggests some white liberationists' willingness to sidestep stringent analysis of their own racial privilege in favor of borrowing black analyses of racial oppression. White gay people in the 1970s could and did draw on culturally current racial analyses of oppression in the effort to articulate their situation in relation to power. But because the tools they borrowed from racial justice movements were developed specifically to analyze oppression, they did not push white people to examine the privilege that typically characterized their own racial situation. Instead, they sometimes encouraged identification with people of color on the grounds of analogous experiences of oppression.

The ethical and strategic problematics of the race/sex(uality) analogy are well known.[31] There is much less discussion of the affective and identificatory patterns that make the analogy possible and pervasive. These are many, and this essay does not attempt a comprehensive overview of their variation in early lesbian and gay historical writing. Instead, this section unpacks two examples of underexamined identification with past forms of nonheteronormative sexuality by white gay and lesbian researchers, sketching out the affective situation that led sincere and committed antiracist white scholars to imagine "the gay and lesbian past" in fundamentally white terms without knowing that they were doing so. My first example is of white gay and lesbian cross-racial identification with Native Americans. I interpret traces of this identification in early lesbian and gay history as suggesting that even deep commitment to exploring the history of "gay" people of color inadvertently could serve to buttress white researchers' ignorance of their own position as a racialized one. The second example is of white gay male identification with racialized class privilege and male dominance; it points to the way in which construing gay history as a form of liberationist activism could have a similar result.

First, then, let's consider the cultural icon of the "gay Indian." Philip Deloria has demonstrated that white Americans in general have long used the image of the Indian to help naturalize their revolutionary claims—think, for instance, of the Boston Tea Party.[32] Native Americans, as indigenes, are easily seen as embodiments of America's primordial essence. As brutally colonized people, they represent the nation-state's suppression and betrayal of that essence. When these two representational traditions are combined, they suggest that the truest Americans are those whom the state bars from exercising liberties that preexist its authority, because those liberties derive directly from nature. Hence the appeal of "Indian" iconography for revolutionaries of many sorts over a span of several centuries. Invocation of Indian-ness enjoyed a countercultural renaissance in the 1960s and 1970s in a way that seems to have fueled white gay identification with the Native American past.

The white iconographic tradition was not the only source for the image of the "gay Indian." During the same years that gay liberation was gathering steam and the first researchers in lesbian and gay history were getting under way, Red Power activists were raising national consciousness about the oppression of Native Americans.[33] By 1975, Native gay activists had developed a powerfully evocative image of an archetypal gay ancestor as part of their struggle to carve out a space for themselves between white gay racism and homophobia in the red power movement.[34] Thus the figure of the "gay Indian" meshed white neocolonial fantasies about "Indianness" with Native cultural memory and activist reclamations of aboriginal tradition for new purposes. The "gay Indian" is a particularly rich and complex racial and sexual image, then, and exploring its circulation in early gay historical writing can provide some clues about how cross-racial identification by whites helped inform the racial analytics of the emerging field.

The first book in the field, Jonathan Ned Katz's *Gay American History*, includes a seventy-page chapter titled "Gay Americans/Native Americans." Katz introduces his material with his characteristic thoughtfulness, cautioning that the sources he excerpts were written by cultural outsiders with broadly imperialist agendas. Katz warns that the sources' meaning is far from transparent: "The sources quoted tell as much, and often more, about the commentator's sentiments about Native homosexuality than they do about its actual historical forms" (423). This warning seems intended both to acknowledge the racism of much of the source literature and to guard against the possibility that contemporary readers will respond to these documents with uncritical identification along the axis of sexual identity. Nonetheless, it also works to initiate and authorize white gay identification with Native Americans across racial lines. Four hundred and twenty-three pages into *Gay American History*, no reasonably attentive reader could have failed to absorb the fact that the vast majority of sources on the white gay past were also generated by cultural outsiders with ideological, political, and religious axes to grind at gay expense. Thus the very unreliability of the primary source record on same-sex erotics and cross-gender presentation in Native cultures may have opened a path for cross-cultural identification for white gay and lesbian researchers: Native Americans of all tribes, and gay people of many immigrant ancestries, shared the experience of being misrepresented by hostile and uncomprehending observers.

Misrepresentation is a common element of minority experience in general. What is notable about gay identification with the Native American past in the 1970s was the way it brought history into the service of liberation. The rich documentary record of European discomfort with the gender and sexual arrangements of many Native peoples provided 1970s gay activists with evidence that what they interpreted as "homosexuality" was a natural, widespread, and honored part of American life until it was suppressed by imperialist forces. Liberation therefore required historical research to recover a precolonial past. Katz describes gay and lesbian history as "part of [gay people's] struggle for social change and to win control over their own lives" before noting that "the colonial appropriation of the continent by White, Western 'civilization' included the attempt by the conquerors to eliminate various traditional forms of Indian homosexuality—as part of their attempt to destroy that Native culture which might fuel resistance—a form of cultural genocide involving both Native Americans and Gay people" (429). The figure of the "gay Indian" condensed a whole series of political claims and beliefs into a single image that justified, even mandated, insurgent political activism to rectify the effects of colonialism.

Historical writing contributed to that insurgency by insisting that present forms of intolerance and inequality mirrored the conquerors' deliberate erasure of the gay/Native past. The historico-political significance of the "gay Indian" is especially prominent in Judy Grahn's award-winning 1984 mythography *Another Mother Tongue*.[35] In a chapter called "Gay Is *Very* American," Grahn asserts that "we have never learned to give proper credit for the ideas and forms of freedom and democratic government learned by the white European forefathers from the Iroquois and other Indian peoples who had created and used them for centuries" (53). In this claim Grahn mobilized the cultural image of Native peoples as both sources and representatives of ancient natural democracy. She then used documents from Katz to suture gender and erotic nonconformity to the postconquest denial of natural rights, declaring, "Modern patriarchal society has usually defined 'natural' to mean rigid adherence to sexually dictated roles delineated by a body of authorities over what constitutes the masculine and what constitutes the feminine sphere of society. The Indian idea of what is natural to a person means what the person's visions and spirits tell her or him to do with life" (58). Her implication is that gay people, like Indians, are throwing off the yoke of colonialism when they reject "rigid adherence" to sexual roles and obedience to gender "authorities" in favor of following their own visions of who they ought to be. Grahn depicts sexual self-determination as inseparable from a democratic political self-rule that she suggests is indigenous to America and natural for authentic citizens. In this formulation, identifying with Native people as the "first Americans" constructs gay people (including Indians) as deserving liberation not in spite of their sexual and/or gender deviance but because of the integrity and core alignment with a primordial vision of America to which it testifies.

Both Katz and Grahn, then, offered their different modes of historical writing as tools with which readers could construct an intersectional politics that did not distinguish between "racial liberation" and "sexual liberation." The value of this construction for the Gay American Indian (GAI) movement was considerable; the first anthology of gay Native writing, *Living the Spirit* (1988), uses a brief excerpt from *Another Mother Tongue* as an epigraph. That anthology opens with Paula Gunn Allen's poem "Some Like Indians Endure" (9–13), which characterizes lesbians and Indians as tenacious survivors and preservers of culture despite the cultural demand that they assimilate: "like indians dykes / are supposed to die out / or forget," but "they remember and they / stay." Gunn Allen's poem suggests that historical memory is a political necessity for dyke/Indian survival, since without it they might "shatter / go away / to nowhere" (12). Although analogies between race and sexuality can become problematic when they obscure real differences in people's needs and relation to power, in this instance the claim to a history of similitude helped gay Native Americans to frame their activism as both authentically Indian and thoroughly gay. For whites, however, identification with the oppression and exclusion experienced by people of color could help legitimize inattention to the real entitlements that flow from whiteness. Thus Grahn's long and lyrical homage to Native American sex/gender systems climaxes with a wistful dream that if she and her (white) first lover had known that Indian cultures honored "gay" people, "much of [their] alienation and terror would have left [them]" (71)—a conclusion implying that the core meaning and larger purpose of Native American history was to comfort white lesbians and gay men with the knowledge that they, "like indians," had both natural and historical rights to a higher status than they presently enjoyed.

Cross-racial identification with gay Native Americans on the grounds of shared political needs for recuperative history therefore could encourage white gays and lesbians to think of their position in terms of unrealized entitlements, rather than in more complex terms of the ways that their real oppressions coincided with their relative access to racial privilege. Where white gay historical identification attached to other whites, this effect was exaggerated. This dynamic is the subject of my second example of underexamined affective investment in "the gay past," this time drawn from Martin Bauml Duberman's contribution to the 1989 anthology *Hidden from History*. In his justly famous "'Writhing Bedfellows' in Antebellum South Carolina: Historical Interpretation and the Politics of Evidence," Duberman performs a quite brilliant analysis of a pair of letters written in 1826 by T. Jefferson Withers to James H. Hammond. In these letters Withers refers to Hammond's sexual proclivities in explicit terms: "I feel some inclination to learn whether you yet sleep in your Shirt-tail, and whether you yet have the extravagant delight of poking and punching a writhing Bedfellow with your long fleshen pole—the exquisite touches of which I have often had the honor of feeling?" (155). In the other letter Withers describes his mental picture of Hammond "charging over the pine barrens of your locality, braying, like an ass, at every she-male you can discover" (156).

Duberman identifies both the explicit content and the breezy tone of these letters as remarkable in their implication that in 1826 elite, white, young, southern men could have sex with men without guilt, shame, romance, or apparent fear about its possible consequences for their careers. Both men's ambitions were rewarded: Hammond became a U.S. senator until South Carolina's secession from the Union, while Withers was a member of the 1861 committee that drew up the governmental structure of the Confederacy. Duberman speculates that "the American South of the latter part of the eighteenth and early part of the nineteenth centuries was (for privileged, young, white males) one of those rare 'liberal interregnums' in our history when the body could be treated as a natural source of pleasure and 'wanton' sexuality viewed as the natural prerogative—the exemplification even—of 'manliness'" (161). Historical research in this area has not yet confirmed or disproved this description of the early Republic, but it is certainly striking for its resonance with gay men's sexual culture in 1970s Manhattan, where Duberman lived when he wrote this article.[36] Indeed, Duberman acknowledges that he finds the Hammond of these letters "admirably playful, exploratory and freewheeling, uninhibited and attractively unapologetic" (159).

I do not point to this resonance in order to discredit Duberman's insight; on the contrary, Duberman's provocative speculation about a culture of elite southern libertinism in the early Republic is an excellent example of the way that identification can sharpen historical perception.[37] Nonetheless it is striking that strong identification with a sexual culture of gratification predicated on the right to absolute dominance over members of weaker classes, sexes, and races did not arouse Duberman's critical interest in entitlement as a significant theme for gay historical investigation. Instead, his analytic focus is on the "politics of evidence." Almost half of "'Writhing Bedfellows'" describes Duberman's frustrated attempts to get formal permission to reprint the Withers/Hammond letters. In the end he published the erotic excerpts "against the wishes of their official custodian" (167), despite deep scholarly misgivings about this course of action. He justifies his decision as an act of political protest:

> I felt it was essential to challenge the tradition of suppressing information which might prove useful to gay people in better understanding the historical dimensions of our experience, the shifting strategies we have adopted over time to cope with oppression, and the varied styles we have developed to express our special sensibilities. If the "lawless" tactics I've resorted to seem extreme to some, well, so is our need. . . . The heterosexist world has long held a monopoly on defining legal and ethical propriety, . . . using them as weapons for keeping us in line by denying us access to knowledge of our own antecedents. (167)

In short, Duberman presents his decision to reprint the letters as a principled blow against the massed forces of heterosexism. Gay history is an activist enterprise as much as a scholarly one, he says, and when social justice needs collide with academic norms, the former should prevail. This stance was, as we've seen, widely shared among lesbian and gay researchers. What this example underscores is the extent to which a commitment to the political value of gay history could draw attention away from the way that identification with oppression allows whiteness to circulate in that history unremarked.

For whom are Confederate statesmen like Hammond and Withers "our own antecedents"? Duberman is not calling elite white gay men to engage with the complexity of their relations to power and privilege, so to embrace these men as "our" ancestors in any celebratory sense, we must be willing to identify with them entirely on the grounds of their libertinism. But if Duberman's speculation about the sexual culture documented in these letters is correct, then Hammond's and Withers' pursuit of pleasure could be so freewheeling *because* their whiteness, maleness, and class status allowed them to "express [their] special sensibilities" without much concern for what lesser people might think or feel about them. To identify with their "attractively unapologetic" libertinism is then also to dream of access to their power.

The racial, class, and gender privilege embedded in this example of gay historical identification is occluded by Duberman's explicit focus on the theme of gay exclusion and the pursuit of history as a form of activism. By emphasizing gay people's "desperate *need*" for history, Duberman participates in the construction of a gay history defined by resistance to oppression *even when its subjects are elite white men.* Seeing gay history as a form of activism entailed, in this instance, a simultaneous denial of and identification with the real power and privilege of people whose sexual freedom stemmed from their position at the top of an extremely hierarchical social and racial order. Despite Duberman's conscious and articulate commitment to racial justice, his equally articulate commitment to history as the practice of liberation leads him to contribute to the construction of a lesbian and gay past that looks very much like an annex to the plantation master's house. Entitlement to history seems like a displacement of, or cover for, entitlement to power. This second example suggests that one of the sources of gay and lesbian history's lack of critical attention to whiteness, paradoxically enough, has been its traditional commitment to resistance against oppression.

When lesbian and gay history began in the mid-1970s its basic claim, that gay people constituted an oppressed cultural minority with a distinct and meaningful heritage, constituted a radical intervention into then-current discourses on homosexuality as psychopathology. In his 1975–76 lectures at the College de France, Michel Foucault described such discursive interventions as "the insurrection of subjugated knowledges." Foucault proposed that such interventions gained critical strength from "coupling together" forms of knowledge that relied on radical applications of conventional scholarly tools, and forms of knowledge "below the required level of erudition or scientificity."[38] In other words, when liberated gay people staged the discursive intervention that became the field of lesbian and gay history, it seemed clear to one of the era's most politically engaged and astute social theorists that this was possible because different modes of knowledge production, some scholarly and some local, were intersecting in a way that had significant epistemological and political consequences. Academic forms of lesbian and gay history drew on the affective potency and political insight of activist approaches;

embodied community knowledges gained (limited) citational support and representational durability as oral history researchers transformed memory and feeling into a print record and as the resulting documentation was preserved in archives.

By the end of the 1980s, however, some of the new forms of knowledge about homosexuality had begun to gain an institutional legitimacy as "history" that did not accrue to others. The increasing dominance of academic empirical standards for lesbian/gay/queer history resulted in the marginalization of mythography's multidisciplinary approaches and affective insights into the processes of racialization and its experiential manifestations. At the same time, historians working with oral narratives and print archives remained in touch with the tradition of gay/lesbian historical activism. These two trends together constituted a new epistemological field that was conventionally scholarly in its citational practice yet simultaneously rooted in GL[BT]/queer community knowledge about and interests in oppression and resistance.[39] That distinctive epistemological configuration helped to shape and limit the racial analyses of lesbian and gay history in the period of its formation through the 1990s and into the new millennium.

As of this writing, it is still difficult to find book-length studies in LGBTQ history that reflect the fact that people oppressed as sexual deviants may also be privileged on racial, as well as on gender and class, grounds. Nonetheless, there are signs of change afoot. At the beginning of the twenty-first century, a handful of historians began to write about whiteness, and white dominance in U.S. culture and politics, as integral to the meaning and experience of (homo)sexuality for white people as well as for people of color.[40] Such emergent engagement received a massive boost from outside the discipline when the "historical turn" in literary criticism and American studies helped support and promote a conceptual shift generated by queer scholars of color who treat race not as an object or a status but as an ongoing process—and the processes of racialization centrally include the social and psychic organization of gender, desire, and intimate relationships.[41] Young historians researching queer subjects are therefore entering the field with a transformed understanding of what it means to study both "race" and "sexuality."

This state of analysis underscores the crucial importance of methodological ecumenicism. If the emergent intersectional history of race and sexuality is to continue to expand and deepen, it must remain alert to the importance of the real range of possible approaches to and presentations of knowledge about the past; literary criticism, creative writing, and cultural studies approaches must be considered as real contributors to the historical project. The field's long tradition of weak attunement to whiteness also raises questions about the politics of history that arise at the intersection of race and sexuality. Like the LGBTQ history with which it overlaps, the history of the race/sexuality nexus in the United States is often motivated by the belief that intellectual work may serve socially progressive ends. As such it may also seek ways to adapt subjugated knowledges to scholarly structures of thought and practice. In doing so, it risks duplicating the gap between good political intentions and the institutionalization of methods and interpretations that are imbricated in the larger culture in which white and heterosexual dominance is normative. Neither the separation nor the intersection of "race" and "sexuality" has predictable and uniform analytic or political effects. No approach to such power-laden topics is inherently progressive. This doesn't mean that historians should abandon the attempt to unravel the intersections of race and sexuality, but rather that we need to think about their political effects in ways that emphasize an ethic of sensitivity to our own continual reinscription in the structures of domination within which we work.

Notes

The author wishes to thank Nan Alamilla Boyd, Mel Y. Chen, Rebekah Edwards, Don Romesburg, and Susan Stryker for their generous engagement with this project.

1. Jonathan Ned Katz, *Gay American History: Lesbians and Gay Men in the U.S.A.* (New York: Avon Books, 1976), 1–2. Subsequent citations in text.

2. Marcus Overseth, *SF Free Press*, no. 3 [1970?], n.p.; Jack Onge, *The Gay Liberation Movement* (Chicago: Alliance Press, 1971), 11. Though Onge spoke of blacks and homosexuals as discrete groupings, there were radical gay and lesbian people of color involved in many liberation movements, a fact that was sometimes acknowledged but more often occluded by just such constructions as analogies between racial and sexual oppression. This mix of acknowledgment and occlusion can be seen in such texts as Donn Teal, *The Gay Militants* (New York: Stein and Day, 1971), where the existence of Third World Gay Liberation is mentioned (in a footnote on p. 158), but where people of color most frequently appear either as analogies (91, 150, 160) or as sources of dissension within gay liberationism (105).

3. Except for one late essay by Bérubé, these independent scholar/activists were less interested in writing about their commitment to antiracism than in incorporating it into their lives and practice. My thanks to Jonathan N. Katz (pers. comm., May 23 2009) for sharing his perception of antiracism's centrality to this founding generation of white gay and lesbian historians. See also Allan Bérubé, "How Gay Stays White and What Kind of White It Stays," in *The Making and Unmaking of Whiteness*, ed. Birgit Brander Rasmussen et al. (Berkeley: University of California Press, 2001), 234–65. The importance of Jewish tradition to many of these radical activist/scholars has not, to my knowledge, been explored.

4. Martin Duberman began his career as a historian of abolitionism with a dissertation on Charles Frances Adams; his second publication was the documentary play *In White America* (New York: Samuel French, 1963), which presents the history of African American struggles for racial justice. John D'Emilio's second publication was an edited collection, *The Civil Rights Struggle: Leaders in Profile* (New York: Facts-on-File, 1979), and his most famous work, *Sexual Politics, Sexual Communities: The Making of a Homosexual Minor-*

ity in the United States (Chicago: University of Chicago Press, 1983), positions gay rights activism of the 1950s in relation to the civil rights movement. See also his *Lost Prophet: Bayard Rustin and the Quest for Freedom and Justice in America* (New York: Free Press, 2003).

5. It was and is rare to find sources that offer unambiguous evidence of same-sex eroticism before the mid–twentieth century, while many of the sources that do exist are uncommunicative about the texture of the experience to the people involved in it or their embeddedness in social worlds. To compound the difficulty, in the 1970s and 1980s almost any less explicit evidence of same-sex eroticism was dismissed as inconclusive or misleading by straight historians and biographers, while many lesbian feminists insisted that genital contact was beside the point and that evidence of same-sex affection and loyalty was more appropriate to a history of women's intimacy. For an incisive discussion of what she named "the historical denial of lesbianism" in extant scholarship, see Blanche Wiesen Cook, "'Women Alone Stir My Imagination': Lesbianism and the Cultural Tradition." *SIGNS* 4, no. 4 (Summer 1979): 718–39. Cook was among those who argued for a definition of "lesbian" that did not require evidence of overt sexual contact but that instead featured commitment to women as life partners.

6. The researchers on whom I focus here addressed themselves to a past they understood as gay and lesbian; I include [BTQ] in brackets to indicate that "lesbian and gay" is not an exhaustive description for the historical subjects in question, though it was treated as such in the literature under discussion.

7. Jim Kepner began the collection that eventually became part of the ONE Institute archive (now the ONE/National Gay and Lesbian Archive, located in West Hollywood) in 1942, but he did not announce the founding of his archive until 1975 or incorporate it until 1979. See the entry for Jim Kepner under the 1940s Timeline at http://www.lgbthistory.org/ (accessed June 16, 2009). The Lesbian Herstory Archives in New York was founded in 1974 (LHA *Newsletter*, no. 1 [1975]); see also the brief institutional history at http://www.lesbian herstoryarchives.org/history.html (accessed June 16, 2009). A number of local history projects began in the 1970s and later provided core collections for archives established or incorporated in the 1980s, after AIDS began to render a new generation acutely sensitive to the ease with which the subculture could be erased from memory and the historical record. For a detailed listing of gay and lesbian archives, see the Society of American Archivists website at http://www.archivists.org/saagroups/lagar/ (accessed January 21, 2016). For instance, see the San Francisco Gay History Project mission statement, San Francisco Lesbian and Gay History Project collection, San Francisco GLBT Historical Society (hereinafter SFGLBTHS), box 1, misc. folder; Chris Czernik, "How the Boston Lesbian History Project Began," *Gay Community News*, Boston, June 16, 1984, 14; Alisa Klinger, "Resources for Lesbian Ethnographic Research in the Lavender Archives," *Journal of Homosexuality* 34, no. 3/4 (1998): 205–35.

8. Joan Nestle, "The Will to Remember: The Lesbian Herstory Archives of New York," *Feminist Review* 34 (Spring 1990): 86–94. Letters in the LHA "Archives Correspondence" files for 1975 and 1976 document similar motivations for the founding of lesbian/gay archives in San Antonio, Texas; Sebastopol, California; Philadelphia, Pennsylvania; and Jacksonville, Kentucky. See also SF Gay and Lesbian Oral History Project meeting minutes (July 15, 1979), SFLGHP Misc. Docs. folder, SFGLBTHS.

9. Nestle, "Will to Remember," 233.

10. Flyer for "Spontaneous Combustion: Two Decades of Police Violence and Gay Rage in San Francisco," with Amber Hollibaugh, Lois Helmbold, Jeffrey Escoffier, and John D'Emilio, SFLGHP collection, box 1, SFGLBTHS. The event was held August 5, 1979. At the end of May, a major confrontation between San Francisco police and the gay community erupted after Dan White, a former police officer who murdered openly gay city supervisor Harvey Milk, was acquitted, and a series of smaller incidents in June meant that the topic was directly relevant to community life. See John D'Emilio, "Allan Bérubé's Gift to History," *Gay and Lesbian Review Worldwide* 15, no. 3 (May–June 2008), http://www.glreview.com/article.php?articleid=58 (accessed June 3, 2008; page no longer available).

11. "Gay Archives" (unsigned editorial), *Body Politic* 10 (1973): 2; "Gay Archives Project Underway" (unsigned editorial), *Advocate*, March 26, 1975, 16; Michael Bronski, "The San Francisco Oral History Project," *Gay Community News*, October 27, 1979, 10; "In Search of Our History: Reclaiming the Past, Documenting the Present" (feature section), *Advocate*, November 12, 1981, 22; Marakay Rogers, "The Search for Gay Roots Needs Your Help," *Gay Paper*, April 1983, 11; Chris Czernick, "How the Boston History Project Began," *Gay Community News* 11, no. 14 (1984): 14; "Make Your Own Archive: History Begins at Home," *Advocate*, May 27, 1986, 32; Scott Wilds, "They Even Want Your Old Love Letters," Philadelphia Lesbian and Gay Task Force *Newsletter*, April 1987, 16; P. Lynch, "Freeze-Framing Our History: A New Slide Program," *Advocate*, October 25, 1988, 78.

12. "History Project promo files—Valencia Rose," Donald Montwill Papers, box 2, SFGLBTHS. Calendars from the Valencia Rose cabaret suggest that staged historical presentations began as part of Pride Month celebrations in June 1983. These events were listed three to four times a month from September 1983 through August 1984, after which they became sporadic.

13. Aurora Levins Morales, *Medicine Stories: History, Culture and the Politics of Integrity* (Cambridge, Mass.: South End Press, 1988), 24.

14. Gloria Anzaldúa, "Border Arte: Nepantla, El Lugar de la Frontera." In *La Frontera / The Border: Art about the Mexico/United States Border Experience*, ed. Natasha Bonilla Martinez (San Diego, Calif.: Museum of Contemporary Art, 1993), 113.

15. Maurice Kenny, "Tinselled Bucks: A Historical Study in Indian Homosexuality," in *Living the Spirit: A Gay American Indian Anthology*, ed. Will Roscoe (New York: St. Martin's Press, 1988), 15, 19. Kenny's piece, the first on its subject matter, is an expansion of a shorter essay originally published in *Gay Sunshine* no. 26/27 (Winter 1975–76), 15–17.

16. Gloria Anzaldúa, *Borderlands/La Frontera* (San Francisco: Aunt Lute, 1987), 104.

17. For examples, see Cherrie Moraga, *Loving in the War Years* (Cambridge, Mass.: South End Press, 1983); Audre Lorde, *Zami: A New Spelling of My Name* (Trumansburg, N.Y.: Crossing Press, 1983); Judy Grahn, *Another Mother Tongue: Gay Words, Gay Worlds* (Boston: Beacon Press, 1984); Paula Gunn Allen, *The Sacred Hoop: Recovering the Feminine in American Indian Traditions* (Boston: Beacon Press, 1986); Anzaldúa, *Borderlands/La Frontera*; Joan Nestle, *A Restricted Country* (Ann Arbor, Mich.: Firebrand Books, 1987); Dorothy Allison, *Trash* (Washington, D.C.: RedBone Press, 1988); and Isaac Julien, *Looking for Langston* (Sankofa Films, 1989). One could argue that many anthologies of "women's" writing spanning the 1980s have a great deal in common with works I've identified as critical mythography (e.g.,

Cherríe Moraga and Gloria Anzaldúa, eds., *This Bridge Called My Back* [Watertown, Mass.: Persephone Press, 1981]; Gloria Anzaldúa, ed., *Making Face, Making Soul* [San Francisco: Aunt Lute, 1990]). They are different primarily in that the single-authored works out of which I've developed a working definition of critical mythography tend to engage more directly and consistently with the relation of the present to the past.

18. Emma Pérez, *The Decolonial Imaginary: Writing Chicanas into History* (Bloomington: Indiana University Press, 2008).

19. Grahn, *Another Mother Tongue*, xii–xiii.

20. "Samuel R. Delany: The Possibility of Possibilities" (interview with Joseph Beam), in *In the Life: A Black Gay Anthology*, ed. Joseph Beam (1986; Washington, D.C.: RedBone Press, 2008), 153.

21. Anzaldúa, *Borderlands/La Frontera*, 104.

22. Isaac Julien, "*Looking for Langston*: An Interview with Essex Hemphill," in *Brother to Brother: New Writings by Black Gay Men*, ed. Essex Hemphill (Boston: Alyson, 1991): "The idea . . . was for the storytelling to actually construct a narrative that would enable audiences to meditate and to think, rather than be told" (177).

23. Martin B. Duberman, George Chauncey, and Martha Vicinus, eds., *Hidden from History: Reclaiming the Lesbian and Gay Past* (New York: New American Library, 1989). The choice of publisher suggests that its intended audience was not solely an academic one: NAL specialized in inexpensive paperbacks with an emphasis on classics, contemporary fine literature, and scholarship; its slogans included "Rich Reading at Low Prices" and "Good Reading for the Millions." On NAL, see its parent company, Penguin USA, at http://tinyurl.com/hdnqzc8 (accessed January 21, 2016), and the description of the publisher in New York University's Fales Library guide to the NAL archives, available at http://dlib.nyu.edu/findingaids/html/fales/nal.html (accessed January 21, 2016).

24. Nan Alamilla Boyd, "Who Is the Subject? Queer Theory Meets Oral History," *Journal of the History of Sexuality* 17, no. 2 (May 2008): 177–89.

25. I mean by this not that mythography is wrong, only that its methods are geared toward truths that differ from those of more-academic histories. Emma Pérez says of Anzaldúa's *Borderlands/La Frontera* that she treated "history as only another literary genre" and suggests that historians focused on "the book's factual errors . . . simply missed the metaphor and read too literally" (*Decolonial Imaginary*, 25).

26. Hence historian Ramón Gutierrez has described Anzaldúa (1987) as "a combination of history (much of it wrong), poetry, essays, and philosophical gems." "Community, Patriarchy, and Individualism: The Politics of Chicano History and the Dream of Equality," *American Quarterly* 45, no. 1 (1993): 63. Will Roscoe's *Changing Ones: Third and Fourth Genders in Native North America* (New York: St. Martin's Press, 1998) offers a fruitful interdisciplinary method for combining mythography's strengths with professional standards of evidence and presentation: "Ethnohistorians utilize historical records, published literature, archives, visual materials and artifacts and consult contemporary members of the communities they study" (19).

27. Ruth Frankenburg, *White Women, Race Matters: The Social Construction of Whiteness* (Minneapolis: University of Minnesota Press, 1993); for the racial self-awareness of

nondominant whites, see John Hartigan Jr., *Racial Situations: Class Predicaments of Whiteness in Detroit* (Princeton, N.J.: Princeton University Press, 1999).

28. John D'Emilio, *Sexual Politics, Sexual Communities: The Making of a Homosexual Minority in the United States, 1940–1970* (Chicago: University of Chicago Press, 1983), 149–53, 223–25. The following paragraph is heavily indebted to D'Emilio's analysis.

29. Kwame Ture (Stokely Carmichael) and Charles V. Hamilton, *Black Power: The Politics of Liberation* (1967; New York: Vintage, 1992).

30. Merle Miller, *On Being Different* (New York: Random House, 1971), 38; quoted in D'Emilio, *Sexual Politics, Sexual Communities*, 2. Donn Teal also describes preliberation homophile activists as pursuing "NAACP-like tactics" (*Gay Militants*, 38). That alignment was a matter more of tactics than of strategies. Gay activists in the early 1970s adopted an aggressively countercultural style, as did black power activists. Nonetheless, the gay liberation movement's early goals included the repeal of sodomy laws, legal protection from employment discrimination, and the removal of homosexuality from the American Psychiatric Association's Diagnostic and Statistical Manual of mental and emotional disorders. Such activities had more in common with the legislative agendas of the NAACP than with black power's attempts to foster economic and cultural self-sufficiency in black communities.

31. bell hooks, *Talking Back: Thinking Feminist, Thinking Black* (Boston: South End Press, 1989), 125; Janet Halley, "Like-Race Arguments," in *What's Left of Theory? New Work on the Politics of Literary Theory*, ed. Judith Butler, John Guillory and Kendall Thomas (New York: Routledge, 2000), 40–74; Siobhan Somerville, "Queer Loving," *GLQ* 11, no. 3 (2005): 335–70. Despite the power of these critiques, it seems to me that identifications across lines of time, race, and state formation can be immensely productive, both politically and intellectually; people who find themselves situated in similar ways vis-à-vis military/governmental and spiritual authorities, as well as formations of capital, can learn from one another's struggles in important ways. The goal, I think, is not to legislate against identification but to remain alert to and respectful of context-specific differences in culture and in relations of power.

32. Philip Deloria, *Playing Indian* (New Haven, Conn.: Yale University Press, 1999).

33. Vine Deloria Jr., *Behind the Trail of Broken Treaties: An Indian Declaration of Independence* (New York: Delacorte Press, 1974); Joane Nagel, *American Indian Ethnic Renewal: Red Power and the Resurgence of Identity and Culture* (New York: Oxford University Press, 1996).

34. Randy Burns, preface to *Living the Spirit: A Gay American Indian Anthology*, ed. Will Roscoe (New York: Macmillan, 1988), 2–3. Burns was (with Barbara Cameron) cofounder of Gay American Indians in 1975.

35. Grahn's *Another Mother Tongue* won the American Library Association's 1985 Gay Book Award, as well as significant praise in the gay press.

36. Some more recent research does suggest that the subject is worth further exploration. See Clare Lyons, *Sex among the Rabble: Gender and Power in the Age of Revolution, Philadelphia, 1730–1830* (Chapel Hill: University of North Carolina Press, 2007).

37. David Halperin describes identification as "a form of cognition" in *How to Do the History of Homosexuality* (Chicago: University of Chicago Press, 2002), 15. See also Carolyn

Dinshaw, *Getting Medieval: Sexualities and Communities, Pre- and Postmodern* (Durham, N.C.: Duke University Press, 1999), 141.

38. Michel Foucault, *Society Must Be Defended: Lectures at the College de France, 1975–1976* (New York: Picador, 2003), 7–8.

39. That distinctive blend of scholarly tools in the service of community interests is vivid in many 1990s monographs; see Elizabeth L. Kennedy and Madeline Davis, *Boots of Leather, Slippers of Gold: The History of a Lesbian Community* (New York: Routledge, 1993); George Chauncey, *Gay New York: Gender, Urban Culture, and the Making of the Gay Male World, 1890–1940* (New York: Basic Books, 1995). A number of more recent works bring fresh research and new perspectives to bear on questions of political activism and the relationship between community and movement formation that have been at the heart of the field at least since D'Emilio's *Sexual Politics, Sexual Communities*; see Marcia Gallo, *Different Daughters: A History of the Daughters of Bilitis and the Rise of the Lesbian Rights Movement* (New York: Seal Press, 2006); [Ann] Finn Enke, *Finding the Movement: Sexuality, Contested Space, and Feminist Activism* (Durham, N.C.: Duke University Press, 2007); and Marc Stein, *City of Sisterly and Brotherly Loves: Lesbian and Gay Philadelphia, 1945–1972* (Philadelphia: Temple University Press, 2004).

40. A particularly important work is Lisa Duggan, *Sapphic Slashers: Sex, Violence, and American Modernity* (Durham, N.C.: Duke University Press, 2000), which makes whiteness and white dominance central to the analysis of the "Sapphic slasher." Her contribution in this regard has not yet had the influence it deserves. Nonetheless, a careful reader can find signs of increasing attention to the whiteness/homosexuality nexus. John Howard, *Men like That: A Southern Queer History* (Chicago: University of Chicago Press, 1999) contains strong, if scattered, discussions of white privilege and white supremacy. Enke, *Finding the Movement*, includes insightful observations about the ways that lesbian style and social space were raced; on whiteness, see esp. 230–37. More recently, Christina Hanhardt makes the intersection of homosexuality and whiteness central to her argument in *Safe Space: Gay Neighborhood History and the Politics of Violence* (Durham, N.C.: Duke University Press, 2013).

41. See Roderick A. Ferguson, *Aberrations in Black: Toward a Queer of Color Critique* (Minneapolis: University of Minnesota Press, 2004); Nayan Shah, *Stranger Intimacy: Contesting Race, Sexuality and the Law in the North American West* (Berkeley: University of California Press, 2011); David Eng, *The Feeling of Kinship: Queer Liberalism and the Racialization of Intimacy* (Durham, N.C.: Duke University Press, 2010).

CHAPTER 3

Race, Class, and the U.S. Supreme Court's Doctrine of Heteronormative Supremacy

MARC STEIN

The U.S. Supreme Court's controversial rulings on abortion, birth control, homosexuality, and obscenity in the 1960s and 1970s are typically regarded as decisions about sex, marriage, and reproduction, not race and class. Yet several of the court's most important decisions on these subjects—including *Griswold, Fanny Hill, Boutilier, Eisenstadt,* and *Roe*—addressed race and class in direct and indirect ways. This essay asks what it might mean to make race and class more central in our interpretations of the court's rulings on sex, marriage, and reproduction during the period commonly associated with the sexual revolution. At the same time, the essay asks what it might mean to make sex, marriage, and reproduction more central in our interpretations of rulings typically classified as decisions about race. For example, scholars frequently present *McLaughlin* and *Loving*, which concerned interracial cohabitation and marriage, as important decisions about race and marriage, but this essay explores their significance for the history of sex and reproduction as well.[1]

For many activists and scholars, it has become increasingly difficult to think about sex, gender, sexuality, class, and race without considering their intersections and interrelationships. Evelyn Brooks Higginbotham, for example, argues that "we must expose the role of race as a metalanguage by calling attention to its powerful, all-encompassing effect on the construction and representation of other social and power relations, namely, gender, class, and sexuality." Siobhan Somerville writes that "questions of race . . . must be understood as a crucial part of the history and representation of sexual formations." While most of the examples used by Higginbotham and Somerville are drawn from the late nineteenth and early twentieth centuries, this essay focuses on intersections of sex, gender, sexuality, class, and race in a set of Supreme Court cases decided in the 1960s and 1970s. These decisions offer important clues about the emergence of new relations and technologies of power in this period.[2]

According to the conventional wisdom about the history of the Supreme Court, the justices most forcefully promoted equal rights in the period that began with the ruling against segregated public schools in *Brown* (1954) and concluded with the decision to overturn restrictive abortion laws in *Roe* (1973). While critics on the right have attacked these rulings as examples of judicial activism, critics on the left have claimed that they did not go nearly far enough in embracing equal rights. My previously published work has argued that the court's decisions in the 1960s and 1970s did not adopt a libertarian or egalitarian doctrine of sexual citizenship. In developing what I call a doctrine of heteronormative supremacy, the court granted special rights and privileges to heterosexual, marital, and procreative forms of sexual expression. This essay argues that the doctrine of heteronormative supremacy was meaningfully classed and racialized.

I label the doctrine "heteronormative" partly because the court privileged heterosexuality over homosexuality, but also because the justices privileged particular forms of heterosexuality. For instance, as the court made clear, laws against nonmarital sex—homosexual and heterosexual—continued to be presumptively constitutional, even as the justices struck down laws against birth control, abortion, and interracial marriage. As for calling this a doctrine of heteronormative "supremacy," I mean to reference a set of discourses and practices that worked to make normative heterosexuality supreme. While allowing for some flexibility and change in what counted as heterosexual and normative, the doctrine was based on the notion that normative heterosexuality had been, was, and always should be favored in society, culture, politics, and law. I also refer to this as a doctrine of heteronormative supremacy to emphasize that the doctrine was based on and related to the doctrine of white supremacy. In this way, my terminology is meant to exemplify one of the essay's main arguments: that the court's decisions about sex, marriage, and reproduction were significantly racialized.

The analysis here suggests several possible avenues for further investigations of how the doctrine of heteronormative supremacy reflected and contributed to the ongoing formation of class and race hierarchies. One of the recurring themes is the use of language about sex, marriage, and reproduction as a technology of race and class. In an era when the court ruled that "race" was a "suspect classification" and subjected "racial classifications" to "strict scrutiny," the justices used coded language about sex, marriage, and reproduction with significantly racialized and classed meanings. The court's use of strict scrutiny for laws and practices that were based explicitly on race encouraged many policy makers and judges to turn to implicitly racialized and classed language. In this context, critical references to nonmarital sex and reproduction functioned in ways similar to conservative discourses about crime, welfare, and taxes: they communicated meaningfully about race and class without appearing to do so.

Griswold (1965)

The *Griswold* litigation was initiated by the Planned Parenthood League of Connecticut, which opened a family-planning clinic in a deliberate effort to provoke a police response and then have the state's restrictive birth control law declared unconstitutional. In its decision, the Supreme Court ruled that the state law, which prohibited the use of birth control, violated constitutional rights of marital privacy. In the court's majority and concurring opinions, most of the justices made passing comments about the legitimacy of laws against nonmarital sex—including laws prohibiting adultery, fornication, and homosexuality—but distinguished these types of statutes from those that interfered with marital rights. The court's ruling was thus based not on an egalitarian or libertarian doctrine of sexual privacy but rather on a doctrine of heteronormative supremacy. According to the majority of the justices, married couples had special rights with respect to sex and reproduction. Given customary prohibitions on same-sex marriage, the court's decision privileged heterosexuality over homosexuality, but it also privileged marital heterosexuality over all other forms of heterosexuality. This was consistent with long-standing U.S. traditions, but in a period of heightened social anxieties about sex, marriage, and reproduction, the doctrine of heteronormative supremacy received firm recognition by the court in *Griswold*.[3]

Theoretically, the doctrine of heteronormative supremacy applied to all U.S. people, but the *Griswold* decision reflected and contributed to the country's ongoing formation of class and racial hierarchies. One of the first issues addressed by Justice William O. Douglas's majority opinion was whether the appellants—Estelle Griswold, the executive director of the Planned Parenthood League of Connecticut, and Lee Buxton, the medical director of the League's clinic—had standing to address the rights of the married women served by the clinic. To establish their standing, Douglas invoked several precedents, including *Barrows* (1953), which had held that "a white defendant, party to a racially restrictive covenant . . . , was allowed to raise the issue that enforcement of the covenant violated the rights of prospective Negro purchasers." Just as a white property owner had standing to raise questions about the rights of prospective black buyers, health care professionals had standing to raise questions about their clients. Put another way, just as prospective black buyers did not speak for themselves in *Barrows*, married women served by Planned Parenthood did not speak for themselves in *Griswold*.[4]

Significantly, the *Griswold* opinions highlighted the professional titles of the two litigants and the marital status of the women they served, but did not address their class background, racial identification, or citizenship status. Historians of the case, however, have determined that while the two litigants were middle-class white U.S. citizens, two of the three married clients whose names Griswold provided to the police were not. When Griswold was initially asked by police for the names of women who had received information and supplies at the clinic, she mentioned two respectable white women who had agreed to this in advance: Joan Forsberg, a graduate of Yale Divinity School, the wife of a Christian minister, and the mother of three children; and Rosemary Stevens, a Yale graduate student and the wife of a Yale professor. Having emigrated from England, Stevens and her husband were not U.S. citizens and told the clinic's lawyer that they "would not want to be deported if they had to testify that they violated the Connecticut birth control statute." According to historian David Garrow, the lawyer "laughingly volunteered that he would happily take that case to the U.S. Supreme Court." This proved unnecessary, as the alien status of Stevens and her husband was ignored in the legal proceedings, though perhaps the lawyer should not have been so dismissive about the vulnerability they might have faced as aliens who had broken Connecticut's law. Indeed, had they not been white British aliens affiliated with a prestigious institution of higher learning, they might have faced more than theoretical vulnerability.[5]

When the police asked for additional patient names, the clinic obliged with Marie Tindall, a thirty-seven-year-old black woman who was married to a social worker. No evidence has been uncovered to suggest that the clinic or its lawyers took race or class into consideration when complying with the police requests, but given the larger cultural context they may have believed initially that judges would be predisposed to side with married white women and then later thought that judges might favor birth control for black women. This is speculative, but what is clear is that in *Griswold* the court ruled that two white citizens had standing to raise questions about the rights of a respectable white citizen, a respectable white alien, and a respectable black citizen.[6]

Beyond the biographies of the case's protagonists, the *Griswold* decision was classed and racialized in other ways. To begin with, the court's discussion of marital privacy was based on a romanticized and idealized conception of marriage that had links to the rise of the bourgeois white nuclear family in the eighteenth and nineteenth centuries. The court did not acknowledge, for example, that in some historical contexts marriage was viewed as an economic relationship, romantic love was associated with nonmarital liaisons, and married couples shared their bedrooms with others.[7] At one point in his majority opinion, Douglas asked with dramatic rhetorical flourish, "Would we allow the police to search the sacred precincts of marital bedrooms for telltale signs of the use of contraceptives? The very idea is repulsive to the notions of privacy surrounding the marriage relationship." He continued, "We deal with a right of privacy older than the Bill of Rights—older than our political parties, older than our school system. Marriage is a coming together for better or for worse, hopefully enduring, and intimate to the degree of being sacred. It is an association that promotes a way of life, not causes; a harmony in living, not political faiths; a bilateral loyalty, not commercial or social projects. Yet it is an association for as noble a purpose as any involved in our prior decisions." Justice Arthur Goldberg's concurring opinion added, "The fact that no particular provision of the Constitution explicitly forbids the State from disrupting the traditional relation of the family—a relation as old and as fundamental as our entire civilization—surely does not show that the Government was meant to have the power to do so." As historians have shown, these ideas about marriage and family are not universal; they are historically and culturally specific and are linked to the rise of the white bourgeoisie.[8]

Also, while the model of a two-parent, child-centered family that practices birth control had cross-class and cross-racial appeal, middle-class whites had a long history of using this model to differentiate themselves from others. This was the case, for instance, in long-standing white middle-class complaints about nonmarital reproduction, single-parent households, and large families in working class, immigrant, and nonwhite communities.[9] Moreover, insofar as rates of formal marriage were higher among middle-class whites than among others, the court's affirmation of marital privacy rights disproportionately favored the country's dominant class and race. At the same time, Justice Byron White's concurring opinion observed that Connecticut's law denied birth control to "disadvantaged citizens," including "those without either adequate knowledge or resources to obtain private counseling, access to medical assistance and up-to-date information." While expressing concern about the "disadvantaged," this comment suggested that the law interfered with their adoption of white middle-class family-limitation strategies. None of this means that the *Griswold* decision was opposed by working-class people and people of color, but it shows that the court's reasoning had class and race connotations.[10]

The race and class implications of the decision are also evident in the language used by the court when referring to "civilized" values. As indicated above, for Justice Goldberg traditional family relations were as old and fundamental as "our entire civilization." Goldberg also cited a well-known dissent by Justice Louis Brandeis that had defended "the right to be let alone" as "the right most valued by civilized men." Using the same key term, Justice Brennan wrote privately to Douglas as the latter worked on his opinion, "In our civilization, the marital relationship above all else is endowed with privacy." As Gail Bederman has pointed out, dominant discourses of "civilization" have been linked with class oppression and white supremacy. Additionally, in repeatedly referring to "our" civilization, "our" society, "our" people, and "our" institutions, the justices were relying on classed and racialized beliefs about other civilizations, societies, peoples, and institutions. At one point Goldberg referenced one such belief when discussing a hypothetical law that would not be constitutional. The hypothetical law declared that "all husbands and wives must be sterilized after two children." Goldberg used this example to challenge the dissenters for suggesting that states could do anything not specifically prohibited by the Constitution, a position he described as permitting "totalitarian limitation of family size." This Cold War formulation referenced U.S. beliefs about foreign countries imagined or known to have such laws.[11]

Finally, the justices decided *Griswold* in the midst of an intensely classed and racialized public discussion about nonmarital sex that was linked with Daniel Patrick Moynihan's controversial report, *The Negro Family*. Moynihan, an assistant secretary of labor in the Johnson administration, argued that the fundamental problem facing the U.S. black community was the "tangle of pathology" produced by low rates of long-term, cohabitational marriages and high rates of promiscuity, illegitimacy, and matriarchal households. Moynihan submitted his report in March 1965, in subsequent months it began to receive attention in the press, and on June 4 some of the report's findings were incorporated into a speech that President Johnson delivered at Howard University. Listening to the oral arguments in *Griswold* on March 29 and working on their opinions in the following months, the justices did not reference the "Negro" family explicitly in their June *Griswold* decision, but in the context of 1965 their celebration of marriage and family and their references to laws against nonmarital sex can be interpreted as having classed and racialized meanings. In effect, *Griswold* used coded language about sex, marriage, and reproduction that favored middle-class whites without appearing to do so. As the justices recognized special rights and privileges for heteronormative sexual expression, they contributed to the reconstitution of race and class hierarchies.[12]

Fanny Hill, *Ginzburg*, and *Mishkin* (1966)

Supreme Court decisions about obscenity are also important to consider when assessing the development of the court's jurisprudence about sex, marriage, and reproduction in the 1960s and 1970s. In three obscenity decisions announced on the same day in 1966, the court extended constitutional protection to materials that had "redeeming social value" but adopted heteronormative standards for assessing social value. The litigation in *Fanny Hill*, which challenged a decision by Massachusetts officials to declare obscene John Cleland's eighteenth-century English novel *Memoirs of a Woman of Pleasure*, was part of a long-term strategy adopted by civil libertarians to restrict the reach of anti-obscenity laws. In this case, the majority of the justices affirmed the court's long-standing position that obscenity was not protected by the First Amendment. But the controlling plurality of three justices now elaborated on the obscenity test announced in *Roth* (1957), which had asked "whether to the average person, applying contemporary community standards, the dominant theme of the material taken as a whole appeals to prurient interest." The key modification introduced in *Fanny Hill* declared that to be judged obscene the material must be "utterly without redeeming social value." Having heard credible evidence of the novel's redeeming social value, the court ruled that it was not obscene.[13]

In contrast to the outcome in *Fanny Hill*, in *Ginzburg* and *Mishkin* the court upheld obscenity convictions. In *Ginzburg* the critical issue was what the justices referred to as "the sordid business of pandering—'the business of purveying textual or graphic matter openly advertised to appeal to the erotic interests of their customers.'" Ralph Ginzburg had been convicted on federal obscenity charges based on the way he marketed a magazine called *Eros*, a newsletter called *Liaison*, and a publication called *The Housewife's Handbook on Selective Promiscuity*. Also at issue were Ginzburg's efforts to mail his materials from Intercourse and Blue Ball, Pennsylvania, and Middlesex, New Jersey, and the fact that his advertisements "deliberately emphasized the sexually provocative aspects of the work, in order to catch the salaciously disposed." According to the court, the "circumstances of production, sale, and publicity" demonstrated that these were "sales of illicit merchandise, not sales of constitutionally protected matter." As for *Mishkin*, this case concerned New York's conviction of Edward Mishkin for publishing and possessing with intent to sell a set of fifty books that addressed sadomasochism, fetishism, and homosexuality. In this case, the court modified the *Roth* test and qualified the *Fanny Hill* holding in deciding that materials aimed at "a clearly defined deviant sexual group" could be found obscene if they appealed to the prurient interests of the members of that group (and not necessarily "the average person").[14]

The obscenity tests announced by the court were heteronormative in theory (insofar as they relied on concepts such as the "average person," "community standards," and "social value") and practice (insofar as heteronormative representations were favored in decisions that used the tests).[15] The tests also were classed and racialized, in part because the "average person" in the United States was white and middle class and because ideas about "community standards" and "social value" were based on middle-class standards and values. For instance, Brennan's plurality opinion referred to experts who emphasized the book's "moral—namely, that sex with love is superior to sex in a brothel," and Douglas's concurring opinion characterized *Fanny Hill* as the story of a "young girl who becomes a prostitute" and then "abandons that life and marries her first lover" when she discovers the "'charms of virtue.'" In both cases, the justices established the novel's "social value" by depicting it as a bourgeois redemption narrative. Moreover, Brennan's opinion relied on the testimony of "experts" who addressed the novel's "literary merit" and labeled the book a "work of art." This rejected the populist conclusion of the state court, which had noted that "the opinions of English professors, authors and critics . . . , no matter how distinguished they may be, cannot be substituted for those of average persons." Instead, Brennan sided with Charles Rembar, the lawyer for the publisher, who had argued, "Appreciation of art and literature can often be gained only through an expenditure of effort; a certain level of cultivation or a certain amount of background may be required. . . . There is no snobbishness in this principle."[16] Notwithstanding Rembar's denial, the court's decision privileged elite perspectives.

While the decision in *Fanny Hill* protected "literature," the decisions in *Ginzburg* and *Mishkin* rejected a different class of materials. The "pandering" test adopted in *Ginzburg* emphasized the "commercial exploitation" of erotica, which reproduced historically bourgeois divisions between the public exchanges of the marketplace and the private intimacies of the home. Writing in the *Atlantic* shortly after the ruling, Jason Epstein detected "class bias" in Brennan's "choice of such prejudicial epithets as 'pandering' and 'the leer of the sensualist,'" which suggested that Ginzburg was a "vulgarian" who "had no right to trade in a market whose delicate and dangerous products must be limited only to gentlemen and scholars." In *Mishkin*, Brennan depicted the books as "cheaply prepared paperbound 'pulps' with imprinted sales prices that are several thousand percent above costs." These rulings were based on class-based distinctions between literature and smut, art and commerce, elite and popular culture, and private consumption and public display.[17]

The rulings also relied on racialized reasoning and rhetoric. In *Ginzburg*, Brennan approvingly quoted the words of Learned Hand, a prominent lower-court judge, who in a different case had upheld a conviction based on the indiscriminate dissemination of materials that "might . . . have been lawfully sold to laymen who wished seriously to study the sexual practices of savage or barbarous peoples." Brennan used this statement to emphasize that the contexts of sale and distribution were important to consider, but the example selected was meaningfully racialized and contributed to ongoing colonial and imperial projects. It is also noteworthy that one of the three items found obscene in *Ginzburg* was an issue of *Eros* that had featured a photographic essay titled "Black and White in Color." Edward de Grazia, who argued several significant obscenity cases before the court in this period, has linked Attorney General Robert Kennedy's political calculations about white voters and politicians in the U.S. South to his decision to prosecute Ginzburg on the basis of the interracial photographs. Before the case was decided, one of Justice John Harlan's clerks noted in a memorandum, "It was probably the picture study of the interracial group that caused all of the excitement; I doubt that there would be any fuss if the pictured couple was of the same color." In another memorandum, one of Chief Justice Earl Warren's clerks confessed that he found the photographic essay "a rather enchanting and even elegant portrayal of interracial love." One of Justice Clark's clerks wrote, "Now I am a genuine southerner, I think, and I realize the implications of encouraging intermarriage, etc. But that is far from calling these things obscene. I really suggest that you take a look at these, for they are beautifully done." In this context, Douglas's dissenting opinion stopped just short of accusing the majority of racism. Discussing *Eros*, Douglas quoted critic Dwight Macdonald, who had stated, "I suppose if you object to the idea of a Negro and a white person having sex together, then, of course, you would be horrified by it."[18]

Various commentators in the 1960s noted that race played a significant role in the 1966 obscenity cases. A letter sent to Harlan after the decision stated, "I gather that color pictures of a Negro man embracing a white woman in 'Eros' produced the demand that Ginzburg be severely punished. Certainly these pictures served to merge the hunt for obscenity with the distaste for desegregation." Ginzburg later was quoted in a *New York Times* interview as saying, "I suppose if it had been a white man and a black woman, nobody would have given it a second thought." In a 1966 *Playboy* interview, Ginzburg was asked "to what extent do you think . . . 'Black and White in Color' . . . was a factor in rousing the authorities against you?" Ginzburg responded, "To a tremendous extent. About three or four days after that issue was deposited in the mails, two members of Congress from the South cried out for my head." *Playboy* also asked Ginzburg, who was Jewish, if anti-Semitism played a role; Ginzburg replied, "I think so, although it's impossible to document."[19] The 1966 obscenity decisions provide additional evidence that the court's doctrine of heteronormative supremacy was influenced by and contributed to emergent class and racial formations. The rulings did not announce explicitly that they favored middle-class white perspectives and values, but this is what they did. Supreme Court decisions on obscenity played a noteworthy role in the reconstitution of class and race hierarchies in the United States in this period.

Boutilier (1967)

The 1967 *Boutilier* decision further developed the doctrine of heteronormative supremacy. In *Boutilier*, the Supreme Court upheld a component of the 1952 Immigration and Nationality Act that provided for the exclusion and deportation of aliens "afflicted with psychopathic personality," which the Immigration and Naturalization Service (INS) interpreted to apply to "homosexuals." Clive Michael Boutilier was a U.S. permanent resident whom the INS decided to deport based on evidence of homosexual "conduct" and "character." The majority opinion by Tom Clark and the dissents by William Brennan and William O. Douglas presented Boutilier as a Canadian national who first came to the United States in 1955 at age twenty-one.

His admission in his 1963 application for U.S. citizenship that in 1959 he had been arrested in New York City on a charge of sodomy, which was later dismissed, triggered the deportation proceedings. Both the majority and the dissenting opinions provided information about Boutilier's sexual history before and after coming to the United States as well as the assessments of two private psychiatrists who denied that Boutilier had a psychopathic personality. None of the opinions addressed Boutilier's class and racial characteristics in explicit ways, though in describing him as Canadian and using his name, which had an English-sounding first-name and a French-sounding last-name, they created an impression that he was white.[20]

While the court's opinions did not say much about Boutilier's class and racial characteristics, the briefs submitted by his lawyers and the statements by his psychiatrists said more. In various ways, Boutilier's defenders tried to emphasize his positive qualities, and some of these efforts relied on class-based narratives. For example, his lawyers and psychiatrists portrayed Boutilier as a member of a struggling Nova Scotia farming family that had migrated to the United States in search of a better life. One psychiatrist noted, "This patient is working steadily as a building maintenance man. . . . Earlier he served as attendant and companion to a man who was mentally ill and the patient performed responsibly." Another observed, "Boutilier has made a good work adjustment in this country. He has held his current job for three years as a maintenance worker with a copper concern. He is well liked, conscientious about his work and concerned with doing a very good job." Boutilier's lawyers, Blanch and David Freedman, pointed out that since coming to the United States Boutilier had worked "steadily" and was "at all times self supporting." These comments were part of a larger effort to depict Boutilier as a respectable and responsible immigrant.[21]

Boutilier's advocates also referenced his race and nationality. One of his psychiatrists described him as a "white male." In the oral arguments, Blanch Freedman's very first words, after the obligatory "if it pleases the Court," declared, "The petitioner is an alien of Canadian nationality." Perhaps no country received more favorable treatment within the U.S. immigration system than Canada, which was seen by the United States as a neighboring country with a predominantly white, Christian, and English-speaking population. Boutilier's advocates hoped to create favorable impressions by depicting him as a white Canadian with respectable and responsible class values. To the extent that the court ruled against Boutilier, the justices made clear that the doctrine of heteronormative supremacy did not necessarily make exceptions based on white privilege or working-class respectability.[22]

Although the court's opinions did not address most of the biographical references to class and race that were made by Boutilier's advocates, one of the key passages in the majority opinion addressed race more directly. Responding to one of the major arguments made by Boutilier's defenders, Clark wrote, "The petitioner is not being deported for conduct engaged in after his entry into the United States, but rather for characteristics he possessed at the time of his entry. Here, when petitioner first presented himself at our border for entrance, he was already afflicted with homosexuality. The pattern was cut, and under it he was not admissible." This was a key point because, according to Boutilier's lawyers, the psychopathic personality legislation did not provide for deportations based on postentry conduct, and if it did, Boutilier had a right to know when he came to the United States that homosexual conduct would make him vulnerable to deportation. Having emphasized that Boutilier was being deported for pre-entry characteristics, Clark proceeded to use a racialized analogy to make the point that Congress had the right to exclude aliens on this basis. According to Clark, "It has long been held that the Congress has plenary power to make rules for the admission of aliens and to exclude those who possess those characteristics which Congress has forbidden. See The Chinese Exclusion Case." After citing *Chae Chan Ping*, an 1889 decision that upheld the Chinese Exclusion Act, Clark continued, "Here Congress commanded that homosexuals not be allowed to enter. The petitioner was found to have that characteristic and was ordered deported."[23] In other words, homosexual aliens were similar to Chinese aliens in the sense that both were defined by characteristics rather than conduct. If Congress could exclude Chinese aliens, it could exclude homosexual aliens.

The timing of Clark's invocation of *Chae Chan Ping* is striking. Congress had repealed the Chinese Exclusion Act in 1943 and abandoned the national-origins immigration system in 1965, yet in 1967 six justices affirmed in *Boutilier* that Congress retained the power to exclude immigrants on the basis of characteristics including race and sexual orientation. The timing is also striking because by the mid-1960s the court regarded laws that classified U.S. citizens on the basis of race as "suspect," which meant they were subject to "strict scrutiny." *Boutilier*, however, did not concern the rights of a U.S. citizen, and while the court found it helpful to make an analogy between a group defined by racial characteristics and a group defined by sexual ones, it distinguished between forms of discrimination that were subject to "strict scrutiny" (such as racial discrimination) and other forms of discrimination (such as discrimination based on sexual orientation and alien status). In *Boutilier*, the court's template for constitutional discrimination against homosexual aliens was constitutional discrimination against Chinese aliens. The heteronormative decision in *Boutilier* relied on a white supremacist precedent; in turn, *Boutilier* could now be cited as a precedent in future cases about race, sexuality, and immigration. *Boutilier* thus is a significant case not only in the history of sexuality but also in the history of race and immigration.

Loving (1967)

In *Loving*, announced shortly after the decision in *Boutilier*, the court overturned state laws that banned marriages between people of different races. In this case, Richard and Mildred Loving challenged a Virginia law that prevented them from marrying because Richard was classified as "white" and Mildred was classified as "colored." The Lovings had returned to Virginia after getting married in Washington, D.C., but in Virginia their marriage was voided, and they were punished for leaving the state to get married and returning to live as a married couple in Virginia. There were two bases for Warren's majority opinion in *Loving*. First, such laws violated the equal protection clause because they constituted "invidious racial discrimination." Second, such laws violated the due process clause because they interfered with the right to marry, which was "one of the 'basic civil rights of man.'" In multiple ways, *Loving* affirmed the special rights and privileges associated with heterosexual marriage. *Loving*, however, also addressed sex and reproduction, and in so doing it contributed to the racialization of the doctrine of heteronormative supremacy.[24]

Loving addressed sex insofar as the decision was based on the notion that the only legal form of sex was marital sex. For decades reformers had argued for legalizing interracial marriage in part by emphasizing that nonmarital sex was illegal, which meant that the only way for interracial couples to have legal sex was to marry. In this and other ways, they explicitly or implicitly accepted the constitutionality of laws against nonmarital sex. In *Naim* (1954), for instance, which was an earlier interracial marriage case, David Carliner argued that "the power of a state to punish adultery and fornication between persons of different races stands on a different footing than any asserted power to prohibit interracial marriages." According to Carliner, who later helped defend the Lovings, "the right to marry is admittedly a fundamental liberty; a right to fornicate is not." In *Loving*, the lawyers for the interracial couple argued that, without the ability to obtain a legally recognized marriage, they were vulnerable to prosecution for "illegal cohabitation" and "fornication." This argument rested on the assumption that such laws were constitutional. The lawyers also argued that antimiscegenation laws "perpetuate and foster illicit exploitative sex relationships" between white men and black women because such laws deprive the latter of the status and protection that comes with marriage. This was based on the assumption that it was constitutional to deny equal status and protection to women in nonmarital relationships. Meanwhile, an *amicus* brief by the Japanese American Citizens League, which had long-standing concerns about antimiscegenation laws, noted that the statute challenged in *Loving* sought "not to deter sexual promiscuity or such similar opprobrious activity but rather the noble and necessary goal common to all persons—'marriage and procreation.'"[25]

On the subject of permissible and impermissible state regulation of intimate relationships, the *Loving* decision repeatedly cited *McLaughlin* (1964), a case in which the justices unanimously overturned a Florida cohabitation law that applied to black-white heterosexual couples who "habitually live in and occupy in the nighttime the same room." White's majority opinion in *McLaughlin* made clear that the court was not overturning Florida's "general" and "neutral" laws against adultery, cohabitation, fornication, illicit relations, lewd and lascivious behavior, premarital sex, and promiscuity, but was rejecting the differential treatment of intraracial and interracial cohabitation. *McLaughlin* and *Loving* thus struck down cohabitation and marriage laws that included explicit race distinctions but left in place laws that privileged marriage and marital sex. According to the logic of *McLaughlin* and *Loving*, Richard and Mildred Loving, if they had had sex or lived together outside marriage, would have been vulnerable to prosecution under race-neutral fornication and cohabitation laws.[26]

Loving also addressed reproduction. The Japanese American Citizens League brief, for example, emphasized the damage done to, and the "stigma of bastardy" faced by, the "illegitimate" children of interracial couples not permitted to marry. As for the Supreme Court decision itself, according to the majority opinion, "The freedom to marry has long been recognized as one of the vital personal rights essential to the orderly pursuit of happiness by free men. Marriage is one of the 'basic civil rights of man,' fundamental to our very existence and survival." Warren's quotation within the quotation was taken from the court's 1942 ruling in *Skinner*, a sterilization decision authored by Justice Douglas, but the remainder of Warren's sentence paraphrased *Skinner*, which had declared, "Marriage *and procreation* are fundamental to the very existence and survival *of the race* [my emphases]." Setting aside for a moment the final three words of this passage, Warren's identification of marriage as fundamental to "existence" and "survival" offered a narrowly procreative conception of marriage and a narrowly marital conception of procreation. After all, while procreation might be necessary for human existence and survival, marriage is not. *Skinner* linked marriage and procreation more explicitly than *Loving* did, but in deleting the explicit reference to procreation, *Loving* arguably strengthened the presumption that marriage was necessary for reproduction and that reproductive marriage was necessary for human existence and survival.[27]

It may seem counterintuitive to argue that a ruling striking down bans on interracial marriage contributed to a racialized doctrine of heteronormative supremacy, but this is what *Loving* did. When Warren invoked the historical rights of "free men" to marry, he was basing the court's decision on a portrait of the past with distinctive racial features. Enslaved people in the United States, for example, did not generally have rights to legal marriage. When Warren argued that "this Court has consistently repudiated '[d]istinctions between citizens solely because of their ancestry' as being 'odious to a free people whose institutions are founded upon the doctrine of equality,'" he again invoked the history of "free people," but this time also erased the history of the court's acceptance and endorsement of racial distinctions. Moreover, this passage quoted from *Hirabayashi*, a ruling that had *upheld* the internment of Japanese Americans during World War II. One of the key words that allowed Warren to cite *Hirabayashi* favorably in *Loving* was "solely." While *Loving*, like *Hirabayashi*, rejected laws based "solely" on ancestry, racial laws justified on other grounds (such as national security) remained constitutional. Another key word—"citizens"—allowed the court to cite *Hirabayashi* favorably in *Loving*, while just three weeks earlier the court noted in *Boutilier* that discrimination on the basis of racial (and sexual) characteristics was constitutional when the discrimination concerned aliens. In other words, Warren's language in *Loving* indicated that, as far as the court was concerned, the decision against miscegenation laws was consistent with decisions favoring Japanese American internment, Chinese immigration exclusion, and immigration restrictions based on homosexuality.

Finally, when Warren's decision in *Loving* excerpted and paraphrased *Skinner* but deleted its reference to the existence and survival "of *the* race," he was citing a case that, in another passage, affirmed "a right which is basic to the perpetuation of *a* race—the right to have offspring [my emphases]." This formulation does not seem to refer to the perpetuation of the *human* race; rather it seems to refer to the perpetuation of each particular race. Elsewhere *Skinner* had expressed concern about "the power to sterilize" because "in evil or reckless hands it can cause races or types which are inimical to the dominant group to wither and disappear." This again means that *Loving* relied on a decision that invoked the reproductive rights of distinct "races" and not the singular human race. Paradoxically, *Loving* struck down laws against interracial marriage on the basis of a racialist precedent that affirmed the right of each race to reproduce itself. *Loving* was not just a decision about race and marriage; it was a decision about sex and reproduction as well. In *Loving*, the court struck down laws against interracial marriage on the basis of conservative ideas about sex and reproduction.[28]

Eisenstadt (1972)

Seven years after the *Griswold* decision, the court ruled in *Eisenstadt* that birth control bans that applied specifically to the unmarried were unconstitutional forms of discrimination based on marital status. *Eisenstadt* was initiated by birth control and abortion rights activist William Baird, who intentionally broke Massachusetts state law by distributing birth control to the unmarried after a speech at Boston University. While the court's decision in *Eisenstadt* was understood by many to have implications for nonmarital sex, the majority opinion by William Brennan indicated that the justices were recognizing the reproductive, not the sexual, rights of the unmarried. Laws against nonmarital sex remained constitutional, even as laws against birth control for the unmarried were struck down. In this way, *Eisenstadt* was consistent with the court's doctrine of heteronormative supremacy. In effect, *Eisenstadt* meant that states could continue to ban nonmarital sex, even if they could not ban nonmarital birth control.[29]

Eisenstadt also addressed class and race, and in so doing linked the doctrine of heteronormative supremacy to the production of class and race hierarchies. For example, the arguments presented by Baird's lawyers included statistics on the high rates of nonmarital reproduction among blacks (said to be more than twice as high among blacks as among whites in Massachusetts) and referred to "the whole social problem of our nation with respect to the poor unwanted child and the welfare mother." Baird's lawyers also argued that the state restrictions on birth control "operate to discriminate against low income and uneducated groups." A brief by Planned Parenthood explained that "since the law requires a doctor's prescription for all contraceptives, poor women . . . are faced with an often insurmountable obstacle to access to contraception." In contrast, "the middle class or wealthy woman who is unmarried can easily go out of state for contraceptive services." Much of the evidence and arguments used by Baird's defenders focused not on matters of reproductive choice for the unmarried, but on the individual and social costs associated with nonmarital reproduction. Overall, the sense conveyed by Baird's defenders was not just that the unmarried, who were understood to be disproportionately working class and nonwhite, should have the right to decide whether to use birth control, but that they should exercise that right.[30]

The Supreme Court echoed these classed and racialized concerns about nonmarital reproduction. Brennan's majority opinion included a passage from the federal appeals court ruling that had argued, "To say that contraceptives are immoral as such, and are to be forbidden to unmarried persons who will nevertheless persist in having intercourse, means that such persons must risk for themselves an unwanted pregnancy, for the child, illegitimacy, and for society, a possible obligation of support." Douglas's concurring opinion emphasized that Baird's speech discussed "overpopulation in the world" and "the large number of abortions performed on unwed mothers." In the context of conservative backlash and the rise of Nixon's "silent majority," these comments about illegitimacy, welfare, overpopulation, and nonmarital reproduction linked race- and class-based anxieties to the reproductive sexual behaviors of the unmarried. The *Eisenstadt* decision thus stands as another example of the ways in which the court's doctrine of heteronormative supremacy played a role in the reconstitution of class and race hierarchies in the United States.[31]

Roe (1973)

One year after *Eisenstadt* was decided, the court announced its decision in *Roe*, its most important and controversial abortion rights case. According to the court, there were three primary interests that had to be considered in resolving questions about the constitutionality of abortion restrictions: the privacy interests of the pregnant woman, the public health interests of the state, and the interests of a "potential life" in life itself. The majority ruled that women's privacy interests were preeminent in the first trimester, subject to the medical judgments of their physicians. These had to be balanced against the state's public health interests in the second trimester, when abortions were said to pose more of a risk to the pregnant woman. In the third trimester (after the point of fetal "viability"), the state's interests in protecting "potential life" became compelling, which meant that more abortion restrictions were permitted.

Roe was consistent with the court's doctrine of heteronormative supremacy in that it was based on a vision of reproductive, not sexual, rights. In several passages the court made clear that its decision did not mean that "one has an unlimited right to do with one's body as one pleases." The justices also did not include "sex" alongside "marriage . . . , procreation . . . , contraception . . . , family relationships . . . , and child rearing and education" when it discussed the parameters of the constitutional right to privacy. Just months later, the court declared in a new obscenity decision, "For us to say that our Constitution incorporates the proposition that conduct involving consenting adults only is always beyond state regulation is a step we are unable to take." In a footnote Chief Justice Warren Burger listed various types of "constitutionally unchallenged" laws involving consenting adults, including laws against adultery, bigamy, fornication, and prostitution.[32]

As was the case with the decisions discussed above, *Roe* illustrates the ways in which the doctrine of heteronormative supremacy was linked to the ongoing formation of class and race hierarchies. Even the name of the case relates to the complexities of class and racial politics. Norma McCorvey became Jane Roe in part because she and her lawyers, Sarah Weddington and Linda Coffee, believed that abortion was a private matter. They could emphasize this by using a pseudonym, which would also spare McCorvey negative publicity. They also may have shared the common view of abortion as shameful and embarrassing. But McCorvey also became Roe because her lawyers were concerned that various biographical features of her life, which could more easily be exposed if her real name were used, might damage their chances of winning.

McCorvey, who describes herself in a 1994 autobiography as "half Cajun and part Indian," had a difficult childhood, did not complete high school, and spent several years in reform school. As a young adult, she was often poor and unemployed. A survivor of physical, sexual, and emotional abuse by family members, sexual partners, and nuns, she had problems with alcohol and drugs and struggled with depression. She had married and divorced, had a history of sexual relationships with men and women, and had worked and socialized in lesbian and gay bars. Twice before, McCorvey had gotten pregnant and given birth, and in both instances she had lost custody of her children. When she became pregnant again, she asked her doctor for an abortion, but he explained that abortions were illegal in Texas, encouraged her to put the child up for adoption, and referred her to a lawyer. When the lawyer asked McCorvey if the pregnancy was a result of rape, she lied, hoping that abortions were permitted in such situations. When he asked about the color of the man who raped her, she avoided answering. Later the doctor told her that the lawyer had said he could not help with an adoption because the child was "probably of mixed race and would be hard to place with white parents." After trying unsuccessfully to self-abort, McCorvey contacted another lawyer, who put her in touch with Coffee and Weddington. At this point, McCorvey was still in her first trimester and hoped to find an abortion provider, but Coffee and Weddington claimed they did not know where she could get an abortion, warned her about the dangers of illegal procedures, and convinced her to become their plaintiff. McCorvey recalls that when she asked when she would be able to have her abortion, Weddington replied, "When the case is over, if we've won." In a 1976 interview, Weddington claimed that before the case reached the court, "We had to face the decision of whether, since it was going to take so long for an appeal, we should make arrangements for her to go outside the state to try and get an abortion. . . . She chose to carry the pregnancy to term because at that point the law regarding abortion was in a nebulous enough state that we were afraid the Supreme Court, if it wanted to, could duck the issue by saying that it was moot because she had been able to get an abortion." According to Weddington, "We explained all that to Jane Roe and told her if she wanted to go, we would help her. But I think even then, she had in some ways a sense of the historic proportion of the case." By the time the court ruled in favor of McCorvey, she had given birth and her lawyers had arranged for the child's adoption.[33]

McCorvey has expressed admiration for her lawyers and pride in her role, but also resentment about the fact that Weddington did not tell her that she herself had gone to Mexico for an abortion several years earlier, did not direct her to an abortion provider, and did not inform her that the litigation process would likely not conclude before it was too late for an abortion. Indeed, if McCorvey had found the abortion referral service that Weddington was assisting in this period, she likely would have had the abortion she wanted. In a 1994 interview, McCorvey complained, "I didn't know until two years ago that she had had an abortion herself. . . . When I told her then how desperately I needed one, she could have told me where to go for it. But she wouldn't because she needed me to be pregnant for her case. I set Sarah Weddington up on a pedestal like a rose petal. But when it came to my turn, well. Sarah saw these cuts on my wrists, my swollen eyes from crying, the miserable person sitting across from her, and she knew she had a patsy." More generally, McCorvey criticizes abortion rights activists for regarding her as "an embarrassment." According to McCorvey, she did not "fit many people's idea of a historical role model," partly because she was a lesbian, partly because she was not "a gentle woman," and partly because she was not "sophisticated." These resentments likely contributed to McCorvey's ambiguous alliance with anti-abortion activists in the late 1990s. Long before this occurred, the story of the relationship between McCorvey and Weddington could easily be read as a story of class and race in America.[34]

Roe was a decision about class and race not only in relation to the biographies of its protagonists but also because the rhetoric and reasoning used by the lawyers and judges addressed class and race. Several briefs offered statistics on and arguments about the large numbers of "unwanted" and "illegitimate" children and stated that many of these children were born to poor women, women on welfare, black women, and teenagers. At the very outset of his majority opinion, Justice Harry Blackmun declared that "population growth, pollution, poverty, and racial overtones tend to complicate and not to simplify the problem" of abortion. Later, in discussing "the detriment that the State would impose upon the pregnant woman," Blackmun noted, "There is also the distress, for all concerned, associated with the unwanted child, and there is the problem of bringing a child into a family already unable, psychologically and otherwise, to care for it. In other cases, as in this one, the additional difficulties and continued stigma of unwed motherhood may be involved." Blackmun expressed concern for "the pregnant woman" and her family, but these types of sentiments led many to accuse abortion rights liberals of advancing race- and class-prejudiced agendas.[35]

As for the "facts" considered by the court, in *Roe* Blackmun provided few details about Jane Roe, other than noting that she was unmarried and pregnant, but in *Doe*, a Georgia case linked to *Roe*, the court observed that Mary Doe had three children, two in foster care and one in the process of being adopted "because of Doe's poverty and inability to care for them." Blackmun also wrote that Doe's "husband recently abandoned her" (though later they "reconciled"), she was now living with "her indigent parents and their eight children," and she had been a "mental patient" at a state hospital. On the one hand, Blackmun expressed the court's sympathy for Doe's difficult situation. On the other, his opinion left the impression that this was the type of woman who should not only have access to abortion but who should have an abortion.[36]

The court also offered classed and racialized arguments in its long discussion of the history of abortion. In this part of his opinion, Blackmun emphasized that

"the restrictive criminal abortion laws in effect in a majority of States today . . .
derive from statutory changes effected, for the most part, in the latter half of the
19th century." But Blackmun reached beyond the United States in his survey of the
history of abortion restrictions; his opinion adopted the ethnocentric practice of
privileging the history of "western civilization." Blackmun's historical survey began
with the Persians, Greeks, and Romans; proceeded through Christian theological and canonical law; continued with English common and statutory law; and
turned finally to "American law." Conceptualizing abortion rights within a narrow
Western civilization framework that privileged particular cultural, religious, and
national histories, the opinion implicitly deemed other histories of abortion less
relevant or irrelevant. Blackmun also surveyed the history of religious perspectives
on abortion but limited his discussion to Jews and Christians. In other words, the
court used an ethnocentric, Judeo-Christian historical framework to support its
abortion rights conclusions. In this way and in other ways, *Roe* was implicated in
ongoing processes of race and class formation in the United States.[37]

In their influential 1986 work *Racial Formation in the United States*, Michael Omi and
Howard Winant explain that they "employ the term racialization to signify the extension of racial meaning to a previously racially unclassified relationship, social
practice or group." It would be a mistake to assert that sex, marriage, and reproduction in the United States did not have racial or class meanings before the Supreme
Court developed its doctrine of heteronormative supremacy, but the analysis above
follows the lead of Omi and Winant, Higginbotham, and Somerville in examining
some of the racial and class meanings of the court's decisions about sex, marriage,
and reproduction in the late 1960s and early 1970s. While these examples can
help illustrate and develop a theoretical understanding of intersections of race
and class with gender and sexuality, they also can contribute to more historically
specific debates about the politics of the post–World War II era. Recognizing the
court's development of a doctrine of heteronormative supremacy in the late 1960s
and early 1970s complicates narratives that emphasize the equal rights politics of
the court during this period and the backlash conservatism of the court in the late
1970s, 1980s, and 1990s. The coded conservative language of race and class that
many scholars associate with the rise of the New Right in the late 1970s, 1980s,
and 1990s was prefigured in the language used by the court during the heyday of
sexual liberalism in the late 1960s and early 1970s.[38]

Confronted by the powerful successes of civil rights activism in the 1950s and
1960s, the Supreme Court attempted to fashion new political compromises that simultaneously granted and limited the equal rights demanded by new social movements. For example, in 1954–55, the court ruled against racially segregated public
schools but permitted implementation delays by calling on local authorities to

proceed with "all deliberate speed." Then in the late 1970s and 1980s, the court further limited progress toward public education equalization by ruling against city/suburban busing plans, university admissions quotas, and school-funding parity schemes.[39] Meanwhile, in the late 1960s and early 1970s, the court recognized new marital and reproductive rights, while limiting progress toward sexual equalization by condoning laws against nonmarital sex, upholding antigay immigration statutes, and adopting sexually discriminatory obscenity tests. Rather than seeing the conservatism of the court's decisions about race and class and the conservatism of its decisions about sex, marriage, and reproduction as parallel developments in the post–World War II era, this essay demonstrates that the court's decisions about sex, marriage, and reproduction participated in and contributed to the development of new forms of race and class governance, just as its decisions about race and class participated in the development of new forms of sexual governance.

Notes

1. This essay is drawn from my work in "Crossing the Border to Memory: In Search of Clive Michael Boutilier (1933–2003)," *torquere* 6 (2004): 91–115; "*Boutilier* and the U.S. Supreme Court's Sexual Revolution," *Law and History Review* 23, no. 3 (Fall 2005): 491–536; "The U.S. Supreme Court's Sexual Counter-Revolution," *Organization of American Historians Magazine of History* 20, no. 2 (March 2006): 21–25; "All the Immigrants Are Straight, All the Homosexuals Are Citizens, but Some of Us Are Queer Aliens: Genealogies of Legal Strategy in *Boutilier v. INS*," *Journal of American Ethnic History* 29, no. 4 (Summer 2010): 45–77; and *Sexual Injustice: Supreme Court Decisions from* Griswold *to* Roe (Chapel Hill: University of North Carolina Press, 2010).

2. Evelyn Brooks Higginbotham, "African-American Women's History and the Metalanguage of Race," *Signs* 17, no. 2 (Winter 1992): 252; Siobhan Somerville, *Queering the Color Line: Race and the Invention of Homosexuality in American Culture* (Durham, N.C.: Duke University Press, 2000), 5. See also Michael Omi and Howard Winant, *Racial Formation in the United States: From the 1960s to the 1980s* (New York: Routledge, 1986), 64.

3. For historical accounts of *Griswold*, see David J. Garrow, *Liberty and Sexuality: The Right to Privacy and the Making of Roe v. Wade* (Berkeley: University of California Press, 1994), 196–269; John W. Johnson, *Griswold v. Connecticut: Birth Control and the Constitutional Right of Privacy* (Lawrence: University Press of Kansas, 2005).

4. *Griswold v. Connecticut*, 381 U.S. 479 (1965), 481. See also *Barrows v. Jackson*, 346 U.S. 249 (1953).

5. Garrow, *Liberty and Sexuality*, 204–6.

6. Garrow, *Liberty and Sexuality*, 208.

7. See Nancy Cott, *Public Vows: A History of Marriage and the Nation* (Cambridge, Mass.: Harvard University Press, 1999); John D'Emilio and Estelle Freedman, *Intimate Matters: A History of Sexuality in America* (New York: Harper and Row, 1988); Hendrik Hartog, *Man and Wife in America: A History* (Cambridge, Mass.: Harvard University Press, 2000); Jacqueline

Jones, *Labor of Love, Labor of Sorrow: Black Women, Work, and the Family from Slavery to the Present* (New York: Basic Books, 1985); Jennifer Nelson, *Women of Color and the Reproductive Rights Movement* (New York: New York University Press, 2003); Dorothy E. Roberts, *Killing the Black Body: Race, Reproduction, and the Meaning of Liberty* (New York: Random House, 1997).

8. *Griswold*, 381 U.S. at 485–86, 495–96. See also Cott, *Public Vows*; D'Emilio and Freedman, *Intimate Matters*; Jones, *Labor of Love*; Nelson, *Women of Color*; Roberts, *Killing the Black Body*.

9. See, in addition to the many examples cited by the sources in note 8, Rickie Solinger, *Wake Up Little Susie: Single Pregnancy and Race before Roe v. Wade* (New York: Routledge, 1992); Rickie Solinger, *Pregnancy and Power: A Short History of Reproductive Politics in America* (New York: New York University Press, 2005).

10. *Griswold*, 381 U.S. at 503.

11. *Griswold*, 381 U.S. at 491, 493, 494, 496–97, 501; William Brennan to William O. Douglas, letter dated April 24, 1965, box 1347, William O. Douglas Papers, Manuscript Division, Library of Congress; Gail Bederman, *Manliness and Civilization: A Cultural History of Gender and Race in the United States, 1880–1917* (Chicago: University of Chicago Press, 1995).

12. See, in addition to notes 7–9, Lee Rainwater and William L. Yancey, *The Moynihan Report and the Politics of Controversy* (Cambridge, Mass.: MIT Press, 1967); Ruth Feldstein, *Motherhood in Black and White: Race and Sex in American Liberalism, 1930–1965* (Ithaca, N.Y.: Cornell University Press), 139–64.

13. *A Book Named "John Cleland's Memoirs of a Woman of Pleasure" v. Attorney General of the Commonwealth of Massachusetts* (commonly referred to as *Fanny Hill*), 383 U.S. 413 (1966), 418–21. See also *Roth v. United States*, 354 U.S. 476 (1957). For historical accounts of these cases, see Edward de Grazia, *Girls Lean Back Everywhere: The Law of Obscenity and the Assault on Genius* (New York: Random House, 1992); Richard F. Hixson, *Pornography and the Justices: The Supreme Court and the Intractable Obscenity Problem* (Carbondale: Southern Illinois University Press, 1996); Charles Rembar, *The End of Obscenity: The Trials of Lady Chatterley, Tropic of Cancer and Fanny Hill* (New York: Random House, 1968); Whitney Strub, *Perversion for Profit: The Politics of Pornography and the Rise of the New Right* (New York: Columbia University Press, 2011); Whitney Strub, *Obscenity Rules: Roth v. United States and the Long Struggle over Sexual Expression* (Lawrence: University Press of Kansas, 2013).

14. *Ginzburg v. U.S.*, 383 U.S. 463 (1966), 465–468, 472, 475; *Mishkin v. New York*, 383 U.S. 502 (1966), 508.

15. See, for example, *Landau v. Fording*, 388 U.S. 456 (1967); *G.I. Distributors v. New York*, 389 U.S. 905 (1967); *Ginsberg v. New York*, 390 U.S. 629 (1968); *Redrup v. New York*, 386 U.S. 767 (1967); *Stanley v. Georgia*, 394 U.S. 557 (1969).

16. *A Book Named*, 383 U.S. at 415–16, 419, 424–25, 446; *A Book Named*, Suffolk County Superior Court, September 3, 1964; Charles Rembar, "Reply Brief for Appellant," *A Book Named*, October 1965, 4–5.

17. *Ginzburg*, 383 U.S. at 466; Jason Epstein, "The Obscenity Business," *Atlantic*, August 1966, 59; *Mishkin*, 383 U.S. at 505.

18. De Grazia, *Girls Lean Back Everywhere*, 504–11; *Ginzburg*, 383 U.S. at 473, 487–88; Nesson to John Harlan, memorandum dated March 15, 1965, box 583, John Harlan Papers,

Seeley G. Mudd Manuscript Library, Princeton University; KZ to Earl Warren, memorandum dated December 2, 1965, box 277, Earl Warren Papers, Manuscript Division, Library of Congress; MWM to Tom Clark, memorandum dated March 13, 1965, box B208, Tom Clark Papers, Rare Books and Special Collections, Tarlton Law Library, University of Texas–Austin.

19. Ward Caille to John Harlan, letter dated March 24, 1966, box 248, Harlan Papers; Ginzburg, cited in Merle Miller, "Ralph Ginzburg, Middlesex, N.J., and the First Amendment," *New York Times Magazine*, April 30, 1972; "Playboy Interview: Ralph Ginzburg," *Playboy*, July 1966, 120.

20. *Boutilier v. Immigration and Naturalization Service*, 387 U.S. 118 (1967). For historical accounts of *Boutilier*, see, in addition to the works cited in note 1, Margot Canaday, "'Who Is a Homosexual?': The Consolidation of Sexual Identities in Mid-Twentieth-Century American Immigration Law," *Law and Social Inquiry* 28 (2003): 351–86; Margot Canaday, *The Straight State: Sexuality and Citizenship in Twentieth-Century America* (Princeton, N.J.: Princeton University Press, 2009), 214–54; William N. Eskridge, "Gadamer/Statutory Interpretation," *Columbia Law Review* 90 (April 1990): 609–81; William N. Eskridge, *Dynamic Statutory Interpretation* (Cambridge, Mass.: Harvard University Press, 1994), 48–80; Joyce Murdoch and Deb Price, *Courting Justice: Gay Men and Lesbians v. the Supreme Court* (New York: Basic Books, 2001), 103–34; Siobhan B. Somerville, "Queer *Loving*," *GLQ: A Journal of Lesbian and Gay Studies* (2005): 335–70.

21. Exhibit 6, Report of Dr. Falsey, March 2, 1964, *Boutilier* case file, 13; Exhibit 7, Report of Dr. Ullman, March 30, 1965, *Boutilier* case file, 15; Blanch Freedman and David Freedman, "Brief for Petitioner," *Boutilier*, 4.

22. Report of Dr. Ullman, 14; Blanch Freedman, *Boutilier* oral arguments.

23. *Boutilier*, 387 U.S. at 123–24.

24. *Loving v. Virginia*, 388 U.S. 1 (1967), 12. For historical accounts of *Loving*, see Rachel Moran, *Interracial Intimacy: The Regulation of Race and Romance* (Chicago: University of Chicago Press, 2001), 76–100; Phyl Newbeck, *Virginia Hasn't Always Been for Lovers* (Carbondale: Southern Illinois University Press, 2004); Peggy Pascoe, *What Comes Naturally: Miscegenation Law and the Making of Race in America* (New York: Oxford University Press, 2009); Renee C. Romano, *Race Mixing: Black-White Marriage in Postwar America* (Cambridge, Mass.: Harvard University Press, 2003), 175–215; Robert J. Sickels, *Race, Marriage, and the Law* (Albuquerque: University of New Mexico Press, 1972); Somerville, "Queer *Loving*"; Walter Wadlington, "The *Loving* Case: Virginia's Anti-Miscegenation Statute in Historical Perspective," *Virginia Law Review* 52 (1966): 1189–223; Peter Wallenstein, *Tell the Court I Love My Wife: Race, Marriage, and Law* (New York: Palgrave Macmillan, 2002).

25. David Carliner, "Reply Brief," *Naim v. Naim*, Virginia Supreme Court of Appeals (1954), cited in Gregory Michael Dorr, "Principled Expediency: Eugenics, *Naim v. Naim*, and the Supreme Court," *American Journal of Legal History* 42, no. 2 (April 1998), 139; Bernard Cohen, Philip Hirschkop, William Zabel, Arthur Berney, Marvin Karpatkin, Melvin Wulf, and David Carliner, "Brief for Appellants," *Loving*, 14, 26; William Marutani and Donald Kramer, "Brief for the Japanese American Citizens League," *Loving*, 9–10.

26. *McLaughlin v. Florida*, 379 U.S. 184 (1964).

27. William Marutani and Donald Kramer, "Brief for the Japanese American Citizens League," *Loving*, 3; *Loving*, 388 U.S. at 12; *Skinner v. Oklahoma*, 316 U.S. 535 (1942), 541.

28. *Loving*, 388 U.S. at 12; *Hirabayashi v. United States*, 320 U.S. 81 (1943); *Skinner*, 316 U.S. at 536, 541.

29. *Eisenstadt v. Baird*, 405 U.S. 438 (1972). For historical accounts of *Eisenstadt*, see Garrow, *Liberty and Sexuality*, 517–44.

30. Joseph Tydings, oral arguments, *Eisenstadt*, November 17, 1965; Harriet Pilpel and Nancy Wecholcr, "Brief for the Planned Parenthood Federation of America," *Eisenstadt*, 5, 20–23, 36–38; Joseph Balliro, "Brief for the Appellee," *Eisenstadt*, 40–41.

31. *Eisenstadt*, 405 U.S. at 452–53, 456.

32. *Roe v. Wade*, 410 U.S. 113 (1973), 152–54, 167–69; *Paris Adult Theatre I. v. Slaton*, 413 U.S. 49 (1973), 65–68. For historical accounts of *Roe*, see Marian Faux, *Roe v. Wade: The Untold Story of the Landmark Supreme Court Decision That Made Abortion Legal* (New York: Macmillan, 1988); Garrow, *Liberty and Sexuality*; Linda Greenhouse, *Becoming Justice Blackmun: Harry Blackmun's Supreme Court Journey* (New York: Holt, 2005), 72–101; N. E. H. Hull and Peter Charles Hoffer, *Roe v. Wade: The Abortion Rights Controversy in American History* (Lawrence: University Press of Kansas, 2001), 89–179; Leslie J. Reagan, *When Abortion Was A Crime: Women, Medicine, and Law in the United States, 1867–1973* (Berkeley: University of California Press, 1997), 165–90, 229–40.

33. Norma McCorvey, with Andy Meisler, *I Am Roe: My Life, Roe v. Wade, and Freedom of Choice* (New York: HarperCollins, 1994), 11, 109, 117, 123; Sarah Weddington, *A Question of Choice* (New York: Penguin, 1992), 52–53; Jeanette Cheek interview with Sarah Weddington, March 1965, Family Planning Oral History Project, Schlesinger Library, Radcliffe College, 24–25. See also Garrow, *Liberty and Sexuality*, 402–5, 439–40, 461; Sarah Weddington, "*Roe v. Wade*: Past and Future," *Suffolk University Law Review* 24 (Fall 1990): 603–4; Hull and Hoffer, *Roe v. Wade*, 2–3; Weddington, *Question of Choice*, 51–57, 256–60.

34. McCorvey, *I Am Roe*, 2. See also *New York Times*, July 28, 1994, C1, C9.

35. Roy Lucas, Sarah Weddington, James Weddington, Linda Coffee, Fred Burner, and Norman Dorsen, "Brief for Appellants," *Roe*, 9, 44; Roy Lucas, Norman Dorsen, Linda Coffee, Sarah Weddington, and Roy Merrill Jr., "Jurisdictional Statement," *Roe*, 15–16; *Roe*, 410 U.S. at 116, 153.

36. *Doe v. Bolton*, 410 U.S. 179 (1973), 185.

37. *Roe*, 410 U.S. at 129. See also 129–52, 160–62.

38. Omi and Winant, *Racial Formation*, 64. See also their discussion of "race and reaction," 109–35.

39. See *Brown v. Board of Education*, 347 U.S. 483 (1954); 349 U.S. 294 (1955); *San Antonio School District v. Rodriguez*, 411 U.S. 1 (1973); *Milliken v. Bradley*, 418 U.S. 717 (1974); *University of California Regents v. Bakke*, 438 U.S. 265 (1978).

PART 2

Beauty and Desire

CHAPTER 4

Early American Bodies

Creating Race, Sex, and Beauty

SHARON BLOCK

In the summer of 2008, the *Los Angeles Times* ran an article about the fallibility of DNA matches. The piece showcased two male felons with "remarkably similar genetic profiles," noting that the odds of unrelated people sharing such markers were extremely low. Nevertheless, the authors concluded that "the mug shots of the two felons suggested that they were not related: One was black, the other white."[1] This conclusion reveals the degree to which modern notions of race have become synonymous with a person's visual image and dominated by a binary monochrome of skin color. These journalists centered their article and presented judgments of the men's blackness/whiteness by sight, translating their beliefs into a racialized reality that was then assumed to be self-evident: a "black" and a "white" person would not be genetically related.

Despite this essay's focus on the eighteenth century, I open with a modern anecdote to note how our current understandings of race still transform bodily features into naturalized fact. Despite scientific and experiential evidence pointing to the fallacy of racial division, many Americans continue to create a racial reality ostensibly based on physical appearance. As Roxann Wheeler has written, black and white have become powerful "cover stories for a dense matrix of ideas as closely associated with cultural differences as with the body's surface."[2] Colonial Americans, too, reinscribed relationships between phenotype and culturally constructed categorization in their daily lives.[3]

This essay uses text descriptions of both purposefully imagined and "real" bodies to unpack how people were raced and gendered in the middle decades (ca. 1750–75) of colonial British America. With a combination of newspaper advertisements for missing persons and almanac discussions of beauty, I apply social and cultural history methodologies to demonstrate how bodies' physical appearances reflected intersecting understandings of gender and race in colonial American print culture.

Exploring a selection of such descriptions reveals how colonists daily constructed the bodies around them. Rather than a straightforward description of discrete, observable features, colonists turned even basic identifying features into reflections of implicit belief systems. Even though missing-persons descriptions were meant to help readers identify individuals, all groups of colonists were not described with equal precision. Whose ethnicity merited regular and whose only exceptional commentary? How were some men's and women's bodies differently represented? More generally, when did colonists focus on what we might group as intrinsic features (e.g., eye color, and, more complicatedly, skin color), on experiential or exceptional markings (e.g., scars, injuries), or on other evaluative criteria?

In the first section, I analyze approximately one thousand runaway advertisements to quantitatively and qualitatively show that men's physical appearance was generally described more specifically than was women's, regardless of ethnicity, and that African-descended female runaways were the least described figures in advertisements overall. Several descriptive categories, including ethnic/national identity, skin color, and eye color, show how even seemingly fixed features were far more variable than we might expect. Ethnicity and national origins were regularly flattened for non-European peoples into the single ahistoric, a-regional descriptor of "Negro." Skin color was not consistently employed in a binary of black and white. Mentions of eye color were infrequent and corresponded to a different color scale than the descriptive terms we tend to use today. Moreover, the importance and regularity of each of these descriptive categories varied according to the sex and race of the individual, again suggesting the cultural uses of even purportedly objective physical features.

Next, I expand the analysis of missing-persons advertisements to what could be categorized as less innate physical features. Discussions of individuals' scars, injuries, and behavior again vary by gender and racial categories. The physical features of African-descended runaways were often less commonly mentioned than were owners' suppositions about what enslaved bodies revealed about character and life experiences. Ironically, African-descended peoples, whose supposedly innate "Negro-ness" structured their life experience in settler colonial society, seemed to be described the least by intrinsic features and the most by the experiences that life—and their slave status—had marked on their bodies.

The final section of the essay shows the impact of such differentially specific bodily descriptions on sexuality, by analyzing colonists' constructions of women's desirability in scores of midcentury almanacs. The space left by un- or underde-scribed bodies allowed women to serve as markers of raced and gendered sexual boundaries. By exploiting the distinction between generic versus individual, and idealized versus lived bodies, colonists made women's generalizable bodies play a very different role from their corporeal bodies. Imagined woman-ness was based on evaluations of female appearance and behavior rather than physical features. However, only some groups of women would be imagined as beautiful and publicly desirable. A century before the solidification of scientific racism, mainstream pub-lic commentaries laid its seeds by creating rhetorical bodies only in conjunction with the textual production of literal bodies.

This research sits at the intersection of studies of sexuality, race, and gender. Bod-ies have played a central role in historical studies of sexuality that trace the ties between sexual acts, sexual beliefs, and the development of racial ideologies in North American history.[4] Literary scholars, too, have investigated the use of, as one writes, "the nonwhite female body [as] the exclusive signifier of race and sexuality," and the ways in which that signification helps to construct political, cultural and class divisions.[5] But much less has been done on tracing the *details* of the bodies that perform sexual acts or represent ideologies. As Mary Fissell rightly encap-sulates the issue, "Bodies are good to think with, but they are also embedded in social practices."[6] If we treat bodies only as transparent entities around which we employ classifications of black/white, male/female as self-evident binary reali-ties, we risk giving short shrift to the daily creation of constructed physicalities. Such naturalized physical descriptions allowed categories of sexual meaning and regulation to be racialized in early America.

To build on our growing understandings of symbolic bodies, I analyze colonial perceptions of the physical bodies on which such views of gender, race, and sexu-ality were constructed. In so doing, I explore potential axes of bodily descriptions that have been lost to us through the overriding violence of racism, asking what happens if we focus on bodies made literal, rather than the assumptions implicit in gendered and raced categorizations. By *not* focusing on texts that are overtly, in Kim Hall's words, "'about' blackness," I discern the multiple intersecting construc-tions of physicality where writers relied on, but did not see the need to explain, the meanings of the bodies they described.[7] Such implicit assumptions are what made bodies useful, to paraphrase Foucault, as part of sexuality's dense networks of power relations. By understanding how early Americans saw the bodies on which they based these foundations of sexual and racial regulation, we can better trace why particular sex-related constructs could be easily naturalized as based in presumed realities of the body. Colonists made their portrayal of the body's surface fit their matrix of ideas, in terms of both sex and race.

Born Bodies: Race, Nationality, and Complexion

Clarence Walker has called for scholars to complicate the association between skin color and race—to analyze the "transhistoric problem of defining what is or has been called 'black' in America."[8] Descriptions of missing persons in colonial America suggest that Walker is right to ask historians to deconstruct our binary assumptions of historic racial boundaries. In advertisements for runaways, the content of ethnic identifiers varied by birthplace and cultural heritage, reflecting a particular imperial order that continued the purposeful dislocation of African peoples from their geographic histories. The imbrication of race, skin color, and identified heritage made descriptions of complexion less obvious dividers than we might expect. Colonists not only saw complexion in a range of gendered hues, but complexion was not exclusively about skin color. Moreover, the expected divisions of "black" and "white" did not yet hold the purchase in eighteenth-century America that they would in later centuries and were not yet a synonym for race.

Runaway slave advertisements have long been a popular source for scholars. Thanks in part to Lathan Windley's multivolume compilation (and more recently, online searchable newspapers), much of the scholarship on slave runaways has focused on the genre of the runaway ad for what it reveals about slavery and enslaved people, especially in the South.[9] Yet some scholars who have focused on descriptions of physical appearance in runaway advertisements tend to take them at face value. While I build on this work, I am also suggesting that we need to move beyond listings of physicalities to include an exploration of the symbolic work done by these bodily descriptions. Moreover, I expand my focus on runaways beyond African American subjects to make direct comparisons to advertisements for European-descended runaways.[10] The nearly one thousand newspaper advertisements that I have examined for this essay primarily address soldiers who had deserted from their military units, runaway servants, and runaway slaves. Such comparisons allow me to more fully interrogate the construction of race via bodily descriptions.

Not all missing persons merited the same level of detail in advertisements. On average, European-descended men garnered the most description, focusing more on basic physical features (e.g., height, eye color) than on features marked on their bodies by life experience or reflected in their character. European-descended women were more likely to be described than African-descended women in most areas, including complexion, body type, hair, eyes, character, face, skin, height, facial features, and speaking patterns. This leaves African-descended female runaways on one end of the spectrum as the least detailed figures overall—even for basic shared features such as height. Perhaps colonists believed that a female laborer traveling to a new community would be more out of place and thus required less description. Yet these patterns showed no change over time, even as increased population would have made identification based just on femaleness more difficult. The comparative lack of so many descriptive features for African-descended women suggests that their female and nonwhite status combined into a totalizing description in and of itself: the identification of a "negro wench" runaway was enough of a particularized description to make other characteristics relatively superfluous. Even if colonists had an ostensible material rationale for needing less description of African-descended female runaways, colonists' textual descriptions still worked to reify divisions of race and gender on the bodies of these women.

When we turn to individual descriptive categories, what we might call national, ethnic, or racial identifiers (e.g., Irish, Negro, mulatto, English, German, Welsh) appeared more frequently than any other physical descriptor for all runaways. African-descended people were described as Negro or mulatto in every single runaway advertisement I examined, while the ethnicity of European-descended runaways was mentioned about two-thirds of the time. These figures were similar for men and for women, reconfirming that colonists saw something we might call heritage or birthplace or nationality as a basic identity marker.

But what exactly did such terms signify? For free people, the term could appear as an adjective (e.g., an Irish servant) or as the listing of the person's place of birth. Military deserters (the majority of whom were notable for their nonresident status) were particularly likely to have their birthplace recorded. *Pennsylvania Gazette* readers learned that deserter Needham Peet was born in London; Alexander Gunnin was "born in Donegall, Antrim, Ireland"; and William Smith was born in Philadelphia.[11] Such comments located these individuals in an imperial world, reflecting possible differences in accent, as well as perceptions about physical appearance and behavior. Where someone came from affected who they were and how they appeared to others.

Yet for enslaved people, birthplace was very rarely mentioned. People of African descent were largely categorized by the imposed category of "Negro," which did not correspond directly to a political state. A "Negro" identity seemed to override any specific differences that might have been indicated by heritage from a particular part of Africa. Occasionally, newspapers specified that a runaway slave was of "this country born," but still usually without more geographic specification—marking only if African-descended people were foreign or domestically birthed.[12]

Thus, for free people, place of birth was a means of understanding one's public presentation of self in an expanding imperial world; for enslaved people, ethnicity was an imposition that marked their exclusion from full membership in that world. "Negro" or "mulatto" were manufactured inventions of who they were, not indicators of the cultural and political collection of individuals to which they related. Thus Daniel could be described as one of three "young Negro" runaways and a few sentences later as "a mulatto fellow," while a European-descended runaway would not be alternately described as English and Irish in the same advertisement. Divorced from a specific locale, African-descended bodies were made to exist outside a notion of geographically bound histories with terms created and imposed by European-descended people. One's heritage was employed in very different ways for free and enslaved people.

But what physical features were the categories of "Negro" or "mulatto" necessarily meant to convey?[13] Perhaps the most common modern association with ethnic/national status—as in the opening *Los Angeles Times* article—is a skin-color designation. Skin color was most commonly discussed as complexion in eighteenth-century newspapers but still carried meanings beyond a location on a color palette. To what degree, then, can we read colonists' use of complexion as skin color, and either as a proxy for race? Because eighteenth-century categories of race, complexion, and cultural belonging were relatively fluid, advertisements used "mulatto" and "Negro" as characteristics intricately related to, but still separable from, skin color. Both could be used to identify a person: Dick was called a "Negroe" yet described as a "dark Mulattoe."[14] Another runaway slave was labeled a mulatto but described as "dark-skin'd," suggesting that factors other than a relatively light skin color led to a mulatto designation.[15] Such overlapping presentations of the relationship between African-descended runaways' appearance and their heritage suggests that we might want to think particularly carefully about the ambiguous relationships between race, skin color and ethnicity in colonial America. Contrary to Paul Gilroy's suggestions that eighteenth-century people were trying to "reproduce blackness and Englishness as mutually exclusive categories," it may be that early Americans were seeing Negro and English (or Dutch or German) as the most parallel of descriptors.[16] Analysis of physical descriptions, not just identity classifications, suggests this more complex picture.

Unlike European identities, which still required an array of physical specificities, Negro-ness appeared to replace a variety of physical feature designations. In fact, European-descended people were much more likely to have the color of their skin described than were enslaved people. The complexions of African-descended people were mentioned in less than one-quarter of the advertisements, while non-Africans' complexions were described over half the time. In other words, the terms *Negro* and *mulatto* implied complexion color as part of their definition—though what color they implied is not as simple as we might think.

European-descended men and women came in a veritable rainbow of complexion colors: black, brown, dark, fair, freckled, fresh, pale, red, ruddy, sandy, and swarthy.[17] Some individuals, presumably falling in between even this array of descriptive categories were identified with qualifiers, diminutives, or combinations of terms: "darkish," "fairish," "very pale," "pretty fair," "fresh dark," or "dark swarthy," just to name a few.[18] These complexion designators did not correspond to any specific European ethnicity. There is also no indication that silence on a runaway's complexion signified a lack of familiarity with the European-descended individual being described. For instance, Hartman Providore, a German deserter from Pennsylvania forces, was described as a smallpox-scarred, brown-haired man who spoke broken English, but his skin color went unmentioned.[19] In other cases, skin color was prominently featured alongside a specific European-descended heritage. James Dunning was a fair-complexioned Englishman, and Jacob Huffman was a German with a brown complexion.[20] Indicating European nationality was neither a prerequisite nor a substitute for describing complexion.

African-descended complexions apparently required little description once the term *Negro* was applied. The most frequently described complexion color of African-descended people was black, but it still appeared in less than 10 percent of slave advertisements (and in about equal numbers for men and women). And rather than a statement of complexion color, these comments were primarily notations of exceptionalism from an understood norm. Runaway slave Jupiter Hazard was "not very black," Jenny was "remarkably black," Tom was "of the blackest sort," and Sam was "not a dark black."[21] All these comments remarked on the color of African skin only in terms of its deviation from an (unstated) expectation.

Perhaps unexpectedly, European-descended runaways were also referred to as having a black complexion—and in those cases, the word was used as a specific color, not in reference to degree of blackness. James Shetingham, an English-born shoemaker, was said to have a "black" complexion, as were German-born Gabriel Earth and runaway convict-servant Charles Lee.[22] A relatively small percentage of European-descended people were described as black complexioned but nonetheless included Irish, Dutch, English, German, and Scottish people—as well as people with no national identity noted. In the mid–eighteenth century, blackness was used for African- and European-descended runaways and still held meaning that crossed racial boundaries.

Unlike black, however, yellow appears virtually exclusively in reference to people of non-European descent, and it was usually used as a color descriptor, not, as black was, in terms of the extent of its variation from a norm (e.g., very black, not very black).[23] Runaway slave Harry Bedlo was "yellow faced," Moses Grimes had a "yellowish complexion," as did Bob (alias Robert Alexander).[24] It is worth noting that all these yellow-complexioned individuals had surnames, which was unusual for people identified as African descended. The atypical inclusion of surnames for enslaved people may suggest a mixed-race background—perhaps with some Native American heritage, as in the case of Jerry Clark, a "Part Indian and part Negroe" slave who was described as "lusty yellow."[25] The description of Josee, a runaway Virginia slave, explicitly contrasted the two colors, stating that she was "rather inclined to a yellow than black complexion." Other slaves were described as "yellow-looking," and even as a "yellow Negro," further complicating the equivalence of "black" with Negro.[26] By the nineteenth century, yellow would increasingly become used in reference to light-skinned, mixed-race people—a means of identifying people who might be called "mulatto." In this period, however, there were still other occasionally used skin-color descriptions—including brown, gray, and as will be discussed below, white—that further suggest the lack of a universally understood language with which to describe the appearance of people of African descent.[27]

It may be that the development of the exclusively used skin-color descriptor *yellow* for African-descended people suggests a need to define African Americans in terms that hold no meaning for European skin color, as "black" plainly did. Or perhaps, since enslaved people had children with an array of American residents—including Europeans and Native Americans—early Americans saw a reason to recognize more visual distinctions among enslaved people. Contemporary publications more commonly associated red or tawny skin-color descriptions with Native Americans, and catalogers in the eighteenth century, such as Linnaeus, associated yellowness with Asian, not African, peoples.[28] This disjuncture between common and scientific characterizations of skin color is suggestive of the nuances of colonial understandings of race, ethnicity, and skin color in early America. Daily shared bodily meanings were not necessarily identical to records of the contemporary elite's explanations of bodily variations.

While *yellow* would eventually become more commonly used to talk about people of combined Euro-American and African descent, it did not become the common descriptor of African American skin color. We could certainly imagine an early America with "red" Native Americans, "yellow" Africans, and "white" Europeans. Yellow might have made sense from a Galenic perspective of the body, which posited that bodies contained four humors, including the yellow bile that was associated with people from hot climates.[29] However, yellow was not the choice made by colonial Americans—and perhaps, surprisingly, neither was white.[30]

Throughout this period, whiteness was virtually absent as a complexion color descriptor in runaway advertisements. In more than nine hundred advertisements, the specific word *white* was used only once as a description of skin color or complexion. A few more advertisements mentioned a "whitish" complexion, which seemed to be associated with an irregular skin appearance, not an inborn skin color. The European-descended runaway John Oulton was described as "whitish" and "much pock marked," while Hannah Camble, a mulatto runaway, was described as being "of a whitich [sic] cast, very much freckled in the face."[31] Both of these advertisements added a derivational suffix to make the less definitive "whitish," rather than the original color term *white*. This happened occasionally with other skin-tone descriptors, but in all these other cases, it was usually a variation on the norm, not a replacement for the original descriptor (e.g., dark and darkish, fair and fairish, light and lightish). Indeed, the only person I have found described as "white" is Annas, a "very white mulatto wench" who ran away from her owner in 1768.[32] While scholars of the nineteenth and twentieth centuries can point to the importance of the development of whiteness as a bonding force among diverse ethnic and class groups, whiteness seemed far from a common descriptive concept for individual European skin color in daily colonial life.[33]

Although descriptions of the complexions of African-descended runaways were relatively uncommon, there was still some variation within them that suggests a continuum, rather than a binary of skin color. Several focused on brightness versus darkness, again suggesting that colonists did not yet see black and white as automatic and exclusive opposites. One owner described Toby, a runaway slave, as "neither a very bright or very dark Mulatto."[34] We might expect the opposite of bright to be dull, and the opposite of dark to be light, but this writer combined the two. These sets of terms could relate to early modern notions of the skin as a clear covering that could reveal, as one scholar has written, "a deeper layer of selfhood" that made inner virtues underneath its cover—as long as the cover was "bright"—as in revealing.[35] In contrast, dark skin, as Thomas Jefferson wrote, "covers all the emotions."[36] Such understandings of complexion contributed to notions of skin as bright or dark, rather than the automatic opposition of black and white to which we have become accustomed.

Other descriptors likewise complicate the notion that complexion referred exclusively to color. Multiple European-descended missing persons were described as having a "fresh" complexion. It is hard to say what exactly colonists saw as a "fresh" or "fresh coloured"—it did not seem to correspond to any particular overall coloring or national heritage among European-descended runaways. European-descended runaways from a variety of regional backgrounds (English, Dutch, Irish, German, Scottish, etc.) were described as fresh colored. Margaret Hurly had a "fresh coloured, dark Complexion," with smallpox scars, while Sarah Robbins was "of a fair complexion, fresh coloured." Thomas Erwin was of a "fresh colour, of a sandy complexion."[37] Thus "fresh" appears to constitute not so much a specific skin color as another skin-related attribute.

The *Oxford English Dictionary* offers a definition of "fresh," in terms of personal appearance, as blooming, looking healthy or youthful, as well as not sullied, bright and pure; full of energy, or of unexhausted fertility. Indeed, one diarist in the period set fresh in opposition to death.[38] How, then, does this complicate our notion of complexion as equivalent to skin color? It does appear that fresh may be a judgment of a state of being, rather than a proximal replication of a color. Yet fresh does not appear completely unrelated to ethnicity: despite the wide array of skin colors associated with freshness, I have yet to find a reference to a Negro- or mulatto-identified runaway as having a fresh complexion. While there does not appear to be any explicit reason for African-descended people not to be described as fresh complexioned, there was something about freshness that early Americans did not map onto African-descended bodies.

The use of the term *fresh* also highlights some of the gendered differences in complexion descriptions. European-descended women were at least twice as likely to be described as having a "fresh" complexion as were European-descended men. Hannah Galley, an Irish servant, was "fresh coloured," and Elizabeth Petters, a Dutch runaway, was "of a fresh complexion."[39] "Fresh" coloring's disproportionate association with European-descended women reminds us of the mutability of complexion beyond visual perception: there is no reason to think that runaway women were inherently more healthy or youthful than runaway men. Perhaps this classification reflects a cultural belief in the perceived greater innocence of (Euro-American) women or a general association of such women with fertility.[40] Regardless, the subjective nature of the classification of skin color is what allows "fresh" to be disproportionately ascribed to European-descended women.

Other gender differences are likewise notable among descriptions of the complexion of runaways. European-descended men were almost three times as likely as European-descended women to be described as having a "black" complexion. Scottish-born Thomas Smith and "Dutchman" Rudolph Buckhouse were both said to have black complexions.[41] European men were not just disproportionately associated with black coloring; they were also almost three times more likely to be described as "pale" than European-descended women were. Thus it appears that edges of the black-and-white spectrum—pale and black—seemed to be the province of European-descended men. Were the extremes—the black and white—so to speak, seen to convey a particular kind of masculinity? Was this an example of the specificity of descriptions that was reserved more for European-descended men? Unlike European-descended men, African-descended slaves, while undeniably seen as black colored, were referred to only in terms of degree of blackness, not by the color on its own.

Other gender differences appear in descriptions of African-descended women and men. While European-descended men and women's complexions were described with the same frequency (both just over half of the time), African-descended men's complexions were noted almost twice as often as African-descended women's (26 percent versus 15 percent). This discrepancy did not appear to be related to a higher percentage of runaway mulatto men; in fact, African-descended women were almost three times as likely to be identified as mulatto than were African-descended men. Thus it appears that the skin-color variation that signified to early Americans possible Euro-African or Native American–African mixed heritage was seen to create an identity for African-descended women ("mulatto") but led to skin-color descriptions for African American men. Women more easily became associated with a totalizing identity, rather than with individual descriptive features.

Like complexion, descriptions of eye color for identification purposes hold some surprises. We might imagine that facial features could be a crucial part of personal identification. Yet eye color was referenced far less frequently than might be expected when compared to its status as a basic feature of twentieth-century identification schema. Eye color could have been an immutable identifier for everyone, yet fewer than one in ten runaways had an eye color listed. Thomas Lassly was known to be five-feet-nine and one-quarter inch, with light hair and a wart on his cheek, and was said to have "tender eyes," but had no eye color mentioned.[42] Thomas Maguire was a twenty-six-year-old Irish deserter who was five-feet-six and one-half inch tall with a smooth face, fresh complexion, curly hair, and unmentioned eye color.[43] Twenty-six-year-old mulatto Milly was of middle stature, with a long, freckled face, but again, no eye color was listed.[44] Clearly, eye color was not omitted because advertisement writers were unfamiliar with particular details of their runaways. Even advertisements for deserters, whose superiors likely benefited from military records filled with vital statistics, still only mentioned eye color in less than one-quarter of the advertisements. In keeping with patterns where European-descended men were described more than were European-descended women, eye color did appear less frequently for European-descended women than men (9 percent versus 14 percent). But even in advertisements for European-descended men, eye color appeared as part of their description with relatively low frequency. The color of one's eyes did not appear to early Americans to be a standard descriptive feature.

This may partly be because colonists saw eye color on a spectrum different from the diverse color range we might use today.[45] As with aspects of skin color, eye color seemed to be constructed on a continuum of light and dark, not a polychrome that included blue, green, and brown. When eye color did merit commentary, it was most likely the descriptor of "grey," which accounted for almost half of all eye colors mentioned. Only a handful of eyes were described as brown, blue, or black, and none as green. It seems that colonists had a different assumed range for eye colors than modern Americans have—any light eye registered as gray (as in not dark/black). This emphasis on light versus dark, rather than an array of colors, hints at a relationship between colonial employment of visual spectrums of bright-dark skin and light-dark eyes.

Even more than skin color, colonists did not see the need to mention the color of the eyes of runaway slaves. Those people who were described as "yellow" or "mulatto"—and might have had equally variant eye coloration—almost always escaped eye color commentary. The only runaway slave whose eye color was mentioned was Moll's: a mulatto woman with brown hair and gray eyes, who, readers were warned, would try to pass for a free woman.[46] In terms of identification, if gray eyes were interpreted as part of a dark-light continuum, then gray eyes, on the light end of the continuum, seemed to be a marker of free status. Thus colonists may not have seen the need to describe the eyes of African-descended runaways, who were the imagined equivalent of enslaved people. Eye color mattered only in people (and even then, infrequently) who were seen to vary on a spectrum that made sense to early Americans.

Thus early Americans saw divisions among groups when describing ethnicity, complexion, and eye color—all attributes that appeared to largely be innate features but were, in actuality, subjective constructions of visualized appearance. The focus of so much of modern racial identities—skin color—turns out to be fairly complex, equivocal, and subjective on numerous fronts. Black and white were not mutually exclusive categories with fixed meanings in mid-eighteenth-century America. Moreover, variations in classifications of skin attributes—such as the overabundance of "fresh" complexions among European-descended women and disproportionate marking of African-descended women as "mulatto"—reminds us not only that skin color and ethnicity were intrinsically subjective but also suggests a gendered commonality: women tended to be assessed, rather than just described. This pattern would continue with more overtly subjective descriptive categories.

Constructing Experience: Injury, Scars, and Behavior

Given that relatively immutable features were subjectively described, we should expect even more variation across groups for features that did not seem to be innate, such as those acquired through lived experience or displayed through social interactions. In this section, I move to focus on several attributes that more clearly reflected life experiences: condition of teeth, evidence of scars, and classification of behavior. Some of these features might not seem to be obvious markers of gender or race, but my analysis reveals how early Americans implicitly inscribed racial and gendered meaning onto bodily descriptions. A focus on the marks that life had left on bodies—whether purposeful or accidental—could provide imagined histories for those who had been forcibly separated from their pasts, could be seen to reveal innate character, or could remind readers of some people's suitability to particularly harsh labor. Moreover, by focusing on the marks resulting from occupation or heritage, some people's bodies—and by extension, the people themselves—were envisioned as far more malleable than those whose bodies did not publicly speak of their life experiences.

In general, advertisers provided more details about free than enslaved people. However, the condition of enslaved people's teeth seemed to be particularly emphasized in runaway advertisements. Although slaves represented less than one-third of advertisements, they account for more than half of the mentions of the condition of teeth. Tony had "lost some of his teeth," Tom was missing some "of his upper fore Teeth," as were Ben, Cyrus, Dick, and Moll.[47] European-descended men's teeth not only were the least frequently mentioned (about a quarter as often as African-descended men), but the focus of the comments differed significantly. When colonists did comment on European-descended men's dentition, they more often focused on innate peculiarities, not tooth loss or damage. One of John Reily's "upper fore teeth stands above the rest," wrote one advertisement. William Hopkins had "short fore teeth," John Shee's fore teeth were "wide apart," and Robert Caten's "upper Teeth . . . [rode] over each other."[48] It is unlikely that all European-descended runaways had healthy teeth; otherwise, it would not have been necessary for one master to note that John Sprague had "good teeth."[49] But advertisers presented African-descended men's teeth in terms of damage and decay, marking the impact of their lived experiences on their bodies, and European-descended men's teeth in terms of individual variation.

Walter Johnson points out the centrality of the examination of mouths in nineteenth-century slave sales, and teeth were used implicitly to distinguish between slave and free in the eighteenth century as well.[50] While it is hard to imagine that any colonists had particularly good dental care by modern standards, it may be that life in slavery resulted in more dental damage. Yet the gendered breakdown of teeth descriptions suggests this is not the entire answer. European-descended women's teeth were discussed in terms and at rates similar to those of African-descended runaway women: Runaway convict-servant Sarah Robbins had "lost some of her teeth," a Dutch woman named Demen Wallbarg had "lost one of her upper teeth," and Elizabeth Morris had "one of her upper teeth remarkably black."[51] Likewise, the descriptions of two runaway enslaved women note that Jude had rotten front teeth, and Moll had broken-off teeth.[52] These similarities in descriptions of teeth across perceived racial lines suggest an exceptional treatment of European-descended men's teeth, rather than a consistently applied racial divide. Also, African-descended men's teeth, though also described in terms of decay and damage, were commented on twice as often as were African-descended women's, again suggesting that writers made gender-influenced choices in their runaway descriptions. Other than European-descended white men, runaways seemed to share in descriptive feature that showcased the effects of life experiences on their bodies.

It may be that colonists gave particular notice to the teeth of commodified human beings precisely because they were seen to represent the potential health and labor value of that individual. But that does less to explain why European-descended female servants' teeth were of significantly more interest than were European-descended men's, and why African-descended women's teeth were of less interest

than African-descended men's. The act of losing teeth—perhaps through an accident or in the course of agricultural labor—may have also been a way of entering life
histories into physical descriptions. Rather than being described by the theoretically
immutable fact of birthplace or nationality, a lack of such particulars left space for
experiential detailing of the bodies of African-descended people and, to a lesser
extent, European-descended women. Such runaways had the world around them
recorded into their bodily descriptions, while European-descended men bodies
seemed to stand alone as individual entities, far less impacted by outside forces.

Similarly, scars were a more prominent feature in African-descended runaway
advertisements than in European-descended advertisements. Almost 20 percent of advertisements for African-descended men and women mentioned some
bodily scarring or marking. This indicated a clear division along racial lines: such
commentaries on European-descended men and women appeared in only about
5–7 percent of their advertisements. It may be that people likely to live a life of
enslavement would more frequently have permanent scars. But the discussion of
scarring marks does not seem to correlate directly to the rates of injuries described:
discussions of European- and African-descended injuries are within a few percentage points of each other, suggesting that scars were a feature that early Americans
chose to focus on when describing their slaves, but not their servants or missing
soldiers. Advertisers chose to focus on scars on African-descended bodies, and
in so doing, created bodies as particularly markable.

Most mentions of scars gave specific details that constructed—or allowed readers to imagine—a life history. Some scars marked a transatlantic journey and sense
of otherness for African-descended people. Phebe had "three or four large Negroe
Scars up and down her Forehead," and Ibbe had "Holes in her ears."[53] Joe, one of
the only slaves identified as a "salt water Negroe man," had "a brass or iron ring in
his left ear," as well as scars on his face and breast that were likely a result of ritual
rather than injury.[54] Coak's scars were obviously ritually made: they were described
as "3 remarkable spots on the upper part of each cheek, near his eyes, supposed
to be marks made in the Negroe country."[55] Some of the "scars" noted on African
bodies were remnants of an African heritage and provided a way to again mark
African slaves with an imagined history outside the bounds of colonial American
settlements. The life experiences of African-descended runaways, made manifest
on their bodies, rather than innate eye or skin color, made them identifiable, making African-descended runaways' otherness animate as members of an African
culture. But even without counting ritual markings, advertisements for African-
descended runaways mentioned scars at least twice as often as did advertisements
for European-descended runaways.

Other comments on scars told individual stories of the enslaved peoples' life
experiences that were not expressly part of an exoticized non-European heritage.

Jupiter had a bare spot on his head from being scalded.[56] Jude had "one of her feet scalded some time ago, and the skin is a good deal thinner than the other."[57] A horse kicked out some of Nann's teeth; she had "two large Scars on one of her Arms below the Elbow, occasioned by a burn, and three Scars on one of her Knees, by the Kick of a horse."[58] Stepney had a large scar on his temple from a burn, and Daniel was ""remarkable scarred on his Shins by Burns and Sores which he receiv'd when young."[59] These descriptions forwarded information beyond what was likely necessary to recognize a scar or a burn. Instead of just listing distinguishing marks, they implicitly reflected the hardships of slavery. Although not expressly about Africanness, such descriptions of scars did point to the racialized experience of slavery by presenting African-descended people as marked by life, not birth: slavery literally formed their bodies. This also meant that while generic descriptions along the lines of Phoebe's "scar on her right eyebrow" did not explicitly include causative stories, they still might believably stoke imaginations about what had happened to these malleable bodies. Unlike other features, both African-descended men and women had similar rates of scars listed, suggesting that a markable body was seen as a consistent feature of life for Africans in America.

Other scars were even more clearly results of a life in slavery. Hannah had "many scars on her back, occasioned by whipping," Boston was "scarified by Whipping," and Dick had been "branded on one of his Shoulders."[60] The inclusion of such details, not immediately visible to a passerby on the street, reflects a sense of entitlement to examine African-descended bodies in order to locate such marks. Given the close proximity in which colonists lived, it is unlikely that scars on the bodies of European-descended servants and soldiers could have easily been unknown to others who had lived with the runaway. A servant's master would likely have known about scars such as the one on an unnamed runaway slave that were "marked under the wasteband of his breeches."[61] Even though corporal punishment was still commonly used for free colonists and soldiers, no advertisements for European-descended people mention scars caused by whipping or branding. But several advertisements do make clear that runaways had experienced corporal sentences. For instance, Alice McCarty, an Irish servant, had apparently "been several times whipped in the workhouse, in Philadelphia, and whipped for theft at the public post," but any resulting scars went unmentioned.[62] The consequences of her misdeeds did not become written on this Irish servant's body the way it would be for enslaved people. Runaway servants or soldiers would likely not have been subject to the kind of physical exams that European-descended colonists could inflict on African-descended bodies, and this created differential knowledge, as expressed in descriptions of free and unfree bodies.

For the most part, comments on the bodies of free people seemed to focus more on inherent features, not on marks of hard-lived lives. Patrick Mannus had a "black hair mole on his right cheek," and Thomas Lassly had "a wart on his right cheek."[63] Almost no European-descended runaways had mentions of burn scars. While slaves may have done more dangerous labor, it is hard to imagine that free people—especially servants and soldiers—did not have some risk of burns from daily work. When writers did take note of injuries to runaways of European descent, they were more apt to mention a recent injury, not a permanent life mark. William Gill, a deserter, had a "cut on his left cheek"; England-born James Margison had a cut on his nose, while Richard Phumphrey and James McFall both had black eyes when they ran away.[64] The distinction between a temporary mark and a permanent scar again differentiated free and enslaved runaways by describing bodies such that life experiences permanently marked African-descended people, while leaving free people as more often, literally, free of the permanent marks of life experience. This set up African-descended bodies as physically malleable—perfect for people whom colonial Americans expected to be slaves.

Beyond descriptions of particular aspects of physical appearance, runaway advertisements regularly included commentaries on individuals' purported character and likely behavior. Such descriptions included comments on alcohol usage, criminal misbehavior, evaluations of the runaway's honesty, social abilities, intelligence, tendency to quarrel, tobacco usage, and exceptional skills. There are no clear patterns of character commentaries across particular European-descended ethnic or skin-color groupings. For instance, there is no indication that a "black" complexion related to negative social stereotypes; such identified people were no more or less likely to receive disparaging comments on their character than were other Euro-Americans. Likewise, people identified as being of Irish descent were no more likely to have comments about their behavior. Indeed, comments on conduct seemed rather unrelated to any particular listed European heritage marker.

However, when overlapping gender and ethnicity, clear variations appear in the use of character commentaries. European-descended men were the least likely to have comments on their character and behavior listed—less than one-fifth of the time. In stark contrast, nearly half of all advertisements that identified runaway women as mulatto included commentary on their character and behavior—the highest percentage of any identifiable group. European-descended women had character commentaries about one-third of the time, as did about one in seven women identified as "Negro." Such variations reflect that bodily evaluations were rarely as simplistic as black versus white or European versus African. Women, already more likely than men to be identified as mulatto, were treated differently from both their African-descended counterparts and European-descended men.

We might think that mulatto women, already identified as a distinct group, would need comparatively fewer individual descriptions. But it seems that once judged as "mulatto," these women merited additional commentaries on their personalities and character—and most of the time, these characterizations were less than positive. Of three mulatto runaways, Hagar Jones was described as "an artful jade," Hannah Cambel was said to be a "bold well tongued hussy," and Violet was supposedly "remarkably artful."[65] The use of terms such as "artful" had clear gender and racial applications: women were five times more likely than men to be described as artful, and African-descended people were three times more likely than European-descended people to be called artful. These patterns again reflect the exceptional ways that European-descended men were textually displayed: their actions were recounted, rather than judged.

Indeed, European-descended women were more frequently described with negative character assessments than with lists of their misdeeds. Eleanor Ferrel seemed to encompass a wide range of unflattering features: she was described as "ill natured, scolding, cursing, swearing, thieving."[66] Sarah Knox was called "a very deceitful, bold, insinuating woman, and a great liar."[67] Many runaway women were characterized as deceitful: Mary Dugan was, like many of her fellow female runaways, said to be "an artful hussy"; Elizabeth Williams was "much given to lying."[68] While all runaways, by virtue of running away, had committed an act against authority, European-descended women may have particularly been seen as engaging in a personalized misdeed. Not only did European-descended female servants abandon their legal and economic responsibilities to their masters, but their defiance of patriarchal mastery also challenged accepted gender dynamics. Thus their actions may have been more easily considered personal affronts that led to their masters' public character attacks.

African-descended people were also particularly likely to be critiqued on their character. A tally of comments on dishonesty confirms this: African-descended women were overrepresented as liars compared to European-descended women. In contrast, African-descended men accounted for about 80 percent of commentaries on men's deceptive character: runaway enslaved men were described as sly and artful, smooth-tongued, accomplished liars, crafty, or cunning.[69] Many of these characteristics undoubtedly came from their efforts toward freedom: Peter was said to be a "cunning artful fellow" who would try to "pass for a free man."[70] African-descended, usually enslaved men, had reason to appear deceitful: slavery, a system of vast power inequities, privileged the judgments and evaluation of masters in ways that even indentured servants did not have to contend with. But advertisers could have chosen just to list the acts of deceit, rather than putting forth frequent character judgments on the deceitful nature of slaves. In so doing, slave owners made personal descriptions into a literal display of their powers to define the very nature of the people they owned.

Similar patterns appear in relation to other character issues, such as criminality. Rather than define European-descended runaway men as criminals, their advertisements seemed to focus on individual crimes they had committed. William Hood apparently stole clothes when he ran away, Thomas Plendible had previously been under suspicion of counterfeiting, and Thomas Douglas allegedly robbed members of his regiment.[71] In contrast, female European-descended runaways rarely had details of their thieving ways included in a description. Instead, they themselves were categorized as "a thief," "a great thief," or, as Rachel Scott was described, "apt to be light fingered," usually without mention of any other specifics.[72] Here again, such women were evaluated rather than described. Criminal behavior resulted in commentaries on European-descended men's specific acts but characterized the nature of the European-descended women.

Whether talking about the condition of teeth, bodily markings, or behavior, descriptions of runaways reveal implicit ideas about the bodies they describe. In all these examples, evaluations of character and behavior presented European-descended men as individuals, while women and people of color became classified with particular identities. Runaway advertisements described European-descended men in the most detail because they were seen to merit treatment as innately individualized. In contrast, European-descended women and African-descended men and women, to differing degrees, became groups who could be more easily created by the world—and people—around them. Being seen as bodily reflectors of experience, rather than individuals with innate identities, had far-reaching consequences. Some of these malleable bodies, already able to be controlled, marked, and evaluated, could then be re-created as symbolic markers for racial, gender, and sexual boundaries in early America.

Beautiful Bodies: Gender, Race, and the Power of Desire

Analyzing the discourse of beauty in colonial print shows how colonists built on their images of individual bodies to conceptualize desirability and attraction along lines of race and gender. Women's bodies, already likely to be evaluated more than described, were further categorized in terms of desirability and attractiveness. Yet not all women appeared beautiful in print. Rather than having physical features define beauty, colonists used beauty to highlight appropriate gender dynamics and mark lines of power and hierarchy.

To undertake an analysis of the use of beauty in print, I examined how colonists wrote about beauty in hundreds of midcentury almanacs, noting whose bodies were and were not discussed as beautiful, and what physicalities, if any, were referenced in relation to beauty. Colonists spent considerable print space talking about beautiful things, people, and ideas. In the middle decades of the eighteenth century, mentions of beauty appeared in up to one-quarter of almanacs.[73] Men virtually never appeared in relation to beauty; references to bodily beauty focused almost exclusively on women. Although colonial Americans wrote about women's beauty without reference to much physical detail, they were relying on images of a European-descended woman in their tales. Indeed, colonists made African-descended women's bodies invisible when discussing the appeal and desirability of beauty. But this was not because beauty was a uniformly positive feature: those women imagined as beautiful in colonial almanacs conveyed messages about the threat that such women could represent to dominant men. Excluding African-descended women from inhabiting the category of beauty thus had less to do with attention to particular physicalities than with racial boundaries that publicly set only European-descended women as potential mates, allowing white women to inhabit a category of wife that explicitly excluded African-descended women. This focus on the power, rather than the physicality, of beauty transformed the evaluation of physical bodies into a means to solidify gender and race via the construction of sexualized desire.

Beauty was used virtually exclusively in reference to women. The very few discussions of male beauty uniformly referred to men with a divine or supernatural nature. A 1762 almanac told the story of a visitation by angels, who "appeared to be like beautiful men."[74] In the retelling of a Native American myth in one eighteenth-century captivity narrative, a male water sprite in the Penobscot River was referred to as "beautiful."[75] These kinds of discussions of male beauty were both rare and limited to supernatural male bodies, not corporeal human men. For colonial Americans, men were not beautiful. This first hint suggests that beauty contains more than a judgment on the symmetry or particular arrangement of physical features. Instead, beauty was an evaluative judgment that purposely excluded male bodies.

While men's bodies rarely appeared in print commentaries on beauty, their actual bodies, it is worth recalling, were described in significantly more detail than were women's bodies in runaway advertisements. Not only did men's descriptions contain more physical information than women's within each ethnic/regional group (European-descended men versus women and African-descended men versus women), but regardless of content, advertisements for female runaways appeared much less frequently than did those for male runaways overall. Even though I explicitly searched for runaway women, men account for about two-thirds of all the runaway advertisements I could identify. While there are a variety of social and economic reasons for this (men were more likely to run away, military deserters were exclusively male, etc.), the result nonetheless had profound cultural implications: women's actual bodies were unlikely to be concretely described in colonial print mediums.

In contrast to the relative paucity of descriptions of female runaways' physical bodies, analysis of beauty discourses suggests that women's abstracted bodies—bodies that were desired, evaluated, used as punch lines or warnings to readers—

appeared relatively frequently in almanacs. Such uses of imagined women's bodies to showcase men's opinions built on the evaluations of actual women's bodies that privileged judgment over description. Colonists would have been more accustomed to seeing evaluations of female bodies than descriptions of their individual features. The comparative scarcity of actual women's descriptions made imagined versions of women—including beautiful women—available for representational purposes.

Colonists engaged in discussions of beauty to do more than comment on a particular physical appearance. Instead, they sought to teach lessons by showing readers the power and danger to men who might mistake women's beauty for evidence of character. *An astronomical diary . . . for the year . . . 1764* discussed beauty a good half dozen times, in ways typical for the time period: there are stories about the beauty of women's bodies; the dangers of outward beauty; the true beauty of the mind; and the contrast of modesty versus beauty.[76] A personified "Beauty" in a South Carolina newspaper in 1772 captured many of the features of beauty discourse in colonial almanacs: "Beauty," Love's daughter, was sent to mankind, and though she "intended well," Vanity, Luxury, and Pleasure made life difficult for those of "her own sex" whom Beauty visited. Ultimately, Beauty lectured humanity about the "calamities a misapplication of [her] gifts ha[d] occasioned," advised them to recognize the value of "Mental Beauty," and threatened to "shun the human race" if they did not.[77] This lengthy allegory, like many shorter almanac stories, ultimately warned readers that trusting women's outward beauty could lead to destruction.

Scores of almanacs told tales of women's beauty in order to provide a lesson to readers. A 1758 almanac's "Rules for taking a Wife" warned that if she "court her fickle Beauty in a Glass, She is for thee, dear Youth, no proper Lass."[78] A 1765 almanac concurred, "If she is enamour'd with her own Beauty . . . turn thy Face from her Charms."[79] One "Lady's Advice to her Son, in chusing a Wife" included "Avoide the fine Lady whose Beauty's her Care, / Who sets an high Price on her Shape and her Air."[80] This theme of the danger of relying on women's apparent beauty was one that would recur again and again. Such writers used beauty to distinguish between virtue and vice, honesty and deceit via an evaluation of women's attractiveness. They did so without referencing specific physical features; rather beauty became the evaluative means to define good and bad, thus turning women's (abstract) bodies into a tool to mark larger social divisions.

The use of beauty as a placeholder for a woman's often duplicitous attractiveness, rather than a judgment on specific physicalities, helps to explain the public exclusion of African-descended women. African-descended people, intended to be enslaved rather than considered potential romantic and marital partners, were purposefully excluded from public acknowledgment of their desirability. Thus the imagined woman behind print discussions of women's beauty was not an inclusive category of womanly physicality; it included within it particular assumptions about race and appearance that constructed an invisibility of race/status in colonial America.

In fact, I could not find a single mention of beauty in relation to a person identified as African-descended in any of the hundreds of almanacs examined. African-descended people were certainly discussed in almanacs—versions of the word *Negro* and *slave* appeared many times in almanacs in this period (the majority of them emphasizing enslavement by referring to "Negroes" for sale or discussing how many slaves one would need to perform particular tasks).[81] But African-descended bodies did not appear in stories about generic women's beauty; such stories relied on an invisibility of whiteness. Scholars such as Jennifer L. Morgan and Stephanie M. H. Camp have shown that English travel writers did associate beauty with African women in earlier centuries.[82] But within colonial print, beauty was used, not as a physical description, but as the potential promise (and danger) of a woman's worth as a wife. African-descended women, not publicly seen to inhabit that category of potential spouse for the American almanac audience, would thus be erased from the womanly beauty that signified attraction to a potential mate. Thus beauty was a female-gendered category that African-descended women could not publicly inhabit for colonial Americans. Beautiful women relied on the invisible privilege of Anglo-American heritage to claim their desirable status, while at the same time carrying the dangerous potential to reverse proper gender norms through deception. This left African-descended women's bodies to perform another purpose in relation to their physical or sexual appeal.

The few references to African-descended women's bodies in mid-eighteenth-century almanacs suggest that colonists also saw a danger in black women's bodies that was beyond particular physicalities. But that danger was not realized through beauty. Rather than endangering men through the trickery of beauty, African American women's desirability degraded the status of the pursuer. A satirical epitaph published as a broadside in the 1760s focused on a "wicked old Lecher / And most abandoned of all Scoundrels That God ever gave Life to," who had committed "every Vice." This included "Black fornication in particular," and obtaining "The Charcoal Charms" of a "Negroe Wench."[83] This condemnation portrayed its subject as a lascivious, immoral, ungodly man with a limitless capacity for vice who seduced unknown numbers of youth to his evil ways and was ostracized by all virtuous men. The specific reference to a "Negroe Wench" and to "black" fornication are the only references to another individual in the lengthy satire. Clearly, her "Charcoal Charms," rather than just her generically female charms, did particular symbolic service here. Rather than evoking sympathy for the (white) man victimized by the deceitful charms of the beautiful (white) woman in other stories, here Africanness is meant to lead the reader to adjudge the man's guilt. Rather than the African-descended woman's charms being located in a desirability that readers might share and thus feel for the male victim's downfall, her race was used as a marker of the man's depravity.[84] Where a (white) woman's appealing, yet duplicitous, body was featured as a warning to men gullible to physical attraction, an African-descended woman's body is presented as fait accompli evidence of a man's irredeemable fall. Moreover, the imagined African-descended women who made up the "black" fornication with this man were epitomized by a color not usually publicly assigned to actual African-descended women. Descriptions of physicality took a backseat to the evaluative uses of women's bodies.

In popular culture, women's bodies appeared to convey a symbolic message by eliminating their corporeal physicalities. Despite the many commentaries on the uses and misuses of beauty, few almanacs made explicit mention of what female beauty should look like. But colonists still held implicit beliefs about the "women" they described as beautiful. Beauty, as a marker of the capability of women to overturn men's patriarchal power in personal relationships, applied only to those women whom European-descended colonists imagined as a racially appropriate wife. Moreover, male almanac writers presented women's beauty in nonphysical terms by relying on the pattern of evaluation of women's physical bodies displayed in runaway advertisements. Images of fictionalized women's bodies thus entered the popular press as vehicles for larger symbolic meanings, particularly in reference to constructions of gender and racial boundaries.

Rather than look at descriptions of corporeal bodies as self-evident, I have, to steal a line from Alexis Shotwell, tried to render eighteenth-century daily descriptions of bodies "differently legible."[85] That new bodily legibility, I argue, meant there was little distinction between the subjectivity of an individual's character, history, and physical features. Runaway advertisements instead reflected the discursive network in which eighteenth-century colonists lived, networks in which they did not have to explain shared linguistic meanings. These cultural constructions of appearance ultimately allowed meanings of gender, race, and sexuality to be indivisibly written onto early American bodies.

I began with ethnicity and skin color because, as the opening modern anecdote shows, these two features have become intertwined symbols of racial difference. Walter Johnson has suggested that "to stabilize the restless hybridity, the infinite variety of mixture that was visible all over the South, into measurable degrees of black and white," in the antebellum south, skin color was read "as a sign of a deeper set of racial qualities."[86] But in the mid–eighteenth century, early Americans did not see black and white as the singular axis on which people were defined. Rather than the *Los Angeles Times*' self-evident assumptions that readers would see black and white in obvious opposition, colonists still did not view individual Europeans as "white" and only infrequently saw the need to comment on African-descended people's skin colors.

Throughout this essay, I ask how, when, and whether we are imposing the categories of whiteness-and-blackness, maleness-and-femaleness anachronistically, in ways that mask, more than reveal, the complexities of bodily interpretations in colonial America. At what point should we suppress individual characteristics to the overriding mantras of race or gender? I suggest that colonists created boundaries implicitly through small descriptive differences in the bodies they regularly described. European- and African-descended missing persons might all have features worth commenting on, but slight variations gave very different meanings to those descriptions. Even similar language (e.g., black complexion) has potentially differing significance when laid on top of colonists' beliefs and assumed knowledge.

Gendered and racial variations in descriptions repeatedly separated immutable characteristics from experiential ones. The physical features of African-descended runaways were less commonly mentioned than were owners' suppositions about what enslaved bodies revealed about behavior, character, and life experiences. For African-descended runaways, an imposed "Negro" status replaced specific physical descriptors and laid the groundwork for further applications of life narratives onto textual recounting of appearance.

Finally, a focus on idealized notions of women's beauty shows that women's actual bodies had comparatively little place in public discourse. While the body has been a constant presence in sexuality studies, it has often been taken as an unproblematized or symbolic placeholder, perhaps unconsciously reflecting, rather than deconstructing, its historic uses. In a modern age where body parts are surgically manipulated, where images of bodies are regularly photoshopped into more pleasing images, and where computer scientists claim the ability to use mathematical algorithms to act as "beautification engines" on human faces, the absence of colonial popular culture commentary on specific physical aspects of beauty is a suggestion of the very long distance we have traveled from the eighteenth century.[87] My analysis of beauty suggests that men's bodies entered public discourse by getting described, while women's bodies were far more likely to enter discourse by getting deployed, often as placeholders to mark the hazard of female desirability. Evaluations of beauty reflected social positioning and fear of inverted gender dynamics and implicitly constructed and enforced racial lines. European-descended women invisibly inhabited the category of beautiful women—not necessarily in positive terms, but with the possibility of sexual and spousal ties to imagined readers. African-descended women, as publicly incompatible partners to European-descended men, were excluded from the category of beauty, not by explicit referral to physical appearance but rather via the symbolic and rhetorical work of the concept of beauty. In so doing, colonial Americans reflected and made real their own judgments under the guise of describing the people around them.

Notes

1. Jason Felch and Maura Dolan, "How Reliable Is DNA in Identifying Suspects?," *Los Angeles Times* July 19, 2008, http://articles.latimes.com/2008/jul/20/local/me-dna20 (accessed April 28, 2010).

2. Roxann Wheeler, *The Complexion of Race: Categories of Difference in Eighteenth-Century British Culture* (Philadelphia: University of Pennsylvania Press, 2000), 2.

3. On constructions of race in the British American colonial period, see Winthrop D. Jordan, *White over Black: American Attitudes toward the Negro, 1550–1812* (New York: W.W. Norton, 1968), 216–65; Ivan Hannaford, *Race: The History of an Idea in the West* (Baltimore: Johns Hopkins University Press, 1996); Kim Hall, *Things of Darkness: Economies of Race and Gender in Early Modern England* (Ithaca, N.Y.: Cornell University Press, 1995); Londa Schiebinger, "The Anatomy of Difference: Race and Sex in Eighteenth-Century Science," *Eighteenth-Century Studies* 23, no. 4 (1990): 387–405; Stephanie M.H. Camp, "Early European Views of African Bodies: Sin and Savagery," in "Black Is Beautiful: An American History," manuscript in author's possession.

4. For example, Sharon Block, *Rape and Sexual Power in Early America* (Chapel Hill: University of North Carolina Press, 2006); Kirstin Fischer, *Suspect Relations: Sex, Race, and Resistance in Colonial North Carolina* (Ithaca, N.Y.: Cornell University Press, 2001); Martha Hodes, *White Women, Black Men: Illicit Sex in the Nineteenth-Century South* (New Haven, Conn.: Yale University Press, 1999).

5. Vera M. Kutzinski, *Sugar's Secrets: Race and the Erotics of Cuban Nationalism* (Charlottesville: University Press of Virginia, 1993), 42. On the genealogy of studies of the body, see Susan Bordo, "The Body and the Reproduction of Femininity," in *Writing on the Body: Female Embodiment and Feminist Theory*, ed. Katie Conboy, Nadia Medina, and Sarah Stanbury (New York: Columbia University Press, 1997), 90–91.

6. Mary Elizabeth Fissell, *Vernacular Bodies: The Politics of Reproduction in Early Modern England* (Oxford: Oxford University Press, 2004), 11. See also Michael Lambek and Andrew Strathern, *Bodies and Persons: Comparative Perspectives from Africa and Melanesia* (New York: Cambridge University Press, 1998), 5, 7, 33.

7. Kim F. Hall, *Things of Darkness: Economies of Race and Gender in Early Modern England* (Ithaca, N.Y.: Cornell University Press, 1995), 14.

8. Clarence E. Walker, *Mongrel Nation: The America Begotten by Thomas Jefferson and Sally Hemings* (Charlottesville: University of Virginia Press, 2009), 30–31.

9. Lathan A. Windley, comp., *Runaway Slave Advertisements: A Documentary History from the 1730s to 1790* (Westport, Conn.: Greenwood Press, 1983). For just some of the work on southern advertisements, see Gerald W. Mullin, *Flight and Rebellion: Slave Resistance in Eighteenth-Century Virginia* (New York; Oxford University Press, 1972); Peter H. Wood, *Black Majority: Negroes in Colonial South Carolina from 1670 through the Stono Rebellion* (New York: Knopf, 1974), 239–68; Shane White and Graham White, "Slave Hair and African American Culture in the Eighteenth and Nineteenth Centuries," *Journal of Southern History* 61, no. 1 (February 1995): 45–76. On northern runaways, see David Waldstreicher, "Reading the Runaways: Self-Fashioning, Print Culture, and Confidence in Slavery in the Eighteenth-Century Mid-Atlantic," *William and Mary Quarterly* 56, no. 2 (April 1999):

243–72, esp. 246; Billy G. Smith and Richard Wojtowicz, *Blacks Who Stole Themselves: Advertisements for Runaways in the Pennsylvania Gazette, 1728-1790* (Philadelphia: University of Pennsylvania Press, 1989).

10. For servant runaways, see Sharon Salinger, *"To Serve Well and Faithfully": Labor and Indentured Servants in Pennsylvania, 1682–1800* (London: Cambridge University Press, 1987). For comparisons of servants and slaves, see Jonathan Prude, "To Look upon the 'Lower Sort': Runaway Ads and the Appearance of Unfree Laborers in America, 1750–1800," *Journal of American History* 78 (June 1991): 124–59; Thelma Foote, *Black and White Manhattan: The History of Racial Formation in Colonial New York* (New York: Oxford University Press, 2004), 190–209.

11. *Pennsylvania Gazette*, December 18, 1760; February 14, 1760; June 14, 1764.

12. *Pennsylvania Gazette*, January 9, 1750; June 6, 1771. For examples of servants referred to this way, see *Pennsylvania Gazette* April 16, 1752; December 23, 1772. There does appear to be a different pattern in the *South Carolina Gazette*, which did, as other scholars have found, specify specific locations within Africa. Because many of these advertisements were put out by workhouses that housed runaways, they may have had more specific information available about the people they described. This difference also likely reflects South Carolina's connections to the Caribbean and Atlantic slave trade. See, for example, Michael Gomez, *Exchanging Our Country Marks: The Transformation of African Identities in the Colonial and Antebellum South* (Chapel Hill: University of North Carolina Press, 1998), 38–40, 138–40.

13. On even modern historians' problematic adoption of "simply a category called 'Negro,'" see Walker, *Mongrel Nation*, 84.

14. *Pennsylvania Gazette*, November 29, 1764.

15. *Virginia Gazette*, October 27, 1752. See also *Virginia Gazette*, January 29, 1767.

16. Paul Gilroy, *The Black Atlantic: Modernity and Double Consciousness* (Cambridge, Mass.: Harvard University Press, 1993), 55.

17. For examples of the variety of complexions, see *Pennsylvania Gazette*, May 29, 1755; June 28, 1764; February 13, 1772; July 16, 1772; June 17, 1756; September 28, 1752; February 12, 1754; August 20, 1761.

18. *Pennsylvania Gazette*, June 21, 1770; June 21, 1753; October 28, 1772; December 18, 1760.

19. For examples of English and Germans with no complexion mentioned, see *Pennsylvania Gazette*, September 4, 1755; June 28, 1764; November 3, 1757; June 9, 1773; June 21, 1759; November 4, 1756.

20. *Pennsylvania Gazette*, September 4, 1755.

21. *Pennsylvania Gazette*, June 13, 1751; August 8, 1771; December 5, 1771; *Virginia Gazette*, May 9, 1755.

22. *Pennsylvania Gazette*, November 3, 1757; March 18, 1756; October 24, 1765.

23. For the one European described as having a yellow complexion, see *Pennsylvania Gazette*, November 8, 1770.

24. *Pennsylvania Gazette*, April 28, 1773; November 25, 1772; December 30, 1772.

25. *Pennsylvania Gazette*, January 20, 1773.

26. *Virginia Gazette*, March 7, 1766. See also *Virginia Gazette*, October 20, 1752; *Pennsylvania Gazette*, July 2, 1772; *Virginia Gazette*, September 5, 1755; February 24, 1766.

27. For example, *Virginia Gazette*, April 18, 1766; *Pennsylvania Gazette*, February 17, 1763.

28. Nathaniel E. Gates, *The Concept of Race in Natural and Social Science* (New York: Routledge, 2014), 67.

29. On early modern geohumoral science, see Rebecca Earle, *The Body of the Conquistador: Food, Race, and the Colonial Experience in Spanish America, 1492–1700* (New York: Cambridge University Press, 2012), 26–32.

30. On interpreting race and color in early America, see Nancy Shoemaker, "How Indians Got to Be Red," *American Historical Review* 102, no. 3 (1997): 625–45; Christopher L. Miller and George R. Hamell, "A New Perspective on Indian-White Contact: Cultural Symbols and Colonial Trade," *Journal of American History* 73, no. 10 (September 1986), 311–28, esp. 323–24. On early modern understandings of the humoral system, see David C. Lindberg, *The Beginnings of Western Science: The European Scientific Tradition in Philosophical, Religious, and Institutional Context, 600 BC to AD 1450*, 2nd ed. (Chicago: University of Chicago Press, 2007), 115–18.

31. *Pennsylvania Gazette*, March 27, 1754; February 24, 1773.

32. *Virginia Gazette*, January 28, 1768.

33. For example, Matthew Frye Jacobson, *Whiteness of a Different Color: European Immigrants and the Alchemy of Race* (New York: Cambridge University Press, 1999); Nell Irvin Painter, *History of White People* (New York: W. W. Norton, 2010); David R. Roediger, *The Wages of Whiteness: Race and the Making of the American Working Class* (Brooklyn: Verso, 1993).

34. *Pennsylvania Gazette*, March 25, 1755.

35. Angela Rosenthal, "Visceral Culture: Blushing and the Legibility of Whiteness in Eighteenth-Century British Portraiture," *Art History* 27, no. 4 (September 2004): 574. For a related argument, see Mechthild Fend, "Bodily and Pictorial Surfaces in French Art and Medicine, 1790–1860," *Art History* 28, no. 3 (2005): 311–39.

36. Thomas Jefferson, *Notes on the State of Virginia*, http://avalon.law.yale.edu/18th_century/jeffvir.asp (accessed January 21, 2016). For Europeans' comments on the brightness of African's skin, see Stephanie M. H. Camp "Early European Views of African Bodies: Beauty," in "Black Is Beautiful: An American History," esp. 9–10, manuscript draft in author's possession.

37. *Pennsylvania Gazette*, June 20, 1754.

38. "Letter from Isabella Marshall Graham, June 08, 1773," in *The Unpublished Letters and Correspondence of Mrs. Isabella Graham, from the Year 1767 to 1814 . . .* (New York: John S. Taylor, 1838), 314.

39. *Pennsylvania Gazette*, September 25, 1755; October 20, 1763.

40. On beliefs about and portrayals of fertility, see Mary Fissell, "Gender and Generation: Representing Reproduction in Early Modern England," *Gender and History* 7 (1995): 433–56; Susan Klepp, *Revolutionary Conceptions: Women, Fertility, and Family Limitation in America, 1760–1820* (Chapel Hill: University of North Carolina Press, 2009).

41. *Pennsylvania Gazette*, November 3, 1757; December 6, 1770.

42. *Pennsylvania Gazette*, October 30, 1755.

43. *Pennsylvania Gazette*, November 7, 1771.

44. *Virginia Gazette*, November 7, 1754.

45. On variation in eye color, see P. Frost, "European Hair and Eye Color: A Case of Frequency-Dependent Sexual Selection?," *Evolution and Human Behavior* 27 (2006): 85–103; R. A. Sturm and T. N. Frudakis, "Eye Colour: Portals into Pigmentation Genes and Ancestry," *Trends in Genetics* 20 (2004): 327–32. On the modern rate of "light" eye color in Europe, see http://www.eupedia.com/europe/maps_of_europe.shtml#eye_colour (accessed January 10, 2010).

46. *Virginia Gazette*, October 27, 1752.

47. *Pennsylvania Gazette*, August 12, 1772; May 12, 1773; July 5, 1770; *Boston Evening-Post*, October 19, 1761; *Pennsylvania Gazette*, May 10, 1770; *Virginia Gazette*, October 27, 1752.

48. *Pennsylvania Gazette*, April 12, 1770; October 28, 1772; August 28, 1760.

49. *Pennsylvania Gazette*, August 19, 1772; see also *Pennsylvania Gazette*, April 2, 1772.

50. Walter Johnson, *Soul by Soul: Life inside the Antebellum Slave Market* (Cambridge, Mass.: Harvard University Press, 2009), 142.

51. *Pennsylvania Gazette*, April 14, 1773; June 10, 1756; October 18, 1750.

52. *Pennsylvania Gazette*, June 29, 1774; *Virginia Gazette*, October 27, 1752.

53. *Pennsylvania Gazette*, September 1, 1763; November 13, 1766.

54. *Pennsylvania Gazette*, September 1, 1773.

55. *Pennsylvania Gazette*, July 11, 1771.

56. *Pennsylvania Gazette*, February 8, 1770.

57. *Pennsylvania Gazette*, June 29, 1774.

58. *Pennsylvania Gazette*, February 14, 1765.

59. *Virginia Gazette*, July 25, 1751; April 10, 1752.

60. *Virginia Gazette*, March 26, 1767; *Pennsylvania Gazette*, October 20, 1773; *Virginia Gazette*, September 25, 1755.

61. *Virginia Gazette*, May 29, 1752.

62. *Pennsylvania Gazette*, November 13, 1766. See also *Pennsylvania Gazette*, July 17, 1755.

63. *Pennsylvania Gazette*, May 8, 1755; October 30, 1755. See also October 3, 1771.

64. *Pennsylvania Gazette*, October 30, 1755; November 3, 1757; February 4, 1752; April 5, 1750.

65. *Pennsylvania Gazette*, February 20, 1772; February 24, 1773; July 4, 1771.

66. *Pennsylvania Gazette*, September 8, 1763.

67. *Pennsylvania Gazette*, February 20, 1753.

68. *Pennsylvania Gazette*, September 22, 1768; February 14, 1771.

69. For example, *Pennsylvania Gazette*, February 13, 1772; September 13, 1750; *Virginia Gazette*, May 30, 1751; *Pennsylvania Gazette*, July 7, 1768.

70. *Pennsylvania Gazette*, June 30, 1773.

71. *Pennsylvania Gazette*, April 9, 1772; March 18, 1756; May 29, 1755.

72. *Pennsylvania Chronicle*, October 19, 1768; *Pennsylvania Gazette*, May 17, 1750; September 22, 1768; May 9, 1771.

73. For instance, of over three hundred almanacs published between 1750 and 1765, sixty-five mentioned beauty in some form. As print culture expanded and almanacs

lengthened, there was a corresponding increase in mentions of beauty; by the last decades of the century, more than one-third of almanacs mentioned beauty.

74. Poor Roger, *The American country almanack, for the year of Christian account 1762* (New York [1761]).

75. John Gyles, *Memoirs of Odd adventures, strange deliverances, &c in the captivity of John Gyles, Esq; . . .* (Boston [1736]), 30.

76. *An astronomical diary; or, An almanack for the year of Christian aera, 1764. . . .* [Boston, 1763].

77. "On Beauty," *South-Carolina Gazette*, October 8, 1772.

78. *Poor Richard improved . . . 1759* (Philadelphia [1758]).

79. *The Wilmington Almanack, or ephemeries, for the year of our Lord, 1766 . . .* (Wilmington [1765]), April. See also *Hutchin's improved. . . .* (New York [1764]).

80. *Father Abraham's almanac, (on an entire new plan.) Fitted for the latitude of Rhode-Island, . . .* (Philadelphia [1761]).

81. For instance, see *The Virginia almanack, for the year of our Lord God 1753. . . .* (Williamsburg [1752]; *The New-York almanack. For the year of Christian account, 1745 . . .* (New York [1744]).

82. Jennifer L. Morgan, "'Some Could Suckle over Their Shoulder': Male Travelers, Female Bodies, and the Gendering of Racial Ideology, 1500–1770," *William and Mary Quarterly* 54, no. 1 (January 1997): 167–92; Stephanie M. H. Camp "Early European Views of African Bodies: Beauty," in "Black Is Beautiful: An American History," manuscript draft in author's possession. Much of the work on black women's sexualized bodies focuses on postcolonial U.S. periods. See Evelynn M. Hammonds, "Toward a Genealogy of Black Female Sexuality: The Problematic of Silence," in *Feminist Genealogies, Colonial Legacies, Democratic Futures*, ed. M. Jacqui Alexander and Chandra Talpade Mohanty (New York: Routledge, 1997), 170–82.

83. *A Conference between the D——l and Doctor D——e. Together with the doctor's epitaph on himself.* ([Philadelphia, 1764]).

84. For a material impact on white men of their alleged sexual relations with African-descended women, see Kirsten Fischer's discussion of slander cases in *Suspect Relations: Sex, Race, and Resistance in Colonial North Carolina* (Ithaca, N.Y.: Cornell University Press, 2002), 150–54.

85. Alexis Shotwell, "Commonsense Racial Formation: Wahneema Lubiano, Antonio Gramsci, and the Importance of the Nonpropositional," in *Race and the Foundations of Knowledge*, ed. Joseph Young and Jana Evans Braziel (Urbana: University of Illinois Press, 1996), 47.

86. Johnson, *Soul by Soul*, 139.

87. On the "beautification engine," see Sarah Kershaw, "The Sum of Your Facial Parts," *New York Times* October 8, 2008, http://www.nytimes.com/2008/10/09/fashion/09skin.html (accessed November 1, 2010). It is worth noting that the computer scientists used only images of "white" faces to create a basis for their mathematical evaluation of attractiveness.

CHAPTER 5

Making Racial Beauty in the United States

Toward a History of Black Beauty

STEPHANIE M. H. CAMP

Physical beauty has never been more widely attended to or more valued by American women and men than it is now. The entertainment-industrial complex trumpets narrow and demanding beauty standards and relentlessly advertises the means—chemical and surgical—to realize them. Ordinary people, for whom expensive surgeries and treatments are out of reach, attempt to depilate, exfoliate, and otherwise manipulate their bodies into compliance with both commercial norms and a variety of American standards of beauty. Class, race, ethnicity, and national origin ensure the coexistence of varied and even conflicting beauty standards in daily life. But among the diverse ideas Americans hold about what makes a body attractive, one idea is more powerful and more encompassing than the rest: that white bodies are the most beautiful.

Black women have a long and troubled relationship with Western concepts of beauty. "Historically," the model-turned-author Barbara Summers has written, "Black women in White America have been called many things: Mammy and mule, radical and religious, Sapphire and sexpot, whore and welfare queen. We have been many others on a too-long list. Beautiful was among the last."[1] The perception of black women's bodies as a problem that cannot be reconciled with Western concepts of the beautiful has proved to be exceptionally tenacious. For at least one and a half centuries, black Americans, among others, have overtly and emphatically challenged what is often called a "white standard of beauty." Yet it persists. How has it managed to endure? Why has it proved so resilient?

This essay argues that the tenacity of this hegemonic beauty ideal arises from the fact that its origins reach far back in time and deep into the nature of American racial formations. Its earliest roots can be discerned in ancient Europe, when Greek and Roman artists had depicted Africans as captives and slaves and as monstrous half-men, half-beasts. Mostly, they were male. By the European Middle Ages, as Christianity swept Europe, ancient fables about frightening creatures of one sort or another in the subcontinent gained new symbolic weight: blackness became increasingly associated with sin. Fearsome, alluring, sinful, blackness was not unlike temptation itself.[2]

But the story here is not one of a long thread of contempt for black bodies. For one thing, ancient Europeans represented sub-Saharan Africans as more than simply monstrous. Distinguished by darker skin, curly hair, and full mouths, Africans were portrayed with classically beautiful human forms. And ancient imaginations saw Africans in a variety of roles: archers, spearmen, mercenaries, entertainers (jugglers, dancers), writers, soldiers, bodyguards, and more. Mixing ancient and medieval legends with newer accounts of travel in Africa, themselves a combination of fact and fantasy, writers in the 1500s and 1600s grappled with the idea of Africa. Lacking recognizable forms of social governance, family organization, and proper religion, the place was chaos. Adding to its chaotic nature were the bodies that peopled the subcontinent—grotesque, disorderly bodies. Africa's people were "men that have but one eye" or "but one foote," headless humans whose eyes and mouths were planted "behind on their shoulders" or "in their breasts." Africans were said to be "all black saving their teeth and a little the palm of their hands." Alternatively, they were also reputed to change color over the course of their lives, from "russet" at birth to "all black" by old age. While not unique in its reproduction of monsters, Africa seemed, relative to other parts of the world, a particularly "fruitfull Mother of such fearfull and terrible *Creatures*," as the English translator Abraham Hartwell wrote in 1597. Africa was wild, and she was a woman.[3]

At the same time, there was a good deal of ambivalence and inconsistency in English and European views of Africans. Africans could also be beautiful. Soft, graceful, shiny, smiling, well-formed—these were descriptors of African women, too. Still, the contradictions of European male ways of seeing Africans would not survive their journeys into the slave trade. By the late eighteenth and early nineteenth centuries, there was an important shift in how Europeans and white Americans thought about black bodies. And it is in that shift that we see the true beginnings of today's racially specific concepts of beauty. Whether the idea manifests as a "white standard of beauty" or its resistant antithesis, "Black Is Beautiful," black and white Americans have, since the early nineteenth century, held fast to the idea of *racial beauty*: the idea that human bodies possess racially specific forms of beauty and ugliness.

From Europe's earliest contacts with Africa and the Americas through approximately the late eighteenth century, Europeans perceived the differences between themselves and those they encountered as arising primarily from social and cultural practices and ideals, notably religious practices and gender ideals.[4] Early modern Europeans took note of physical differences, and they invented the language of color that persists to this day. But they did not conclusively believe that the cultural and social differences they found so striking arose from (equally striking) bodily variation. In the eighteenth century, enlightened "environmentalism" ruled the day. Geography and environment were said to shape human cultures, societies, and even bodies: Africa's sun and heat produced the "Negro's" dark skin and wide nose no less than his passions and indolence. Europe's frosts drew out the beard, and courage and industry.

Between the late eighteenth century and culminating in the mid-nineteenth, a new way of thinking about racial difference emerged in the United States.[5] This new conception of difference prioritized, more than ever before, biology and anatomy. In the wake of the American Revolution, slaveholders and nonslaveholders alike wrestled with the tensions inherent in the coexistence of environmentalist ideas of racial difference and the institution of slavery. Environmentalism implied that people could be anything, or almost anything, depending on their circumstances. The triumph of varied Enlightenment ideals in the American Revolution, the French Revolution, and the Haitian Revolution only aggravated the problem. Black slavery had never needed to be defended before, or even explained. But during the Age of Revolution, some Americans were asking questions, others were freeing their slaves, and the northern states and Britain gradually but steadily abolished slavery. Southern slaveholders felt compelled to explain to themselves and others why slavery was justified in the modern era. Key to their defense of slavery was a reassignment of racial difference from the environment to the body—in particular, to the body's physiognomy.

Since we are the heirs of this "unthinking" choice, it might appear to be obvious that race is based on appearance. But in fact, there were other classification schemes. Enlightenment-era racial writers might have elected to follow the example of a thinker like William Petty, a noted English scientist of the mid–seventeenth century. In his analysis of living creation, he agreed with many others that, on the basis of physiognomy, humans appeared to be closest to apes. But Petty wondered if perhaps animals and humans shouldn't be categorized by other features. He considered ordering humans and animals by voice, in which case the animal that was closest to humans was the parrot. If intelligence were the criterion, he argued that elephants were next to man in rank.[6] Petty's wide-ranging speculations did not catch on, however, and the classification of humankind according to looks took hold.

During the Age of Revolution, decision makers and opinion shapers in the emerging United States paradoxically institutionalized both the principles of political modernity and a new and much harder form of racism: white supremacy. The Enlightenment's rage for order, comparison, measurement, and classification reconceptualized and reshaped older notions of racial difference. After the late eighteenth century, racial difference was no longer seen as primarily cultural, religious, or environmental. Instead, it was increasingly understood among men of science that race was located in the body. Racial scientists (a broad term that included academics, medical doctors and amateurs) examined bodies inside and out in search of the source of race. The question for the nineteenth century was, *Where*, exactly, did race reside if not in climate or culture? The skin? The brain or skull? The blood? The hair, limbs, or jaw? Americans embraced one or a collection of these body parts as the locus or loci of racial essence.

Aesthetic interpretations of the body were a central pillar in the emerging biological definition of race. Modernity not only spurred the production of a biological concept of race, but it did so in a way that was fundamentally aesthetic. Modern ideas of racial difference were ideas about beauty, *hierarchical* ideas about beauty.[7] In turn, Western concepts of beauty did more than embellish the emerging view of biologically distinct "varieties" of humankind. Ideas about beauty and ugliness defined one way of thinking about the world's people and human inequality. Cornell West has made this same point. "The very structure of modern discourse," he has written, "*at its inception* produced forms of rationality, scientificity, and objectivity as well as aesthetic and cultural ideas which require the constitution of the idea of white supremacy." "The controlling metaphors, notions and categories of modern discourse," West continues, "produce and prohibit, develop and delimit, specific conceptions of truth and knowledge, beauty and character, so that certain ideas are rendered incomprehensible and unintelligible. . . . One such idea that cannot be brought within the epistemological field of the initial modern discourse is that of black equality in beauty, culture, and intellectual capacity."[8]

Entangled with modernity itself are aesthetic values that have excluded black bodies from the realm of the beautiful. Indeed, this exclusion was constitutive of modern interpretations of human inequality; the turn to linking perceptions of essential concepts of physical beauty and ugliness to inner human nature and character marked a turning point in the history of American racism.

Beauty and racism have an ugly history. It is such an ugly history that comparatively few historians have tackled it directly, especially in the centuries before emancipation freed black entrepreneurs, journalists, and activists to promote black standards of beauty.[9] The early history of the subject is painful, shameful, and, consequently, often taboo. But exploring it rewards us with a deeper understanding of the social and cultural processes that invented and constantly remade the idea of race in the United States. The sociologists Michael Omi and Howard Winant call this process "racial formation," a very useful shorthand.[10] Race and the body parts it gives social meaning to are historically contingent phenomena, as historians of racial formation have shown over the past twenty-five years or so. And there is no better lens through which to chronicle the mutability of race than another moody and somatic social category: beauty.

But if the history of beauty and slavery is an ugly one, it cannot also be said that it was linear. Perceptions of African and black appearances changed in tandem both with shifts in definitions of beauty and with the rise and development of racial slavery. Beauty and race, we all know, are highly mutable concepts. What counts as beautiful or "Other" in one place and time can seem quite surprising in another. What has been less explored in United States history is the history of their interdependence. For the categories of beauty and ugliness were a vital source of fuel for the long and dynamic process of making and remaking race and slavery. And in the shift from enlightened environmentalism to biological determinism, beauty's importance deepened. As race moved into the body, the ostensible beauty or ugliness of that body was no longer considered superfluous or even coincidental. Beauty and race became two entangled categories through which bodies were grouped and ranked and through which race was made.

Nowhere are these vicissitudes more apparent than in the work of nineteenth-century racial scientists. Take, for example, the adventures of skin color. In 1851, the Louisiana physician and racial researcher Samuel Cartwright wrote, "It is commonly taken for granted that the color of the skin constitutes the main and essential difference between the black and white race."[11] By the nineteenth century, it was equally taken for granted that the black/white difference in skin color was also a difference in beauty. In this regard, many Americans were no doubt following Thomas Jefferson's lead. In 1785, Jefferson wrote in *Notes on the State of Virginia*, "[The] first difference which strikes us is that of color." This most striking difference was also, for Jefferson, the most important of the many differences distinguishing black from white: "Is this difference of no importance? Is it not the foundation of a greater or less share of beauty in the two races? Are not the fine mixtures of red and white, the expressions of every passion by greater or less suffusions of color in the one, preferable to that eternal monotony which reigns in the countenances, that immovable veil of black which covers all the emotions of the other race?"[12] For Jefferson, as for many racial thinkers after him, the category of beauty and its antipode, ugliness, provided the language for the invention and description of physiological racial difference. And for Jefferson, skin color was the defining feature, the most "important" site of "difference" and the principal source of "beauty." Jefferson measured the beauty of skin color by its shade, because shade produced, according to Jefferson, emotional transparency or inscrutability.

At the same time, many nineteenth-century racial scientists seemed to make it their project to disrupt the hegemony of skin color as the locus of essential racial difference. Cartwright, for instance, was critiquing what he saw as an overreliance on skin color. After pointing out that skin color was commonly assumed to be the "main and essential difference" between black and white people, Cartwright went on to say, "There are other differences more deep, more durable and indelible . . . than that of mere color."[13] In fact, in the nineteenth century, racial beauty and ugliness were promiscuous concepts, ones that mingled with many features other than skin color. Beauty, ugliness, and racial otherness resided together everywhere in the face and head and all over the body as evidence of European excellence and of black otherness and inferiority. Among the more important of the "Negro's" distinctive body parts were the foot (big, flat, and ugly), the leg (too long and too thin), the arm (also too long and too thin), and the hand (once again, too long and slender). The head came in for special attention. The skull itself was the subject of an entire discipline, phrenology, which studied the skull's capacity, its weight, and the beauty of its form. After the skull, the most attended-to feature of the head was not the eye, the lips, or even the nose. It was the jaw.

Prognathism, the presence of a strong, long, or forward-jutting jaw, was reputed to be common among blacks, many of the globe's other "inferior" races, and, unsurprisingly, apes. Nineteenth-century phrenologists drew on the work of the influential eighteenth-century anatomist Petrus Camper, who "discovered" the nasal index and the facial angle. Camper was a Dutch professor of surgery, anatomy, and botanics who spent most of his career at the University of Groningen. In 1792, he published his research on the facial angle and nasal index, and the work was translated into English two years later. The nasal index measured the angle of the nose—the degree to which the bridge of the nose reclined or formed a straight, vertical line. And the facial angle measured the angle of the face as a whole by examining the relation of the chin, jaw, and forehead to one another. The highest facial index, ninety degrees, was realized only by ancient Greek sculptures of gods and philosophers. Modern Europeans had an average facial index of eighty-five. The "Negro" had a facial index of seventy, less than halfway between the facial index of orangutans (fifty-eight degrees) and Europeans.[14] Indeed, according to Camper's measurements, European and African facial angles were actual opposites of each other: "Let the face of an European be first sketched, and by inverting the mode, the physiognomy of a negro will be obtained."[15] Camper's way of framing their opposition, though, hinted at a particular complementarity. Of all the races in the world, the European and the African had facial profiles that fit each other, negatively. They completed each other.

Camper's primary concern was to discuss "the beautiful, as manifested in the human figure, and particularly in the head" and to give to "the beautiful" a mathematical rationality. His main goal was not to rank humankind. Nonetheless, he *did* rank humankind according to the facial angle and nasal index. His schema identified Jews as the most "distinguishable" of the world's "nations" and marked the "negro" as the inverse of the European. His rankings were, in his judgment, strongly shaped by the environment (by food and climate) —not by biology alone. Importantly, the categories of difference that Camper identified were not, in his mind, permanent or even biologically based. Camper was an environmentalist: "Food and climate frequently co-operate; but we cannot suppose them productive of a different race. Black, tawny, and white men are simply varieties; they do not constitute essential differences. Our skin is precisely the same contexture with that of the negro; but it is not of so deep a dye."[16] So it is quite ironic that Camper's work linking aesthetics with human ranking would actually influence the nineteenth century's essentialist pairing of appearance and destiny as much as it did.

Racial scientists drew on Camper's description of the nasal index and facial angle, but they ignored his environmentalism and his anti-essentialism. They concurred with Camper that Africans were a disproportionately prognathous race but took the point much further. For some, like the Mobile, Alabama, doctor Josiah Nott, prognathism itself constituted a racial "type," one that was the opposite of the Caucasian type and one that was coterminous (but not synonymous) with the "Negro" type: both types shared the problem that their "intellect" "corresponded with their inferior physical developments."[17] For others, especially phrenologists, prognathism was an essential element of black physiognomy, a crucial part of what their research was finding to be the overall misshapen, undersized, and primitive skull of the Negro. Prognathous jaws ended prematurely in chins that were too "small"; they extended upward into "low receding foreheads" and defined heads that were, all in all, entirely too "long and narrow."[18] The supposedly undeveloped intellect that lay inside black skulls was as visible to racial scientists in the faulty lines that described the misshapen jaw and head as in the numerical measurements of brain weight and skull size. American ethnologists were interested in accomplishing a number of goals in their research. They wanted to establish essential, biological differences between black and white people; to prove black physical and intellectual inferiority; to defend slavery; and, in many cases, to establish that black people were not members of the human species. The aesthetics of the jaw enabled them to accomplish many of these goals through a somatic shorthand: they made the jaw an aesthetic measurement of intelligence.

Besides the jaw, there were other features that garnered attention for their beauty, or their ostensible lack thereof. Some racial observers felt that the truest and "most constant characteristic of the negro conformation" was the hair.[19] Others believed that distinction belonged to the voice. "There is a peculiarity in the Negro voice by which he can always be distinguished," James Hunt told his audience at the annual meeting of the London Anthropological Society in 1863. "This peculiarity is so great that we can frequently discover traces of Negro blood when the eye is unable to detect it. No amount of education or time is likely ever to enable the Negro to speak the English language without this twang. Even his great faculty of imitation will not enable him to do this."[20] For Hunt, even if any or all other racial traits could be shed through imitation or passing, there was no getting away from the "twang" of the black voice. It was incumbent on interested parties to use their many senses to suss out the unmistakable stain of black ugliness, whether it be barely visible in the texture of hair or almost inaudible in the tone of the voice.[21]

Few American racial scientists made skin color the central quality that Jefferson had believed it to be. Fewer still made claims of constancy for skin color like those made about hair and voice. They couldn't. Interracial rape and sex had produced generations of mixed-race black people. The clarity and simplicity of what a black body was—which was never fixed or simple—was never more troubled than it was by the 1850s. Famous cases of racial passing (like that of the runaways William and Ellen Craft in the 1840s), accounts, and widely circulated photographs of white-looking slave children (like that of Mary Mildred Botts in the mid-1850s), and legal suits brought by black slaves who claimed they were white and therefore free (such as the case brought to court by the blond-haired, blue-eyed Alexina Morrison in the 1850s) drove home to all who heard of them the extent to which the skin color of some enslaved black people was becoming so light as to be indistinguishable from white skin.[22] What Samuel Cartwright called the "pervading darkness" may have tinted, as he argued, the body's membranes and muscles, vapors and fluids, but it could no longer be trusted to suffuse the skin consistently.[23] Thus Cartwright's interest in "differences more deep, more durable and indelible . . . than that of mere color." And also James Hunt's interest in alternative features that would "discover traces of Negro blood when the eye is unable to detect it."[24]

There is, of course, a great irony in this story, one that is most evident when we listen to the views of the enslaved on the subject of beauty. On the one hand, most white Americans screened the appearances of African and black people through the concept of racial beauty and perceived in them proof of blacks' intellectual and anatomical primitiveness. According to official pronouncements from much of white America, black beauty was a contradiction in terms. On the other hand, the enslaved knew those pronouncements to be shallow in the extreme. Many white southern men hotly desired enslaved women; raped some of those they owned, managed, or were served by; and paid sensational prices for women they called "likely" or "handsome" or, most of all, "fancy"—but never "beautiful."[25] Black women had, in the minds of racial writers, a convenient double character: "likely" and repulsive, female and sexually available.[26] Western men have for millennia considered female beauty to be a danger to the men who fell victim to womanly seduction. But enslaved women and men considered female beauty in a slave to be a danger to the *woman*. "If God has bestowed beauty upon [an enslaved girl], it will prove her greatest curse," the ex-slave autobiographer Harriet Jacobs wrote in 1861. "That which commands admiration in the white woman only hastens the degradation of the female slave."[27] Jacobs's interpretation of beauty is echoed extensively throughout the autobiographies of former slaves in the nineteenth century.

So, beauty had a saturnine temperament in the context of American slavery. Its many moods manifested in the variety of body parts enlisted in the making of modern race. Racially meaningful beauty or ugliness resided in the face, the skull/head, the foot, the arm, and elsewhere. Beauty's volatility was visible as well in the range of roles that it played. For beauty appeared in such varied guises in nineteenth-century America as evidence of black alterity and inferiority (in racial science, for instance); as an extremely desired feature (in slave traders' records); and as a danger, the "greatest curse" to enslaved women (in slave narratives).

Beauty mattered. It mattered to nineteenth-century defenses of slavery and their influence on modern, biological ideas of race. And it would continue to matter. Nineteenth-century Americans created the idea of racial beauty, and racist ideologues made it hegemonic: most white Americans assumed that Europeans represented the epitome of physical excellence. Nineteenth-century Americans solidified the idea of "racial beauty": hierarchical beauty ideals that prized features believed to be specific to one or another race. But was "racial beauty" the same as a "white standard of beauty" or a white supremacist beauty ideal? To answer that question, let's consider another version of racial beauty, an interpretation that both reshaped the principal idea and upheld it.

In a speech delivered in 1854, the revered black abolitionist Frederick Douglass lampooned the "scientific moonshine" that attempted to separate the physiology of sub-Saharan Africans and their descendants from "every intelligent nation and tribe in Africa" and, of course, the world. He critiqued the presentation of data and portraits as "distorted." "If, for instance," Douglass wrote, "a phrenologist or naturalist undertakes to represent in portraits, the differences between the two races—the negro and the European—he will invariably present the *highest* type of the European and the *lowest* type of the negro." Douglass may have critiqued racial scientists' data, but he did not reject the use of aesthetics or essential features to judge races. Instead, he argued that better studies would be produced by including pictures of representative heads from prominent black abolitionists. These pictures would give a better "idea of the mental endowments of the negro." If this were done, Douglass conceded that "negroes answering the description given by the American ethnologists and others" would be found. But so would "every description of head . . . ranging from the highest Hindoo Caucasian downward." Douglass roundly rejected white supremacist claims that beauty and intelligence adhered to white bodies only. But he nonetheless accepted and even promoted the connection between attractive appearances and "mental endowments." Moreover, he also shared white supremacists' veneration of "Caucasian" beauty.[28]

Frederick Douglass was revered in the black community, then as now, but he was not unchallenged on the beauty question. "I believe in insurrections—and especially those of the pen and of the sword," the black abolitionist John S. Rock avowed in a speech he delivered in March 1860.[29] And not only the pen and the sword: Rock believed in the "moral insurrection of thought."[30] One of Rock's more revolutionary thoughts was his early and ardent love of black beauty. "If any man does not fancy my color, that is his business, and I shall not meddle with it. I shall give myself no trouble because he lacks good taste," he quipped in 1858.[31] Black physiognomy was graced with "the fine tough muscular system, the beautiful, rich color, the full broad features, and the gracefully frizzled hair" ostensibly characteristic of black people. When he compared beautiful black bodies with "the delicate physical organization, wan color, sharp features and lank hair of the Caucasian," Rock felt compelled to conclude that "when the white man was created, nature was pretty well exhausted—but determined to keep up appearances, she pinched up his features and did the best she could under the circumstances."[32] Rock's audiences ate it up, laughing with pleasure throughout his speeches. It was not just that Rock mocked white appearances while mainstream American society celebrated them as superior to all others on the face of the planet. Audiences basked in Rock's confidence in black intelligence, character and, perhaps most insurrectionary of all, black physiognomy. "I not only love my race, but am pleased with my color," he told one audience. His "love" of black people and black physical beauty made his activist work on behalf of the race "my duty, my pleasure and my pride."[33] Rock saw his political activism as work that would help uplift the black community economically and educationally. One result of such uplift would be a revolution in how black bodies were perceived. When "we become educated and wealthy, [. . .] then the roughest looking colored man that you ever saw or ever will be will be pleasanter than the harmonies of Orpheus, and black will be a very pretty color. It will make our jargon, wit; our words, oracles; flattery will then take the place of slander, and you will find no prejudice in the Yankee whatever."[34] Yet, for all his insurrectionary thoughts and words about black beauty and his de-linking of blackness from badness, Rock, like Douglass, never questioned the assumption that race was a biological category, one visible to the naked eye in people's physical appearances. Like Douglass, Rock accepted the idea of racial beauty, if only to turn it on its head.

The history of black beauty demonstrates that the aesthetics of the body have ruled the formation of "whiteness" and "blackness;" it reveals the vicissitudes in what body parts have mattered historically, and why. The body parts and zones that mattered the most to one set of people at one moment did not necessarily continue to matter at a different time or in a different place. For example, during the early modern period, African women's alterity was identified, in part, by breasts depicted by male travelers as immodestly exposed and unattractively long.[35] But by the nineteenth century, black women's breasts had all but disappeared as signs of difference among white male writers and ordinary people alike. And the body parts that would come to matter after emancipation (for instance, penises in the aftermath of Reconstruction, or black women's bottoms in the late twentieth century) were far less meaningful in earlier periods. Like ideas of what constituted a race, judgments about what made one or another race beautiful or ugly changed over time.

Historicizing the idea of black beauty also contextualizes one of slavery's most enduring and pernicious legacies: a white supremacist beauty myth. The concept of racial beauty is not a transhistorical phenomenon, no matter how hegemonic and seemingly natural it appears to be today. Rather, it came into being when the body was transformed from a reflection of environment into the source of character, ability, and destiny. The body's beauty ceased to be incidental, ornamental, or superfluous: beauty became, along with the body's other physical attributes, entangled with the American idea of race itself. The entanglement of beauty with biological race had been centuries in the making. Beauty had long been linked with difference of all sorts, including proto-racial difference. But when race came to be seen as a biological category, something new happened: it came to be seen as an unavoidable product of the natural world. The body's beauty or ugliness came to reflect a creature's unchanging place in that natural world, its permanent superiority or inferiority. To return to the question posed at the beginning of this essay: why has a white standard of beauty proved so resilient in the face of sustained critique? The difficulty in overturning white supremacist versions of racial beauty is not only that the critique comes from the social margins. Nor is it solely due to the long duration of prejudices against bodies categorized as black. It is also that beauty was and is a constitutive element in the making and meaning of race itself. To dismantle racial beauty would entail a transformation, if not the dissolution, of American ideas of race. It would also mean releasing the equally essentialist idea of racial beauty, even its resistant version of Black Is Beautiful.

Notes

Stephanie M. H. Camp submitted this essay before she passed away. Jennifer L. Morgan and Sharon Block lightly edited the essay in order to prepare it for final production, preserving her voice and ensuring that her contribution appeared in the volume.

1. Barbara Summers, *Black and Beautiful: How Women of Color Changed the Fashion Industry* (New York: Amistad, 2001), xiii.

2. Frank M. Snowden, "Iconographical Evidence on the Black Populations in Greco-Roman Antiquity," in *The Image of the Black in Western Art*, vol. 1, *From the Pharaohs to the Fall of the Roman Empire* (New York: William Morrow, 1976), 135–238; Jean Devisee, *The Image of the Black in Western Art*, vol. 2, *From the Early Christian Era to the "Age of Discovery"* (New York: William Morrow, 1979), 62–64.

3. Snowden, "Iconographical Evidence"; Devisee, *Image of the Black*, 2:62–64; Eldred D. Jones, *The Elizabethan Image of Africa* (Charlottesville: University of Virginia Press, 1971); Patricia Parker, "Fantasies of 'Race' and 'Gender': Africa, *Othello* and Bringing to Light," in *Women, "Race," and Writing in the Early Modern Period*, ed. Margo Hendricks and Patricia Parker (London: Routledge, 1994), 84–100; Kim F. Hall, *Things of Darkness: Economies of Race and Gender in Early Modern England* (Ithaca, N.Y.: Cornell University Press, 1995); Alden Vaughn and Virginia Mason Vaughn, "Before Othello: Elizabethan Representations of Sub-Saharan Africans," *William and Mary Quarterly*, 3rd ser., 54, no. 1 (January 1997): 19–44; Sue Niebrzydowski, "The Sultana and Her Sisters: Black Women in the British Isles before 1530," *Women's History Review* 10, no. 2 (Summer 2001), 187–211; Ann Korhonen, "Washing the Ethiopian White: Conceptualizing Black Skin in Renaissance England," in *Black Africans in Renaissance Europe*, ed. T. F. Earle and K. J. P. Lowe (Cambridge: Cambridge University Press, 2005). "One foot," "ne eyes," "mouth behind their shoulders," "russet," and Abraham Hartwell quotes in Hall, *Things of Darkness*, 26, 40; "all black," "mouth and eyes in the breasts" quotes in Jones, *Elizabethan Image of Africa*, 5; Francis Bacon ("regions of the material globe") quoted in Parker, "Fantasies of 'Race,'" 86–87.

4. Jennifer L. Morgan, "'Some Could Suckle over Their Shoulder': Male Travelers, Female Bodies and the Gendering of Racial Ideology, 1500–1770," *William and Mary Quarterly*, 3rd ser., 54, no. 1 (January 1997): 167–92; Kathleen M. Brown, *Good Wives, Nasty Wenches and Anxious Patriarchs: Gender, Race, and Power in Colonial Virginia* (Chapel Hill: University of North Carolina Press, 1996).

5. On shifting notions of black bodies, see George Frederickson, *The Black Image in the White Mind: The Debate on Afro-American Character and Destiny, 1817–1914* (1971; Middleton, Conn: Wesleyan University Press, 1987); Seymour Drescher, "The Ending of the Slave Trade and the Evolution of European Scientific Racism," *Social Science History* 14, no. 3 (Fall 1990): 419–20; Joyce E. Chaplin, "Slavery and the Principle of Humanity: A Modern Idea in the Early Lower South," *Journal of Social History* 24, no. 2 (Winter 1990): 302–3; Gregory P. Downs, "University Men, Social Science, and White Supremacy in North Carolina," *Journal of Southern History* 75, no. 2 (May 2009): 267–304.

6. Terence Wilmot Hutchison, ed. *Sir William Petty: Critical Responses* (Hove, England: Psychology Press, 1997), 27–28, also cited in Winthrop Jordan, *White over Black: American Attitudes toward the Negro, 1550–1812* (Chapel Hill: University of North Carolina Press, 1968), 225. "Unthinking decision" is Jordan's famous description of colonial Virginia's turn to racial slavery. On early modern human-animal taxonomies, see Roxann Wheeler, *The Complexion of Race: Categories of Difference in Eighteenth-Century British Culture* (Philadelphia: University of Pennsylvania Press, 2011), 29–31.

7. Nell Irvin Painter has recently written about white beauty and its links to white supremacy. Painter, *The History of White People* (New York: W. W. Norton, 2010).

8. Cornel West, "A Genealogy of Modern Racism," in *Race Critical Theories: Text and Context*, ed. Philomena Essed and David Theo Goldberg (Malden, Mass.: Blackwell, 2002), 90–91.

9. Scholarship on black physical beauty prior to the twentieth century includes Sylvia Ardyn Boone, *Radiance from the Waters: Ideals of Feminine Beauty in Mende Art* (New Haven, Conn.: Yale University Press, 1986); Patricia Morton, *Disfigured Images: The Historical Assault on Afro-American Women* (New York: Greenwood Press, 1991); Morgan, "'Some Could Suckle'"; Joyce Chaplin, *Subject Matter: Technology, the Body, and Science on the Anglo-American Frontier, 1500–1676* (Cambridge, Mass.: Harvard University Press, 2001); George Brooks, *Eurafricans in Western Africa: Commerce, Social Status, Gender, and Religious Observance from the Sixteenth to the Eighteenth Century* (Athens: Ohio University Press, 2003).

10. Michael Omi and Howard Winant, *Racial Formation in the United States: From the 1960s to the 1980s* (New York: Routledge and Kegan Paul, 1986). The editors of this piece would like to add to this list the following scholars, whose work directly or indirectly concerns questions of race and beauty: Sharon Block, "Making Meaningful Bodies: Physical Appearance in Colonial Writings," *Early American Studies* 12 (2014): 524–47; Jim Downs, *Sick from Freedom: African American Illness and Suffering during the Civil War and Reconstruction* (New York: Oxford University Press, 2012); Ann Fabian, *The Skill Collectors: Race, Science, and America's Unburied Dead* (Chicago: University of Chicago Press, 2010); Daina Raimey Berry, "'We Sho Was Dressed Up': Slave Women, Material Culture and Decorative Arts in Wilkes County, Georgia," in *The Savannah River Valley up to 1865: Fine Arts, Architecture, and Decorative Arts*, ed. Ashley Callahan (Athens: Georgia Museum of Art, 2003), 73–83; Michael Sappol, *A Traffic of Dead Bodies: Anatomy and Embodied Social Identity in Nineteenth-Century America* (Princeton, N.J.: Princeton University Press, 2002).

11. Samuel A. Cartwright, "Report on the Diseases and Physical Peculiarities of the Negro Race," *New Orleans Medical and Surgical Journal* 7 (1851): 692.

12. Thomas Jefferson, *Notes on the State of Virginia*, ed. David Waldstreicher (1785; Boston: Bedford/St. Martin's, 2002), 177–78.

13. Cartwright, "Report on the Diseases," 692.

14. Petrus Camper, *The Works of the Late Professor Camper, on the Connexion between the Science of Anatomy and the Arts of Drawing, Painting, Statuary, &c., &c. in Two Books*, ed. Thomas Cogan (London: J. Jearne, 1821), 9, 34–44, 50.

15. Camper, *Works*, 51.

16. Camper, *Works*, 32, 20, 9, 28.

17. Josiah Nott, *Two Lectures on the Connection between the Biblical and Physical History of Man* (New York: Bartlett and Welford, 1849), 22.

18. "Small" chin, Samuel Morton, *Crania Americana* in *American Theories of Polygenesis*, ed. Robert Bernasconi (1839; Bristol: Thoemmes Press, 2002), 6; "low receding foreheads," Louis Buchner, cited in James Hunt, "The Negro's Place in Nature" (New York: Van Evrie, Horton., 1864), 22; "long and narrow" heads in Morton, *Crania Americana*, 6.

19. Hermann Burmeister, *The Black Man: The Comparative Anatomy and Psychology of the African Negro* (New York: W. C. Bryant, printers, 1853), 12.

20. Hunt, "Negro's Place in Nature," 10.

21. Mark M. Smith has explored the many senses beyond sight used to create and re-create race in *How Race Is Made: Slavery, Segregation, and the Senses* (Chapel Hill: University of North Carolina Press, 2006).

22. Walter Johnson, "The Slave Trader, the White Slave and the Politics of Racial De-termination in the 1850s," *Journal of American History* 87, no. 1 (June 2000): 13–38; Mary Niall Mitchell, *Raising Freedom's Child: Black Children and Visions of the Future after Slavery* (New York: New York University Press, 2008), 59–87; James Downs, "Rethinking the One-Drop Rule: The Proliferation of Racial Categories after the American Civil War," unpublished essay in the author's possession.

23. Cartwright, "Report on the Diseases," 692.

24. Cartwright, "Report on the Diseases," 692; Hunt, "Negro's Place in Nature," 23.

25. Walter Johnson, *Soul by Soul: Life inside the Antebellum Slave Market* (Cambridge, Mass.: Harvard University Press), 113; Edward E. Baptist, "'Cuffy,' 'Fancy Maids,' and 'One-Eyed Men': Rape, Commodification, and the Domestic Slave Trade in the United States," *American Historical Review* 106, no. 5 (December 2001): 1619–50.

26. Morgan, "'Some Could Suckle,'" 16.

27. Harriet A. Jacobs, *Incidents in the Life of a Slave Girl*, written by herself (Boston, 1861), 46, http://docsouth.unc.edu/fpn/jacobs/jacobs.html (accessed January 19, 2016).

28. Frederick Douglass, "The Claims of the Negro Ethnologically Considered: An Address Delivered in Hudson, Ohio, on 12 July 1854," in *The Frederick Douglass Papers*, ed. John W. Blassingame (New Haven, Conn.: Yale University Press, 1979), 502, 507, 510–11, 513–14.

29. John S. Rock, speech delivered at the Meionaon, March 5, 1860, in *The Abolitionist Papers*, ed. C. Peter Ripley (Chapel Hill: University of North Carolina Press, 1992), 5:59.

30. Rock, speech delivered at the Meionaon, *Abolitionist Papers*, 5:59.

31. John S. Rock, speech delivered at Fanueil Hall, March 5, 1858, http://tinyurl.com/hvthb39 (accessed September 23, 2008).

32. Rock, speech delivered at Fanueil Hall, Boston, March 5, 1858.

33. Rock, speech delivered at Fanueil Hall, Boston, March 5, 1858.

34. Rock, speech delivered at the Meionaon, *Abolitionist Papers*, 5:64–65.

35. Morgan, "'Some Could Suckle.'"

CHAPTER 6

The Soul of the Boy Was . . . Aztec

Race and Sexuality in Ramón Novarro's Self-Narrative

ERNESTO CHÁVEZ

On October 31, 1968, Americans awoke to news of the death of one of Hollywood's faded celluloid heroes, Ramón Novarro. As the *Los Angeles Times* reported, "Ramon Novarro, a swashbuckling star of silent films and early talkies who later became a television character actor, was found beaten to death . . . at his home in the Hollywood Hills. He was sixty-nine. A lifelong bachelor, he lived alone. Police said he was killed after a violent struggle, which left over-turned furniture and splotches of blood in three rooms of his home in Laurel Canyon. The killer apparently was a man. He apparently knew Novarro."[1] Eventually the investigation into his death revealed that Paul Robert Ferguson, a male hustler, had killed Novarro on the night of October 30, 1968. On the evening that it happened, Ferguson had called Novarro to offer his services, and the actor had invited him to his home. Ferguson arrived a while later with his brother, Thomas, who was visiting from Chicago. After a few drinks, Paul and Novarro went into the bedroom to engage in sexual activities. When Thomas happened to pass by and observed them kissing, Paul panicked and began beating Novarro, leaving him unconscious.[2] They then fled the scene. Novarro eventually died of asphyxiation; he choked on his own blood. These disclosures in effect "outed" Novarro as gay, and the image of the shy recluse and devout Catholic that he had constructed and worked so hard to maintain was unraveled as the details of his death were disclosed.[3] Most Hollywood insiders knew what the world learned at his death: that Novarro was gay even in his heyday, although the press and the film industry long kept his secret. His brutal death made public what he had tried his whole life to keep hidden.

Most popular depictions of Novarro focus on the way he died and present him as an unfortunate victim of his era, I would like to propose a counterpoint to this standard narrative of Novarro's life and death, one that depicts him as a vibrant historical actor rather than as a tragic movie star. In order to do this, this essay focuses on the construction of Novarro's star image in order to show how the themes of race, religion, and sexuality played out in his life and how he deployed and performed them at various times. Although the themes interconnect, I believe that the construction of his star image was predicated on his homosexuality. His death revealed once and for all how he had lived his life, yet those readers privy to queer cultural codes in the early twentieth century would have been able to detect the gay traces in the fan magazine and periodical literature written about Novarro. At a moment when ethnic Mexicans faced intense racism, Novarro was able to deploy his race in a positive manner, and in so doing he portrayed himself as a different kind of Mexican who posed no threat to the social order but instead could be assimilated into, as one contemporary journalist noted, "a red-blooded-go-getting American."[4]

Like that of most movie stars, Novarro's image was carefully constructed in order to make him more appealing to the public, especially to heterosexual women, who were the main consumers of films and fan magazines. In order to keep these women interested in the gay actor, the studio, his publicists (most notably Herbert Howe, who plays a substantial role in what follows), and Novarro himself relied on three interconnecting themes to present the star to the public: his middle-class Mexican status, his Roman Catholicism, and his sensual yet pure body. These texts disclose what the queer studies theorist Eve Koslowsky Sedgwick, in another context, identified as a "performative aspect" that in effect reveals "closetedness." According to Sedgwick, "Closetedness itself is a performance initiated as such by the speech act of a silence . . . in relation to the discourse that surrounds and differentially constitutes it."[5] The silences regarding Novarro's private life played a significant role in the construction of his public life, or rather how that life was depicted, and give us a glimpse into how he managed to remain true to himself even while lying about who he really was. Interpreting these sources in this manner allows us to comprehend how Novarro's sexuality proved to be an asset that allowed him to forge his place in the motion-picture industry despite the intense racism that existed in Hollywood and across the United States in the mid–twentieth century.

Although the content of Novarro's stardom was unique, the form was common. According to film scholar Richard Dyer, stars are a "structured polysemy" who embody a "finite multiplicity of meanings," so that "some meanings and affects are foregrounded and other masked or displaced." Dyer argues that even while stars have a "'real' individual 'existence' in the world," they navigate between that reality and their stardom through what he calls "magical synthesis."[6] Yet I would argue that the contradictions in Novarro's life were not reconciled. Instead, given the racism and homophobia of the era in which he lived, he was unable to do so, and his inability to reconcile his public persona with his homosexuality eventually led to alcoholism, a secret life, and a violent death. Rather than dwell on the tragedy of his life, however, I would like to focus on the forces that came together to construct Novarro's stardom.

In order to understand who Novarro was, a bit of background is required. Novarro was part of the wave of immigrants who fled their native land during the Mexican Revolution of 1910 and traveled north to the United States. He was born Ramón Gil Samaniego on February 6, 1899, in Durango, Mexico, into a middle-class family, one of ten children of a dentist and his wife. Although he lived a more privileged life than most in Mexico, as a child Novarro aspired to be in motion pictures, so he left home in 1916 to come to Los Angeles and try his luck in the film industry. In 1922 director Rex Ingram gave him a role in his film *The Prisoner of Zenda* and signed Novarro to a two-year contract but urged him to change his name to something more "pronounceable." The actor chose the moniker Novarro and went on to appear in this director's productions of *Trifling Women* (1922), *Where the Pavement Ends* (1923), *Scaramouche* (1923), and *The Arab* (1924). Appearing in these productions gave Novarro real visibility and in 1923 led to a contract with Metro Pictures, the forerunner of Metro-Goldwyn-Mayer (MGM). The following year MGM's production chief offered Novarro the lead in *Ben-Hur*, and with its release in late 1925, Novarro become a star and a movie legend.[7] Novarro went on to appear in other films and made the transition from silent films to "talkies" in 1929. After he lost his contract with MGM in 1935, Novarro began a semi-successful career as a singer, made a few films with Republic Pictures, and wrote and directed a Spanish-language film, *Contra la Corriente* (1936). He continued to appear in minor films and on television until shortly before his death in 1968.

Although the film industry reflected and perpetuated the nation's racial discourses, when it came to homosexuality Hollywood was more tolerant than the rest of the United States. Film historian Ronald Gregg argues that in the 1920s motion-picture producers, publicists, and journalists began to cater to sophisticated Americans who embraced the contribution of gays and lesbians in films. Novarro might have been discriminated against because of his race and sexuality outside the film industry, but within Hollywood his Mexicaness and homosexuality worked together in an imbricated manner to allow for his rise and success.

It was within this setting that Rex Ingram not only "discovered" Novarro but also initiated the construction of his star image and set the tone for others. Although Ingram was married to actress Alice Terry, it was rumored that he might have been gay or perhaps bisexual. Whether Ingram was attracted to Novarro sexually is not known, although we do know that he at least tolerated the actor's homosexuality. In 1923 Ingram hired the man who would be most responsible for constructing Novarro's star image, Herbert Howe. As Novarro's publicist, Howe soon began writing articles about the star that hinted at his infatuation with him. According to Howe, the two men first met in 1922, when he interviewed him in New York soon after the star completed *Where the Pavement Ends*, but it wasn't until a year later, in November 1923, when they sailed to Cherbourg, France, together en route to the set of Ingram's film *The Arab* in Tunis, that he got to know Novarro. For the next five years, Howe would let his readers know that he and Novarro were best friends. What started out as a professional relationship turned into a personal one that, if one believes Howe's articles, had many ups and downs. Evident in most of the columns he wrote about Novarro was his infatuation with him and also hints of a possible intimate relationship. Howe's revelations about his close friendship with Novarro were easily passed off as tidbits aimed at women, who composed the majority of the movie-going public and fan magazine readership. These sorts of publications, as film scholar Gaylan Studlar argues, "evidence a desire for intensification of the cinematic signifier, for a revelation of the 'truth' behind the screen."[8]

This kind of revelation is exactly what occurred in Howe's pieces on Novarro. His first article appeared in *Photoplay* magazine in June 1923 and seems to have derived from an interview he conducted with Novarro in December 1922, before they set sail for Cherbourg. Titled "What Are Matinee Idols Made Of?," the piece starts off by informing readers that "it's the woman who pays and pays for the upkeep of the Hollywood beaux," meaning that a matinee idol must make sure that he plays to the women. Yet although Howe was seemingly concerned with helping women to understand Novarro, one could argue that it is he who was fascinated with him even as his article seems to reveal much about Novarro, if one reads closely. "Since Ramon Novarro is the latest to win queenly favor and the attendant royal swag," Howe wrote, "I sought from him the secret, hoping to tip off some fellow man, who, like myself, may have a heart of gold that he hasn't been able to cash."[9] The word *queen*, which still today identifies an effeminate gay man, may be one of those clues; according to historian George Chauncey the expression was already in use.[10] The same might be said of coded words like "the secret" or "some fellow . . . like myself." So it is possible that Howe was hinting that he was gay and wanted to win Novarro's favor, masking his desire as simply another revelation aimed at Novarro's admirers. Reading the piece with Eve Sedgwick's directive to be mindful of how silences reveal the closet, it may be that Howe's words illuminate a potentially more complex relationship between journalist and star.[11]

Howe built on others' notion that Novarro was a different kind of Mexican, not the "dirty" kind familiar to filmgoers but a more palatable one. According to

Howe, "You could tell from a glance that he's clean and wholesome." He continued: "It is hard to write about one of these upstanding whole-wheat boys. My sympathies are with the criminal classes. And Ramon is not one of these, even though he is a Hollywood resident and a Mexican. Not that I mean any disparagement of Mexicans. I may want to take flight over the border myself one day." Novarro had clearly gained a fan in Howe. For not only did the journalist report that the actor was wholesome and devoted to his family, but he also described Novarro's physical features. He wrote: "Ramon has the finest, clearest black eyes I ever saw outside the countenance of a Neopolitan bambino." When Novarro responded to a question, Howe noted that "there was a contraction of his upper lip, a thin upper lip."[12] It resembles multimillionaire John D. Rockefeller's thin upper lip, Howe explained, as he revealed that Novarro had signed his own million-dollar contract with Metro Pictures (an obvious exaggeration given what we know about Novarro's salary at the time), but we're still left with Howe staring at Novarro's lips.

Acting as both publicist and journalist, Howe mentioned Novarro in columns and in stories every chance he got. The way he wrote about Novarro, nonetheless, was quite different from how he depicted other movie stars. Howe had earlier worked as a publicist for actors Antonio Moreno and Malcom McGregor, and his stories about them and others were usually chatty and full of "intimate" information, as were most fan magazine articles.[13] Yet Howe's pieces about Novarro presented him, as he later said, "as Galahad in contrast to the 'Latin Lovers'—a new type of high distinction." Seeing Novarro as Galahad from Arthurian legends allowed Howe to emphasize Novarro's purity, his nobility, and even his piety; according to Howe, "Ramon's interest in religion was natural."[14]

From 1924 to 1928, Howe regularly mentioned Novarro in his columns in *Photoplay*, the *Los Angeles Times*, and the other periodicals for which he wrote. *Photoplay* let its readers know about the special relationship between the two men. In 1925 Howe's *Photoplay* column and other articles reported on Novarro's experiences in Europe while filming *Ben Hur*. Howe also accompanied Novarro on this trip to Europe, as publicist, journalist, and companion; while there he provided his readers with intimate details of the actor's life. With the approaching release of *Ben Hur*, the topic of Novarro's "Aztec ancestry" became prominent. As Howe wrote in the October 1925 issue of *Motion Picture Classic*, "Long before I knew Ramon well, . . . I was struck by the fact that the soul of the boy was not Spanish or Mexican, but Aztec."[15] This description of Novarro is unusual but might be read as an attempt to show once again that he was Mexican, yet not like other Mexicans. However, it was likely a total fabrication, given that Novarro's family was from northern Mexico and probably did not possess any Aztec heritage, and the information about his Aztec background was "unrevealed by Novarro" himself. Still, it represented another kind of fantasy upon which white fans could fixate.[16] In the same issue, both Howe and

Los Angeles Times columnist Harry Carr discussed Novarro's Aztec "heritage." According to Carr, through Novarro "an ancient Aztec civilization is speaking to us."[17] Howe even took Carr's suggestion a bit farther, saying: "Harry Carr's astute and immediate observation of the Aztec note in Novarro has been sufficient to plunge me into an exploration of Aztec history."[18] He described at length how Novarro was linked to the ancient Aztecs:

> One legend served to impress me with the good fortune of Novarro in being born today instead of a thousand years ago, for the fate of it unquestionably would have been his. The most famous of all Aztec sacrifices was that which took place once a year when the victim was the handsomest youth of the nation. The priests who made the selection insisted on his being physically perfect, without a single blemish and in possession of all the graces of youth. . . . When the final hour came he said goodbye to his sweethearts and, decorated with flowers, took his place on the sacrificial stone. Then a priest dressed in red drove his knife into the breast of the youth and pulled out his heart. It was held aloft before the eyes of the people and they fell on their knees in adoration. Later on the body was cut into pieces and distributed to a favored few, who cooked and served it on their tables as the tidbit of the year. I say this undoubtedly would have been Novarro's fate a thousand years ago, but isn't that his fate today—the fate of the popular idol? The heart is dragged out and held up for moment's brief adoration, then quickly devoured by the worshippers.[19]

Even when comparing Novarro to an Aztec man, it was not to any ordinary Aztec. To be sure, the passage is full of racist notions, which was typical during this era. Nonetheless, Howe's discussion of Novarro's Indian heritage was far more benevolent than the way in which the Native American roots of most Mexicans were depicted at the time. Howe's depiction of Novarro's body and how it signified his race is fascinating in itself, but it is also intriguingly queer. Novarro is both exoticized and eroticized.

The concern with Novarro's body, his sexuality, and his race was also evident in Howe's attempt to write Novarro's biography two years later. Titled "On the Road with Ramon Novarro," it appeared in *Motion Picture* magazine as a five-part series from February to June 1927. It was a further attempt to shape Novarro's stardom, and as with Howe's other articles, it gave intimate details of Novarro's life that revealed the author's infatuation with him.[20] Even more than his other pieces, it is full of coded queer language. Howe began by telling how he and Novarro first met; according to Howe they had dinner together the evening before they arrived in France and "then decided to stay up all night and receive Europe in the dawn." Howe added: "I must have touched a secret spring to his confidence for that evening was of charmed revelation, thru [*sic*] which I saw the substance of his character."[21]

In addition to a queer subtext, however, one can read Howe's words as evidence that Novarro's bodily beauty emerged as an object of desire in ways that allowed him to transcend his racial self and, with it, overcome the deeply racist impulses not only of his American fans in the early twentieth century but also of those who wrote about him. In the second installment of "On the Road," for example, Howe quoted *Los Angeles Times* columnist and screenwriter Harry Carr, who said that, "Ramon Novarro is a romantic hero to women, but he is a man's friend. And his appeal to men, strangely enough, is on account of his spiritual qualities. He has the body of a young Hercules and a mind unsoiled by the smut of the world."[22] This depiction of Novarro's "unspoiled" body is especially fascinating given that in October 1924, just three years before the piece was published, Los Angeles experienced an outbreak of pneumonic plague that lasted into the beginning of 1925 and was blamed on Mexicans living in the city. The fact that 90 percent of the forty people who died during the epidemic were ethnic Mexicans, coupled with racist perceptions of the Mexican population as a whole, ensured that even many uninfected Mexican Americans were fired from their jobs and that dwellings in Mexican neighborhoods were "disinfected" or torn down.[23] These fears would still have been current as Howe wrote. Mexican bodies were also often viewed as bearers of tuberculosis.[24] In contrast, for Howe, Novarro was something completely different, "born into that prolonged romance, which is old Mexico, blended out of Spanish and Aztec traditions with Oriental antecedents. Ramon's daily life ha[d] been an intensely pictorial drama."[25]

As Howe's writings make clear, it was Novarro's good looks and the journalist's fascination with them that allowed him to depict Novarro as a different kind of Mexican, a clean one who had been transformed into an American, an ethnic assimilation that was otherwise impossible for most Mexicans. It appears that the collaboration and close friendship between Novarro and Howe ended sometime in 1928. In a *Photoplay* article from November of that year, Howe discussed his adventures in Mexico but never mentioned Novarro.[26] When Novarro did appear in Howe's pieces after 1928, the assessment of both his career and his life was a bit nasty. These feelings notwithstanding, it appears that he and Novarro remained friends for the rest of Howe's life. While others have suggested that the demise of the close friendship between Howe and Novarro stemmed from personal rather than professional reasons, I would like to suggest that the two aspects were inextricably linked. Novarro's public image in the early part of his career was rooted in his private life; his sexuality not only allowed for the construction of his star image but also facilitated his success in another way. While some viewed Rudolph Valentino as an agent of miscegenation because he married white women, in contrast, Novarro, as a confirmed bachelor, one who had no thoughts of marriage and in fact never seriously dated a woman, posed no threat to the racial order.[27]

For the rest of his life, Novarro would continue to build upon the star image that Howe and others had helped him to construct, one that centered on his body and his religious devotion. Evidence of this can be found in the March 1930 issue of *Physical Culture* magazine. In an article titled "My Strength Gave Me My Career," Novarro (given the awkward writing style, he may have actually written it) outlined his physical regimen and the philosophy behind it. As he wrote, " The body is a temple. It is the earthly home of which God has given us. Therefore to keep it in perfect condition is a sacred duty. We clean out material houses. Why should we not give to our real home—the body—the same sincere care and attention."[28] Yet the article did not shy away from his racial background. When discussing his diet, he remarked, "Dinner [consists of] soup, a reasonable portion of meat and fresh vegetables. Always beans. We are Mexican!"[29]

As his career waned, however, and so too his body, Novarro began emphasizing his Catholic devotion more and more. We see this new emphasis beginning in the October 1928 issue of *Photoplay*, which featured a story announcing that Novarro would remain in the movies, despite the advent of sound. His devotion to his Catholic faith and especially the notion that he was interested in the priesthood and thought about joining a monastery would remain a constant feature in articles about him for the rest of his life. According to Novarro, he wondered if God would reprimand him for not using his talents and so decided that, "to go into the priesthood in order to avoid the worries of the world make me a coward rather than a helper for my religion."[30] Rather than join the priesthood, Novarro continued to work in films, but he tried to have more control over the kinds of parts he could get. By the 1930s, the advent of talking pictures, the waning interests in the Latin lover, and, perhaps as in the case of gay MGM star William Haines's career, the adoption of the Hollywood Production Code, which caused a decline in the use of queer codes to promote stars, diminished Novarro's status.[31] In 1935 Novarro and MGM decided that it would be best to terminate his contract, which relegated him to find employment at the lesser Republic Pictures and later to work independently.[32]

With the advent of the Second World War, Novarro attempted to join the U.S. military. He petitioned the Mexican government in August 1942 to allow him to retain his natal citizenship while serving in the United States, but the American armed forces seem to have rejected him, perhaps because of his age (he was forty-three by this time) or perhaps because he had recently been arrested for drunk driving.[33] A month later he tried to enlist in the Mexican army and met with the Mexican president, Manuel Avila Camacho, who persuaded him that he might better serve the war effort by acting in films.[34] Novarro appeared in *La Virgen que Forjó una Patria*, released in 1943, in which he played Juan Diego, the Indian who allegedly witnessed the apparition of the Virgin of Guadalupe in 1531.[35] It turned out to be his only Mexican film, despite his telling the *Saturday Evening Post* that he wanted to direct and act and distribute "Mexican films in the United States and Latin America."[36]

The same *Saturday Evening Post* article also featured Novarro's take on marriage and demonstrates the role that Novarro continued to play offscreen, hiding his homosexuality by acting the confirmed bachelor. When asked ten years earlier about matrimony, he had replied: "Women—phooey." At that time he had declared: "Beautiful women? Sure. And they're charming too. But marriage—not as long as I'm still acting." His views on marriage had not changed much by 1944, and he referred to it as "a mistake [he] did not make." The article then went on to explain that Novarro was "extremely devoted to his family, sharing a Los Angeles home with his mother."[37]

In the last decade of his life, Novarro still maintained the star image that he had helped craft so long ago. At this point, his piety took center stage. According to syndicated columnist Bill Slocum, who interviewed him in 1962, "God is much in his talk." Novarro claimed that he had "tried to become a Jesuit. And then a Trappist." In an attempt to infuse humor into the thought of being a monk, Novarro added: "Imagine an actor taking a vow of silence." He continued: "But I was 48. They said I was too old. They were right."[38] A similar religious motif appeared three years later, in September 1965, in Bill Kennedy's Mr. LA column. Talk of the actor's piety seemed to be part of a script, a performance that was perhaps aimed at deflecting discussion of other aspects of his life. Novarro repeated almost verbatim what he had said in 1962: "I tried to become a Jesuit, but they said I was too old, and of course they were right." He continued: "And then I contemplated the life of a Trappist monk."[39] As if on cue, Novarro even repeated the punch line he had used three years earlier: "Imagine an actor taking a vow of silence." Despite this religious motif in his interviews, Novarro also tried to sustain his image as a ladies' man, if in a comic manner. He told the *Los Angeles Times*: "The ladies are the same today as they were in 1925, except when they swoon over me now someone has to help them get up."[40]

Throughout his career, Novarro carefully controlled how he presented himself to the public. He was less successful managing his various interactions with the law, yet there was still a performative aspect to these reports. Already in 1931, Novarro was involved in an automobile accident that made the papers. During that incident and during another in 1934, it was reported that Novarro was not driving the vehicle, yet he was held responsible for the other party's injuries. Because he was under contract with MGM, the studio probably determined how the incident was reported and dealt with legally, as was typical for the era. In 1941 he was arrested for an altercation with police when driving while intoxicated; he pleaded guilty, although he claimed he was not.[41] Six months later, in April 1942, he was arrested again for drunk driving. In typical Novarro fashion, he told the police that he was upset because he had quarreled with his girlfriend. These drunk-driving incidents continued, and he was charged once again in June 1943.[42]

The incidents of drunk driving reemerged in 1959 and continued into the 1960s. Given what we know about how Novarro died, it is quite possible that he drove drunk while he pursued sex. Novarro biographer André Soares claims that Novarro frequently paid for sexual companionship; in the summer and fall of 1968, that is, in the months before he was killed, Novarro wrote close to 140 checks ranging between twenty and forty dollars made out to "gardeners" and "masseurs."[43] Hiring Paul Ferguson, the hustler who killed him, seems to be part of a larger trend that turned tragic. In the end, Novarro's determination to hide his homosexuality unraveled.

The obstacles Novarro faced as a Mexican and a gay man in the Hollywood film industry could be viewed as what the performance scholar José Esteban Muñoz has called "disidentification." According to Muñoz, disidentification "is a strategy that tries to transform a cultural logic from within, always laboring to enact permanent structural change while at the same time valuing the importance of local or everyday struggles of resistance."[44] It would be overstating Novarro's actions to say that he was trying to enact permanent structural change; however, it does seem that he was engaged in everyday struggles of resistance. His name change, for example, and especially his efforts to present himself as a different kind of Mexican might be seen not simply as self-serving but also as an attempt to present the ethnic Mexican community in a better light. Although some might argue that Novarro was simply an accommodationist, it seems that his experience was more nuanced. Muñoz claims that "disidentification negotiates strategies of resistance within the flux of discourse and power." In this regard, Novarro's interactions with Howe and the movie industry in general, private and public, personal and professional, were negotiations with power. Despite the fact that Novarro was a star, he was still a Mexican-born star, and given Hollywood's racial attitudes, which were a reflection of, and in turn projected those of, the nation in general, he remained in a precarious position.

Novarro's stardom was constructed out of the complicated reality of his life: he was presented as a respectable Mexican while still possessing a sensual body, and as a not-so-secret Aztec while remaining a hidden homosexual. Even at the end of his career, Novarro emphasized his devout Catholicism while downplaying his drunk-driving record and disguising his search for sexual gratification.[45] Looking at depictions of Novarro in the popular press and on the screen allows us to see the interrelated categories of race and sexuality in the making of his star image. Although he died brutally and tragically, it is my hope that we concentrate on his life and recognize how his sexuality facilitated his ability to forge a place for himself in the film industry despite the rampant racism that existed. Rather than perpetuate the standard narrative of Novarro's life that begins with great talent and promise and ends with his death as a lonely old man paying for sex and a victim of murder, one that ultimately remained fixated on his body, I would like to rethink the narrative so that Novarro emerges as a historical actor who lived a purposeful life rather than a faded movie star who had little control over his destiny.

Notes

Adapted from "'Ramon is not one of these': Race and Sexuality in the Making of Silent Screen Star Ramón Novarro's Star Image" by Ernesto Chavez, first published in *Journal of the History of Sexuality* 20, no. 3 (September 2011), 520–44. Copyright © 2011 by the University of Texas Press. All rights reserved.

1. Jerry Cohen and Dial Torgerson, "Found in Hollywood Home," *Los Angeles Times*, November 1, 1968, 1.

2. It was first reported that the Ferguson brothers beat Novarro in attempt to find the whereabouts of five thousand dollars they believed he had hidden in a safe. However, in a 1998 interview with André Soares, Paul Ferguson claimed that he had made up the story. Instead, he said that the reason he beat Novarro was because he felt Catholic guilt about kissing the actor in front of his brother, which was transformed into violence. If this is true, it seems ironic, given that Novarro was a devout Catholic and probably felt guilty himself about being gay. See André Soares, *Beyond Paradise: The Life of Ramon Novarro* (New York: St. Martin's, 2002), 294.

3. Although the term "outing," denoting "the intentional exposure of secret gays by other gays," as *Time* reported, was not coined until 1990, it is suitable to use it to refer what occurred when Novarro died. See William A. Henry III, Andrea Sachs, and James Willwerth, "Forcing Gays out of the Closet," *Time*, January 29, 1990. See also Diane Fuss, introduction to *Inside/Out: Lesbian Theories, Gay Theories*, ed. Diane Fuss (New York: Routledge, 1991), 4–5.

4. Herbert Howe, "On the Road with Ramon Novarro," pt. 4, *Motion Picture*, May 1927, 96.

5. Eve Koslowsky Sedgwick, *Epistemology of the Closet* (Berkeley: University of California Press, 1990), 3.

6. Richard Dyer, *Stars*, 2nd ed. (London: British Film Institute, 1998), 3, 26.

7. George C. Pratt, "'It's Wonderful How Fate Works': Ramon Novarro on His Film Career," *Image: Journal of Photography and Motion Pictures of the International Museum of Photography at George Eastman House* 16, no. 4 (1973): 17; Soares, *Beyond Paradise*, 1–11, 55, 112–15, 192.

8. Gaylyn Studlar, "The Perils of Pleasure? Fan Magazine Discourse as Women's Commodified Culture in the 1920s," in *Silent Film*, ed. Richard Abel (New Brunswick, N.J.: Rutgers University Press, 1996), 291.

9. Herbert Howe, "What Are Matinee Idols Made Of?," *Photoplay*, April 1923, 41.

10. George Chauncey, *Gay New York: Gender, Urban Culture, and the Making of the Gay Male World, 1890–1940* (New York: Basic Books, 1994), 16.

11. Eve Kosofsky Sedgwick, *Epistemology of the Closet* (Berkeley: University of California Press, 1990), 3.

12. Sedgwick, *Epistemology of the Closet*, 3.

13. For more articles by Howe on other male stars, see his "The Unretouched Por-traiture," *Motion Picture Magazine*, February1921, 24; "A Tribute from a Friend," *Photoplay*, March 1923, 37; "What Chance Has a Man in Pictures?," *Photoplay*, January 1924, 57, 103; and "He's the Whole Show," *Photoplay*, May1925, 39, 105.

14. Herbert Howe, "Hollywood's Hall of Fame," *New Movie Magazine*, August 1931, 62–63.

15. Harry Carr and Herbert Howe, "What Is the Mystery of Ramon Novarro?," *Motion Picture Classic*, October 1925, 76.

16. Manuel Reyes, "Ramon's Ancestors Greeted the Mayflower," *Photoplay*, November 1925, 46. Although the article was attributed to Manuel Reyes, it may well have been written by Howe given that this is the only article that Reyes wrote for *Photoplay* or any other fan magazine.

17. Carr and Howe, "What Is the Mystery?," 72.

18. Carr and Howe, "What Is the Mystery?," 76.

19. Carr and Howe, "What Is the Mystery?," 76.

20. Howe had already ghostwritten Valentino's life story for *Photoplay* in 1923, told in Valentino's own voice. See Emily W. Leider, *Dark Lover: The Life and Death of Rudolph Valentino* (New York: Faber and Faber, 2003), 78.

21. Herbert Howe, "On the Road with Ramon Novarro: The Romantic Life Story of Novarro," part 1, *Motion Picture*, February 1927, 19.

22. Herbert Howe, "On the Road with Ramon Novarro," part 2, *Motion Picture*, March 1927, 27.

23. William Deverell, *Whitewashed Adobe: The Rise of Los Angeles and the Remaking of Its Mexican Past* (Berkeley: University of California Press, 2004), 182–206.

24. Emily K. Abel, "From Exclusion to Expulsion: Mexicans and Tuberculosis Control in Los Angeles, 1914–1940," *Bulletin of the History of Medicine* 77, no. 4 (2003): 834.

25. Herbert Howe, "On the Road with Ramon Novarro," part 4, *Motion Picture*, May 1927, 96.

26. Herbert Howe, "An Innocent Gringo in Mexico," *Photoplay*, November 1928, 65, 106.

27. Studlar makes the point that Latin lovers after Valentino were de-eroticized and made wholesome, but she never connects this image directly with Novarro's sexuality ("Discourses of Gender and Ethnicity," *Film Criticism* 13, no. 2 [Winter 1989]: 30).

28. Ramón Novarro, "My Strength Gave Me My Career," *Physical Culture*, March 1930, 52.

29. Novarro, "My Strength," 143.

30. Ruth Biery, "Why Ramon Novarro Decided to Remain in the Movies," *Photoplay*, October 1928, 58, 102.

31. Ronald Gregg, "Gay Culture, Studio Publicity, and the Management of Star Discourse: The Homosexualiztion of William Haines in Pre-Code Hollywood," *Quarterly Review of Film and Video* 20, no. 2 (2003): 93.

32. Soares, *Beyond Paradise*, 205, 220.

33. "Novarro Asks Army Service," *Los Angeles Examiner*, August 6, 1942.

34. "Novarro to Join Mexican Army," *Los Angeles Examiner*, September 15, 1942.

35. "Ramon Novarro in Mexican Film," *Motion Picture Herald*, November 7, 1942.

36. William Krehn, "Where Is . . . Ramon Novarro?," *Saturday Evening Post*, January 15, 1944. In contrast, Dolores Del Rio (who was Novarro's second cousin) made several Mexican films after her career in American film waned; see Mary C. Beltrán, *Latina/o Stars in U.S. Eyes: The Making and Meanings of Film and TV Stardom* (Urbana-Champaign: University of Illinois Press, 2009), chap. 1.

37. "'Fool to Wed,' Says Novarro," *Los Angeles Examiner*, February 20, 1934.

38. Bill Slocum, "Keeping It Brisk: It Took Him 63 Years, but Novarro Made It," *Hearst Headline Service*, April 18, 1962.

39. Bill Kennedy, "Mr. L.A.: The Sunset Years," September 28, 1965, Novarro Clippings File, Margaret Herrick Library, Academy of Motion Picture Arts and Sciences, Los Angeles.

40. "Novarro Has 'Em Swooning," *Los Angeles Times*, June 1, 1965.

41. "Novarro Pays Liquor Fine," *Los Angeles Times*, October 30, 1941. See also Allen R. Ellenberger, *Ramon Novarro: A Biography of the Silent Film Idol, 1899–1968* (Jefferson, N.C.: McFarland, 1999), 148–49.

42. "Ramon Novarro Released on Bail," *Los Angeles Times*, April 16, 1942, 20; "Novarro Put under Strict Probation in Drunk Driving," *Los Angeles Times*, April 30, 1942, A3; "Novarro Faces Jury Trial," *Los Angeles Times*, June 16, 1943, A 10.

43. Soares, *Beyond Paradise*, 269–70.

44. José Esteban Muñoz, *Disidentifications: Queers of Color and the Performance of Politics* (Minneapolis: University of Minnesota Press, 1999), 11–12.

45. His devotion was undoubtedly sincere, and he left large sums of money to the Catholic Church at his death. The *Hollywood Citizen-News* reported on November 14, 1968, for example, that Novarro left $15,000 in his will to St. Anne's Catholic Church.

PART 3

Subjectivities

CHAPTER 7

Power and Historical Figuring

Rachael Pringle Polgreen's Troubled Archive

MARISA J. FUENTES

It may be precisely due to Rachael Pringle Polgreen's "exorbitant circumstances" during her life as a free(d) woman of color in late-eighteenth-century Bridgetown, Barbados, that her narrative has not changed since she appeared in J. W. Orderson's 1842 novel *Creoleana*.[1] Apart from an important critique by Melanie Newton of the political and historical context of *Creoleana*, Polgreen's life story—her triumphs, extraordinary relationships, and visual depictions have not altered since the nineteenth century. Thus the archive and secondary historical accounts beg reexamination. She was a woman of color, a former slave turned slave owner, and many stories circulate that she ran a well-known brothel without much legal controversy.[2] The persistent historical representations of her life draw from an archive unusual for many free(d) and enslaved women of color in eighteenth-century slave societies. Polgreen left a will, and her estate was inventoried by white men upon her death—a process reserved primarily for the society's wealthier (white) citizens. Her relationships with elite white men and the British Royal Navy are well documented in newspaper accounts and most significantly, in the nineteenth-century novel written by a resident of Bridgetown who may have been well acquainted with Polgreen. In the 1770s and 1780s, Polgreen appears in Bridgetown's tax records as a propertied resident, and her advertisements in a local newspaper allude to the importance she placed on property. From a caricatured 1796 lithograph to the folkloric accounts of Prince William Henry's (King William Henry IV) rampage through her brothel, Polgreen's story has in many ways been rendered impermeable, difficult to revise, and overdetermined by the language and power of the archive.

The archive conceals, distorts, and silences as much as it reveals about Rachael Pringle Polgreen. *Creoleana*, in which a "complete" dramatized life story of Polgreen is narrated, provides a tantalizing solution to gaps and uncertainties for historians who struggle with the fragmented and fraught records of female enslavement marked by the embedded silences, the commodified representations of bodies, and the epistemic violence of slavery's archive. However, for Polgreen, it is perhaps her hypervisibility in images and stories that continues to obscure her everyday life, even when the archive appears to "substantiate" certain aspects of that life. I contend that such powerful narratives, visual reproductions, and archival assumptions erase the crucial complexities of her personhood and obfuscate the violent and violating relationships she maintained with other women of color in Bridgetown's slave society. The challenge, then, is to track power in the production of her history while recognizing that Polgreen's historical visibility is also an erasure of the lives of those she enslaved.

In the scholarship of slavery and slave society in Barbados, Polgreen and other free(d) women of color are centered on narratives about business acumen and entrepreneurship. Several historians discuss the significant role that prostitution played in the local and transnational market economy. Indeed, in many of the eighteenth-century Caribbean and metropolitan Atlantic port cities, prostitution was rampant and served a significant mobile military population as well as providing local "entertainment."[3] "During the 1790s," Melanie Newton states, "the symbol of nonwhite business success in Barbados was the female hotelier."[4] A number of free(d) women found slave owning and prostitution economically viable routes to self-sustenance as they and other free(d) people of color in slave societies were systemically excluded from many other roles and opportunities.[5] Though many references of free(d) women of color mention their involvement in the sexual economy of port cities, we must also note that in Bridgetown there was a unique demographic of a majority white female population by the beginning of the eighteenth century. This white female (and mostly slave-owning) majority tended to own more women than men and set the precedent for the selling and renting out of enslaved women for sexual purposes.[6] Moreover, in a town setting with little arable land, white women profited from a surplus of domestic laborers by hiring them out to island visitors.[7] It is thus within this environment of slaves, sailors, Royal Navy officers, and other maritime traffic in Bridgetown's terribly bustling port that Rachael Pringle Polgreen made her living.

Polgreen necessarily appears in histories of gender and slavery in Barbados as she lived a remarkable life within a slave society. However, the other enslaved and freed women who lived in similar circumstances during her time are eclipsed and silenced by her seductive narrative. This essay tracks how material and discursive power moves through the archive in the historical production of subaltern women.[8]

Moreover, revisiting the documentary traces of Polgreen's life and death illuminates several contradictions or historical paradoxes that make it problematic to characterize Polgreen or enslaved and free(d) women's sexual relations with white men as unmediated examples of black female agency. How does one write a narrative of enslaved "prostitution?" What language should we use to describe this economy of forced sexual labor? How do we write against historical scholarship that too often relies on the discourses of will, agency, choice, and volunteerism, which reproduce a troubling archive that cements enslaved and free(d) women of color in representations of "their willingness to become mistresses of white men."[9] If "freedom" meant free from bondage but not from social, economic, and political degradation, what does it mean to survive under such conditions?

In an analysis of the processes by which Polgreen is historically confined, I challenge previous assumptions about her lived experiences by attending to the ways in which enslaved and free(d) women enter history.[10] The first part of this essay sets the scene of Barbados and Bridgetown in the late eighteenth century in order to give context to the lives of these Afro-Barbadian women. I next reexamine the secondary literature and present new archival traces of Polgreen's material life to reveal an image incommensurate with a triumphant narrative. Engaging with secondary sources on Barbados illuminates the specific gendered and sexual representations of women in Caribbean slave societies and examines how these images are reproduced in the historiography. Presenting previously unexamined archival material from Barbadian deeds and British parliamentary debates on Caribbean slavery, this essay presents the ways in which Polgreen's "agency" depended on the sexual subjugation of other black women and supported a system of slavery established and perpetuated by the white colonial authority. At stake in this discussion of Rachael Pringle Polgreen's power (inhabited and represented) is the desire to make plain how the archive and historical production facilitate the survival of particular stories and the erasure of others.

By the mid– to late seventeenth century, Barbados was considered the "crown jewel" of the English Caribbean colonies. As the first point of embarkation for British slaving vessels and a significant port of call for the British military, the colony of Barbados was pivotal in the networks of trade and profit that propelled England into economic prosperity. According to Richard Dunn, Barbados dominated the sugar and shipping markets beyond any other British colony.[11] In order to sustain sugar production, Barbados planters and merchants bought into and sustained the trade in African captives throughout the seventeenth and eighteenth centuries. By 1670, Barbados was firmly established as an economy dependent on enslaved labor.[12] Bridgetown, the capital port city in which Rachael Pringle Polgreen resided, received hundreds of ships a year laden with material products and captive Africans, who supplied the labor for sugar works plantations as well as domestic labor in town settings. Although demographic sources are rare for the eighteenth century, Melanie Newton estimates that "by 1789 . . . there were at least 62,115 slaves, 16,167 whites, and 838 free people of color in the island."[13] In the 1770s and 1780s, Bridgetown's free population of color remained relatively small but had experienced significant growth by the turn of the nineteenth century.[14] There a small group of "free colored" men and women survived through economic activities including store keeping, huckstering, shipbuilding, and in some cases prostitution. The military infrastructure built to support the British Royal Navy in and around Bridgetown perpetuated the demand for an informal sexual economy beyond that which the white Barbadian slave owners already seized from enslaved women's bodies. As a former slave of a white owner who was possibly her own father, it is probable that Polgreen herself experienced the typical sexual violations inherent in slave societies.[15]

The gender demographics of Barbados and Bridgetown were unique for a Caribbean colony. Though enslaved men tended to dominate in British plantation societies, there is evidence that Barbadian planters sought to balance the sex ratios among the laboring African population, and according to one historian, the island had actually attained a majority female enslaved population by the early eighteenth century.[16] Moreover, and equally anomalous, white women constituted a slight majority among the white population during the same period (51 percent according to the 1715 census) and remained so until the era of emancipation (1834–38).[17] In Bridgetown, these female majorities influenced the character of urban slave society. For example, Hilary Beckles's scholarship challenges Caribbean historiography that focuses on the planter "patriarch," showing that "58 percent of slave owners in [Bridgetown] were female, mostly white . . . [and] women owned 54 percent of the slaves in town." Furthermore, he points out that "white women also owned more female slaves than male slaves."[18] Thus female slave owners like Polgreen made up much of the landscape of urban life.

Due to a shift in Caribbean historiography in the late 1980s, the subject of gender and slavery has received a considerable amount of attention. The scholarship of Hilary Beckles and Barbara Bush opened a field into the study of enslaved and free(d) women of color across the Caribbean. Out of this commendable effort emerged several studies in which enslaved and free(d) women were "centered" in historical scholarship.[19] For studies focused on Barbados specifically, Jerome Handler's two publications, *The Unappropriated People: Freedman in the Slave Society of Barbados* (1974) and "Joseph Rachell and Rachael Pringle-Polgreen: Petty Entrepreneurs" (1981), laid the blueprint for later discussions of Rachael Pringle Polgreen, free women of color, and prostitution.[20] "The first of the Bridgetown taverns owned by a freedwoman," Handler asserts, "appears to have begun operating in the early

1780s and [was] said to have belonged to Rachael Pringle Polgreen."[21] Handler's discussion continues by recounting Polgreen's enslavement by William Lauder, her freedom, and her rise to "business" woman—a story drawn primarily from the nineteenth-century novel *Creoleana*: "Born around 1753, Rachael was the daughter and slave of William Lauder, a Scottish schoolmaster, and an African woman whom he purchased not long after emigrating to Barbados around 1750. . . . [By] her 'juvenile days,' Rachael was a 'remarkably well-made, good-looking girl, possessing altogether charms that . . . awakened the libidinous desires of her [father,] who made many . . . unsuccessful attempts at her chastity.'"[22]

In describing her adult life, Handler uses *Creoleana* to explain that "Rachael was bought from her father, and then manumitted, by a British naval officer whose mistress she had become; the house he provided for her in Bridgetown ultimately became her *celebrated* "Royal Navy Hotel . . ." At her death in 1791, Rachael owned 'houses and lands' and nineteen slaves, six of whom were to be manumitted by the terms of her will."[23] Understandably, subsequent historical work has drawn extensively on Handler's authority on Polgreen and free(d) people of color in Barbados.[24] Indeed, several texts mention Polgreen's property accumulation, her relationships with white male elites, her shrewd business management, and her demurring yet assertive challenge to the Prince of England.[25] Barbados historian Pedro Welch examined Rachael Pringle Polgreen's emergence as a property owner, using the St. Michael levy books from 1779, to describe the economic possibilities available to enslaved and freed women in town.[26] For Welch, Polgreen exemplified resistance. Based on the logic of capitalism, he contends that hoteliers' property-ownership "managed . . . to challenge the economic hegemony of whites." Welch also argues "that even where alternatives might have existed some slave and free coloured women either prostituted themselves or provided prostitution services for the financial and status gains which derived from such activities."[27] Perhaps more attentive to the coercive nature of sex and status in a slave society, Hilary Beckles distinguishes rape from "the commercialisation of slave women's sexuality as cash-receiving prostitutes."[28]

While contemporary historians of Barbados have rightly characterized Polgreen as part of a "colored elite" who owned property—including slaves—and were able to maintain a standard of living comparable to their white counterparts, they do not deal critically with the ways in which "discourses of seduction obfuscate the reality of violation."[29] By this, I mean to problematize how studies of slavery might too easily equate black female agency with sexuality. Discussions of black women, free or enslaved, using white men as an avenue to freedom often erase the reality of coercion, violence, and the complicated positions black women were forced to inhabit in this system of domination. It is interesting to note that alongside a breadth of scholarship about free(d) and enslaved women and their profit from sexual relations during slavery, there has not been equally consistent attention to the ways in which white and black free(d) and enslaved men benefited from these relations. It would seem, based on the current scholarship, that women of color wielded an inordinate amount of power in these sexual encounters. What is necessary in these interpretations is teasing out how discourses of "resistance," "sexual power," and "will" shape our understanding of female slavery. How is *will*, as Hartman asks, "an overextended approximation of the agency of the dispossessed subject/object of property or perhaps simply unrecognizable in a context in which agency and intentionality are inseparable from the threat of punishment?" What kind of power is gained from the systematic sexual violation of other women? What does this reveal about slavery's system of domination, and within it, Rachael Pringle Polgreen's role?

Michel-Rolph Trouillot writes of historical power, arguing that history represents both the past (facts and archival materials) and the story told about the past (narrative).[30] Polgreen's archival remains and the histories written about her clearly represent this interaction between the processes of historical production and demonstrate her limited power in self-representation (epitomized by her status as a woman of color, her illiteracy, her former enslavement, and her engagement in the sex trade). More recent historical work has ascribed Polgreen agency due to her material success. Throughout her life and after her death, she served the agendas of divergent political discourses, used in the nineteenth century as a motif to remind white society that black women's sexuality must be contained; later, for the post-colonial Barbados elite, she exemplified loyalty to England, accommodation, and peaceful negotiation.[31]

What documents and processes, then, informed the making of archival records that fashion "truths" about her experiences? What does it mean that discourses of commodity (that is, her material accumulations) constitute the most accepted sources of Polgreen's significance? In other words, Polgreen's inner self—her fears and confidences—remain difficult to retrieve using documents produced within a slave society limited by capitalist and elite perspectives.[32] A critical reengagement with the sources elucidates her complicated life situation.

Although no existing birth record survives, historians contend that Rachael Pringle Polgreen was born Rachael Lauder sometime around 1753.[33] Her burial was recorded on July 23, 1791, at the parish Church of St. Michael.[34] At her death, her estate was worth "Two Thousand nine hundred & thirty Six pounds nine Shillings four pence half penny," an amount comparable to a moderately wealthy white person living at the same time.[35] According to her inventory, along with ample material wealth in the form of houses, furniture, and household sundries, Polgreen owned thirty-eight enslaved people: fifteen men and boys, and twenty-three women and girls.[36] In her will Polgreen freed a Negro woman named Joanna, bequeathing to her an enslaved Negro woman named Amber.[37] Joanna was also given her own son, Richard, who was still enslaved. Polgreen also freed a "mulatto" woman named Princess and four "mulatto" children (not listed in familial relation to any "parents"). Polgreen ordered that the rest of her estate—including William, Dickey, Rachael, Teresa, Dido Beckey, Pickett, Jack Thomas, Betsey, Cesar, a boy named Peter, and nineteen other enslaved people—was to be divided among William Firebrace and his female relatives, William Stevens, and Captain Thomas Pringle, all white people with whom she had social ties. The bequest (the enslaved as property) was to them and "their heirs forever."[38]

This information survives precisely because of the value placed on property. Thus, produced through her materiality, Polgreen's archival visibility relies on the logic of white colonial patriarchal and capitalist functions, reproducing the terms of the system of enslavement. Her burial in the yard of the Anglican Church of Saint Michael did not, as a triumphant narrative might argue, exemplify transcendence over racial and gendered systems of domination but rather illustrates the power of her social connections, without whose permission a church burial would not have been granted. We may speculate on the limited degrees of her integration into the white Anglican religious community of Bridgetown, given her profession as a brothel owner. We can also surmise that Polgreen's participation in the sociality of slave ownership and the general acceptance of her economic position by the white community granted her unusual power.

Beyond her will and estate inventory, another remarkable surviving document is a lithograph produced by the English artist Thomas Rowlandson and printed in 1796.[39] It pictures a large and dark-skinned Rachael Pringle Polgreen seated in front of a house purported to be her "hotel." Her breasts are revealed through a low cut dress as she sits open-legged and bejeweled. In the background of the lithograph are three other figures, a young woman and two white men. The young woman is pictured similarly dressed. Her bodice is cut lower, however, than that worn by the seated Polgreen. She stares, almost sullen-faced, at a large white man appearing in the rear of the picture in a tattered jacket and hat.[40] Observing the young woman from the right side of the picture is a younger white man wearing a British military uniform. He is a partial figure, shown in profile only. A sign posted behind Polgreen reads: "Pawpaw Sweetmeats & Pickles of all Sorts by Rachel PP."[41]

In 1958, an anonymous editorial preceded the first "scholarly" article about Polgreen in the *Journal of the Barbados Museum and Historical Society*. The editorial reads the image as a narrative about her life, contending that "a gifted [caricaturist] such as Rowlandson would not . . . have placed as a background to the central figure of Polgreen in her later and prosperous years characters such as 'a tall girl in a white frock,' etc. and an officer looking through a window, which had no relation to her or to her career."[42] In the writer's view, the figures in the background represent a young Polgreen, averting the repulsive advances of her master-father. The young military man represents her "savior," Captain Pringle, the man who is credited with granting her freedom. Corresponding with the most pervasive narrative about her life, Polgreen is said to have taken the name Pringle after Captain Pringle, who allegedly purchased her from her father-master, William Lauder (d. 1771). After settling Polgreen in a house in Bridgetown, Captain Pringle left the island to pursue his military career, and in his absence, Rachael Pringle took the name of Polgreen.[43]

The editorial does not, however, read into the explicit sexual tone of the sign posted above Polgreen. "Pawpaw, Sweetmeats & Pickles of all Sorts" advertised more than the culinary items available for purchase. Free(d) and enslaved women in towns played a significant if not dominant role in the informal market economy, selling a variety of ground provisions to locals and incoming ships, and the sign above Polgreen clearly situates her within a well-established market system. She can easily assume the part of a market woman seated outside her "shop."[44] However, the artist's phallic references on the sign also allude to the sexual services offered inside. The language of the consumption of "sweetmeats and fruits" worked to both mask and advertise the sexually overt activities within the tavern. At the same time, the image reinforces the positionality of enslaved black women as sexually available, consenting, consumable, and disposable. Many of Rowlandson's works depict London and other maritime scenes, filled with sexual references.[45] These include sailors and prostitutes in various sexual acts and stages of undress. It may not be surprising then, to find him dedicating an entire collection to what was then described as "erotic" art.[46] Rowlandson's caricature of Rachael Pringle Polgreen depicts an extravagant woman of color in various stages of her life. In one frame Polgreen is racialized, discursively and visually sexualized starting from her younger lighter self to an older, darker, larger self seated in the foreground. This visual production represents Polgreen's race, gender, and sexuality and a complete narrative of her life story *as the artist* imagined her.

The material fragments of Polgreen's existence evident in her will, inventory, and this visual depiction exemplify Trouillot's concept of archival power.[47] Operating on two levels, archival power is present in influencing what it is possible to know or not to know about her life. In the first instance, power is present in the making of the archival fragments during her particular historical moment. Her will, recorded by a white male contemporary, leaves evidence only of what was valued in Polgreen's time—the material worth of her assets in property. She left no diary or self-produced records.[48] Also, as illustrated by the lithographic representation, Polgreen's image and life history were imagined by an Englishman whose own socioeconomic and racial reality limited and informed what he produced about a woman of African descent.

In 1842, nearly fifty-one years after Polgreen's death, *Creoleana, or Social and Domestic Scenes and Incidents in Barbados in the Days of Yore*, by J. W. Orderson, was published in London. Orderson was born in Barbados in 1767 and grew up in Bridgetown. His father, John Orderson, owned the *Barbados Mercury* (a local newspaper), and J.W. became its sole proprietor in 1795.[49] Thus he would have been a teenager when many of the events he wrote about in *Creoleana* occurred, although he wrote about them when he was seventy-five years old. It was likely, as evidenced in numerous newspaper advertisements that Polgreen made in his paper, that J. W. Orderson knew her.[50]

It is important to read *Creoleana* as a "romantic," "sentimental" novel of its time, for the historical context in which the novel was written is as pertinent as Orderson's characterization of Polgreen. The novel was, as Newton suggests, both "a revision of slavery and a moral reformist tale to guide behavior in postemancipation society."[51] Slavery and apprenticeship had officially been abolished in the British colonized Caribbean by 1842, only four years prior to its publication. Orderson was clear about his nostalgia for a time in which the enslaved were "happier" in their bondage than in freedom.[52] Melanie Newton's critical reading of the novel illuminates the consequences of Polgreen's historical (re)production, "In the postslavery era, as had been the case during slavery, stereotyped and sexualized representations of women of color, especially the 'mulatto' woman, often served as the means through which white reactionaries expressed both antiblack sentiment and fear of racial 'amalgamation.'"[53]

Acknowledging the pro-slavery project constituent to such representations raises questions about how to use a text like *Creoleana* as a primary source for Polgreen's historical reality. This is not to dismiss completely the novel's potentially historically informative qualities but rather to offer insight into its distorting representations of Polgreen. At the moment when the British and North American antislavery movement was storming across the Atlantic and into the Caribbean, Orderson articulated his pro-slavery beliefs while condemning the "perversion" of interracial sex.[54] In a pamphlet published in 1816, Orderson responded to British parliamentary debates concerning the abolition of slavery in Britain's colonies, but his remarks center specifically on the growth of the free population of color in Bridgetown: "Particularly with the staff of the army, who at one period, in the civil department especially, introduced a more bold and licentious intercourse with these [black and 'colored'] women than had before been ever tolerated, and which, unhappily for the morals of society, has left its baleful influence on the manners of all the youth of the West Indies, who formerly were in some measure guarded against the bad example of the irregularities of their fathers."[55] Using less symbolic language than the novel to describe his abhorrence of interracial sex, Orderson strongly expresses his moral outrage. Blaming the military, perhaps to avoid implicating his planter friends, he remarks upon his belief of the moral decline of white society through the "licentious intercourse" with women of color. More importantly, his language serves to silence any coercion on the part of the men he accuses. By using the term "irregularities" to expose the white men presumably responsible for upholding the paternalistic role of moral exemplar, Orderson essentially silences the women of color sexually coerced by white men and erases even the possibility of their violations.

Creoleana centers on the lives of two white characters, Jack Goldacre and Caroline Fairfield. A young "mulatto" girl named Lucy is a shadow character of Caroline, whose tragic death had resulted from her "voluntary" sexual encounter with an Irishman. Lucy's story remains encapsulated in an oft- reproduced trope of the virtuous white woman and the "tragic mulatta" (read as illicit interracial sex, immorality, and death). Though Rachel Pringle Polgreen is not a main character of the novel, Orderson includes a brief life-sketch of her bondage, abuse, humiliation, redemption, and triumph. "'Miss Rachael,' as *par excellence* . . . was the daughter and slave of the notorious William Lauder, a Scotch schoolmaster and an African woman he owned."[56] Orderson describes how Polgreen was frequently abused by her owner-father, a result of her physical "charms that touched not the heart, but awakened the libidinous desires."[57] The author imagines Lauder's many "unsuccessful attempts on her chastity" and recounts his resort to public punishment by the town "jumper" for her disobedience.[58]

It is necessary here to interrogate the possibilities of what Lauder's sexually violent relationship to his "daughter" exposes, as well the absence of previous scholarly attention to these incidents. What does the narrative of incest reveal about the author of Polgreen's "history," the depths of her subjection, and the erasure of her African mother? What of the liminal place in which her incestuous experiences remain, encapsulated within a novel (and perhaps Rowlandson's lithograph) but consequently outside historical "reality?" What also is at stake when the representations of such violent acts continue to elude the historian's critical gaze? Orderson regards the act of incest upon one's family member as the point at which the brutal nature of slavery is illuminated: "Lauder's conduct to his offspring, is a damning proof how debasing to the human mind is the power given us over our fellow creatures by holding them in bondage! The ties of consanguinity were all merged in the authority of the master, and he saw but the slave in his own daughter!"[59] This particular narrative, upon closer examination, lays bare Polgreen's body, her violations and subjugations, as well the complete erasure of her mother—compounding the powerlessness of these enslaved women.

The legal parameters of slavery and the violence that protected its existence severed the ties of "family" for the enslaved.[60] Elucidating a complicated formulation, literary scholar Hortense Spillers touches on the nature of female enslavement, sexual violation, and the disruption of the "family" in slavery. The act of incest relies on a recognizable and legal biological bond that the laws and logic of slavery make impossible. The role and relationship of the "father" to the "daughter" in this instance, Lauder to Polgreen, are confused and denied here. Essentially, incest performed or threatened in a system of slavery with "its imposed abeyance of order and degree" cannot really exist. Or, in Spillers contention, this moment can speak for or illuminate the extant "losses" of family and "confusions" of the status of the enslaved person as both object and subject—person and property.[61] Polgreen was at once nonhuman, daughter, woman, chattel, and sexual object. Ultimately, it is only through the revelation of her abuses and the desecration of her body that Polgreen becomes a subject through a sentimental novel. Thus the act of incest provokes recognition of Polgreen's humanity that is at the same instant destabilized by the laws of slavery.[62]

Immediately following Orderson's discussion of incest, his sensational account of Polgreen's whipping implicitly sexualized her body, connecting it to her rescue by a white seaman: "She was already 'tucked up,' in the indecorous manner of those days, and the brutal hand of the mercenary whipper, armed with the fatal 'cowskin,' stretched forth to lay on the unpitying merciless lash, when a British tar! A gallant seaman rushed on the relentless executioner, seized the whip from his grasp, and rescuing his panting victim, carried her off in triumph amidst the cheers of a thronging multitude!"[63] Orderson ends Polgreen's story with the visit of England's Prince William Henry (who later becomes King William IV) to the island in 1789.[64] As Barbadians celebrated the prince's presence by illuminating the town with lights, he used Polgreen's Hotel as his on-land base from which to make his rounds dining with various planters and merchants. During his visit, the prince led a regiment on a drunken rampage through Polgreen's hotel, destroying nearly all her property by "breaking the furniture, &c., . . . The very beds [were] cut up, and their contents emptied into the street, and the whole neighbourhood strewed with feathers."[65] As a final act, epitomizing the pinnacle of colonial power, "he bid [Polgreen] 'good night,' and to crown his sport, upset her and chair together, leaving her unwieldy body sprawling in the street, to the effable amusement of the laughing crowd."[66] Polgreen's narrative response, through Orderson's ventriloquism, leaves her in her place, "calling out in her sweetest dulcet tones, 'Mas Prince! Mas Prince; you come ma-morning, to see wha' mischief you been do!'"[67] In closing, Orderson tells of Polgreen's industriousness, how she took immediate account of the damage to her property and sent a bill to the prince upon his departure from the island—"which was duly paid."[68] Not allowing the reader to remain long with her humiliation and abuse, Orderson's narrative forces Polgreen into an embodiment of triumph and guile. Through *Creoleana*, Orderson produces a distorted, disfigured, and silenced Polgreen, creating an almost unchangeable snapshot of Polgreen's (imagined) intimacies by fixing her into a bounded frame of identity. For historians this novelistic representation has become the central understanding of her identity—its power so pervasive as to inform most other historical representations of her life.[69]

The power of this novelistic representation has proven seductive, and several attempts have been made to historicize Polgreen's encounter with the prince. An editorial published in the *Barbadian* (1842) acknowledged the publication of *Creoleana* and provided circumstantial evidence to support the novel's depiction of events. Yet the editorial powerfully (re)fixes Polgreen's bodily image within the text of the newspaper and into the nineteenth century:[70]

> Many of the scenes [Orderson] has remarked *we* have a distant recollection of. We well remember the wild frolics and pranks of Prince William Henry . . . who probably little thought that one of the Barbadians would, at this distant period of 55 years, amuse the world with his mischievous tricks at old Rachael Lauder's alias Rachael Pringle. We perfectly recollect this immense mass of flesh (she was nearly as big as a sugar hogshead) walking with the Prince, actually leaning on the Royal Arm, and accompanied by other Naval Officers, and a host of mulatto women.[71]

Here Polgreen's archive is reproduced through an anonymous editorial. Its reference to her as "an immense mass of flesh" serves as a postmortem dehumanization that becomes her mytho-history, and the despicable captivation she inspired in Barbadian lore implacably passes through time. Polgreen is transparently despised in this moment of recollection, "actually leaning on the Royal Arm," as the author of this editorial degrades the memory of her. He shifts our understanding away from Orderson's victim-to-trickster representation to a Polgreen whose arrogance and audacity violated nineteenth-century mores.[72] Aghast at the possibility that a woman of color would take such liberties with royalty, the editorial's author discursively caricaturizes Polgreen and implicitly disempowers her role in relation to a figure such as the late king. Moreover, in this nineteenth-century moment, Polgreen's body is aged and reduced to mere flesh, "as big as a sugar hogshead," refiguring the terms of her commodified captivity—literally and symbolically. Reducing Polgreen to an object of commerce, the editorial deconstructs Orderson's representation of her as embattled yet empowered.

Perhaps unsettling Orderson's novel as mere fiction, another important trace of Polgreen reveals an advertisement she had placed in the *Barbados Gazette* of January 31–4 February 4, 1789:

> Lost by subscriber, a small filigree waiter, scalloped round the edge, and bordered with a vignette, seven silver table spoons, seven tea-spoons; marked S.B. in a cipher, also two dessert spoons marked R.P. in a cipher. Whoever had found the same, and will deliver them to her or the printer of this paper, shall receive FOUR MOIDORES reward, or, in proportion part. Silver-Smiths and others are requested to stop the above articles if offered for sale.
>
> RACHAEL-PRINGLE POLGREEN[73]

These articles, according to Barbados historian Neville Connell, may represent the "contents emptied into the street," during the prince's violent sweep through the hotel.[74] This archival fragment coincides with Prince Henry's 1789 visit, possibly imbuing Orderson's account with some historical veracity. The historical interest in this story still concerns the value that Polgreen placed on property.

Tracing the manner in which Polgreen enters the historical record and accounting for the power with which her story is reproduced allows us to understand the productive nature of history—and illuminates what is silenced in the process. The following archival pieces were created in the midst of the transatlantic abolition movement, and while debates over ending the slave trade raged in the chambers of the British Parliament. Historians have noted that "abolitionist literature frequently contained gruesome depictions of drunkenness and acts of cruelty, especially rape and flogging, being committed against slaves, usually by white men."[75]

In an interview between a British military officer named Captain Cook and members of the Privy Council taken in 1791, a harrowing image of Polgreen appears. It reads:

[Captain Cook, of the Eighty-Ninth Regiment of Foot, called in and examined]
Were you ever in the West Indies?
Yes.
When, and in what islands?
In the years 1780 and 1781, in Barbados, St. Lucia, St. Christopher's &c.
Did the Negro Slaves in general appear to you to be treated with mildness or severity?
In the towns I thought with very great severity.
Do any particular instances occur to you of [slaves] being treated with severity?
Many; one was an instance of a female Slave belonging to a woman named Rachael La[u]der, who I saw beat in a most unmerciful manner; She beat her about the head with the heel of her shoe, till it was almost all of a jelly; she then threw her down with great force on a child's seat of a necessary, and there attempted to stamp her head through the hole; she would have murdered her had she not been prevented by the interposition of two officers. [The girl's] crime was, not bringing money enough from aboard ship, where she was sent by her mistress for the purpose of prostitution.[76]

Although the following fragment cannot necessarily be characterized as abolitionist propaganda, it does characterize Polgreen's violent power exercised against another woman of color.[77] The system of slavery in which Polgreen operated provided her the power to enact violence upon the bodies of those she enslaved. This incident described by a British naval officer reveals both Polgreen's power and the limits of her power. It is not known whether she was indicted for the beating of this enslaved woman, but the toleration of "prostitution" within the city and her position as a slave owner supports the assumption that she retained a form of power over her slaves similar to that of white slave owners. From the details Captain Cook provides about a "child's seat of a necessary [toilet]" and the fact that two other military "officers"—not the town's constable—intervened, it is possible that this violent scene occurred inside Polgreen's hotel. The officers, like Captain Cook (probably patrons of the brothel), were struck by the extreme violence perpetrated by Polgreen against this unnamed woman and eager to recount this story.

In a gesture toward an alternative image of Polgreen's constructed history, we might also ask if this fragment draws us nearer to the otherwise invisible women she owned and the nature of their sexual labor tragically encapsulated by the "libidinal investment in violence" characterizing so much of slavery's archives.[78] For the woman beaten by Rachael Pringle Polgreen, the labor demanded by her enslavement would have required her to find transportation (most likely by row boat) to the unknown lawless space of the ship in harbor, in order to secure a willing white patron who would pay to use her body sexually.[79] Not satisfying the patron could result in returning to her owner without the expected compensation. Moreover, due to her enslaved status, this beaten woman could never guarantee payment for her services in such a society. There were no laws to protect even Polgreen's expectation of profit.

The intensity of the beating also suggests a passion that went beyond the recovery of money, a willingness to murder a woman on whose productive value she relied. Generally, violence against one's own property was not punishable by law, but Polgreen maintained her economic interests outside the law, which did not support her status as "citizen." Due to her own liminality, Polgreen effected her own discipline: she was her own overseer, labor negotiator, and slave master. After further examination, this incident also reveals the nature of Polgreen's agency, one that depended on the subjugation of others. What does this scene expose about the very nature of this slavery? What does it mean that the beaten woman's labor required daily access to her sexualized body? What are the configurations of her labor—her enslavement? How can we make careful distinctions between the "jobbing" slaves in town who scrambled for windows of autonomy in an urban landscape and the women forced to sell their bodies only for the material gain of their owners? Through the enslaved women she owned, Polgreen amassed a small fortune. Her "production of pleasure" for the sailors and military men she entertained, as well as the sexual labor she demanded from her slaves, hint at the many layers of her agency. The women she owned were forced into an "economy of enjoyment" that they did not control. The performative nature of such an economy—"pleasurable" sexual service—must be carefully interrogated.

If we consider the brothel as a microcosm of racial and gendered social relations of eighteenth-century Barbados, we might understand it as a site where varying degrees of power are played out. Polgreen inhabited a liminal space within larger Bridgetown society. Though free, she was a woman of color whose racial, gendered, and sexual markers confined her to a particular economic function. She could have never inhabited the role of "wife" as did white women of her time, and she sustained a vulnerability to white society's legal and social regulation and control of black bodies. Through her will, we understand she made connections with elite white males and their families. She also acquired the means to survive at a higher economic level than many of her free peers. This, too, depended on her buying into a system of slavery from which she was not far removed. Within her brothel, then, racial and gendered meaning (that is, hierarchies based on race and gender) sustained her liminal place within Bridgetown while further subjugating the women and men she owned.

Henri Lefebvre argues that "the city and the urban cannot be understood without *institutions* springing from relations of class and property."[80] The brothel, then, might be imagined as a space where "that zero degree of social conceptualization" is articulated.[81] The institution of the brothel cannot be imagined as space where enslaved women were empowered by the mode of (sexual) production. Imagining the space in this way extricates both the site of the brothel and the women who labored therein from the social and racial hierarchies that made the brothel possible in the first place. These relations between enslaved sexual laborers and their patrons depended on degrading racial and gendered codes that placed enslaved women in subjugation and rendered them lascivious, sexually deviant, and whorish. Moreover, "sexual intercourse, regardless of whether it is coerced or consensual, comes to describe the arrangements, however violent, between men and enslaved women."[82] And in the historical literature, sexual intercourse becomes the means by which power is ascribed to enslaved women.[83]

The transatlantic context of prostitution illuminates the expectation of the men who employed enslaved and free women for sexual services. By the late eighteenth century, prostitution was widespread in English port cities such as London and Liverpool. London in particular experienced a rise in hotels known throughout the city as "houses of ill-repute."[84] In the mid–eighteenth century, boroughs such as Covent Garden gained a reputation for an overabundance of "disorderly women," and maritime slang depicted illicit sexual activity. Artwork by William Hogarth and Thomas Rowlandson, for example, represent tavern culture, "loose women," sailors, and prostitutes with sexually suggestive captions such as "Jack got safe into port with his prize," and "Launching a Frigate."[85] The sailors and military men sailing to the West Indies carried expectations of paid sexual services based on their experiences with prostitutes in such English cities. Most of the prostitutes who worked in London were lower-class white women. They, too, provided pleasure to meet the expectations of their patrons. Central to my argument is the strikingly different nature of enslaved prostitution; in the case of enslaved women, their racial, gendered, and non-class status kept them in a particularly subaltern position. These acts of sexual servitude thus reproduced not an equal relation of power but rather that of owner and owned, patriarch and submissive female. In essence, enslaved women forced to prostitute themselves for the pleasure of white males (re)produced degrading and violent racialized inequality. For the enslaved black women forced to labor in this particular manner, their "personal desire or erotic interests" could not exist.[86] These enslaved women were forced to serve the desires of the paying male without compensation and without a guaranteed avenue to "freedom." It is precisely due to the type of labor extracted from an enslaved female body that denies the possibility of pain or pleasure, rape and violence. I argue therefore that we cannot collapse this particular form sexualized labor into definitions of "prostitution," for it more closely resembles ritualized rape, and we must be critical when ascribing agency to enslaved women in these contexts.

We clearly see through this meditation how silences in the archive of women of color in slave societies bury the narratives of the most subaltern. Overshadowed by Polgreen's metanarrative of material success, nearly all the women she owned disappear as quickly as they are mentioned in her will. This essay therefore presents new research from late-eighteenth-century deeds that enable a fuller revision of Polgreen's narrative by shifting the focus to a woman she owned. As stated previously, in her will Polgreen requested that four women be freed upon her death. One of the women, Joanna (who was given her own still-enslaved son and also a woman named Amber) appears several times in succession in the register of deeds for this period. There are many aspects of Joanna's and Amber's lives that we will never know. Indeed, Amber disappears completely from the historical record. These fleeting glimpses through a historical aperture that closes too fast make it nearly impossible to string events together in a neat narrative. Nevertheless, the information in these documents and the time frame of their production allude to Joanna Polgreen's destitute circumstances in "freedom," her complicated labor negotiation and relationship with her former owner, the role of the military in the support and perpetuation of brothel culture, and the vulnerability of free people of color to white legal and economic power.

On July 20, 1793, two years after Rachael Pringle Polgreen's death, Captain Henry Carter ("mariner") and William Willoughby ("gentleman") gave a deposition affirming that in 1779 or 1780, "they knew a certain Negro or Mulatto Slave named Joanna who had been the property of Rachael Pringle Polgreen & by her Sold or conveyed to one Joseph Haycock who was a Servant to General Ackland or Soldier in the Regiment. . . . And that the Said Joseph Haycock did manumit and set free by Deed of Manumission the Said Joanna now known by the name of Jo-anna Polgreen."[87] Carter and Willoughby made this deposition to act as witnesses to Joanna's freedom, as "they ha[d] heard & been told by the Said Joanna Polgreen that it [was] alleged that her manumission was lost in the Hurrycane" of October 1780, and so "at her particular request the Deponents came forward to prove and maintain the freedom of the Said Joanna Polgreen."[88]

At first glance this deposition appears to support the narrative of enslaved women and their "room to maneuver" toward freedom in an urban slave society.[89] Consistent with the literature on the military in Barbados and the sexual uses to which enslaved women were subjected, Haycock likely met Joanna in Polgreen's brothel and arranged for her purchase. Joanna's agency here might be easily linked with her ability to achieve her freedom through her sexual interactions with white men. However, another deed recorded earlier complicates what "freedom" actu-ally meant for many black women and reveals the cost of their survival in this slave society. On December 3, 1783, three years after her freedom was "secured," Joanna set her mark of *X* to a deed asking Rachael Pringle Polgreen to legally and formally honor a contract of indenture while supplying Joanna with food, drink, and clothing: "I the underwritten do by these Presents Bind myself in the Capac-ity of an apprentice for and during the term of Twelve years from the date hereof unto Mrs. Rachael Pringle Polgreen . . . to be in her Service and Direction. . . . And the Said Rachael Pringle Polgreen do by these presents for the respect She bears [Joanna] do hereby agree for her better maintenance to find her Victual, and Drink & [a] couple Suits of Decent apparel for her."[90]

Based on this evidence, we must assume that if Haycock did in fact free Joanna, he apparently did not provide for her maintenance. Joanna must not have been able to survive on her own. The dates of these documents and the time frame of their production allude to Joanna's destitute circumstances in "freedom," which forced her to commit herself back into an unusually long (twelve-year) indenture binding her again to Polgreen.[91] We can speculate that Joanna's use of this legal avenue stemmed from a mistrust of Polgreen's verbal promises. The language, "for the respect she bears for her," appealed to Polgreen's conscience to honor Jo-anna's request for material support. That it was necessary to ask for clothing and food forces us to consider whether Polgreen adequately provided for her slaves. It is curious too, that Joanna took Polgreen's last name, perhaps to establish her status as a free black woman. However, Joanna Polgreen's short-lived "freedom" (1779–80 to 1783) and her "voluntary" indenture challenges narratives of success and privileges afforded to free(d) women of color in the urban context.

In his short biography of Rachel Pringle Polgreen, historian Jerome Handler described Joanna's relationship to Rachel Polgreen in the following terms: "Two other slaves [Richard and Amber] were bequeathed to a *slave* woman [Joannah]

who *won* her freedom under the terms of Rachael's will."[92] But these additional
sources show that Joanna's freedom was not so easily "won" nor retained. What
then, did "freedom" mean in such a society? Joanna sought to indenture herself in
1783 for the period of twelve years. Polgreen died before the end of Joanna's contract, and in her will freed her "Negro Woman Joanna" with no language clarifying
the nature of Joanna's status. Was she to be freed from contract or from slavery?
Perhaps, even more troubling, Joanna sought to substantiate her freedom based
on circumstances outside of Polgreen's will—from her manumission by Joseph
Haycock around 1780. Had she been freed in Polgreen's will, there would have been
no need for Joanna to elicit the testimony of two white men in an effort to prove
her free status—this status of freedom always ever under suspicion and under the
threat of being stolen. If the executors of Rachael Pringle Polgreen's will had in
fact performed her bequests, then Joanna would have been freed in 1791, thereby
terminating the labor contract she had negotiated in 1783.

In many ways the certain details of Joanna's life have been eradicated by the
processes of historical production. As Trouillot makes clear, "power is constitutive
of the story."[93] One final source provides a glimpse of an otherwise invisible person,
raising more questions than the document will answer. On August 1, 1800, Joanna
freed her son, Richard Brathwaite, "for Divers good causes & considerations . . . and
in consideration of the Sum of Ten Shillings to [her] in hand paid by Wm. Gowdey
Joslyne for the use and Purpose of [her] manumitting and freeing him."[94] It may
have taken Joanna nine years to secure her freedom or the money to free her son
from slavery.[95] She may have sold her body in order to sustain herself. We do not
know the identity of Richard's father nor her relationship with William Gowdey
Joslyne. It is clear, however, that Joanna's enduring persistence freed her son, and
their relationship may have shaped the circumstances surrounding the previous
deeds.

Given Joanna's complicated labor negotiation and relationship with her former
owner, the role of the military in the support and perpetuation of enslaved brothel
culture, and the vulnerability of free people of color to white legal and economic
power, I ask us to reexamine what it means to valorize Polgreen's "successes" in
the face of the violence she may have endured herself in slavery and certainly the
violence she may have perpetuated. Planters, merchants, white elites, and the
British colonial government created a system of economic development that set
the terms of success in Barbados: slave ownership and material accumulation
based on white supremacy and the bodily exploitation of "other(ed) humans." This
system also depended on a systematic sexual exploitation of enslaved women.
The military complex, sustained by the British Royal Navy, whose presence in the
eighteenth-century West Indies protected British economic and political interests,
was serviced by the informal sexual economy of enslaved prostitution.

Central to debates on "enslaved agency" and resistance in contemporary scholarship on slavery are the ways in which agency has been gendered and sexualized concerning enslaved women and women of color in slave societies and their sexual relations with white men. Moreover, even a feminist intervention on the definitions of agency might be revised if we focus specifically on Rachael Pringle Polgreen. Polgreen's status rested on the axis of different types of power. First, the archive that produces the record of her material life was created and sustained by white colonial power. This power is replicated in subsequent narratives of her lived "experiences" in the secondary literature. Also, the power attributed to Polgreen as slaveholder and brothel keeper must be understood within the context of the processes (techniques, mechanisms, and strategies) that enable a formerly enslaved woman to own other women of similar racialization and to coerce them into a sexual economy from which the benefits for them were not necessarily freedom and economic independence.[96] It is not my intention to separate Polgreen from the system of racial and gendered domination within which she lived. Instead, I want to emphasize the particularities of that system that rendered her choices and the limits of her actions therein. A glance back at the system of slavery operating in eighteenth-century Bridgetown reveals the racial and gendered hierarchies in place (where white male supremacy dominated and black women were placed at the bottom of the social hierarchy) and the implicit (white) societal desire for a sexual outlet for white men, both resident and transient. Polgreen's power and agency "are not the residue of an undominated self that existed prior to the operations of power but are themselves the products of these operations."[97] In other words, Polgreen's economic and social power was produced by the system of slavery in place and was not harnessed by her in an effort to subvert that system.[98]

The scholarship on Rachael Pringle Polgreen centers on her success as a businesswoman. Certainly, she was an iconic figure whose life story has captured historians' attention into the twenty-first century. Yet I would argue that understanding how she came by her "success" is just as important as the unusual position she occupied in eighteenth-century Bridgetown—a quintessential slave society ruled by the commodification of black bodies. If Polgreen's success depended on owning slaves and the forced sexual labor she demanded from the women she enslaved, then those enslaved women's stories are also vital to understanding the nuances of gender and power in slave societies.

In this essay I contend that knowing more about Rachel Pringle Polgreen's relationships with the women whose labor she owned changes the way we imagine Polgreen and also questions narratives of black women's "success" within slave societies. But even more, unraveling Polgreen's seemingly unyielding story forces us to also reconsider how we produce histories of enslaved and free(d) women of color in the Atlantic world using archives that significantly limit our efforts to access their lives.

Their core experiences, shaped by sexual violence and impossible choices, are not necessarily fully elucidated by progressive notions of agency. Without discounting the imperative in historical scholarship since the 1960s to recover enslaved agency against attempts to render the enslaved as passive and utterly dominated, I ask us to consider now what other facets of enslaved lives we can discover beyond these heroic stories of resistance and survival. Agency cannot be examined outside the constraints of slavery's systematic mechanisms of domination. Joanna's desperate circumstances, read in tandem with Polgreen's success, make it difficult to write of Polgreen separate from her troubling power. Despite the effort to recover enslaved women from the "archive's mortuary," those most disposable in their exchangeability and commodification—the thirty-seven other men, women, and children owned by Polgreen at her death—remain confined by slavery's archive.

Notes

Reprinted from *Gender & History*, 22, no. 3 (November 2010): 564–84.

1. I take this quote from Saidiya Hartman, "Venus in Two Acts," *small axe* 26 (June 2008), where Hartman describes how the invisibility of enslaved women in the archive is sometimes disrupted by "an act of chance or disaster" (2). This essay is an attempt to point out exactly how Rachael Pringle Polgreen comes to be known—at different moments reified and at others despised or celebrated but all of which characterize her in a spectacular manner. J. W. Orderson, *Creoleana: Or, Social and Domestic Scenes and Incidents in Barbados in the Days or Yore and The Fair Barbadian and Faithful Black*, ed. John Gilmore (Oxford: Macmillan, 2002). Only Caribbean historian Melanie Newton has critiqued Orderson's *Creoleana* (1842) through a contextual examination of the politics, biases, and debates that infused his novel. See Melanie J. Newton, *The Children of Africa in the Colonies: Free People of Color in Barbados in the Age of Emancipation* (Baton Rouge: Louisiana State University Press, 2008), 258–62. I employ the term *free(d)* here and throughout the essay to refer to the status of people of color like Polgreen, who became free through manumission, in an effort to encompass the varied possibilities of "status" in Bridgetown's slave society.

2. See Orderson, *Creoleana*. See also Jerome S. Handler, *The Unappropriated People: Freedmen in the Slave Society of Barbados* (Baltimore: Johns Hopkins University Press, 1974); Roger Norman Buckley, *The British Army in the West Indies: Society and the Military in the Revolutionary Age* (Gainesville: University Press of Florida, 1998); Hilary McD. Beckles, *Centering Woman: Gender Discourses in Caribbean Slave Society* (Kingston: Ian Randle, 1999); Pedro Welch and Richard Goodridge, *"Red" and Black over White: Free Coloured Women in Pre-Emancipation Barbados* (Bridgetown: Carib Research and Publications, 2000); Newton, *Children of Africa*; Pedro Welch, *Slave Society in the City: Bridgetown, Barbados 1680–1834* (Kingston: Ian Randle, 2003).

3. See Handler, *Unappropriated People*; Buckley, *British Army in the West Indies*; Beckles, *Centering Woman*; Welch and Goodridge, *"Red" and Black over White*; Newton, *Children of Africa*; Pedro Welch, *Slave Society in the City*.

4. Newton, *Children of Africa*, 61.

5. Free(d) and enslaved women's predominant participation as "hucksters" in the informal produce and commodity markets in town exemplified the alternative to prostitution. See Newton, *Children of Africa*.

6. See Hilary Beckles, "White Women and Slavery in the Caribbean," *History Workshop Journal* 36 (1993): 66–82.

7. Hilary Beckles, *Natural Rebels: A Social History of Enslaved Black Women in Barbados* (New Brunswick, N.J.: Rutgers University Press, 1989), 143–44.

8. Gayatri Spivak, "Can the Subaltern Speak?," in *Marxism and the Interpretation of Culture*, ed. Lawrence Grossberg and Carl Nelson (Urbana: University of Illinois Press, 1988): 271–315.

9. Buckley, *British Army in the West Indies*, 165.

10. Hartman, "Venus in Two Acts," 6.

11. Richard Dunn, "Barbados Census of 1680: Profile of the Richest Colony in English America," *William and Mary Quarterly*, 3rd ser., 26 (1969): 8–9, cited in Handler, *Unappropriated People*, 8.

12. See Beckles, *Centering Woman*; Richard Dunn, *Sugar and Slaves: The Rise of the Planter Class in the English West Indies* (Chapel Hill: University of North Carolina Press, 1972); Handler, *Unappropriated People*; and Welch, *Slave Society in the City*.

13. Newton, *Children of Africa*, 27.

14. Handler, *Unappropriated People*, 15–28; Newton, *Children of Africa*, 27–28.

15. For the original iteration of this narrative, see Orderson, *Creoleana*, 76.

16. Beckles, *Natural Rebels*, 9. See also Jennifer L. Morgan's *Laboring Women: Reproduction and Gender in New World Slavery* (Philadelphia: University of Pennsylvania Press, 2004), wherein her careful research reveals planters' in Barbados (and later the Carolinas) pattern of reliance on an enslaved female workforce for both labor and reproduction (84–85).

17. Beckles, *Natural Rebels*, 14–15.

18. Beckles, "White Women and Slavery," 69–70.

19. See Beckles, *Natural Rebels*; Barbados Bush, *Slave Women in Caribbean Slave Society, 1650–1838* (Kingston: Heinemann, 1990). While Beckles's work seeks to make the lives and resistances of a black female majority in Barbados historically visible, Bush thematically characterizes the lives of enslaved women throughout the Caribbean, highlighting the specific roles that enslaved women inhabited primarily on the plantation. It must also be noted that Deborah Gray White's text, *Ar'n't I a Woman? Female Slaves in the Plantation South* (New York: W.W. Norton, 1985), pioneered in the effort to document the experiences of enslaved women in the antebellum United States.

20. Handler, *Unappropriated People*; Handler, "Joseph Rachell and Rachael Pringle-Polgreen: Petty Entrepreneurs," in *Struggle and Survival in Colonial America*, ed. David Sweet and Gary Nash (Berkeley: University of California Press, 1981), 376–91.

21. Handler, *Unappropriated People*, 134.

22. Handler, "Joseph Rachell and Rachael Pringle-Polgreen," 383.

23. Handler, *Unappropriated People*, 134–35.

24. See, for example, Beckles, *Centering Woman*; Welch, *Slave Society in the City*; Newton, *Children of Africa*.

25. See Orderson, *Creoleana*; Sir Algernon Aspinall, "Rachel Pringle of Barbados," *Journal of the Barbados Museum and Historical Society* 9, no. 3 (May 1942): 112–19; Joel Augustus Rogers, *Sex and Race: Negro-Caucasian Mixing in All Ages and All Lands* (J. A. Rodgers, 1944); Neville Connell, "Prince William Henry's Visits to Barbados in 1786 and 1787," *Journal of the Barbados Museum and Historical Society* 25, no. 4 (August 1958): 157–64; Handler, *Unappropriated People*; Karl S. Watson, "The Civilised Island: Barbados a Social History, 1750–1816" (PhD diss., University of Florida, 1975); F. A. Hoyos, *Barbados: A History from the Amerindians to Independence* (London: Macmillan, 1978); Handler, "Joseph Rachel and Rachel Pringle Polgreen"; Hilary Beckles, *Black Rebellion in Barbados: The Struggle against Slavery, 1627–1838* (Bridgetown: Antilles Press, 1984); Beckles, *Natural Rebels*; Bush, *Slave Women in Caribbean Society*; Bernard Bailyn and Philip D. Morgan, eds., *Strangers within the Realm: Cultural Margins of the First British Empire* (Chapel Hill: University of North Carolina Press and Institute of Early American History and Culture, 1991); Christine Barrow, *Family in the Caribbean: Themes and Perspectives* (Princeton, N.J.: Markus Wiener, 1998); Buckley, *British Army in the West Indies*; Verene Shepherd, *Women in Caribbean History: The British-Colonised Territories* (Kingston: Ian Randle, 1999); Lennox Honeychurch, *Caribbean People* (Cheltenham, England: Nelson Thornes, 2000); Warren Alleyne, *Historic Bridgetown* (St. Michael: Barbados Government Information Service, 2003); Felicity Nussbaum, *The Limits of the Human: Fictions of Anomaly, Race, and Gender in the Long Eighteenth Century* (Cambridge: Cambridge University Press, 2003); Welch, *Slave Society in the City*; David Barry Gaspar and Darlene Clark Hine, eds., *Beyond Bondage: Free Women of Color in the Americas* (Champaign: University of Illinois Press, 2004); Pamela Scully and Diana Paton, eds., *Gender and Slave Emancipation in the Atlantic World* (Durham, N.C.: Duke University Press, 2005); "Rachel Pringle, the Notorious Barbadian Madamme," http://tinyurl.com/zf37rjs (accessed January 21, 2016); Cecily Jones, *Engendering Whiteness: White Women and Colonialism in Barbados and North Carolina, 1627–1865* (Manchester: Manchester University Press, 2007); Newton, *Children of Africa*.

26. Welch, *Slave Society in the City*, 170.

27. Welch, *Slave Society in the City*, 48 and 89.

28. Beckles, *Centering Woman*, 22–23.

29. See Saidiya Hartman, *Scenes of Subjection: Terror and Self-Making in Nineteenth-Century America* (New York: Oxford University Press, 1997); Darlene Clark Hine, "Rape and the Inner Lives of Black Women in the Middle West: Preliminary Thoughts on the Culture of Dissemblance," in *Words of Fire: An Anthology of African American Feminist Thought*, ed. Beverly Guy-Sheftall (New York: New York Press, 1995), 380–88.

30. Michel-Rolph Trouillot, *Silencing the Past: Power and the Production of History* (Boston: Beacon Press, 1995), 29.

31. I thank anonymous reviewer 2 for bringing this important historiographical point to my attention.

32. Hartman, *Scenes of Subjection*, 10.

33. Handler, "Joseph Rachell and Rachael Pringle-Polgreen," 383. See also the introduction to the edited edition of *Creoleana*, in which Gilmore makes reference to another version of Polgreen's possible origins: "Her master [not William Lauder] came from Windward, [St. Philip Parish, a rural parish on the south coast of the island] was indicted or punished for stealing a cow, and [Rachael] continued to reside in Bridgetown," 236.

34. Records of Baptisms and Burials, St. Michael Parish Church, July 23, 1791, RL1/5: 538, Barbados Department of Archives, hereinafter referenced as BDA. William Lauder was her owner; her last name was presumably given by him.

35. Estate inventory of Rachael Pringle Polgreen, August 13, 1791, BDA. For a discussion of the monetary accumulation of free women of color in Bridgetown, see Welch, *Slave Society in the City*, 166–81.

36. This calculation is based solely on Polgreen's estate inventory. Based on his reading of Polgreen's will, Jerome Handler writes in *Unappropriated People* that Polgreen owned nineteen. In order to address this inconsistency, I used the inventory list as opposed to the more general language of Polgreen's will, wherein she refers to her unnamed enslaved people (those not explicitly freed) as "All the Rest, Residue and Remainder of my Estate, real and personal, here or elsewhere." Will of Rachael Pringle Polgreen, July 21, 1791, RB6/19: 435–36, BDA.

37. In various documents, including Polgreen's will and deeds in which Joanna appears, her name is spelled both with and without an *h*.

38. Will of Rachael Pringle Polgreen, July 21, 1791, RB6/19:435–36, BDA. In an attempt to track the manumissions of the women Polgreen requested be freed in her will, I traced manumission payments in the St. Michael Parish Vestry Minutes from 1780 through 1788 and 1789 through 1805. Any slaveholder wishing to manumit an enslaved person was to pay fifty pounds to the church vestry in the parish where she or he resided (this fee was raised to three hundred pounds in 1800 to discourage manumissions). I found no evidence that such manumission fees were paid for those Polgreen wished to free during the above-mentioned years. I could speculate that the individuals may appear in a deed, or their freedom effected through means that would have avoided payment of manumission such as willing them to others as enslaved but with the understanding they were to live as "free"; as J. W. Orderson explains, "White men, who in general (it being often a stipulation with their favourite) purchase [enslaved women] of their owners, in many instances their own parent,—and subsequently giving a certificate on the back of the deed of sale, annulling their right of property in the person of their favourite, in like manner give them a freedom not recognized by the laws." Orderson, *Cursory Remarks and Plain Facts Connected with the Question Produced by the Proposed Slave Registry Bill* (London: Hatchard, Piccadilly; Hamilton, Paternoster Row, and J. M. Richardson, 1816), 16, New York Public Library, hereinafter referenced as NYPL).

39. See John Gilmore, "A Note on the Illustrations," in Orderson's *Creoleana*, viii; Handler, *Unappropriated People*, 135.

40. Gilmore, introduction to *Creoleana*, 1–18.

41. Aspinall, "Rachel Pringle of Barbados," 114.

42. Editorial, "Polgreen of Barbados," *Journal of the Barbados Museum and Historical Society* 9, no. 3 (May 1942): 109.

43. We know very little of how she acquired this name. In the historical works that write of Rachael Pringle Polgreen, none have ventured to discover Mr. Polgreen's identity. For a summary sketch and unverifiable speculation of his life, see John Gilmore's notes to *Creoleana*, 235–39. Additionally, a James Polgreen appears in the Bridgetown levy records in 1780 as the owner of several properties, but no clear linkage between he and Rachael Pringle

Polgreen has been established. It is possible, however, that Rachael Polgreen forged a relationship with a Mr. Polgreen similar to her "relationship" with Captain Thomas Pringle.

44. See Beckles, *Natural Rebels*, 72–89; Newton, *Children of Africa*, 34–35, 105–6. Similar to the experiences of free women of color in the United States during slavery, free(d)
Afro-Barbadian women faced stigmatism for their "public" visibility. Due to racial and
gendered stereotypes of their immorality stemming from their public roles as market
women and tavern keepers, some Afro-Barbadian women sought to distance themselves
from these images through philanthropic and religious work. I thank anonymous reviewer
2 for bringing this point to my attention.

45. Thomas Rowlandson (1757–1827) was a half-French, half-English portrait and
landscape painter and social satirist painter. He was a contemporary of William Hogarth,
whose work influenced many of Rowlandson's scenes of Georgian English life.

46. Editorial, "Polgreen of Barbados."

47. Trouillot, *Silencing the Past*, 28–29.

48. Polgreen signed her will with an *X*, indicating that she was likely illiterate.

49. Gilmore, introduction to Orderson's *Creoleana*, 3.

50. Though Polgreen lacked literacy, she clearly understood the power of the written word. Over the course of three years, she placed at least three advertisements in the
Barbados Gazette or the General Intelligencer, the first of which appears in the January 26–30,
1788, edition advertising a lost gold ring. The next was an advertisement for lost silver-
ware, January 31–February 4, 1789, *Barbados Gazette or the General Intelligencer*. Finally, she
advertised for a raffle of "paintings in oil" as well as her hosting a portrait taker named
T.G., who offered accurate portraits to customers "nothing required," February 4–7, 1789.
Bridgetown Public Library, hereinafter referenced as BPL.

51. Newton, *Children of Africa*, 259.

52. See Orderson, *Creoleana*, 91–92, describing the tale of a young African boy named
Prince who in the service of a ship is given the chance to return to his kinsmen in "Da-
home." Instead of accepting freedom, Prince returns to Barbados and enslavement, pro-
claiming that "he liked the white people's ways, and their victuals and dress, and all that
something in backara country, which he no have in he own." As a moral lesson directed
at the antislavery debate, Orderson offers that recollection "to the consideration of the
Anti-Slavery Society, and generally to the friends of the African race" (*Creoleana*, 91–92).

53. Newton, *Children of Africa*, 259. See also pages 259–62, where Newton critically
engages the gendered and racial context and content of Orderson's *Creoleana*.

54. See also Gilmore, introduction to Orderson's *Creoleana*, 13.

55. Orderson, *Cursory Remarks*, 16, NYPL.

56. Orderson, *Cursory Remarks*, 16, NYPL.

57. Orderson, *Cursory Remarks*, 16, NYPL.

58. Orderson, *Creoleana*, 76. The town "jumper" referred specifically to a person who
earned money by being hired to whip "disobedient" slaves. This man was hired by particular owners or went door-to-door inquiring of the residents if they had slaves to be
punished. The "jumper" was also ordered by the town governmental authorities (mag-
istrates, judges, etc.) to whip particular slaves as punishment if they were found guilty
of particular actions that violated the Barbados Slave Codes. Pedro Welch contends that

"in Bridgetown, and elsewhere in the Caribbean, the occupation of the driver [in the context of a plantation] was replaced in the urban context by that of 'constable,' or 'jumper'" (*Slave Society in the City*, 13).

59. Orderson, *Creoleana*, 76.

60. Hortense Spillers, "'The Permanent Obliquity of an In(Pha)llibly Straight': In the Time of the Daughters and the Fathers," in *Black, White, and in Color: Essays on American Literature and Culture* (Chicago: University of Chicago Press, 2003), 249.

61. Spillers, "'Permanent Obliquity,'" 249.

62. See also, Doris Garraway's discussion of incest and miscegenation in the eighteenth-century French Caribbean. In *The Libertine Colony: Creolization in the Early French Caribbean* (Durham, N.C.: Duke University Press, 2005), Garraway argues that incest perpetuated by the white father-master against his "mixed-race" daughter-slave was inherent "in a society where white men placed themselves in the position of symbolic fathers of all the races, and biological fathers of free people of color in particular, while at the same time erecting a cult of desire around mixed-race women and fantasizing their effective sterility, [in such a society] the structure of interracial desire was decidedly incestuous" (34).

63. Orderson, *Creoleana*, 76–77.

64. Orderson, *Creoleana*, 76–78.

65. Orderson, *Creoleana*, 78. See also Connell, "Prince William Henry's Visits," 157–64.

66. Orderson, *Creoleana*, 79.

67. Orderson, *Creoleana*, 79.

68. Orderson, *Creoleana*, 79.

69. See for example, Handler, *Unappropriated People*; Welch, *Slave Society in the City*.

70. This editorial, found in the original 1842 issue of the *Barbadian*, was located with information gleaned from Neville Connell, "Prince William Henry's Visits."

71. Editorial, May 21, 1842, *Barbadian*, BPL.

72. Gilmore, introduction to Orderson's *Creoleana*, 16.

73. "Advertisement by Rachael-Pringle Polgreen for a lost gold ring," in *Barbados Gazette or the General Intelligencer*, Saturday, January 31, to Wednesday, February 4, 1789, BPL. This advertisement was also found with information from Connell's "Prince William Henry's Visits," 164.

74. Orderson, *Creoleana*, 78; Connell, "Prince William Henry's Visits," 164.

75. Newton, *Children of Africa*, 169.

76. Testimony gathered by the Privy Council of the British Parliament on the slave trade and slavery in the colonies, *House of Commons Sessional Papers of the Eighteenth Century*, ed. Sheila Lambert (Wilmington, Del.: Scholarly Resources, 1975), 82:203. Rachael Pringle Polgreen remains an elusive figure in the archives and more-recent historical accounts. Her names alone leave the scholar perplexed about how she referred to herself. Throughout her archive, she is referred to as Rachael Pringle, Rachael Pringle Polgreen, Mrs. Pringle Polgreen (in one newspaper advertisement referring to her hotel), and Rachael Lauder. According to the novel and subsequent historical accounts, William Lauder owned Polgreen before she acquired her freedom from Captain Thomas Pringle. In this particular archival document, she appears as Rachael Lauder, though one can speculate

that many who knew her referred to her as Rachael Pringle. In the 1842 newspaper editorial, the anonymous author refers to her as "old Rachael Lauder," perhaps to discount her self-naming as she took the last names of elite white men with whom she was allegedly involved. The fact of her multiple namings in various sources reflects perfectly the archival power to which Polgreen had little access.

77. *House of Commons Sessional Papers*, ed. Lambert.

78. Hartman, "Venus in Two Acts," 5.

79. See the Estate Inventory of Rachael Pringle Polgreen, 1791, BDA. At the time of her death, she also owned three boats.

80. Henri Lefebvre, *The Production of Space* (Oxford: Blackwell, 1991), 106, emphasis in original.

81. Hortense Spillers, "Mama's Baby, Papa's Maybe: An American Grammar Book," in *Black, White, and in Color: Essays on American Literature and Culture* (Chicago: University of Chicago Press, 2003), 206.

82. Hartman, *Scenes of Subjection,* 85.

83. See, for example, Handler, *Unappropriated People*; Douglas G. Hall, *In Miserable Slavery: Thomas Thistlewood in Jamaica, 1750–86* (Kingston: University of the West Indies Press, 1999); Buckley, *British Army in the West Indies*.

84. See Tony Henderson, *Disorderly Women in Eighteenth-Century London: Prostitution and Control in the Metropolis, 1730–1830* (New York: Pearson Education, 1999).

85. See, for example, David Dabydeen, *Hogarth's Blacks: Images of Blacks in Eighteenth-Century English Art* (Athens: University of Georgia Press, 1987); Osbert Sitwell, *Famous Water-Colour Painters: Thomas Rowlandson*, vol. 6 (London: The Studio Limited, 1929).

86. Julia O'Connell Davidson, "The Rights and Wrongs of Prostitution," *Hypatia* 17, no. 2 (2002): 86.

87. RB3/40: 442, Recopied Deed Record Books, BDA.

88. RB3/40: 442, Recopied Deed Record Books, BDA.

89. See Welch, *Slave Society in the City*, 89.

90. RB3/40: 441, Recopied Deed Record Books, BDA.

91. Typically indenture contracts for this period were between four and seven years. I thank my colleague Gunther Peck for bringing to my attention the significance of the unusually long time frame of this indenture.

92. Handler, "Joseph Rachell and Rachael Pringle-Polgreen," 387, my emphasis.

93. Trouillot, *Silencing the Past*, 28.

94. Deeds RB3/40: 445, Recopied Deed Record Books, BDA.

95. At this time manumission fees in the amount of 50 pounds were paid to the parish church vestry. Manumission fees would be raised in 1801 to 300 pounds for female slaves and 200 for male.

96. Saba Mahmood, *Politics of Piety: Islamic Revival and the Feminist Subject* (Princeton, N.J.: Princeton University Press, 2005), 17.

97. Mahmood, *Politics of Piety*, 17.

98. Mahmood, *Politics of Piety*, 5–9.

CHAPTER 8

The Curse of Canaan; or, A Fantasy of Origins in Nineteenth-Century America

BRIAN CONNOLLY

Writing on race in 1915, W. E. B. Du Bois came to the so-called curse of Canaan, the biblical story that had been associated with the origins of racial difference and justifications of the enslavement of Africans for several centuries. It was a curious moment in the history of race—most historians would argue that by the nineteenth century the curse was declining in significance, replaced in large part by newer, scientific accounts of race, such as climatological theories, comparative anatomy, polygenism, and ethnology. Indeed, Du Bois seems to accord the curse little lasting significance: "The biblical story of the 'curse of Canaan' (Genesis IX, 24–25) has been the basis of an astonishing literature which has to-day only a psychological interest." And, elaborating a bit, Du Bois rejected its historical veracity: "The biblical story of Shem, Ham, and Japheth retains the interest of a primitive myth with its measure of allegorical truth, but has, of course, no historic basis."[1] Du Bois would go on to account for race in somewhat different terms, but we would be rash—overdetermined by the historiography and the imperatives of modernity—to think that he was simply dismissing the curse as an atavistic trace.

"Psychological interest," "primitive myth," "allegorical truth," "astonishing literature"—these all suggest something else. Not only did the curse of Canaan still have force in the making of race in the early twentieth century—Du Bois was not alone in referring to it—but these terms also suggest that Du Bois might have thought more of it than he let on. As the literary critic Peter Coviello has argued apropos *The Souls of Black Folk*, Du Bois "labors to produce in it an account of an awful power, condensed and expressed in 'race,' that gauges its terrible efficacy and scale while recalling at all points that it lies categorically beyond the reach of any power to determine, conclusively, the nature of any person's relation to the forces of his or her own world."[2] If Du Bois is thinking of race in this manner—and Coviello is persuasive that he is—then all those terms of seeming dismissal might actually point to ways of thinking "categorically beyond the reach of any power to determine." If this is the case, then the curse of Canaan, rather than an atavistic trace, might be a key to an analytics of race.

What, however, was the curse of Canaan and what astonishing thing, in its status as primitive myth, allegorical truth, and psychological interest, can it tell us about race? The curse of Canaan (or curse of Ham, or Noah's curse, the naming of which suggests, in part, whether one emphasizes punishment, transgression, or law, respectively) derived from a story in Genesis and had been called upon, since at least the fifteenth century, to justify the enslavement of Africans. The story recounted the first postdiluvian episode in the life of Noah and his three sons, Ham, Shem, and Japheth. As the story appears in Genesis, in the days after the flood, Noah, who had planted a vineyard, found himself, at the end of a day, inebriated. In such a state, he fell asleep naked in his tent. Sometime after this his son, Ham, "saw the nakedness of his father" (which carried with it sexual connotations that became a frequent centerpiece of later hermeneutics) and, instead of respectfully covering his father's body, went and found his brothers in order for them to see their father in this less-than-authoritative state. Instead of joining in Ham's ridicule, however, Shem and Japheth chose to walk backward with a garment to cover Noah, "and they saw not their father's nakedness." Noah awoke the next day aware of Ham's transgression of filial duty and so cursed Ham's son Canaan to be the servant of servants, in particular to Shem and Japheth, both of whom had received blessings.[3]

The tendency of much writing on the curse of Canaan is to treat it as part of a centuries- (or millennia-) old narrative tradition. Thus, as David Goldenberg writes, "This biblical story has been the single greatest justification for Black slavery for more than a thousand years."[4] Werner Sollors, taking the history of the curse as a continuous, if quite complicated, interpretive history argues that, while including issues of "class structure, or human weakness," it was primarily concerned with slavery and "the origin of black skin color."[5] What these critics suggest is that, despite important historical differences, the long interpretive history of the curse is a relatively continuous history, one bounded by and grounded in the original text. This would constitute a history, then, that moves through Jewish, Christian, and Muslim exegeses, through fifteenth- and sixteenth-century justifications of the enslavement of Africans, and up through nineteenth-century iterations that attempt to make sense of racial difference in the era after democratic revolutions and of scientific racism. Historical specificity matters—and certainly most scholars simply fit a small piece into this larger epic—but it is the long interpretive tradition that has generally conferred meaning.

There are dissenters from this logic, most notably Benjamin Braude, who argues that the printing press constituted a dramatic rupture in the history of the Bible and the history of the curse.[6] And there are those, like Stephen R. Haynes and Sylvester Johnson, who devote substantial works to nineteenth-century American accounts of the curse.[7] I argue that the nineteenth century also constituted a rupture, but one of a different sort. By the late eighteenth century, most readers consumed the curse via an interpretive text, which is to say that one's encounter with Ham, Noah, Canaan, transgression, punishment, and law did not come in Genesis but rather in texts like Josiah Priest's *Slavery, as It Relates to the Negro* or Ottobouh Cugoano's *Thoughts and Sentiments on the Evil of Slavery*. Second, in the era of scientific racism, the curse offered a theory of racial origins at a moment when biblical histories were not taken as unquestioned truth. But it did provide a fantastical theory of hereditary descent and race that complemented new scientific accounts of race and held out for white pro-slavery writers the force of racial purity in the face of the social facts of interracial sex and for black ethnologists the possibility of racial identity grounded in interracial sex and thus the impossibility of racial purity, and by extension, racial hierarchies.

Finally, given that most scholars have focused on slavery, one needs to ask whether slavery required the curse of Canaan for its justification, or if, by the nineteenth century, this rationale worked to occlude other, more pressing, issues in the curse. While slavery was certainly a central question, it was the articulation of racial difference that was paramount. The curse offered a theory of race, and at times it was deployed in a manner that acknowledged that Japheth, and not Japheth and Shem, was at the top of the hierarchy. For instance, in 1868 Lydia Maria Child invoked the curse in *An Appeal for the Indians*: "And we 'nail it with Scripture,' just as we did our enslavement of the negroes," Child wrote. "'Japhet shall be enlarged, and inhabit the tents of Shem, and Canaan shall be his servant.' If the white man is Japhet, all I have to say is, he behaved in a rascally manner toward Shem and Canaan."[8] However, because the curse was usually invoked in the context of slavery, the mechanics of racial difference operated around a black/white binary, with Ham/Canaan on one side, Shem/Japheth on the other (even as Shem was never quite white). Taken together, the persistence of the curse in the nineteenth century was an effect not of its long exegetical history but rather of the way it provided an origins story of racial difference that tied sex, reproduction, kinship, and family together.

If we can comfortably call this a social construction, we must also note that it was a fantasy by which race was (and is) structured from generation to generation in terms of kinship and biology.[9] It was, then, a theological site of race striated by biology, sex, and reproduction. Indeed, insofar as we write histories of race in North America that note the increasing atavism of the curse of Canaan in the nineteenth century, we fail to consider the ways in which the curse figured the hereditary structure of race itself, a notion that persisted in the seemingly more modern scientific racism. To get at this, it might be best to forego the familiar essentialist-constructionist binary and turn instead to the psychoanalytic concept of fantasy, which points to a psychical reality that can be reduced neither to biology nor to culture. Race as fantasy thus offers a way of making sense of its persistent force, a mechanism for thinking about how power works and is articulated as a means of making sense of the world while simultaneously subjecting us. It also makes sense of why such seemingly problematic categories hold an appeal to a wide spectrum of subjects. The curse of Canaan as one of the primary modes of race as fantasy allows us to think about how a wide spectrum of subjects imagined the origins of humanity and racial difference and how seemingly outmoded ways of apprehending the world continued to structure even the most fervently progressive notions of science and human history.

As in many biblical stories, much of the efficacy of the narrative lay in its ambiguity, making it ripe for embellishment over centuries. Perhaps most obviously, there is no mention of anything suggesting race or skin color. While an exegetical practice had developed that linked the word "Ham" to blackness, this was by no means apparent in the narrative, nor did it enjoy widespread consensus in the nineteenth century. The other explanation of the link between Ham and Africa derives from the claim concerning the sons of Noah that "of them the whole earth was overspread." By the nineteenth century, the most common understanding was that Japheth and his descendants populated Europe, Shem and his descendants populated Asia and the Americas, and Ham and his descendants populated Africa. Indeed, at the end of the genealogy of the families that derived from Shem, Ham, and Japheth, we find, "These are the families of the sons of Noah, after their generations, in their nations; and by these were the nations divided in the earth after the flood" (Genesis 10:32). Thus the punishment of servitude meted out against one of Ham's sons, Canaan, combined with the geographic dispersal of Ham and his descendants to Africa, worked to justify the enslavement of Africans. Or, recursively, the transatlantic slave trade secured the relationship between Ham and Africa. While there was much disagreement about the particulars, especially regarding which descendants populated which portions of each continent, the broad dispersal was consistent through nearly every iteration of the curse.

If the absence of any explicit mention of race constituted one generative difficulty, another emerged around the figure of Canaan. Put simply, Canaan was punished for his father's transgression. In many accounts of the narrative, Canaan was not even born at the time, and thus this ambiguity in Genesis gave license to significant exegetical elaboration. Moreover, given that the curse of Canaan was frequently treated as both central to the justification of African slavery and as the most egregious and arbitrary action in the narrative, some commentators claimed that Noah was not actually cursing Canaan but rather in uttering "cursed be Canaan" demonstrating his prophetic powers—as anyone in the nineteenth-century with passing familiarity with the Bible would have known, the Canaanites were, indeed, a wicked people.[10] Rather than cursing Canaan, Noah was foretelling the coming wickedness of one of Ham's sons and his descendants.[11] While this does not change the racial order that emerged from the narrative, it does suggest that the odd temporality of the narrative itself was both in the order of the curse/prophecy and in the recursive claims about slavery and race, from the contemporary to the ancient and back again.

Perhaps most importantly, despite the centrality of sexual reproduction to the production of racial difference, there were no women in these accounts. Women were, of course, there—the narrative of Noah and the flood is nothing if not a heteronormative remaking of the world ("But with thee will I establish my covenant; and thou shalt come into the ark, thou, and thy son, and thy wife, and thy sons' wives with thee. And of every living thing of all flesh, two of every sort shalt thou bring into the ark, to keep them alive with thee; they shall be male and female" [Genesis 6:18–19]). But in the part of the narrative that concerns us here, that of Ham and his transgression and punishment, there is no mention of women. Strikingly, women were an absent presence in the (re)production of race. Striking, perhaps, but telling—this is where the turn to psychoanalysis, and fantasy specifically, in elaborating the workings of race finds its warrant.

As a project of nineteenth-century racialized kinship, the curse of Canaan was also a project in making a universal notion of humanity, riven, of course, by difference. In one sense, this was a polemical project, aimed, by midcentury, against polygenism, which claimed that there were multiple creations and thus made Africans not only "inferior" but of another type entirely. Against this, the curse of Canaan, whatever its justifications of slavery and racial hierarchies, was a project in universal humanity. As such, one should read it as part of the project of elaborating the conditions of the "human family," a project led by the ethnographer Lewis Henry Morgan, who, in John Lardas Modern's words, was engaged in an exercise of producing "a universal code that determined particular ways and means of being human."[12] Unlike Morgan, whose evolutionary schema elaborated various forms of kinship that would be progressively dropped as societies evolved toward the nuclear family, the curse of Canaan set the family as the universal form of kinship. As Mark Rifkin has written, "Populations are racialized through their insertion in a political economy shaped around a foundational distinction between public and private spheres, with the latter defined by a naturalized, nuclear ideal against which other modes of sociality appear as lack/aberrance."[13] By the nineteenth century, the curse of Canaan naturalized the nuclear ideal riven by racial difference by situating it at the postdiluvian origins of humanity.

To place the curse of Canaan in a genealogy of the human and universal humanity suggests something unsettling. Recently, the historian Walter Johnson has cautioned against blithe, unreflective uses of humanity in writing the history of slavery. Johnson insists that "dehumanization" is the wrong way to think about slavery, averring instead that "slaveholders were fully cognizant of slaves' humanity—indeed they were completely dependent upon it. But they continually attempted to conscript—simplify, channel, limit, and control—the forms that humanity could take in slavery."[14] Another way of putting this is that slavery and racial fantasies like the curse of Canaan are not dehumanizing, which suggests that they are aberrations in the utopian, emancipatory project of being human. Rather, they are integral moments in that genealogy, in which case, if the curse of Canaan is one theory of universal humanity, then what is it, precisely, to be human?

Despite its association with racial hierarchies and slavery, the curse of Canaan and its fantasy of racial origins were not confined to pro-slavery writers. Indeed, it was nearly as frequently engaged with by both white antislavery writers and writers of the black diaspora. While theirs was a critical engagement, refuting the conclusions of African savagery and barbarism that pro-slavery writers produced and endorsed, they nonetheless turned to the curse and the Noahic genealogy of race to make claims on humanity. Although they frequently did so in terms suggesting that sexual reproduction was not such a neat affair when it came to racial purity, and that turning to biblical genealogies of race provided evidence not of the separate posterities of Shem, Japheth, and Ham but of their mutual, reproductive entanglement, they nonetheless did not get outside the universalizing impulses that an attachment to Noah provided. The curse of Canaan proved an efficacious fantasy of race regardless of one's position on slavery.

While the curse has a history that stretches across centuries and has frequently been apprehended over the *longue durée*, I am less interested in the long history of the curse than in its significations and efficacies in the age of scientific racism. I am also more concerned with the multiple deployments of the Noahic genealogy of racial difference. In thinking of the curse of Canaan as one particularly powerful fantasy of race, we can also think of race as a kinship system and the theories needed to sustain that fantasy. If the fantasy persisted as a common explanation of both racial difference and the enslavement of Africans, it was also a fertile field for the critical theorizations of race proffered by black ethnologists. The curse of Canaan has, for the most part, been confined to histories of race and slavery, which is more than understandable. However, it should be as much a part of histories of sexuality, family, and kinship. Indeed, the Noahic genealogy perpetuated by the curse of Canaan was both an articulation of universal humanity figured in familial terms—all people could be traced back to a founding family, or, in the words of the mid-nineteenth-century minister Philip Schaff, humanity was "the future posterity of the three patriarchs of the human family"—and, in its narrativization of the origins of race, the introduction of difference into that universal humanity.[15] In other words, it was kinship with difference. This fantasy was the field in which identities were forged, subjugations articulated, and desire structured. And by making the familial form universal and perpetuated by the (sovereign and nonsovereign) sexual transmission of race, it held out a singular humanity cut by racial inequality.

Race as Fantasy

For the past several decades a small (but growing) cadre of critics have been calling for a turn to psychoanalysis as an analytic through which to think about race. This has been a tense call—as Jean Walton wrote in 1995, "Psychoanalysis has not been seriously considered a likely arena for the exploration and critique of racialized constructions of subjectivity."[16] Hortense Spillers has similarly noted this tension, with a particular attention to African American history: "Little or nothing in the intellectual history of African Americans within the social and political context of the United States suggests the effectiveness of a psychoanalytic discourse, revised or classical, in illuminating the problematic of 'race' on an intersubjective field of play, nor do we know how to historicize the psychoanalytic object and objective, invade its hereditary premises and insulations, and open its insights to cultural and social forms that are disjunctive to its originary imperatives."[17] Spillers, Walton, and others have, of course, done much to change this.[18] They suggest that psychoanalysis, while focused on the irresolvability of sexual difference, also allows us to begin to make sense of the immovability of race. Which is to say, if we have demonstrated over the last several decades that race is "socially constructed" and historically contingent, neither approach seems capable of accounting for the implacable persistence of race. As Kalpana Seshadri-Crooks writes, "The investment we make in appearance is beyond simple historical or material explanation, and . . . only by exploring the psychical import of race . . . could [one] hope to understand its resilient non-sense."[19] It is, perhaps the "non-sense" of race that makes the curse of Canaan, which scholars have called "strange and confusing" and marked by "oddities and difficulties," a particularly fecund site for exploring race as fantasy.[20] Indeed, even in the nineteenth century, commentators on the curse noted its non-sense. As one antislavery author wrote in 1862, "The prophecy concerning Ham is obscure and obviously elliptical."[21]

The psychoanalytic concept of fantasy is one way of getting at the psychic *and* material dimensions of race. Indeed, a quick perusal of Christopher Lane's introduction to *The Psychoanalysis of Race* suggests as much—fantasy is one of the most frequently used terms.[22] As any number of psychoanalytically oriented critics have noted, fantasy means something quite particular when addressed in this register.[23] Which is to say that it is not just an escapist imagination. As Joan Wallach Scott puts it, we should "consider fantasy as a formal mechanism for the articulation of scenarios that are at once historically specific in their representation and detail and transcendent of historical specificity."[24] One might see the curse of Canaan in such a description, for it attains a historical specificity in its articulations; the nineteenth-century version is not, despite the appearance of similar source material, the same as the sixteenth-century version. This has to do with contemporary concerns over the articulation of race, science, and slavery in the nineteenth century, with the changing deployments of kinship and sexuality. But it also transcended history, in this case by creating an alternative historical narrative that created an immovable field in which historical experience was articulated. The curse of Canaan worked and appealed to both racist and antiracist writers precisely because it made race a transhistorical, immutable (or mutable) given. It provided an air of certainty and transcendence in the face of chaos and confusion and the more implacable social conditions of race.

Fantasy, as an analytic concept, has specific defining aspects, several of which are relevant here. Before turning to the fantasmatic nature of the curse, we might do well to deal with these briefly and schematically. First, fantasy, as Slavoj Žižek notes, "constitutes our desire, provides its co-ordinates; that is, it literally 'teaches us how to desire.'"[25] As an originary story of racial difference, one that relied on the continuity of sexual reproduction, the curse of Canaan was pedagogic, teaching racially pure desire even as it was confronted with the supposed horror of the real: interracial sex. Second, fantasy occludes some antagonism by narrativizing it. In this sense, one might think here of racial difference, which could only be figured as racial antagonism—the curse of Canaan narrativized this so that an originary racial unity existed, which was then disrupted by Ham's transgression, so that racial difference has an origin. But, and this is quite central both to fantasy and the curse itself, that lost object (in this case racial purity/unification) only came into being at the moment of its purported loss. As Žižek puts it, "The lost quality emerged only at this very moment of its alleged loss. . . . Narrativization occludes this paradox by describing the process in which the object is first given and then gets lost."[26] The curse of Canaan was, at its core, a story about the origins of racial difference that predominantly presupposed a time in history in which there were no races, only one race (whether it was "red" or "white," is, for the moment, beside the point), a moment that was lost at precisely the moment in which the world was remade after the flood. The story of Ham, Canaan, and Noah marked not only the emergence of racial difference and the loss of racial unification but also the possibility that something like racial unification could be thought. And finally, fantasy is about the installation of the Law of the Father, which in this case is also the law of racial difference.[27] As Žižek observes, "The phantasmic narrative does not state the suspension-transgression of the Law, but *the very act of its installation*, of the intervention of the cut of symbolic castration—what the fantasy endeavors to stage is ultimately the 'impossible' scene of castration."[28] While fantasy is often associated with the pleasure of transgression, Žižek directs us to the fact that fantasy stages the installation of law and thus teaches us how to desire. Is not the curse of Canaan, in its simplest sense, a story about the installation of law? Ham's transgression brings with it a punishment that also instantiated the law of racial difference, and every iteration was inscribed within this constellation of transgression, law, and punishment.

Moreover, that Law, turning on the actions of the Father (Noah), who is both the father of those children and the Symbolic Father, pertains to the world of sons and brothers, thus demonstrating the ultimate precariousness of the Father. Whatever Noah's role in the production of racial difference—and while Noah was central to the linking of Ham, Canaan, Africa, and slavery, his role in the production of racial difference is much more variable—it is a world in which he has no place. That this scenario resonates with the crimes of the primal horde in Freud's *Totem and Taboo* should be obvious, thus suggesting another transhistorical feature of the fantasy. But it also resonates with a historically specific feature of the late-eighteenth- and early-nineteenth-century United States: republicanism. The American Revolution has been frequently described as a revolt against patriarchal authority, specifically one in which the sons revolt against the Father (King) and the Mother (England).[29] Yet, as Dana Nelson notes, this was by no means the end of the reign of men—it simply replaced the rule of the father with the rule of the sons. As Nelson writes, "Deference to biological fathers was no longer axiomatic, but conditional"—one might say that postrevolutionary America was potentially Hamitic.[30] But, as Nelson points out, the various groups making claims on political belonging—women, free blacks and the enslaved, Native Americans, the propertyless—were to be managed by what she calls "national manhood," which "promised counterphobically to manage anxieties about masculine rivalry unleashed . . . by nascent practices of radical democracy."[31] Nelson writes of the "racial purification" of national manhood (republicanism) as whiteness by reference to scientific texts, but we can also see the ways in which the curse of Canaan, with its genealogy of a world of men descended from three originary brothers, managed the potentialities of the enslaved through a racial order that rejected the transgressive acts of Ham. The curse of Canaan, then, was an adjunct of white national manhood, or republicanism.

To turn to the curse of Canaan is at once to think about the narrativizing of the origins of racial difference and its inimitable imbrication in inequality and domination *and* to sidestep the question of the "actual" origin of race. Put differently, the curse is a story about the origins of race that does not compel the historian to determine the originary moment of racial difference, does not compel one to determine whether race or slavery came first. Rather, it is a primary fantasy, which in the words of psychoanalysts Jean Laplanche and J.-B. Pontalis, "lies beyond the history of the subject but nevertheless in history; a kind of language and symbolic sequence, but loaded with elements of imagination; a structure, but activated by contingent elements."[32] This allows us to think through what is at stake in these fantasmatic scenes of origin—why do a variety of nineteenth-century U.S. Americans find this biblical story a compelling narration of race?

This may be compelling, insofar as it goes, but it does not necessarily suggest why fantasy would be more effective than terms such as *myth* or *discourse*. However, psychoanalysis privileges the problem of sexual difference, captured perhaps most famously in Lacan's aphorism, "there's no such thing as a sexual relationship," and given the centrality of reproduction and the absence of women in the curse, fantasy becomes indispensable.[33] As Joan Wallach Scott puts it, "Sexual difference [is] a permanent quandary—because ultimately unknowable—for modern subjects."[34] In the psychoanalytic register, this is precisely because the phallus, the master signifier, is disruptive, a signifier of an impossible wholeness that can never be attained (because, in the end, as Freud, Lacan, and many others have noted, the phallus is not the penis but rather associated with the mother before the Oedipus complex and castration, a fantasy of wholeness that was also a misrecognition). As Lacan has written, in his well-known distinction between "being" (feminine) and "having" (masculine) the phallus, even having is an illusion, "derealized . . . by the intervention of a 'to seem' that replaces the 'to have', in order to protect it on the one side, and to mask its lack in the other."[35] Thus securing a whole, unified subject, fully male or fully female, constituted and realized in a relationship between the two, is an impossibility that fantasy works to resolve but always, in the end, of necessity, fails.

For Scott, "gender is the attribution of meaning to something that always eludes definition," that something being sexual difference. We might also think of race in this way, as an attempt to resolve sexual difference and assign meaning. This was certainly part of Frantz Fanon's project—one need only think of the status of the phallus in *Black Skin, White Masks*.[36] As Kaja Silverman has written, "The distinction between 'blackness' and 'whiteness' can also be traced back to a kind of castration crisis. . . . The binaries of race find their necessary support in the one that creates gender."[37] Given that Ham's transgression certainly revolved around the status of the phallus, it is striking that the curse has not been met with psychoanalysis before now. Indeed, one could certainly read Noah as the phallus, and Ham's transgression as the unveiling of the phallus, thus revealing the phallus's emptiness.[38] Moreover, the curse of Canaan, in its emphasis on sexual reproduction and its jarring absence of women, encourages such an analytic move. And it is one that forces us to think about what Lee Edelman and Lauren Berlant have called the sovereignty and nonsovereignty of sex.[39] Race, and especially the racial purity associated with the curse of Canaan, relied on a fantasy of the sovereignty of sex, captured by the absence of women. White writers repeatedly produced versions of the curse that spoke of the posterity of Ham, or Shem, or Japheth while also occluding the role of women in the reproduction of race. A sovereign notion of sex that tied race back to an originary set of men functioned by obscuring relationality. Black writers, in offering their critiques, situated racial order in Noah's family but insisted on the relationality, or nonsovereignty, of sex to refute notions of racial purity and hierarchy embodied by the language of posterity.

Pro-slavery

The contours of the fantasy were elaborated by pro-slavery writers and contested by antislavery writers and black ethnologists. While the racial origins that the curse provided were used by the various conflicting groups, producing an emergent consensus on racial origins, I will treat them separately so as to interrogate the fantasy and its ruptures. The familial origins of racial difference were paramount: if race had come to structure normative familial, marital, and sexual relations through division, its origins, in the curse, were inside, not outside, the family. In this case, Matthew Estes's 1846 book, *A Defense of Negro Slavery, as It Exists in the United States*, was perhaps exemplary, as it negotiated the tensions between midcentury scientific racism and biblical narratives. Estes, a resident of Columbus, Mississippi, was quite optimistic that his book would have a wide audience. His optimism was ill-founded, as he would go into debt to his publisher, but he did synthesize the prevailing biblical and scientific views of the day.[40] Estes acknowledged Johann Blumenbach's scientific notion of five races (Caucasian, Malay, Mongolian, American, and African), but nonetheless reduced them to the tripartite distinction of the Noahic genealogy.[41] "This division [that of Blumenbach] may be reduced to three . . . springing from the three sons of Noah: Shem, Ham, and Japheth."[42] In effect, Estes reduced Blumenbach's quintet, which while organized around the Caucasian as the original human type was nonetheless not hierarchical and was founded in geographic dispersal, to a trinity that stemmed from one family and its transgressions and punishments. Moreover, when Estes wrote, in defending the enslavement of Africans, that Canaan was "one of the acknowledged progenitors of the African race," he contributed to the fantasy of racial purity enabled by the structure of the curse. Africans were enslaved because of Canaan—they were direct descendants of him, regardless of the condition of any reproductive partners. Here, Estes established the patrilineal fantasy of racial purity.

References to and accounts of the Noahic origins of racial difference were littered across the pages of the *African Repository and Colonial Journal*, one of the central sources of colonizationist thought in antebellum America. For instance, as one writer noted in 1840, "The world may be regarded as a great plantation, given at the first to ADAM, and afterwards inherited by NOAH, as the only surviving Patriarch of ADAM'S family. This great landed estate was thenceforward divided among the three sons of NOAH—and became three plantations: Europe becoming in the allotment of Providence, the portion of Japheth, Asia of Shem, and Africa of Ham."[43] The familial racial distribution of the world was clear here, as was its genealogy of ownership, and while the author was using the term *plantation* in its older sense of something being founded, it is impossible to read plantation outside the discourse of slavery.

Despite the intervening millennia, this was the end of the division of the world into patriarchal plantations. Afterward, world history was determined by the fates of the three patriarchs, and "marvelously different have been their fortunes."[44] As expected, "the darkest of the three, have been those of the younger branch—the more reckless and dissolute HAM." This fate was sealed in the transgressions and punishments of Noah's family and then in the reproductive logic of generations: "In this line is illustrated from the first and awful accumulation of crimes bequeathing its bitter income of righteous moral abandonment from sire to son, and from generation to generation, as long as revelation and history continue to hold their light upon the scene. In their curse-bound inheritance, the seed 'unto the flesh' was sown by them early. And the harvest of barbarism, oppression and death has been long. More than four thousand years have this African family been gathering it in. 'Servants of servants' have they truly been."[45] The history of the world was set in the racial ordering of Noah's family and then perpetuated along racial lines from generation to generation.

Those who turned to the curse of Canaan and its Noahic genealogy to justify both slavery and racial hierarchy wrote in a language that presumed that something like a pure race could be transmitted intact across generations. In doing so, we can see the way in which race as fantasy constructed a tightly wound narrative that worked to occlude antagonism and structure desire. As Joan Scott writes, "It extracts coherence from confusion, reduces multiplicity to singularity, and reconciles illicit desire with the law. . . . In the fantasy scenario, desire is fulfilled, punished, and prohibited all at once, in the same way that social antagonism is evoked, erased, and resolved."[46] We have seen the common features of the narrative, the coalescence of transgression, punishment, and law, and the figuring of social antagonism. But to think of the way that social antagonism is evoked, erased, and resolved, we need to turn to the way reproductive sex and race figured in the curse. Over its long history, the curse has been suffused with sexual interpretations, particularly around Ham's transgression. However, as Stephen R. Haynes notes, "One searches in vain among [nineteenth-century] comments on Genesis 9 for an explicit statement that Ham's transgression was in any way sexual."[47] While Haynes notes the exception of Josiah Priest, in another way the curse of Canaan and the Noahic genealogy of race that it perpetuated were entirely about reproductive sex. How was race, and in particular a notion of racial purity, perpetuated? It was in this fantasy scenario, which turned on the language of "posterity," in which the problem that sex posed to racial purity was evoked, that the long, ambiguous, and vexed history of interracial sex was erased, and thus the possibility of racial purity and the perpetuation of racial hierarchies was maintained. Moreover, we should read this as one moment in the deployment of sexuality, wherein we find "a political socialization achieved through the 'responsibilization' of couples with regard to the social body as a whole."[48] The curse of Canaan provided a deep history and originary fantasy for the legal, social, and political maintenance of intraracial and broadly endogamous sex.

Indeed, one might read the curse and its notion of race and slavery as the corollary to another, legal, configuration of race, slavery, women, and reproduction. The legal configuration of the heritability of slavery through the woman's reproductive body, that the condition of the child follows the condition of the mother (*partus sequitur ventrem*), first established in 1662 in Virginia, privileged women in the making of race and slavery.[49] Here, moreover, white men, slave masters, could act as they would, on their patriarchal authority, and ensure that the rape of an enslaved woman always produced an enslaved, black child. The curse, on the other hand, created a fantasmatic scenario in which race was produced and reproduced through the actions of men, with posterity obscuring the relational act of sexual reproduction and the role of women in this process. Both ensured a sovereignty in sex of the white man.

This fantasy of racial purity constituted in the curse rested on the language of posterity. However, rather than ascribing blackness/slavery to the enslaved black woman's reproductive body and whiteness/freedom to the free white woman's reproductive body, the curse, in its tripartite racial schema, attributed racial purity to the productive force of the three original men. This turned on the absence of women in these accounts. The three races of the world were commonly referred to as the posterity of Shem, the posterity of Japheth, and the posterity of Ham. As H.R. observed in the *African Repository* in 1855, "The posterity of Ham seem not to have confined themselves to Africa."[50] Even in an instance where the accepted geographic dispersal was being questioned, the idea that there was a "posterity of Ham" that could mingle with the "posterity of Shem" remained intact. This was the most integral part of the fantasy itself. It laid out a vision of global history determined in the family of Noah, and it elided the uncertainty of all social, cultural, familial, and sexual relations with the neat order of posterity. Indeed, believing in the force of the curse's posterity, the colonizationist author Joel Parker wrote in 1849 (all evidence to the contrary), "If we give the utmost freedom to all, the white race must be free to choose such conjugal and other intimate social relations as are most agreeable to their tastes. They will never unite themselves with a caste which is physically and mentally inferior to their own, especially when marked by such a broad and unmistakable distinction as black and white."[51] The curse effectively occluded contemporary, profane social relations and relied on the patrilineality of the fantasy. To write of posterity also secured a patrilineal order of race; while the reproduction of race from generation to generation—that is, the making of posterity itself—may have required women as sexual partners or wives, women were mostly absent. Indeed, it was at the rare moments in which women did appear that the fragility of this racial logic was perhaps most evident.

Josiah Priest, for instance, captured this logic effectively in assuming that racial separation was a part of God's law: "It cannot be supposed for a moment, that Noah would allow the three distinct complexions, or races of his family to mingle or amalgamate, for he knew it was God who had produced for a wise purpose, these very characters; amalgamation, therefore, would certainly have destroyed what God so evidently had ordained and caused to exist. . . . These were to be kept sacredly asunder, and pure from each other's blood forever."[52] This language provided a sacred law of racial difference and racial purity that countered the social fact of interracial sex. Indeed, Matthew Estes implied as much, noting, "Sexual crimes [by which he meant interracial sex] are considered unusually common in the Slave States of this Union. I . . . have admitted to its existence to some extent; but have denied, and will deny again, that we are guilty to the extent charged upon us by our opponents."[53] Interracial sex was a political threat in this fantasy scenario because it suggested the impossibility of referring to the Noahic genealogy as evidence of nineteenth-century racial hierarchies since presumably no one could have claimed a "perfect genealogy" back to Shem, Ham, or Japheth. Here, then, social antagonism like that registered by Estes was occluded and resolved by fantasy.

This sense of "posterity," the possibility of transmitting and maintaining the racial purity and hierarchies associated with the three patriarchs of racial difference, was also important to the formation of the state in the nineteenth century. As Michel Foucault has written, "Racism is born at the point when the theme of racial purity replaces that of race struggle, and when counterhistory begins to be converted into a biological racism. . . . State sovereignty thus becomes the imperative to protect the race."[54] The linking of racial purity to the state was clear in one of the most incendiary Supreme Court decisions of the nineteenth century. In Roger Taney's infamous opinion for the majority in *Dred Scott v. Sanford* (1856), he wrote that "a negro of African descent, whose ancestors were of pure African blood . . .

were not intended to be included, under the word 'citizens' in the constitution."[55] Thus, as we well know, not only the enslaved but anyone of African descent were excluded from full citizenship, based on the fantasy of the transmission of "pure African blood." This linked racial purity to state sovereignty on the eve of the formal dissolution of the union, but in figuring this purity one did not necessarily need to rely on the "medico-normalizing techniques" associated with scientific racism, since these notions had already been articulated in the writings on the curse. Indeed, it was perhaps not an accident that Taney's prose at times sounded similar to those writings. For instance, as it was common to find writers referring to Ham's or Shem's or Japheth's "posterity," so too did Taney, in writing of those counted as citizens at the time of the adoption of the Constitution, state that "it was formed by them, and for them and their posterity, but for no one else."[56] Just as one could conceivably trace the pure posterity of Shem, Ham, and Japheth, so too could one trace the pure posterity of proper (white) U.S. citizens.

Such an interpretation is bolstered by an 1863 printing of Taney's opinion. Published by the New York physician J. H. van Evrie, it included an introduction by Van Evrie and an appendix by the influential southern physician and race scientist Samuel Cartwright. In the appendix, Cartwright turned to the language of Canaan and in doing so gave substance to Taney's "pure African blood." "The blackness of the prognathous race," Cartwright wrote,

> Known in the world's history as Canaanites, Cushites, Ethiopians, black men or negroes, is not confined to the skin, but pervades, in a greater or less degree, the whole inward man down to the bones themselves, giving the flesh and the blood, the membranes and every organ and part of the body, except the bones, a darker hue than in the white race. Who knows but that Canaan's mother may have been a genuine Cushite, as black inside as out, and that Cush, which means blackness, was the mark put upon Cain? Whatever may have been the mark set upon Cain, the negro, in all ages of the world, has carried with him a mark equally efficient in preventing him from being slain—the mark of blackness. The wild Arabs and hostile American Indians invariably catch the black wanderer and make a slave of him instead of killing him, as they do the white man.[57]

Cartwright, in what was certainly one of the more confused passages in the history of the curse, provided a physiological substance to the Noahic genealogy, and in binding it with Taney's opinion also bound the language of the curse and its posterity to the formation of the racial state.

As the language of posterity suggests, the notion of racial purity that animated the efficacy of the curse of Canaan relied on the lineal transmission of race from generation to generation through sexual reproduction. To write of Hamitic, Shemitic, and Japhetic descendants, then, presumed that the racial inheritance could be passed, uninterrupted, from generation to generation. This identified a certain type of individual sovereignty—sexual reproduction required two partners, and thus the possibility of racial purity perpetuated by the curse of Canaan was always under threat from sex itself—and thus interracial sex was a threat to humanity's racial origins. The curse, in its language of posterity, handled this by occluding women. In this fantasy, if sexual reproduction was implied, it was only men—Ham, Shem, Japheth—who produced and reproduced race. Women were absent almost entirely from the accounts proffered by those perpetuating this racial order and hierarchical justification of slavery.

As a contributor to the *American Phrenological Journal* asked in 1868, "If the curse of Noah (as many thousands contend) made Ham black, where did he get his negro wife?"[58] This author went on to propose a different origin of the races, but even for those who held to the Noahic genealogy, the idea of racial purity was troubled by the idea of woman. An abolitionist, writing in the Congregationalist quarterly *New Englander* in 1862, raised the issue implicitly. Without refuting the Noahic origins of race, the author questioned the possibility of racial purity, demanding that advocates of the curse "admit the ethnological assumption that the negroes of the United States, and not the negroes only but the mulattoes, quadroons, octoroons, and all others who cannot prove the absolute purity of their descent from one or both of the two older sons of Noah, are of the race of Ham, and are, therefore, subject to the curse."[59] What this author addressed, of course, was the notion that for the reproduction of race actually to take place, one needed not just Ham, Shem, and Japheth, but women as well. And in their posterity, all interracial sex between the Hamitic and either of the other races resulted in descendants who continued to be deemed Hamitic.

One of the *New Englander* author's targets was the Louisiana pro-slavery writer John Fletcher, in particular his 1852 book *Studies on Slavery, in Easy Lessons*. Fletcher, unlike most pro-slavery writers, addressed the threat that interracial sex and marriage posed to the fantasy of racial origins and thus attempted to account for Ham's wife. Fletcher's account of Noah, Ham, and Canaan was perhaps the most outlandish of any version of the fantasy elaborated in the nineteenth century, but in its outlandishness, in its "non-sense," it accounted for precisely what was at stake in race making at that moment. Rather than finding the origins of racial difference entirely within the Noahic genealogy, Fletcher claimed racial difference could be traced back to Cain (an argument not confined to Fletcher). Indeed, blackness was "the mark" of Cain, according to Fletcher, and thus black skin was the mark of Cain's iniquity. Interracial marriage, according to Fletcher, was in part the cause of the flood itself. Writing of marriages between "sons of God, those of the race of Seth" and "daughters of men . . . females of the race of Cain," Fletcher claimed that "immediately upon the announcement that these two races thus intermarry,

God declares that his spirit shall not always strive with man, and determines to destroy man from the earth."[60] Of course, claiming that the origins of blackness lie with Cain, and that Noah was of the line of Seth, Fletcher was left with the problem of how blackness as a mark of iniquity of a race, inherited from Cain, could have survived the flood.

Like Josiah Priest, who claimed that Ham's transgression was incest with his mother, Fletcher did not find Ham's transgression—witnessing a drunk, naked Noah—to be enough to warrant such punishment. Given that interracial marriage had brought about the deluge, it is unsurprising, perhaps, that Fletcher claimed it was Ham's interracial marriage to a descendant of Cain that brought about the perpetual bondage of Africans. Fletcher argued, in a circuitous, elusive manner (that the *New Englander* abolitionist called "in some respects the silliest, and as a whole the most unreadable") that Naamah, the daughter of Lamech and the last descendant of Cain mentioned in Genesis (4:22), was Ham's wife, thus uniting the races of Seth and Cain after the flood. So the curse on Canaan, that of servitude, followed from the interracial sex of his parents, which perpetuated the black mark of the lineal descendants of Cain. As Fletcher wrote of the curse, "Where are we to look for such a cause, unless in marriage? And with whom could such an intermarriage be had, except with the cursed race of Cain?" Furthermore, what is of particular interest here, beyond Fletcher concocting an elaborate genealogy of racial difference and enslavement tied to interracial sex, was the way that he moved, seamlessly, almost unconsciously, from fantasy to social reality. The marriage of Ham and Naamah began as a counterfactual—"in case the supposed marriage of Ham with the race of Cain be true"—and became social fact: "the wife of Ham must have been black." Fletcher's fantasy mimicked the larger structure of race as fantasy, in which the curse of Canaan in nineteenth-century America produced a kind of social reality.

Antislavery

These familial origins of racial difference were not confined to those defending slavery and colonization. Indeed, early black ethnologists figured similar familial constellations of racial difference. As the former slave and minister James W. C. Pennington wrote in 1841, "The human family was not only dispersed from Babel, but it was also *divided* into sections. These sections had respect to the original sons of Noah."[61] Martin Delany, in his *Principia of Ethnology* of 1879, wrote in a similar vein. Delany, like many others, noted the original unity of humanity in Adam and Eve: "And from the Garden of Eden to the building of the Tower, there certainly was but one race of people known as such, or no classification of different people."[62] In this, Delany struck a chord similar to that of the pro-slavery writer Josiah Priest, who argued in 1843 for a common human origin, and that that common origin was marked by a "bright florid red" complexion that changed to the "dark hue of common copper" as a result of sin.[63] Nonetheless, for Pennington, Delany, Priest, and countless others, there was once, in the deep history of humanity, a commonality marked by the absence of racial difference.

However, this common humanity, this sameness, was destined, as Delany noted, to be divided. "To separate this family was the paramount object," Delany wrote, "and to sever their interest in each other was necessary to this separation."[64] For Delany, this family, destined for separation, was also of mixed complexion: "These three sons of Noah all differed in complexion, and proportionate numbers of the people all differed as did the three sons in complexion."[65] Marking this flexible difference of complexion, one that was present at "the Tower," according to Delany, he nonetheless attributed great force to the family of Noah, and does so in one of the most compelling articulations in the entire history of the Noahic genealogy of race. "On leaving the ark, they were one family, relatives, continuing together as 'one people,' all morally and socially blind and ignorant of any difference of characteristics personal, or interests general, as much so as a family of children with themselves toward the family, till years of maturity brought about a change. Hence, when the confusion took place, their eyes became open to difference in complexion with each other, as a division, preferring those of their kind with whom they went, permanently uniting their destiny."[66] For Delany difference did not simply exist; rather, it came into existence at the moment of its perception. The varying complexions of Noah's family were there prior to their recognition, but they did not constitute difference until "their eyes became open to difference." Thus, for Delany, a unified human family simply existed; indeed, it was the condition of existence. Difference, then, was historical, tied to an event that changed perception.

The notion of a unified familial existence was common to the discourse on the curse of Canaan and spread across antebellum American ethnology and ethnography. Pennington, for instance, wrote of the human family at the moment of creation: "With this, then, as the root of all true history of the human family, we find ourselves at this remote distance, in point of time, from the moment of creation, constituting a part of the vast race of the original two, and one of the most peculiar of the classes into which *the race* is divided." The race, here, was the human race, and the classes were those of racial difference. What Pennington offered his reader was an explanation of "the causes of the diversity of the human species."[67] One can see this language of a universal human family across a broad spectrum of works in this period, and perhaps nowhere more influentially than in the ethnographer Lewis Henry Morgan's *System of Consanguinity and Affinity in the Human Family*, which attempted to demonstrate the originary and future unification of humanity through an evolutionary scale of kinship systems.[68] As the literary critic

Marc Shell has written of the human family, "The universalist asserts the apparently philanthropic and comforting view that all human beings are fellow family members. . . . Yet the trade-off for this universalist sentiment is . . . a characteristic psychological disquietude and political instability."[69] While the curse of Canaan and its Noahic genealogy trafficked in both disquietude and instability, it is worth noting that this familial-universalist rendering of humanity was constituted in a narrative that both introduced difference into Noah's family, a difference that required separation, and was, in its common tie to Ham's or Canaan's transgression, a justification of hierarchical orderings of difference, but one that, for the most part, continued to present a vexed universal human family, in contradistinction to those midcentury polygenists who denied the humanity of Africans and in doing so wrenched away the language of common humanity.[70]

Nearly every writer, regardless of where he or she fell on the spectrum of thought on the curse, followed the migrations of Shem, Ham, and Japheth to explain the racial peopling of the earth. We might take Quobna Ottobouh Cugoano's pamphlet of 1791, *Thoughts and Sentiments on the Evil of Slavery*, as exemplary in this instance. Cugoano, writing simultaneously as "A Native of the Gold Coast" and a Christian, took the Noahic genealogy of racial difference as a historical given. "As all the present inhabitants of the world spring from the family of Noah, and were then all one complexion," Cugoano wrote, "there is no doubt, but the difference which we now find, took its rise very rapidly after they became dispersed and settled on the different parts of the globe."[71] While Cugoano goes on to suggest, in line with much Enlightenment thinking on race in this period, that racial difference was geographic and climatological, he nonetheless refers it all back, ultimately, to "the work of an Almighty hand."[72]

As Martin Delany argued,

> Of one thing we are morally certain, that after the confusion of tongues, each one of these three sons of Noah, turned and went in different directions with their followers. . . . And there can be no reasonable doubt . . . that these people were all of the same complexion with each of the sons of Noah whom they followed. . . . And it will not be disputed, that from then to the present day, the people in those regions where those three sons are said to have located—the three grand divisions of the Eastern Hemisphere: Asia, Africa and Europe—are . . . of the distinct complexions of those attributed to Shem, Ham and Japheth. And this confusion of tongues, and scattering abroad in the earth, were the beginning and origin of the races.[73]

While many black writers detached Africans from Canaan or disavowed the curse, some simply acknowledged it yet did not see it as determinative of the present condition of enslaved Africans. With racial difference both the work of God and a response to climate, Cugoano turned to the curse, admitting that "there [could] be no doubt, that there was a shameful misconduct in Ham himself," and that "Africa, in general, was peopled by the descendants of Ham." Moreover, the descendants of Canaan were to be the servants of the descendants of Shem and Japheth. In Cugoano's version, Canaan was there at the moment of Noah's indiscretion; indeed, it was Canaan's "rude audacious behavior" and Ham's "obloquy" that brought Noah's curse on Canaan. So here it was Canaan's transgression and Ham's failure to uphold the dictates of patriarchal authority that structured the curse. The Canaanites, as in all versions (in this both an incontrovertible "fact" and a consistent part of the fantasy), "became an exceeding wicked people, and were visited with many calamities."[74]

As any number of scholars have noted, early black ethnologists like Robert Benjamin Lewis and Hosea Easton did not so much refute the Noahic genealogy of racial difference as they reformulated the moral valence of the curse of Canaan. This occurred in a variety of ways, from noting the civilizational glories of Egypt to claiming the curse had nothing to do with blackness or skin color to the idea that the curse was ended with the extermination of the Canaanites. But in thinking about the curse of Canaan and its Noahic genealogy of racial difference, which was invoked so many times by white writers not only to justify the enslavement of Africans but also to make claims for the transhistorical purity of race, we should also be struck by both the insistence on racial mixing and the impossibility of racial purity in late-eighteenth- and nineteenth-century black diasporic writings. In this, then, we might think of these writers, in different and not always confluent ways, as operating within the terms of the fantasy in order to constitute recognizable racial identities while also undoing them. We might, in other words, see black ethnology's engagement with the Noahic genealogy as what Žižek refers to as "the empty gesture."[75]

The empty gesture is not something to be casually dismissed but instead is a radical act. "This paradox of willing (choosing freely) what is in any case necessary, of pretending (maintaining the appearance) that there is a free choice although in fact there isn't, is strictly co-dependent with the notion of an empty symbolic gesture, a gesture—an offer—which is meant to be rejected: what the empty gesture offers is the opportunity to choose the impossible."[76] In the face of increasingly inflexible racial boundaries, what these black writers and critics of the curse of Canaan frequently offered was the empty gesture of the impossible, an origins of race that begins with interracial sex, making the fantasy of racial purity that the Noahic genealogy perpetuated an impossibility in itself. For race to work its subjugating function, this gesture had to be rejected precisely as it exposed the system of race for the fantasy that it was (and is). It also offers a way of thinking about African diasporic engagements with the curse and Noahic genealogy in the nineteenth century. These engagements frequently took the form of focusing on

Egypt and/or Ethiopia—if Egyptian or Ethiopian civilization (identified with two of Ham's other sons, Mizraim and Cush, respectively) could be tied to Ham and Africa, then the association of Africans with the doomed posterity of Canaan and slavery could be refuted.[77] Others refuted the logic of the curse itself, pointing to various holes in the biblical narrative. While these were certainly important points of black ethnology, they also obscure another way of considering this engagement. The "choice" to work within the Noahic genealogy was precisely not a choice at all; by the nineteenth century race was a primary means of social and political intelligibility precisely as it was a structure of domination. With the curse and its Noahic genealogy the most pervasive articulation of the origins of racial difference, not to choose to operate and identify within its terms was no choice at all. But in making that nonchoice, African American critics of the curse made "the empty gesture," a conscious acknowledgment that racial purity, which so many white writers used the curse to signify, was impossible, often from the earliest moments of postdiluvian human history. Instead, interracial sex was the condition of humanity, and the Noahic genealogy demonstrated this; according to many of these writers, precisely as race came into being the boundaries were crossed in the kind of reproductive sex that made nations.

Here we might turn back to Cugoano's engagement with the Noahic genealogy. While he noted that the Canaanites were destroyed by a series of peoples, from Chederluomer, a descendant of Shem, through to the Greeks, the Romans, and the Turks, Cugoano does not count them, to an individual, completely exterminated. Rather, he matter-of-factly undercuts the claims of racial purity that structured so many other accounts of the curse. "Many of the Canaanites, who fled away in the Time of Joshua," Cugoano wrote, "became mingled with the different nations, and some historians think that some of them came to England, and settled about Cornwall; so that, for any thing that can be known to the contrary there may be some of the descendants of that wicked generation still subsisting among the slave-holders in the West-Indies."[78] Even if Cugoano began with a theological-climatological origin of racial difference, he nonetheless took the time to undercut the idea of racial purity. He goes on to give a brief overview of the peopling of Africa, from Noah's "olive-black complexion" to Noah's other noncursed children and the mixing of nations (races) that made that history. For Cugoano, the Noahic genealogy structured racial difference, but given that it was also a story of common, universal humanity, it militated against racial purity.

James W. C. Pennington also refuted the common white understanding of the curse of Canaan and the origins of Africans *and* situated racial difference in the Noahic genealogy. In doing so, he turned to racial mixing, the familial language of race, and a muted sense of the possibility of racial purity. In this, we can see that even those moments in which the boundaries of the fantasy were shown to be unstable were comfortably aligned with the fantasy of transhistorical racial purity. Unlike Cugoano, who presumed that contemporary Africans were the descendants of Canaan but that the notion of racial purity was an historical impossibility, Pennington refuted the association of Africans with Canaan. Or, more precisely, he associated those sub-Saharan Africans who had been enslaved in the transatlantic slave trade with Ethiopia and Cush, one of Ham's other sons who had not been cursed. Racial difference, for Pennington as for so many other nineteenth-century writers on race, had its origin with Noah and his family. "The human family was not only dispersed from Babel," Pennington wrote, "but it was also *divided* into sections. These sections had respect to the original sons of Noah." Thus race was a mark of difference internal to a global-universal system of kinship, a difference within the same. Pennington immediately, however, distinguished contemporary Africans from Canaan: "We came from Noah through Ham, and from Ham through Cush." Yet, importantly, Pennington qualified this, noting that it was not a case of pure racial origins; rather "*We are properly the sons of Cush and Misraim amalgamated.*"[79] The phrasing here suggests a contradictory notion of race and history. On the one hand, contemporary Africans were, for Pennington, the descendants of the amalgamation of Cush and Misraim, and thus the notion that one could trace racial origins back to a pure origin, as in Cugoano and others, was challenged. On the other hand, in relying on patronymics, the amalgamation, as stated, suggests not only both incest and homosexuality but also that a people, as in the people of Cush and Misraim, can be reduced to their patriarchs. The fantasy thus created a notion of racial purity quite powerful for making sense of history, one tied to the force of patronyms and patriarchs, even when the fantasy was being cut. Put differently, while to a different end, women were still absent from the fantasy. As in the work of white pro-slavery writers, this was the history of Man as the occluded reproductive history of men.

This was even more apparent in a distinction Pennington made between Carthaginians and Ethiopians. Pennington did not refute the curse of Canaan; rather, he acknowledged it but distinguished contemporary Africans from Canaan. This presented a problem, however, for thinking of Africans as encompassing a continent *and*, like several other early black ethnologists, desiring to claim Egypt as part of the African inheritance. For Pennington contemporary Africans could claim an Egyptian heritage because they were the products of Misraim, who settled in Egypt, and Cush, who settled Ethiopia. Historically, according to Pennington, "it is beyond all dispute certain that Misraim settled Egypt, as it is also that Cush settled Ethiopia."[80] This left North Africa and the Carthaginians, who most certainly occupied the continent of Africa but were just as certainly, for Pennington, descendants of Canaan. The force of Pennington's critique here relied on rejecting the association between contemporary Africans and Canaan—to admit Carthaginians as ancestors was to insert Canaan into African genealogy. For Pennington, however, there was no historical evidence of amalgamation. "There is no evidence that they ever amalgamated with the Ethiopians as did Egyptians." And that is the end, for Pennington. While he uses "amalgamation" to refute the transhistorical force of racial origins, he also upholds something of that fantasmatic force, albeit within more politically efficacious terms.

Cugoano and Pennington were not alone in this project. Alexander Crummell's critique, for instance, rested on the fact that the mobility of persons did not end with the initial scattering. "The fact should not be forgotten that the blood of the Canaanites was more mingled with that of Europeans," Crummell wrote, "than with Africans; for they formed more colonies in Europe than Africa, and their influence was stronger in Europe than in Africa."[81] In this, then the curse should have registered, if at all, with Europeans, not Africans. In arguing against the polygenist H. Buckner Payne (Ariel) that "the Negro" was indeed "the progeny of Ham," Robert Young turned to interracial sex for proof. "A white man associates with a negro woman. What is the offspring? If the Negro is a beast, the issue ought to be a *hybrid*, and worse than a hybrid—*a monster*. But we know that the offspring is a fertile, prolific Mulatto. And this very test will satisfy any scientific man in the world that the Negro is a *variety* of the human *Species*."[82] Again, interracial sex belied the possibility of pure races and thus a racially pure state.

Not all who trafficked in the Noahic origins story absented women from the (re)production of race. The African American minister and abolitionist Henry Highland Garnet recounted the familiar division of the races and the world, but after making familiar claims such as "Ham was the first African," he turned to the sexual violence of slavery in a manner that undercut the fantasmatic language of the curse. "Our sisters ever manifesting the purest kindness . . . are unprotected from the lusts of tyrants. . . . Driven into unwilling concubinage, their offspring are sold by their Anglo Saxon fathers. To them the marriage institution is but a name, for their despoilers break down the hymenial alter and scatter its sacred ashes on the winds."[83] Here the social fact of the rape of enslaved women was broached in relation to the fantasmatic scenario of the curse and its posterity in way that cut the fantasy. Here Garnet sounded more like Harriet Jacobs or Maria W. Stewart, who emphasized the sexual violence of enslavement. And, as Garnet continued, "This western world is destined to be filled with a mixed race. . . . It matters not whether we abhor or desire such a consummation, it is now too late to change the decree of nature and circumstances."[84] This followed from the universal humanity, the familial origins, of the curse.

The force of race as fantasy relied on its familial configuration of humanity, one that, precisely in its universalizing gesture potentially exceeded its racism and justification of slavery. For its patrilineal defense of racial hierarchy and purity it relied, as we have seen, on what we might call the sovereignty of sex. Lee Edelman has written of "the subject's fantasmatic sovereignty," a phrase that binds the psychic life of the subject to the machinations of political.[85] It was, at its core, a fantasy of control and whiteness: in the nineteenth-century United States, it was the fantasy of the liberal subject, who deployed reason to control the excesses of desire and thus achieve an autonomous freedom. The racial fantasy that was the curse of Canaan, in its depictions of racial purity and posterity, rested on both individual and racial (collective) sovereignty. Sex, however, was (and still is) relational, and black ethnologists and antislavery writers deployed sex as a critique of the fantasy of racial purity and potential disruption of sovereignty, but did so, for the most part, in the terms of the fantasy. As Lauren Berlant (in this instance, Edelman's coauthor/conversationalist) writes of the "nonsovereignty" of sex, "Both politics and pedagogy emerge from within the disturbing encounter of these various modes of being incomplete, contradictory, out of control. Nonsovereignty can engender different atmospheres and potentials, and the structures of self-discontinuity and the place of fantasy in shifting, remediating, and revisceralizing its threat are more than extraneous noise and variation, are not always only failed attempts at adequation or mastery, and where all kinds of significant transformations happen."[86] Or, in Frederick Douglass's words, "If the lineal descendants of Ham are alone to be scripturally enslaved, it is certain that slavery at the south must soon become unscriptural; for thousands are ushered into the world, annually, who, like myself, owe their existence to white fathers, and those fathers most frequently their own masters."[87]

By the turn of the twentieth century, the utility of the curse of Canaan would seem to have been exhausted in the project of race making. Yet an exchange in 1900 and 1903 between Charles Carroll, a polygenist minister from Missouri, and the Baptist minister W. S. Armistead, suggested otherwise. The exchange was striking for a number of reasons: by the early twentieth century the curse still had an explanatory force; Carroll's iconoclastic insistence on polygenesis, which had gone out of favor in the face of social Darwinist arguments; and Armistead's use of the Noahic genealogy as a humanitarian argument against Carroll's vitriolic racism. In doing so, the exchange gestures at the ways in which the curse of Canaan was as much a fantasy of the human as anything else, and the ways in which the human was not necessarily an emancipatory category.

For Carroll, the curse of Canaan, which had once been the primary theological justification of racial inequality and the enslavement of Africans, was a "monstrous theory . . . conceived in . . . and handed down to us from, the dark ages of ignorance, superstition and crime."[88] The theory was monstrous, according to Carroll, precisely because if one accepted it, then one had to acknowledge the kinship between white, black, and God. "We are emphatically taught that there is no kinship between man and the animals," Carroll wrote, "but that the kinship is between God and man."[89] The implication, for Carroll, was that to explain racial inequality and the treatment of people of African descent required excluding them from the human family, for to accord them a place in the human family, as the curse of Canaan did, was also to acknowledge their equal kinship with God.

The problem with this vision was that it not only violated an unstated ethics of kinship but that it also undercut the possibility of racial purity, all of which turned on the necessity of interracial sex. I quote at length in order to demonstrate the way in which Carroll apprehended the impossibility of transhistorical racial purity, an impossibility that rested on the necessity of interracial sex in the originary fantasy, once one acknowledges the necessity of women.

> Having consented to believe all this absurdity, in order to accept the best explanation which the modern clergy has offered us as to the origin of the negro, we should be excused for indulging the hope that our credulity has been sufficiently taxed, and that no further draft would be made upon it; but this fond hope, however comforting, was but born to be blighted; a glance at the scriptural narrative reveals the fact that Noah manifested no disposition to visit this dire calamity upon any other individual than Canaan; there was no female cursed and changed into a negress to mate with Canaan, and thus enable him to produce a progeny of negroes. Hence, he had no alternative than to take a wife from among the whites, for he was the father of the Canaanites; the offspring resulting from this union would not have been negroes, but half castes—mulattoes. These, upon reaching maturity, would not have taken husbands and wives from among their brothers and sisters, but would have intermarried with the whites; the offspring resulting from these unions would not have been negroes, but three-quarter white. Thus, through their intermarriage with the whites, each succeeding generation of the descendants of Canaan would have grown whiter, and their hair straighter, until, in the course of time, it would have been difficult, if not impossible, for the ordinary observer to distinguish them from pure whites, and when Canaan had lived out his days and died, he would have been the last, as the clergy would have us believe he was the first negro, and the presence of the negro in subsequent ages would remain unexplained. Hence, whether we view this most important subject from a scriptural, or from a scientific standpoint, it at once becomes plain that the negro is not the son of Ham.[90]

The passage is long and convoluted, but at its core is the puncturing of the fantasy—racial purity, as conceived by the curse of Canaan, was an impossibility, precisely because of the "nonsovereignty" of sex. Where most writers relied on the patriarchs and thus could conceive of Africans as the posterity of Ham, Europeans as the posterity of Japheth, and Asians as the posterity of Shem, Carroll insisted that they must be the posterity of Ham and a woman. And in this, for Carroll, racial purity, to which he was vehemently committed, was no longer secure. Thus the title of his book, *The Negro a Beast*, was his response to the possibility of interracial sex and the absence of racial purity.

In 1903 W. S. Armistead published his response to Carroll, refuting his argument at every turn. Armistead attempted to undercut Carroll on every issue, beginning with Carroll's claim that Adam and Eve were white. Armistead, like others before him, including Josiah Priest, insisted that the original pair were red.[91] But this does not make the white and black races, the European and the African, any less human. Indeed, Armistead's account was one of both the infinite variety of the human complexion and the infinite power of God to make humans as he pleased. Indeed, the postdiluvian peopling of the earth and the racial difference that marked this geographic distribution were an effect of God's will. "Reaching the Noachian age," Armistead wrote, "God, consulting 'His will and pleasure,' determined, the deluge passed, to change the order of things, partitioning the earth, and assigning the different continents, then known, to people differing in characters (complexion and pilious [pileous] systems), and speaking no longer the same language."[92] Indeed, Noah's three sons were the conduits through which this population dispersal was to be accomplished. "God caused Noah to beget three sons—one for each continent—each with characters (complexion and pilious systems) entirely different, but exactly fitted to the continent He designed them to populate."[93] Thus the scattering of peoples over the earth and racial difference were not the effect of a curse but the result of God's sovereign decision to create Shem, Ham, and Japheth as different races to facilitate that scattering. This explanation insisted that the human family, in its originary, postdiluvian form, accommodated racial difference.

Ham, then, was the father of the black race not because of his transgression but because God made him, and thus his descendants, physiologically adapted for life in Africa. Ham, Armistead wrote, "with descendants, was certainly given Africa, 'the dark continent,' so-called from being populated by his descendants, *alias* black people, *alias* negroes . . . that continent being exactly adapted to settlement by black people and no other, shows that Ham was a negro or black man." Of course, Armistead displayed a form of circular reasoning here—Africa is associated with blackness because Ham and his descendants settled there, and Ham is certainly black because only black people could have lived in Africa. But what was also important here was that, in figuring the Noahic genealogy as a claim for an expansive, racially diverse humanity, Armistead absented women from the procreative history of Ham and his descendants, one that Carroll had noted was necessary to believe in the Hamitic genealogy. Ham's "descendants have all been of that color, and from a time immemorial. . . . He and his offspring had of necessity to be blacks or negroes from the pilious system found among them, such a pilious system always accompanying a black complexion. . . . He and his offspring had to be negroes or blacks to enable God to consummate His plans of populating the whole earth then known."[94] Here we find Ham, producing offspring and descendants, all of whom are black, in the absence of women. The production of racial purity relied, again, on the fantasy of sovereign procreative sex in the absence of women. And unlike most of the writers who took up this position, Armistead did this as a humanizing gesture against Carroll's polygenism.[95]

If Armistead turned to the Noahic genealogy to assert the humanity of people of African descent in the face of Carroll's dehumanizing discourse, he nonetheless did not discount the curse of Canaan. Indeed, Armistead accounts for a variety of instances in which all of Ham's descendants were subjugated by the descendant of Shem and Japheth, with the United States becoming the fulfillment of the curse. "Here in the United States, we have had a most remarkable fulfillment of the Noachian curse. . . . The history of this country shows that, when discovered, it was populated by a 'red people'—the Indian—people evidently descended from Shem. When the whites—Japheth's descendants—overran it, they drove out the Indians who dwelt in tents, and for over two hundred years had negroes, Ham's descendants, as servants; thus fulfilling the prophecy: 'Japheth shall dwell in the tents of Shem, and Canaan shall be his servant.' We repeat, it is a matter of undoubted history that all the nations of the earth, of Shemitic or Japhetic descent, have participated in Hamitic enslavement."[96] Which is to say, in short, that the humanizing gestures that Armistead trafficked in were neither emancipatory nor egalitarian. Indeed, writing in the midst of the consolidation of Jim Crow, Armistead presented an expansive vision of humanity that was as much a justification of racial subordination.

The curse of Canaan and the recitation of the origins of racial difference in Noah's family were a complex story of race, sex, kinship, and the human. Indeed, as we trace this story anecdotally and read it in relation to the polygenist arguments of the mid-nineteenth-century American school, we can see the Noahic genealogy as a narrative of universal humanity, something that the black ethnologists picked up on in their insistence on racial mixing. We might then think of polygenesis not only in terms of the narrative of scientific racism but also as an attempt to curb the broad universalism in the Noahic genealogy. If the origins of racial difference were frequently narrated as the product of Ham's transgression, they were based on the fundamental humanity of everyone involved—it would be difficult to claim the inhumanity of Ham, even if one conceded that he was a transgressor, a family criminal. In this, we find a universalism that encompasses sameness in familial terms and difference in racial terms.

The disagreements of Carroll's and Armistead's texts suggest the extent to which the curse of Canaan was a fantasy of the human as much as it was a justification of both slavery and racial inequality. I say this not to suggest that this is a useful source of humanitiarianism, but instead to suggest that it is a moment, an event even, in the genealogy of the human that cautions against the emancipatory hopes of a universal humanity. It suggests that natural rights are not the only source of a universal humanity and that certain visions of this universalism can comfortably accommodate inequality. Here, as in Armistead's text, the humanity of the curse of Canaan is tied to the origins of racial difference and racial inequality. However, in making this fantasy one that turns on sex and its erasure, we can see, in the works of the black ethnologists like Pennington and Crummell, that the relationality of sex and the acknowledgment of that relationality, was the source of a more expansive and emancipatory notion of humanity.

Notes

I would like to thank Joan Scott, Greta Lafleur, and Britt Rusert for reading earlier drafts, as well as audiences at the Institute for Advanced Study, Fordham University, and the University of California–Santa Cruz for particularly insightful feedback.

1. W. E. B. Du Bois, *The Negro* (1915; New York: Oxford University Press, 1970), 11.

2. Peter Coviello, "Intimacy and Affliction: Du Bois, Race, and Psychoanalysis," *MLQ: Modern Language Quarterly* 64, no. 1 (March 2003): 9.

3. The King James Version, which would have been the version most familiar to many nineteenth-century Americans, reads as follows:

And the sons of Noah, that went forth of the ark, were Shem, and Ham, and Japheth: and Ham is the father of Canaan.

These are the three sons of Noah: and of them was the whole earth overspread.

And Noah began to be an husbandman, and he planted a vineyard:

And he drank of the wine, and was drunken; and he was uncovered within his tent.

And Ham, the father of Canaan, saw the nakedness of his father, and told his two brethren without.

And Shem and Japheth took a garment, and laid it upon their shoulders, and went backward, and covered the nakedness of their father; and their faces were backward, and they saw not their father's nakedness.

And Noah awoke from his wine, and knew what his younger son had done unto him.

And he said, Cursed be Canaan; a servant of servants shall he be unto his brethren.

And he said, Blessed be the LORD god of Shem; and Canaan shall be his servant.

God shall enlarge Japheth, and he shall dwell in the tents of Shem; and Canaan shall be his servant.

(Genesis 9:18–27)

4. David M. Goldenberg, *The Curse of Ham: Race and Slavery in Early Judaism, Christianity, and Islam* (Princeton, N.J.: Princeton University Press, 2003), 1.

5. Werner Sollors, *Neither Black nor White, yet Both: Thematic Explorations of Interracial Literature* (New York: Oxford University Press, 1997), 86.

6. Benjamin Braude, "The Sons of Noah and the Construction of Ethnic and Geographical Identities in the Medieval and Early Modern Periods," *William and Mary Quarterly* 54, no. 1 (1997): 103–42.

7. Stephen R. Haynes, *Noah's Curse: The Biblical Justification of American Slavery* (New York: Oxford University Press, 2003); Sylvester Johnson, *The Myth of Ham in Nineteenth-Century American Christianity: Race, Heathens, and the People of God* (New York: Palgrave Macmillan, 2004). Witness Haynes, for instance, who gives both specificity to the nineteenth century and situates it in a long historical arc: "By locating American readings of Genesis 9 within the history of biblical interpretation, the distinctive features in proslavery versions of the curse are clarified. Overwhelmingly, these reflect two concerns that pervaded antebellum slave culture—honor and order" (8).

8. Lydia Maria Child, *An Appeal for the Indians* (Wm. P. Tomlinson, 1868).

9. The conflation of kinship and biology in sexual reproduction was what led the anthropologist David Schneider to reject the intellectual edifice of kinship altogether. As Schneider writes in answer to why kinship was "regarded as a privileged system": "The clue to this answer comes from the fact that kinship has been defined in terms of the relations that arise from the processes of human sexual reproduction. Human sexual reproduction has been viewed by anthropologists as an essentially biological process, part of human nature, regardless of any cultural aspects which may be attached to it." For Schneider, this presumption undergirds a kind of Western epistemological imperialism, converting the ethnographic facts from varied cultures around the world into the language of kinship, which was grounded in two related Western assumptions: "Blood Is Thicker than Water" and "The Genealogical Unity of Mankind." That the curse of Canaan also rested on these two assumptions suggests the way in which kinship, rather than being derived, prima facie, from social facts, was and is a disciplinary apparatus for making subjects. David M. Schneider, *A Critique of the Study of Kinship* (Ann Arbor: University of Michigan Press, 1984), 165.

10. Nineteenth-century print culture, especially evangelical print culture, was littered with accounts of the wickedness and destruction of the Canaanites. While it is beyond the scope of this essay, it would be interesting to interrogate the uses of the Canaanites in the nineteenth-century United States, uses that would certainly intersect with the curse of Canaan but cannot be reduced to this racial fantasy. For one instance of just how far the Canaanite metaphor was extended, there was this account of a mob in Canaan, New Hampshire, in 1836, with the title "The Canaanites Again." "Canaan [N.H.] has been again disgraced by a mob.—Its object was to maintain the 'union,' by violating the Constitution. The illegal efforts of the mob, failing it putting down the abolitionists, and did nothing more than prove, that Canaan is scarcely yet redeemed from the darkness of heathenism." "The Canaanites Again," *Philanthropist*, November 25, 1836, 3.

11. This position was scattered through various antislavery writings. It was particularly efficacious because one could then argue that the Canaanites were punished and cite copious biblical evidence. See, for example, [Isaac Anderson], *Address Delivered by a Member of the Manumission Society, on the 17th of August 1817* (Knoxville, Tenn.: Manumission Society, 1817).

12. John Lardas Modern, *Secularism in Antebellum America* (Chicago: University of Chicago Press, 2011), 184.

13. Mark Rifkin, *When Did Indians Become Straight? Kinship, the History of Sexuality, and Native Sovereignty* (New York: Oxford University Press, 2011), 11.

14. Walter Johnson, *River of Dark Dreams: Slavery and Empire in the Cotton Kingdom* (Cambridge, Mass.: Harvard University Press, 2013), 207–8.

15. Philip Schaff, "Slavery and the Bible," *Mercersburg Review* (April 1861): 288.

16. Jean Walton, "Re-placing Race in (White) Psychoanalytic Discourse: Founding Narratives of Feminism," *Critical Inquiry* 21, no. 4 (Summer 1995): 776.

17. Hortense Spillers, "'All the Things You Could Be by Now, If Sigmund Freud's Wife Was Your Mother': Psychoanalysis and Race," in *Female Subjects in Black and White: Race, Psychoanalysis, Feminism*, ed. Elizabeth Abel, Barbara Christian, and Helene Moglen (Berkeley: University of California Press, 1997), 135.

18. See also Anne Cheng, *The Melancholy of Race: Psychoanalysis, Assimilation, and Hidden Grief* (New York: Oxford University Press, 2001); Ranjana Khanna, *Dark Continents: Psychoanalysis and Colonialism* (Durham, N.C.: Duke University Press, 2003). This has been a particularly fraught engagement for historians, who still seem to work overly hard to erase the stain of psychohistory. That this has impoverished historical writing both on race and more generally is the unstated wager of this essay.

19. Kalpana Seshadri-Crooks, *Desiring Whiteness: A Lacanian Analysis of Race* (New York: Routledge, 2000), 2.

20. Mia Bay, *White Image in the Black Mind: African-American Ideas about White People, 1830–1925* (New York: Oxford University Press, 2000), 29l; Sollors, *Neither White nor Black*, 81.

21. "Noah's Prophecy: 'Cursed Be Canaan,'" *New Englander* (April 1862): 341.

22. Christopher Lane, "The Psychoanalysis of Race: An Introduction," in *The Psychoanalysis of Race*, ed. Christopher Lane (New York: Columbia University Press, 1998), 1–37.

23. The most important works on fantasy include Jacqueline Rose, *States of Fantasy* (Oxford: Clarendon Press, 1996); Slavoj Žižek, *The Plague of Fantasies* (London: Verso, 1997); Maria Torok, "Fantasy: An Attempt to Define Its Structure and Operation," in Nicholas Abraham and Maria Torok, *The Shell and the Kernel: Renewals of Psychoanalysis*, trans. Nicholas T. Rand (Chicago: University of Chicago Press, 1994), 27–36; Jean LaPlanche and J.-B. Pontalis, "Fantasy and the Origins of Sexuality," *International Journal of Psychoanalysis* 49, no. 1 (1968): 1–18.

24. Joan Wallach Scott, "Fantasy Echo: History and the Construction of Identity," in *The Fantasy of Feminist History* (Durham, N.C.: Duke University Press, 2012), 49.

25. Žižek, *Plague of Fantasies*, 7.

26. Žižek, *Plague of Fantasies*, 13.

27. Indeed, the curse of Canaan, in its particulars, mimics Lacan's writings on the Law of the Father, or, the Name of the Father. Here, we might see Noah as analogous to the symbolic father in Lacan's writings. The symbolic "Father may be regarded as the original representative of the authority of the Law," and in this one can see Noah, who seems to be the authority of the Law but, given its beguiling nature, he is rather the representative of that authority. Moreover, the "true function of the Father . . . is fundamentally to unite

(and not to set in opposition) a desire and the Law." See Jacques Lacan, "The Subversion of the Subject and the Dialectic of Desire in the Freudian Unconscious," in *Ecrits: A Selection*, trans. Alan Sheridan (New York: W.W. Norton, 1977), 311, 321. Here, not only Noah but also Shem, Ham, and Japheth function as the progenitors of a law of racial difference and, in articulating the law also aim to teach one how to desire racially, thus attempting (but always failing) to unite desire and the Law. Finally, as Lacan notes, the symbolic father is the fundamental element in the structure of the symbolic order: the symbolic order of culture is distinguished from nature by the centrality of patrilineality. Patrilineal order, as not only Lacan but many feminist critics have noted, must be cultural and is marked by an insistent uncertainty. The curse of Canaan makes race, and the inheritance of racial purity in particular, a patrilineal order—one is Hamitic, Shemitic, or Japhetic, a fantasy of racial order that is dependent on men only. That women, white and black, were often ascribed the position of interrupting racial order in the eighteenth and nineteenth centuries only further bolsters this claim. See Jacques Lacan, *The Psychoses*, trans. Russell Grigg (New York: W. W. Norton, 1993).

28. Žižek, *Plague of Fantasies*, 14.

29. See, most influentially, Jay Fliegelman, *Prodigals and Pilgrims: The American Revolution against Patriarchal Authority* (New York: Cambridge University Press, 1982).

30. Dana D. Nelson, *National Manhood: Capitalist Citizenship and the Imagined Fraternity of White Men* (Durham, N.C.: Duke University Press, 1998), 35.

31. Nelson, *National Manhood*, 38.

32. Jean Laplanche and J.-B. Pontalis, "Fantasy and the Origins of Sexuality," *International Journal of Psycho-analysis* 49, no. 1 (1968): 10.

33. Jacques Lacan, *On Feminine Sexuality, the Limits of Love and Knowledge, 1972–1973— Encore: The Seminar of Jacques Lacan, Book XX*, ed. Jacques-Alain Miller, trans. Bruce Fink (New York: Norton, 1988), 12.

34. Joan Wallach Scott, "Introduction: 'Flyers into the Unknown,'" in *Fantasy of Feminist History* (Durham, N.C.: Duke University Press, 2011), 6.

35. Jacques Lacan, "The Signification of the Phallus," in *Écrits: A Selection*, trans. Alan Sheridan (New York: W.W. Norton, 1977), 289.

36. Frantz Fanon, *Black Skin, White Masks* (New York: Grove Press, 1967).

37. Kaja Silverman, "Girl Love," *October* 104 (Spring 2003): 19.

38. There has been much speculation about Ham's transgression; most scholars concur that seeing Noah naked was not enough to warrant such severe punishment. The most common speculations concern castration, paternal incest/sodomy, and maternal incest. While speculating on Ham's transgression lies beyond the scope of this essay, it also seems beside the point, missing the specific insights of Du Bois, that the power of the curse in the making of race lay in its allegorical, psychological, and mythic resonances. Moreover, such speculation treats Noah, Ham, and Canaan as real people, referents who can be documented, rather than as parts in a fantasmatic constellation. Again, psychoanalysis helps here, in seeing that the story is in part about the status of the phallus. As Lacan writes, the phallus "can play its role only when veiled." Ham's transgression, in seeing Noah drunk and naked and not attempting to restore the veil, was in seeing

the authority of the father unmasked, the realization that Noah's masculinity is not and cannot be the phallus. Whether this was paternal or maternal incest or castration is irrelevant from the standpoint of the fantasy—they all signify the same unveiling. Lacan, "Signification of the Phallus," 288.

39. Lauren Berlant and Lee Edleman, *Sex, or the Unbearable* (Durham, N.C.: Duke University Press, 2014), 66–72.

40. Johanna Nichol Shields, "Writers in the Old Southwest and the Commercialization of American Letters," *Journal of the Early Republic* 27, no. 3 (Fall 2007): 487–90. Estes's failure in the publishing world was likely more a function of the regional nature of mid-nineteenth-century print culture than evidence of a lack of interest in his writings on race.

41. Johann Blumenbach, "On the Natural Variety of Mankind, Third Edition (1795)," in *The Anthropological Treatises of Johann Friedrich Blumenbach*, trans. and ed. Thomas Bendyshe (London: Longman, Green, Longman, Roberts, and Green, 1865), 264–65. Blumenbach did not traffic in scriptural explanations of racial difference, nor did he explicitly attempt to refute them. As he wrote, blackness had been linked to Cain, Ham, and Ishmael, but it was not his "intention either to support or refute these opinions, but rather to deduce [his] conclusion from matters of fact" (368). It is this kind of writing that supports claims that the curse and scriptural explanations of racial difference waned in the nineteenth century; however, simply because one strain of scientific taxonomy of race chose to move from "facts" rather than scripture does not mean that the scriptural was of less importance. As we see in Estes and others, one could easily, if contradictorily, merge the two perspectives.

42. Matthew Estes, *A Defense of Negro Slavery, as It Exists in the United States* (Montgomery, Ala.: Press of the "Alabama Journal," 1846), 49–50.

43. "Africa and Her Children, and Her Prospects," *African Repository and Colonial Journal* 16, no. 20 (October 15, 1840), 317.

44. "Africa and Her Children," 317.

45. "Africa and Her Children," 317.

46. Scott, *Fantasy of Feminist History*, 51.

47. Haynes, *Noah's Curse*, 69.

48. Michel Foucault, *The History of Sexuality*, vol. 1, *An Introduction*, trans. Robert Hurley (New York: Vintage, 1978), 105.

49. Kathleen M. Brown, *Good Wives, Nasty Wenches, and Anxious Patriarchs: Gender, Race, and Power in Colonial Virginia* (Chapel Hill: University of North Carolina Press, 1996), 107–36.

50. H.R., "The Land of Ham; or Africa: Her Curse and Her Cure," *African Repository* (October 1855): 298.

51. Joel Parker, "Hope for Africa: A Discourse Delivered in the Clinton Street Church," *African Repository and Colonial Journal* (July 1849): 202.

52. Priest, *Slavery*, 72.

53. Estes, *Defense of Negro Slavery*, 153.

54. Michel Foucault, *"Society Must Be Defended": Lectures at the College de France, 1975–1976*, trans. David Macey (New York: Picador, 2003), 81.

55. *Dred Scott v. Sanford* 60 U.S. 400, 404 (1856).

56. *Dred Scott*, 60 U.S. at 406.

57. Samuel Cartwright, "Natural History of the Prognathous Species of Mankind," in *The Dred Scott Decision*, 2nd ed. (New York: Van Evrie, Horton, 1863), 47.

58. "Origin of the Races—White and Black," *American Phrenological Journal* (February 1868): 78.

59. "Noah's Prophecy: 'Cursed Be Canaan,'" *New Englander* (April 1862): 341.

60. John Fletcher, *Studies on Slavery, in Easy Lessons* (Natchez, Miss.: Jackson Warner, 1852), 231.

61. James W. C. Pennington, *A Textbook of the Origin and History of the Colored People* (Hartford, Conn.: L. Skinner, 1841), 9.

62. Martin R. Delany, *Principia of Ethnology: The Origins of Races and Color*, 2nd rev. ed. (Philadelphia: Harper and Brother, 1880), 14.

63. Josiah Priest, *Slavery, as It Relates to the Negro, or African Race* (Albany, N.Y.: C. Van Benthuysen, 1843), 20.

64. Delany, *Principia of Ethnology*, 20–21.

65. Delany, *Principia of Ethnology*, 21.

66. Delany, *Principia of Ethnology*, 21–22.

67. Pennington, *Textbook*, 6.

68. Lewis Henry Morgan, *Systems of Consanguinity and Affinity in the Human Family* (Lincoln: University of Nebraska Press, 1997); Thomas Trautmann, *Lewis Henry Morgan and the Invention of Kinship* (Berkeley: University of California Press, 1987). On the perpetuation of racial difference in Morgan's ostensibly universalist project, see Brian Connolly, *Domestic Intimacies: Incest and the Liberal Subject in Nineteenth-Century America* (Philadelphia: University of Pennsylvania Press, 2014), 210–21.

69. Marc Shell, "The Want of Incest in the Human Family: Or, Kin and Kind in Christian Thought," *Journal of the American Academy of Religion* 63, no. 3 (Autumn 1994): 625.

70. See, for instance, J. C. Nott and George R. Gliddon, *Types of Mankind: Or, Ethnological Researches* (Philadelphia: Lippincott, Grambo, 1855).

71. Quobna Ottobouh Cugoano, *Thoughts and Sentiments on the Evil of Slavery* (London, 1791), 11.

72. Cugoano, *Thoughts and Sentiments*, 12.

73. Delany, *Principia of Ethnology*, 21–22.

74. Cugoano, *Thoughts and Sentiments*, 15.

75. Žižek, *Plague of Fantasies*, 27.

76. Žižek, *Plague of Fantasies*, 27.

77. Bay, *White Image in the Black Mind*, 27–30; Bruce R. Dain, *A Hideous Monster of the Mind: American Race Theory in the Early Republic* (Cambridge, Mass.: Harvard University Press, 2002), 126–28.

78. Cugoano, *Thoughts and Sentiments*, 15–16.

79. Pennington, *Textbook*, 12, emphasis in original.

80. Pennington, *Textbook*, 21.

81. Alexander Crummell, "The Negro Race Not Under a Curse," in *The Future of Africa* (New York: Charles Scribner, 1862), 340.

82. Robert A. Young, *The Negro: A Reply to Ariel* (Nashville, Tenn.: J. W. M'Ferrin, 1867), 12.

83. Henry Highland Garnet, *The Past and the Present Condition, and the Destiny, of the Colored Race* (Troy, N.Y.: J. C. Kneeland, 1848), 8, 15.

84. Garnet, *Past and the Present Condition*, 26.

85. Berlant and Edelman, *Sex, or the Unbearable*, 2. The book is an extended conversation between Berlant and Edelman, so each contribution is clearly marked.

86. Berlant and Edelman, *Sex, or the Unbearable*, 67.

87. Frederick Douglass, *Narrative of the Life of Frederick Douglass, An American Slave*, ed. Deborah McDowell (1845; New York: Oxford University Press, 1999), 17.

88. Charles Carroll, *The Negro a Beast; or, In the Image of God* ([1900]; Miami: Mnemosyne, 1969), 75.

89. Carroll, *Negro a Beast*, 28.

90. Carroll, *Negro a Beast*, 78–79.

91. W. S. Armistead, *The Negro Is a Man* (Tifton, Ga.: Armistead and Vickers, 1903), 1.

92. Armistead, *Negro Is a Man*, 99.

93. Armistead, *Negro Is a Man*, 100.

94. Armistead, *Negro Is a Man*, 103.

95. It is worth noting that Armistead, more than almost any other writer, was prone to insistent contradiction. And in this regard he was no different: after insisting that all the offspring of Ham were "negroes or blacks," Armistead writes that "so many different people from Ham shows that God, in his case also, followed His custom of developing a number of different nations from a single pair, Ham and his wife." That the introduction of diversity into the offspring of Ham accompanies a direct reference to his wife simply illustrates the fragility of the fantasy of racial purity. Armistead, *Negro Is a Man*, 103.

96. Armistead, *Negro Is a Man*, 105.

CHAPTER 9

Mapping Sex, Race, and Gender in the Corps of Discovery Expedition

WANDA S. PILLOW

The 1804–6 Corps of Discovery Expedition, commissioned by President Thomas Jefferson and led by Meriwether Lewis and William Clark, is celebrated and heralded as an epic tale of Manifest Destiny and a defining American event.[1] Bestselling historical works, romance novels, children's books, Hollywood movies, and yearly reenactments along the trail tell tales of the bravery, vision, and brilliance of Lewis and Clark. They also increasingly focus on Sacajawea, the young Lemhi Shoshone woman who, with her then infant son, Baptiste, accompanied the expedition.[2] Twenty-nine additional men made up the permanent party of the Corps, including Charbonneau, a French Canadian trader and Sacajawea's "husband," and York, Clark's Black African slave.[3]

The Corps in its makeup and interactions with Native communities offers a unique opportunity to examine stories of encounter and critically reread what becomes visible when the "fantastic conflation" of gender, race, colonialism, and sex are centered in an analysis of the journey.[4] Lewis and Clark's journal entries about sexual activity during the expedition and later interpretations of these entries offer a mapping of the lingering "intimate relations" of colonialism.[5] The journals provide a lens into the "intimate interactions of ordinary people" who were, it could be argued, under extraordinary circumstances.[6]

The presence of York and Sacajawea on the expedition has posed particular problems for scholars. Given their absence in the archive—anything known about York and Sacajawea is always filtered through another, whether journal entries,

letters, or pieces of oral history—how does history account for a slave and an indentured teen mother as part of an American "Corps of Discovery"? Sacajawea's
and York's positions as "captives" within the Corps, as servant and slave, provoke
questions of what happens when we look at the expedition, at Lewis and Clark,
at Native encounters through an Indian woman *and* a black man? How are stories
of sexual encounter based on exchange or trade complicated by the presence of
Sacajawea and York? Did Sacajawea's presence, as a Native woman, affect constructions of York's blackness? And how did York's presence alongside Indigenous
peoples contribute to racial demarcations during the expedition and affect later
interpretations?

These questions highlight specific challenges in attempting to think through the
multiple margins in this project with subjects like Sacajawea and York. Lewis and
Clark's journals contain few references to either Sacajawea or York, their absence
an indicator of social relations of the time. Yet we also know that such subjects
simultaneously bore a hypervisibility, overburdened by racial and colonial discourses and images that produce and sustain systems of control and domination.[7]
This tension between absence and hyperpresence is particularly evident in interpretations of York and Sacajawea after the expedition, whether they are ignored,
distorted, or reclaimed.[8]

Mapping these tensions through Sacajawea and York requires a broader and
more in-depth rereading of the archive—a reading against the grain of what is
simultaneously present and absent. Saidiya Hartman describes this process as
an encounter with "the constraints and silences imposed by the nature of the archive," a condition that necessitates a reading "best understood as a combination
of foraging and disfiguration."[9] Such an approach involves not simply a search for
Sacajawea and York in the archive but an archival mapping of the social and cultural conditions shaping how Sacajawea and York have been ignored, storied, and
represented, as an Indian woman and a black man, since the expedition.

This framework raises more possibilities than can be discussed in one essay.
Here, then, the emphasis is specifically on what would it mean to take seriously
Thomas Lowry's comment that during the twenty-six month expedition "sex was
never far from center stage."[10] Focusing on this assertion takes sexual stories seriously as a specific project of modernity and builds on cultural histories detailing how relations of power shaped categories of race and gender and reinforced
institutions and practices of colonialism, slavery and conquest.[11] Although this
essay does not directly debate existing narratives of sexual conquest as cultural
exchange or trade, reading sex through Lewis and Clark's journals and tracing how
Sacajawea and York have been present or absent in interpretations of key journal
entries offers a rereading of how gender, race, and colonialism continue to operate
through sexual stories.

Thus this essay places Sacajawea and York alongside reproductions of sexual stories of the Corps, primarily stories proliferated in the late twentieth century, a time of renewed interest in the expedition leading up to the bicentennial celebrations in 2004. Here, for example, the interest is not in proving or disproving that the expedition for York was "the time of his life" but rather tracing how such a declaration gains currency and why it matters. While concerned with representation of margins, the methodology of this project is concerned not with recuperating a voice for York and Sacajawea but rather with writing in their existence and acknowledging how their presence marked the Corps and has tangled our subsequent understanding of it.

Using Eve Sedgwick's discussion of "male homosocial desire" to analyze sexual narratives of the Corps helps identify how the specificity of sexual colonial constructions reinforce "structures for maintaining and transmitting patriarchal power."[12] The addition of York and Sacajawea into the "erotic triangle" of (white) homosocial solidarity also demonstrates how deeply narratives of repulsion and attraction are embedded in colonial and racial desire.[13] Three mappings begin this analysis: mapping the Corps as a sexual (white) homosocial journey; mapping constructions of York's black masculinity; and lastly mapping Sacajawea's presence and absence in these spaces detailing how she has been sexually domesticated by homosocial interpretations.

Mapping Sex and White Homosocial Spaces

Thomas Lowry states that "sex is the long ignored theme of Lewis and Clark and their immortal journey.... Sex is ... the gigantic fact that all agree to ignore."[14] While Lowry's statement is compelling, it is not accurate. Acknowledgment of sexual relations between the Corps expedition and Native women was included in the earliest histories, and these relations continue to be mentioned. However, what is missing in this attention is an explicit analysis of sex, the meaning of sexual relations during the expedition, and the legacy of the most often circulated sexual stories.

The reader of Lewis and Clark's journals does not have to look far before finding evidence of sex. Out of all the entries describing Native peoples, over one-quarter refer to sexual encounters between Corps men and Native women. By the time of the expedition, narratives of sexual encounters between settlers and Natives were an established literary genre and circulated in print media. Interracial sexual unions across the colonies established new social orders as the legality of such relations were debated in courts of law, whose decisions determined status and rights. Tales from previous explorers, hundreds of years of colonial encounters with Native peoples along the northern and southern coasts and inland areas, and prescriptive racial boundaries set by slavery preceded the expedition by many years.[15]

Thus by the time the Corps set forth, Indian people figured prominently in the early-nineteenth-century American mind and imagination, and contrasting images depicted Native peoples as generous, honest, and brave or as lazy, dirty, and dishonest savages.[16] Approximately one-fourth of the permanent party of the Corps was made up of explorers and trappers, men who had interacted with Native communities before the expedition, and at least three men were identified as having French Canadian fathers and Native mothers. Sexual expectations and attitudes about sex before and during the expedition would have been influenced by all these factors and by colonial and racial tropes prevalent at the time.

Prior to the expedition, Lewis and Clark exchanged correspondence detailing minute particulars for the journey but did not write about their preparations for sex. This omission may indicate how taken for granted and inevitable sexual encounter as part of the journey was viewed, because prepared for sex they were. As Lowry explains, "The explorers anticipated and expected sex and venereal disease. . . . Their medicine chests were filled with venereal remedies."[17] Such preparation attests to the sexual knowledge of the time, and "venereal disease"—specifically syphilis—was the most frequently described ailment in Lewis and Clark's journals.

Lewis in particular was interested in treatments for sexually transmitted diseases. During the expedition he carefully recorded incidences and descriptions of venereal disease found among Native communities and displayed curiosity about Native remedies. He penned this journal entry at Fort Clatsop on January 27, 1806:

> Goodrich has recovered from the Louis veneri which he contracted from an amorous contact with a Chinnook damsel. I cured him as I did Gibson last winter by the uce of murcury. I cannot learn that the Indians have any simples which are sovereign specifics in the cure of this disease; and indeed I doubt very much wheter any of them have any means of effecting a perfect cure. when once this disorder is contracted by them it continues with them during life; but always ends in decipitude, death, or premature old age; tho' from the uce of certain simples together with their diet, they support this disorder with but little inconvenience for many years, and even enjoy a tolerable share of health; particularly so among the Chippeways who I believe to be better skilled in the uce of those simples than any nation of Savages in North America.[18]

It is difficult to have an exact count of how many men of the Corps were treated for venereal disease during the expedition. Lowry asserts that Lewis and Clark must have "treated many, perhaps most, of their men for the effects of venereal disease," and some include Lewis in this estimate.[19]

While discussion and evidence of venereal disease during the expedition provides a way to mark sex along the trail, it is the more nuanced commentary of sexual relations that is of interest here, the slippages in the journals when Lewis and Clark step away from scientific language to describe Native peoples and sexual encounters, such as Lewis's use of "damsel" and "Savages" in the cited journal excerpt. In the following discussion I review the most commonly referenced passages from Lewis and Clark's journals: October 1804, September 1805, and January 1805, which have recirculated in scholarly and popular history texts creating and establishing white homosocial narratives of understanding about the Corps and sex.

The expedition set off outside St. Louis, Missouri, on May 14, 1804, and sexual relations between Corps members and Native women began within one month of the journey's beginning. Clark's journal entry of October 1804 describes the Arikara, noting: "Their womin [were] verry fond of caressing our men &c," and relations continued while the party spent winter near the Mandan-Hidatsa villages (in what is now the Bismarck, North Dakota, area). From December 1804 to April 1805, Lewis and Clark established a camp, Fort Mandan, across the river from the main Mandan village, where over four thousand people lived—a population at that time larger than St. Louis or Washington, D.C.[20] Their journals note regular visits with the village—for trade, socializing, and sexual relations—and include repeated notations stating, "Some of the party came home & Some stayed all night." The first venereal complaints appear by mid-January 1805, and by September 19, 1805, Lewis reports: "Brakings out, or irruptions of the Skin, have also been common with us for some time."[21]

One of the most commented-on passages from Clark's journal concerns a Mandan ceremony. On January 5–7, 1805, Corps members were invited to witness a Buffalo Dance, a three-night ritual to ensure hunting success, which included sexual relations as a practice of transferring successful hunting power. Clark describes the ritual as "a curious Custom [in which] old men arrange themselves in a circle & after Smoke a pipe. . . . the young men who have their wives back of the circle go to one of the old men in a whining tone and (request) the old man to take his wife (who presents necked except a robe) . . . if the Old man (or a white man) returns to the lodge without gratifying the man & his wife, he offeres her again and again." Clark states, "All this is to cause the buffalow to Come near So that they may kill thim" and elaborates, "We Sent a man to this Medisan last night, they gave him 4 Girls."[22]

Clark's journal entry is the only description of the dance, and this passage has undergone multiple edits. First published in Nicholas Biddle's 1814 edition, the passage was translated into Latin and included additional text from Biddle's interview with Clark after the expedition. Later the passage was left out of an 1893 reprinting of the journals, only to be reinserted in later editions. The Moulton editions, published 1983–99, include the passage, retaining Biddle's addition of "(or a white man)," thus assuring the place of white men as "Big Medicine" in expedition lore. As if the convoluted history of the journals is not enough, interpretations of Clark's description are flagrantly exaggerated, ascribing race and gender social normativity to what by the late twentieth century had become a highly eroticized event from 1805.

Consider for example these statements: "The Americans were said to be 'untiringly zealous in the attracting of the cow' and in transferring power," and "as the drumbeat became more insistent and the chanting swelled, one of the youngsters would approach an old man and beg him to take his wife, who in her turn would appear naked before the elder."[23] While these descriptions, found in best-selling histories and repeated in scholarly works, partially reflect Clark's journal entry, they move into almost salacious detail: "To the great luck of the enlisted men, the Mandans attributed to the whites great powers and big medicine. . . . One unnamed private made four contributions. Sure enough there was a good buffalo hunt a few days later."[24] These reinterpretations are also prevalent in educational material found on the PBS Lewis and Clark website, one of the most utilized resources by teachers and students:

> Some of these guys were just tottering old men, they could hardly move. And the girl would be there, half dressed or not dressed at all. And the brave would offer the wife to the old man, who was supposed to go outside the lodge in the terrible cold North Dakota winter and have a sexual intercourse which would transfer power to the young man and help bring back the buffalo. Some of these old men weren't up to it. The brave would then be on his knees, begging, "You've got to do it." The men of the expedition were a part of that, too. They also were begged by the braves to go out with their wives and transfer that power.[25]

Such representations are abundant. The following, one example of many, is available and authorized by its inclusion in the Journals of the Lewis and Clark Expedition website:[26] "The enlisted men meanwhile were cementing relations in their own way. For the first time in almost a year there were plenty of women around with whom they could satisfy pent-up sexual energies without restraint. Male relatives raised few objections, token payments sufficed, and the women, according to both Clark and Ordway, were for the most part handsome, clean, lively, and lecherous."[27]

The wink, wink—men will be men—characterizations of Lewis and Clark's journal entries reinforce present-day colonial understandings of and homosocial fantasies about the expedition. Certainly Lewis and Clark wrote out of the colonial frameworks of their time. Their writings depict Native peoples as savage and primitive and focus on instrumental interactions of trade and cooperation. While providing some quasi-ethnographic detail, both captains replicate ideologies of their time in describing Native peoples as "Dirty, Kind, pore, & extravegent" and repeatedly referring to Native women as "drudges" and "low." Lewis and Clark's journal entries also demonstrate attempts to navigate each tribal nation's sexual cultural traditions. In August 1805, Lewis remarks on the Shoshone:

> The chastity of their woman is not held in high estimation, and the husband will for a trifle barter the companion of his bead for a night or longer if he conceives the reward adequate; tho' they are not so importunate that we should caress their women as the sioux were and some of their women appear to be held more sacred than in any nation we have seen I requested the men to give them no cause for jealousy by having connection with their women without their knowledge, which with them strange as it may seem is considered as disgracefull to the husband as clandestine connections of a similar kind are among civilized nations. To prevent this mutual exchange of good officies altogether I know it impossible to effect, particularly on the part of our young men whom some months abstanence have made very polite to those tawney damsels.[28]

Similarly after a visit from a Chinook party in November 1805, Clark writes: "Those people appear to View horedom Sensuality as a necessary evile, and do not appear to abhore this as Crime in the unmarried females."[29] However, an early incident at Fort Mandan offers a glimpse at how the captains and their men may have misunderstood and misread Native cultural norms with sexual openness. John Ordway, a sergeant in the Corps, purportedly had relations with a Mandan woman outside the Buffalo dance ritual. This breech led to a threat to kill Ordway and a demand of trade goods from Lewis and Clark. Lewis and Clark diffused the situation, and as Lewis's passage above demonstrates, the captains did caution their men to pursue sexual relations without causing jealousy, although most of these admonitions were also related to containing or limiting venereal outbreaks. For example, in March 1806, Lewis writes of the long recovery of "so many of our party" after contact with a certain group of Chinook women, noting, "I therefore gave the men a particular charge with respect to them which they promised me to observe."[30]

There is much in the journals' entries to contribute to understandings of colonial constructs of gender, nation, and status, but scholarly works and best-selling histories, which have shaped how America thinks about, understands, and teaches the expedition, have ignored such complexities. Consider how best-selling author Stephen Ambrose describes the sexual encounters of the Corps: "Some tribes were pretty chaste and, and had a high morality. And other tribes the morality was looser."[31] Such statements clearly mark understandings of Native traditions and rituals through Eurocentric definitions of behavior and create assumptions about American Indian cultures, without any analysis of colonialism.

By the end of the twentieth century, interpretations of Lewis and Clark, references to the Corps and sex were flattened to homosocial narratives of male bonding. Key to homosocial retellings is an ennobling of Lewis and Clark as a certain class of white men by removing them from direct interactions in sexual relations. Lewis and Clark have been accepted as narrators only, never participants; they observed "their men in numerous sexual encounters" and effectively managed Native peoples and their men through multiple sexual encounters and treatment of venereal diseases.[32]

In this way, Lewis and Clark become omnipresent narrators. The absence of an explicit record of their participation in sexual activity is taken as evidence that they did not engage.[33] Thomas Slaughter explains this willingness of history to not record Lewis and Clark as sexually active because "it is important to the expedition's historians that Lewis and Clark practiced sexual restraint during the journey.... Abstinence, at least from relations with racially darker women, is also a defining characteristic of the heroic type of which Lewis and Clark are ideals."[34] Not having sex becomes one of the key distinguishing qualities of Lewis and Clark, separating them as white American men of honor. In this narrative, Lewis and Clark practiced restraint over base sexual needs, marking them superior to their men and Native peoples.

The desire to leave Lewis and Clark out of stories of sexual encounter maintains their elite status and contributes a unique hierarchy to the homosocial tellings related to the expedition. Accepting Lewis and Clark as authors and never participants establishes their white authority and allows consumers of the expedition to separate Lewis and Clark from the contradictions and discomfort surrounding the colonial sexual relations of the expedition, the "dirty secrets."

Male historians in particular have accepted Lewis and Clark's supremacy, recasting the expedition as a uniquely male journey into the wilderness, "the greatest camping trip of all time, the greatest hunting trip of all time, but so much more."[35] These tellings turn the expedition into a homosocial tale of friendship and bonds. Ambrose writes eloquently on this topic:

> What Lewis and Clark and the men of the Corps of Discovery had demonstrated is that there is nothing men cannot do if they get themselves together, and act as a team. Here you have thirty-two men who had become so close, so bonded, that when they heard a cough at night they knew instantly who had a cold. They could see a man's silhouette in the dark and know who it was. They knew who liked salt on his meat, and who didn't care. They knew who could get a fire going the quickest on a rainy morning. Around the campfire, they got to know about each other's parents and loved ones, and each other's hopes and dreams. They had come to love each other to the point that they would sell their lives gladly to save a comrade. They had developed a bond. They had become a band of brothers, and together they were able to accomplish feats that we just stand astonished at today.[36]

Ambrose gives credit to the moral superiority of Lewis and Clark in being able to form these tight bonds and describes their friendship as based on love explaining,

"At its height, friendship is an ecstasy. For Lewis and Clark it was an ecstasy, and the critical factor in their great success."[37]

The "ecstasy" of male bonding on the expedition creates an "interdependence and solidarity" necessary to (white) homosocial narratives and reaffirms Lewis and Clark's superiority.[38] York's blackness and slave status are absent from Ambrose's paean; in these narratives, he is rolled into "the band of brothers," and Sacajawea is the absent/present female that homosocial patriarchal power organizes around. However, what happens when York's presence and blackness must be accounted for? And how is Sacajawea made female? The following discussion continues to map sexual narratives of the expedition, tracing how York and Sacajawea's presence complicates homosocial interpretations of Lewis and Clark's journal entries.

Mapping York's Black Masculinity

Tracing York through expedition journals and later writings is a foraging through absences, tropes of blackness, and perpetuations of myths. A scan of history books include the following themes presented as facts about York: York was "dark as ink" and large and "strong as an ox," an "Adonis sculptured in ebony."[39] York possessed great sexual prowess and was a skilled dancer; he was the expedition clown; he fathered several children with Native women and after the expedition became an Indian chief; he was a buffoon and later in life a drunk; he was Clark's entrusted friend and freed after the expedition only to regret his freedom because he was unable to manage his own welfare.[40] Despite the fact that most of these characterizations are unsupportable or have been disproven as myths, they continue to be circulated.

We do know that York was born into slavery to Clark's family and raised with Clark as his personal slave. We know little about York's appearance, and there is no record of what he thought about his experiences on the expedition. Clark's decision to take his slave on the expedition was not due to his enlightened sense of fairness, but was likely a nondecision; where a gentleman slave owner went, so too did his "manservant." References to York in the expedition journals confirm that he continued to serve at Clark's bidding. York obeyed on the trail; there is no evidence that he did not. He was a part of hunting parties, but we do not know where he slept or ate his meals during the journey. In the intimacy of the expedition, York's role could not have been easy; he was a Black man, a slave in status to all other Corps members, but he was also Clark's entrusted man, and this may have protected York from mistreatment.

By the time the expedition settled into the Fort Mandan village for winter camp, Lewis and Clark were aware of the keen interest of Native people in York. While the belief that Native people would treat white men like gods was a common narrative of early colonial settlers, by the time of the expedition Native-settler contact had developed other forms of ceremony and trade-economy relations. Lewis and Clark, as white American ambassadors, prepared to meet Native leaders with presidential medals, flags, and other gifts. There was a definite hierarchy in the Corps; it was organized and run as a military unit with divisions of labor and status, which yielded certain privileges along the trail and determined payment afterward.

York, however, had no official status in the Corps and received no compensation for his role on the expedition. Yet, as Clark's slave, he was expected to perform multiple duties and accompanied Clark everywhere, including to meetings with Native leaders. Typically Native scouts announced the presence of the Corps, or word of its impending arrival would reach a village through other means. Lewis, Clark, York, and chosen members of the Corps, some until Charbonneau's hire serving as interpreters, entered a village for council—a time of talk, gift and trade exchange, and negotiations. Communication occurred through gesture, sign language, and drawings, and often required three-part translations, from English to French to Native languages and then back again. Through these meetings, which brought together intersections and margins of nation, status, slave relations, and racial classification, we can begin to identify the cracks that York's presence rendered and how these fissures have been written otherwise after the expedition.

As noted earlier, York's presence as a shadow of Clark was not out of the ordinary. York, like Native women and children, would have been on the periphery of council meetings, a nonentity until there was a demand for him to perform a service or meet a need. Clark and Lewis's first awareness of Native interest in York occurred during meetings with the Arikara in October 1804, and there is evidence that they used this interest during the remainder of the expedition to establish relations with Native communities. On October 9, 1804, Clark writes: "—the Indians much asstonished at my Black Servent and Call him the big medison, this nation never Saw a black man before."[41] On October 15, he notes: "Those people are much pleased with my black Servent."[42] Clark again remarks, eleven days later, "[The Mandans] appeared delighted with the Steel Mill which we were obliged to use, also with my black Servent."[43]

This interest at times moved York from periphery to center, but always under white eyes. Two occurrences described in Lewis and Clark's journals point out how this occurred. One involves York reportedly being "examined" by Native people, and the second involves York being ordered to dance. Certainly both of these occurrences are highly charged and encoded with racial meaning; however, consideration of what Lewis and Clark recorded versus what has been proliferated from these accounts demonstrates how racialized markings of York's masculinity have become even more entrenched two hundred plus years after the expedition.

The first incident, which has incited multiple retellings, occurred after Clark began to notice Arikara interest in York, and he describes a large crowd of Arikara, who "all flocked around him & examind. him top to toe."[44] Clark does not mention how or where this scene took place—were they walking through the village or in a council meeting? Nor do we know whether Clark ordered York to stand and allow examination, but we do know that Clark and other Corps members allowed this examination to occur and that York in this way became visible to the expedition journal writers. By 1908, this scene was reimagined as York "stripped down bare" and immortalized in Charles M. Russell's painting, a mass-produced depiction of York stripped of his shirt as Indian men try to rub the blackness off his skin.[45]

Hold onto this image of York stripped and examined as we move to the second occurrence, dancing. Although in Lewis and Clark's journals, there are only two references to York dancing—and in each he is "ordered" to participate—later representations of York as the main entertainment during the expedition become explicitly tied to his hypersexualization. This is not to deny that York being ordered to dance marked a racialized experience for those observing, an issue I discuss later, but the expedition journals clearly mark the prevalence of music and dance as common to the Corps and an activity in which most of the men, including Lewis and Clark, participated. Several notations in the journals refer to men from the Corps playing instruments and dancing for Native people. During the expedition, music and dancing served as entertainment as well as forms of social interaction and diplomacy with Native communities.

Reporting on New Year's Day celebrations in 1805 at Fort Mandan, Clark writes: "I found them much pleased at the Danceing of our men, I ordered my black Servent to Dance which amused the Croud verry much, and Some what astonished them, that So large a man Should be active."[46] What is interesting in this passage is that York was *not* initially participating; he was not a part of the Corps dancing but rather was on the side. York could participate only when ordered to perform by Clark. He only became visible to Clark when Clark noticed Native interest and played with that interest by ordering York into the central spotlight.

While later interpretations of Clark's passage tend to leave out "ordered" and assign York agency in choosing to dance, the recognizable trope of the "black-faced minstrel" remains prevalent.[47] Consider this commonly accepted rewriting of Clark's entry: "York was irrepressible. He hammed it up; he flexed his muscles, rolled his eyes, growled, and displayed himself to the curious bystanders."[48] Another interpretation in the same vein reads: "He was a slave. We know he was big. We know he was very athletic. He was a great dancer. He was devoted to William Clark."[49] Such flattened interpretations support white homosocial tellings of the Corps.

We cannot know if York "was a great dancer" and "athletic"—at one point in the expedition journals, Clark describes York as "fat"—but assignment of tropes of "black" characteristics, including submissive loyalty, are accepted as fact.[50] In

214 • WANDA S. PILLOW

this way, the interest of Native peoples in York, as evidenced in five journal entries over the twenty-six-month expedition, has been rewritten in ways that maintain York as spectacle through white eyes and reinforce commonly accepted tropes of hyperracialized and sexualized viewing of black bodies and specifically black masculinity. These repeated tropes and images—York stripped down for examination and York as dancer/performer—reinforce racial stereotypes, and Russell's visual image yields a striking similarity to the practice of examining African Americans on the slave auction block. Tribal nations, particularly those west of St. Louis, would not have had this context in which to put York's display, but for Lewis and Clark and other Corps members, the spectacle of York on display for examination and entertainment was normalized by racialized attitudes and practices of a slave economy.

Further, when we step back from this scene and observe Lewis and Clark observing Native peoples observing/examining York, we see how reinterpretations of this display participate in and continue a viewing that reproduces a racial order of Lewis and Clark's supremacy that has continued over two hundred years after the expedition. In present-day interpretations, what is left unexamined in these scenarios is how Lewis and Clark and the other white men are not simply passive observers but participants in the construction of the spectacle they believe they are observing. Not only did they observe and witness York on display as a natural, assumptive role for a black slave, but depictions of Native people's naive, childlike curiosity about York's blackness further allow and affirm their white superiority in the moment and with repeated readings and viewings in perpetuity.

Perpetuation of existing racialized tropes has played a significant role in talk about York and sex. Although there is absolutely no mention in the original journals of York engaging in sexual relations during the expedition, published notes from an 1810 Nicholas Biddle interview with Clark and extrapolation from the references to Native "interest" in York quoted above, have overwhelmingly been taken up and used to reproduce York as emblematic of black sexual prowess and depravity. Biddle added his paraphrased notes to the published edited journals of Lewis and Clark in 1814, quoting Clark as stating: "The black man York participated largely in these favors; for, instead of inspiring any prejudice, his color seemed to procure him additional advantages from the Indians."[51] Many scholarly and popular texts do not clarify the origin of specific statements about York, leading the reader to assume that quotes are direct descriptions from the original expedition journals, when in reality much of the detail about York is based on Biddle's interviews with Clark.

The truth of whether York engaged in sexual relations with Native women during the expedition will remain speculative and is not the primary question here; rather the focus is on what narratives have circulated and what they produce. While Clark does mention Native reference to York as "big medicine," the journal also states,

"Every thing which is incomprehensible to the indians they call *big medicine,* and is the opperation of the presnts and power of the *great sperit.*"[52] Counter to this definition, interpretations of York as "big medicine" have attributed this solely to evidence of his black physical strength and sexual proficiency. The attention and interest in York by Native peoples are narrowed to white colonial conceptions of race and sex. In best-selling histories and scholarly works, York's subjectivity is repeatedly attributed and limited to his sexual aptitude, and conjectures are presented as occurrence: "The Indians love him, and the Indian women especially loved York and he took full advantage of that so that on many occasions York would be missing that night and he would be in the lodge with one of the Indians. Sometimes with the Indian husband standing guard while the business was completed."[53]

A 2001 publication offers the following depiction: "York, fat, tall and enormously strong, was a favorite," furthering emphasizing that although Clark and Lewis could control his behavior, they could not put a damper on "his unflagging sexual prowess."[54] Several texts, in a fit of white homosocial camaraderie, jokingly refer to Clark's notation that after a stretch of extreme cold, "my Servents feet also *frosted* & his P—s a little," with one scholar editorializing: "If one can believe the numerous stories over the next forty years regarding Indians who looked a lot like York, it would appear that he made a full recovery."[55] Consider also this more racially charged conclusion: "His [York's] kinky-haired progeny were traceable among the Indian tribes contacted by the Expedition all the way to the Pacific."[56]

The prevalence of white, male, homosocial talk about York's sexuality creates and reinforces entrenched ideologies of the black man's uncontrollable, animal-like sexuality, while at the same time retaining white, male, civilized superiority. Key to this formation is the acceptance of Lewis and Clark's white sexual purity during the expedition, thus allowing a focus on and fetishization of black-on-brown sex. York's hypersexuality—evidenced by his "kinky-haired progeny"—is celebrated only because in these tellings he is having sex with Native women, who are thus also positioned as hypersexual and animal-like in their morals and needs.[57]

Discussion of York's sexual prowess cannot be read as a disruption of whiteness because it is written and proliferated through white homosocial gazes that maintain status and control. York's sexuality is both titillating and a warning, a performance to control, always observed and channeled through white eyes. One way critical discussions of York's presence have been controlled is by rampant portrayals of the expedition as "the time of his life." In this representation, York's ability to engage in sexual relations with Native women is most frequently cited as evidence of his freedom on the trail and of the Corps as an early exemplar of American equality.

In these tellings, economies of slave relations are removed from the expedition. To imagine York having sex, one must also imagine that he was free to leave

Clark's side and pass into Native villages, for a few hours or for the night. While the expedition did likely stretch conditions of social relations, there is no mention of York ever being on his own—except on one occasion when he became "lost" from a hunting party. Every mention of York and his activities places him within a group or within sight of Clark or another white man. Despite this, repeated commentary encourages present-day audiences to look at York's experiences on the expedition as evidencing "a world of lightened enslavement."[58] Ambrose asserts, "York had a great time on the expedition."[59] Another scholar argues: "It does not take a flight of imagination from these sources to surmise that York's expedition was personally transforming and empowering."[60]

Focusing on York's supposed free access to sexual encounters ignores and makes invisible his daily status and lived conditions as a black man who was a slave. These depictions seem written as an attempt to counter the fact that after the expedition Clark did *not* release York from slavery. By summer of 1809, Clark wrote his brother that he had refused to send York to join his wife, who was also a slave. Clark wrote that York became "insolent and sulky," and he resorted to giving York "a Severe trouncing" and locking him away for an unspecified period of time. Soon afterward, Clark hired York out to a "severe master," and it is unclear if York ever received his freedom.[61] Homosocial narratives of the expedition make invisible the complexities of what York's presence can yield about racial constructs of blackness and ignore what York's presence does to whiteness and postcolonial understandings of slavery.

Mapping a Domestication of Sacajawea

In the above mappings, Sacajawea becomes necessary to the formation of a white homosocial space and to further define York's blackness. Although she was pregnant when Lewis and Clark met her, she is never depicted as having sex, either in expedition journals or in scholarly texts written after the journey. She is always defined against and through her relationships with white men and is further defined by readings of the sexual encounters of the Corps.

Native women were integral to colonial relations; they were often the "middle ground" between males and cultural exchanges.[62] A strong body of work has articulated the complexities of these spaces.[63] However, Sacajawea, with few exceptions, has been described as if such work had not been produced. Due to the absence of critical engagement of Sacajawea's presence, homosocial narratives write her as if "colonial depictions of Indian women and their sexual relations became a means of imagining, planning, and explaining colonization."[64] What if, instead, Sacajawea were written as an Indian woman "negotiating some of the dramatic social, economic, and cultural effects of colonization."[65] Were Native women utilizing mechanisms of survival, or were they traitors, helpmates to Manifest Destiny, or creating new associations?

Discussion of Sacajawea occurs at the intersections of these depictions. On the journey, she occupied multiple contradictory middle grounds as well as margins; the complexity of these positions offer places to trace the intricacies of how gender and race entered into Lewis and Clark's accounts and the interpretations that came afterward. Similar to the case of York, an insertion of Sacajawea's Native female identity as an active presence into expedition journals and later interpretations allows additional mapping of how "the concept of margins [allows us] to pose new questions about colonial experiences."[66]

By the time of the expedition, Indian women were commonly understood through two distinct tropes: one, the Native woman as primitive, overworked, quasi slaves of Native men, the "squaw drudge"; and simultaneously, Native women as sexually appealing "damsels" eager to engage with white men. As indicated earlier, writings about the Corps replicate established views of Native women as "lustful and devoid of restraint . . . willing to prostitute themselves . . . in return for a few glass beads or other trifles."[67] Sacajawea's subjectivity seems to have escaped being contained within these constructions, but if so, why? Because she is not represented as a sexual damsel, should we assume that she was free from sexual approaches or colonial violence?

I form this question knowing it is unanswerable in the archive, but do so to highlight how much has been assumed in writings and constructions of Sacajawea. Once we place Sacajawea and her presence actively back into the daily life on the trail, we face the complexities her presence created for the Corps, and many omissions become apparent. For instance, we know nothing about her sexual encounters during the expedition, and while it has been assumed that she would not have been expected or required to have sexual relations after the birth of her son, by the end of the expedition, Baptiste was almost two and a half years old. We do not know how she was thought about, fantasized about, or acted upon by the men in the Corps or what she thought of them. We do not know where Sacajawea was when the men of the Corps were in council or dancing or having sex, or where she slept at night. Although it has been suggested in some interpretations, we do not know if Lewis and Clark announced Sacajawea off limits to sexual advances from the Corps men to keep control during the expedition or out of some measure of respect to Charbonneau, a white, albeit non-U.S. American, man who owned her and was referred to as her husband. Sacajawea, who like York was literally property of whiteness, occupied a complex marginal position.

While Sacajawea is absent from sexual stories and thus virginal in the record, we should not assume this absence is an innocent representation. In other words, why has there been such a need to describe and uphold Sacajawea differently from other Indian women of her time? The answer seems obvious. Like Pocahontas, Sacajawea is a symbol of the U.S. national imagination and its romance with the story of a young Native woman's relationship with white men. Sacajawea has been rewritten as an "Indian maiden" and used to affirm the white colonial national interests of Manifest Destiny, rewritten as a (white) feminist heroine and most recently as a multicultural object.[68]

The discrepancy between these constructions and her absence in the archive is glaring. Lewis and Clark's notations on Sacajawea concern the following: giving birth, carrying out tasks, participating in a few key events, and health. In the journals she is referred to as "squar" or as "Janey," the name given to her by Lewis. Certainly Sacajawea's inclusion on the expedition was indicative of her low status. Lewis and Clark would not have imagined or entertained a white woman joining the expedition and certainly not one with an infant. The fact that Sacajawea accompanied the expedition within two months of giving birth is not testimony to some enlightened view of Lewis and Clark, a myth perpetuated in popular representations, but rather evidence that it was only and exactly because they saw her as less than a woman, as a "squaw," as "savage," that her presence could be accepted.

Given the lack of formative information about Sacajawea in the expedition journals, it is useful to consider how she has been domesticated by texts after the expedition and how this domestication performs a whitening of Sacajawea that provides a counterpoint for York's blackness/slave status and reinforces homosocial narratives.[69] While Lewis and Clark rarely mention Sacajawea's roles, later interpretations of the expedition imagine and rewrite Sacajawea as the feminine, womanly presence that soothed the men and brought a civilized tone to their camp. Central to this move is a containment of Sacajawea's roles on the expedition. Within Corps literature there has been a shifting debate about whether Sacajawea served as an actual guide to Lewis and Clark—did she point the way? The past two decades have seen a shift toward clearly limiting her role and capacity as a guide and explorer.

Dayton Duncan, best-selling author of expedition books, coauthor of the award-winning *Corps of Discovery* film made with Ken Burns, and prominent contributor to the companion PBS website, which provides curricula linked to national and state history standards for K-12 public schools, sums up the debate about Sacajawea's roles this way: "She was an important person on the expedition. Her role's been romanticized and exaggerated. She was not a guide for the expedition. . . . But she helped find some food."[70] While Duncan is accurate in stating that Sacajawea has been a "romanticized" figure, the recent trend to diminish her roles also achieves certain outcomes. Once Sacajawea is contained through domestication, accounts of her can become more generous, and here her role in a white, male, homosocial patriarchy is apparent: "Having said she wasn't the guide, what she was was the cement. I believe really very strongly that having her along made that expedition. Just think about sitting around the campfire in Dakota on a May evening in 1805, and here is a girl with a baby at the breast, and that's a reminder to these young lions who are ready to take on the world, and to maybe kill a grizzly bear that day, that there is hearth and there is home, and there is more to life than the ultimate camping expedition, and I think it had a really positive and powerful effect on them to have her along."[71]

In these narratives, Sacajawea is used to represent home, femininity, purity and motherhood, and in this role turn the Corps into an extended family (with York perhaps on the fringes of the family?). Domesticating Sacajawea, positioning her as occupying spaces between civilization and savageness, places her within a comfortable colonial model of gender roles and reinforces the homosocial and masculinity narratives presented here.[72] In this domestication, Sacajawea retains early-twentieth-century constructions of her purity.[73] Ambrose echoes this theme, setting aside any ideas that Sacajawea, as an Indian woman, was impure, noting there was "never a hint of this teenage girl causing any problem, and these are thirty-two healthy young men, but there's never a hint of her causing a problem."[74]

Poetic, interpretive license is also taken to give voice to a Sacajawea who finally finds herself at peace "being with the White men."[75] Similar to narratives of York's "freedom," twentieth-century accounts find the need to make sense of Sacajawea's status, especially the problematic question of why, when the expedition in August 1805 met her Shoshone band and family, she didn't leave the expedition and remain with her people. Ignoring Sacajawea's status as an indentured Native woman with a male child, who was "half-white," current narratives explain Sacajawea's "choice" to stay with the expedition as a story of childhood displacement, after which she found a home and her people with whiteness and in the Corps.

This theme is furthered by repeated references to an infatuation or romance between Sacajawea and Clark or Sacajawea and Lewis. Lewis and Clark seem interchangeable in these narratives; what is important is that Sacajawea is presented as someone who understandably finds herself attracted and devoted to either man as an exemplar of the white American male. Just as important to this story line is that Sacajawea each time, regardless of the object of her affection, recognizes that the relationship cannot be, that it would not be fair to Clark or Lewis, because she would never truly fit within a white woman's world.[76]

Nowhere in Lewis and Clark's journals or in Biddle's interviews is there evidence of any such sentiment or relationship between Sacajawea and either captain. Parallel to interpretations that ignore the conditions of slavery, an agreement between Clark and Charbonneau (and Sacajawea) to place Baptiste with Clark and send him to St. Louis Academy, a Jesuit Catholic school, has been misused as proof of friendship, rather than what it was: a social contract of colonialism replicating common practices of removal of certain "half Indian" children from their Native cultures to be educated in white systems (a practice that formed the basis for widespread implementation of Indian boarding schools sixty years later).[77]

Likewise depictions of a domesticated Sacajawea cannot be extrapolated from Lewis and Clark's journals and stand in stark contrast to other Native women encountered by the Corps, who were described in animalistic terms and interpreted as having loose morals. Refreshed domesticated representations serving homosocial tellings continue to render Sacajawea's daily lived experiences as less than compelling. If she is not a guide, interpreter, or love interest of the captains, her life remains invisible and discounted under gender normativities. What would it look like to rethink Sacajawea within her identities and contexts: as Native woman, servant, mother, sexual object, caregiver, harvester, cook, trader, and interpreter? What would be challenged and altered if through these identities Sacajawea was also written as an explorer? The hierarchy of Lewis and Clark as the only true knowers and explorers would have be to rethought and rewritten.

Placing Sacajawea and York side by side in these interpretations yields further cracks in homosocial narratives. How did Sacajawea and York encounter and experience each other? Did they at times share similar duties and roles and share margins of domesticity? Teasing these absences out will take more foraging in the archives, but the domesticizing of Sacajawea in texts after the expedition mark York in his absence. A whitening domestication of Sacajawea contributes to a valorization of white men on the expedition, particularly Lewis and Clark, as well as reinforcing, in romanticized ways, traditional domesticate gender roles.

This gendered social order framework placed on the Corps maintains domestic arrangements, including slavery. Sacajawea's middle ground as a gendered racial subject allows her to be used to meet a discursive need; she can be whitened in ways that cannot be performed on York's body. Domesticating Sacajawea delimits seeing her presence as a disruption leading to complexities along the trail and in our readings of the journey afterward.

Mapping Sexual Stories: Reading Absences and Presence

This essay begins to explore how readings and understanding of the Corps expedition are challenged when Sacajawea and York are centered as presences in the daily lived experiences along the trail and within popular interpretations produced after the expedition. By specifically examining the production of sexual intimacies and relations reported in the journals, we see that York and Sacajawea's depictions demonstrate how white homosocial narratives are created and repeatedly circulated in U.S. popular imagination and racial discourse.

Faced with subjects who are both absent from the archive yet proliferated in interpretations requires shifting from attempts to prove or disprove common notions about the expedition—Were Lewis and Clark abstinent? Was the expedition for York "the time of his life"? Did Sacajawea lead the way?—to tracing how such articulations and debates gain currency and why it matters. This approach works to interrupt the proliferation of the "it may not be exactly true, but it makes a great story" narratives about the Corps and examine how retellings of sexual encounters during the expedition "remain entangled within a politics of domination."[70]

Paying attention to the marginal or absent yet at times hypervisible positionalities of York and Sacajawea offers insights into how their complex identities have been used to define the expedition and present Lewis and Clark as exemplars of white American men. Interpretations of the expedition depend on and deploy margins and marginality of race and gender through York and Sacajawea as a way to explain a palatable colonialism that keeps margins contained. Mapping this process points to and provides insight into historical contradictions of social constructs and their relevancy for our own time. Although as Gerald Vizenor states Lewis and Clark needed and "wanted to be *seen* by tribal people on their expedition," as "their mission would have been threatened not by the presence of the other, but by the absence of the tribes," York and Sacajawea, as expedition participants, have been simply and violently removed, inserted, or distorted from the record to suit white homosocial and colonial, racialized tellings.[79]

Methodologically, this project seeks another kind of remembrance, one that acknowledges the embodied social relations of subjects such as Sacajawea and York, so that the complexities of their presence begin to be actively accounted for in colonial histories and present-day constructions.

Notes

1. See Stephen Ambrose, *Undaunted Courage* (New York: Touchstone/Simon and Schuster, 1996); Dayton Duncan and Ken Burns, *Lewis and Clark: The Journey of the Corps of Discovery* (New York: Knopf, 1997); Eva Emery Dye, *The Conquest: The True Story of the Adventures of the Lewis and Clark Expedition* (Chicago: A. C. McClurg, 1902); David Holloway, *Lewis and Clark and the Crossing of North America* (New York: Saturday Review Press, 1974).

2. See Nancy Frazier, *Sacajawea: The Girl Nobody Knows* (New York: David McKay, 1967); Grace Raymond Hebard, *Sacajawea* (Glendale, Calif.: Arthur H. Clark, 1933); Joyce B. Hunsaker, *Sacagawea Speaks: Beyond the Shining Mountains with Lewis and Clark* (Guilford, Conn.: TwoDot Book/The Globe Pequot Press, 2001); Donna Kessler, *The Making of Sacagawea: A Euro-American Legend* (Tuscaloosa: University of Alabama Press, 1996).

3. Lewis and Clark's designation of Sacajawea as Charbonneau's "wife" was indicative of their nomenclature and a term they applied to Native women whom they saw to be another man's property. While their designation has been repeated without question

and certainly some relations between Native women and European men were legally or culturally recognized, we know that Sacajawea as a young teen joined Charbonneau's household as his servant and second Native "wife" when he purportedly won her in a bet. See Sharon Block, *Rape and Sexual Power in Early America* (Chapel Hill: University of North Carolina Press, 2006); Anne-Marie Plane, *Colonial Intimacies: Indian Marriage in Early New England* (Ithaca, N.Y.: Cornell University Press, 2000).

4. Except in direct quotes, I use the terms "Native," "Indigenous," "Nation," and "Indian" interchangeably. None of these terms is unproblematic. My varying use is a reminder that the Indian, as represented in narratives of the Corps, is always already a simulation infected with colonial desire. Gerald Vizenor, *Fugitive Poses: Native American Indian Scenes of Absence and Presence* (Lincoln: University of Nebraska Press, 1998). The quotation is from Anne McClintock, *Imperial Leather: Race, Gender and Sexuality in the Colonial Context* (New York: Routledge, 1995), 4.

5. Ann Laura Stoler, *Carnal Knowledge and Imperial Power* (Berkeley: University of California Press, 2002), 1.

6. Kirsten Fischer, *Suspect Relations: Sex, Race, and Resistance in Colonial North Carolina* (Ithaca, N.Y.: Cornell University Press, 2002), 1.

7. McClintock, *Imperial Leather*.

8. Attempts to reclaim York and Sacajawea often reproduce romanticized narratives and distortions about their lives. For analysis, see Robert B. Betts, *In Search of York: The Slave Who Went to the Pacific with Lewis and Clark* (Boulder: University Press of Colorado, 2000); Michael Heffernan and Carol Medlicot, "A Feminine Atlas? Sacagawea, the Suffragettes and the Commemorative Landscape in the American West, 1904–1910," *Gender, Place and Culture* 9, no. 2 (2002): 109–31; Sally McBeth, "Memory, History, and Contested Pasts: Re-imagining Sacagawea/Sacajawea," *American Indian Culture and Research Journal* 27, no. 1 (2003): 1–32; Wanda S. Pillow, "Searching for Sacajawea: Whitened Reproductions and Endarkened Representations," *Hypatia* 22, no. 2 (2007): 1–19.

9. Saidiya V. Hartman, *Scenes of Subjection: Terror, Slavery, and Self-Making in Nineteenth-Century America* (New York: Oxford University Press), 12.

10. Thomas P. Lowry, *Venereal Disease and the Lewis and Clark Expedition* (Lincoln: University of Nebraska Press, 2004), 58.

11. Regarding taking sexual stories seriously, see Michel Foucault, *The History of Sexuality* (New York: Vintage Books, 1990); Ken Plummer, *Telling Sexual Stories: Power, Change and Social Worlds* (New York: Routledge, 1995). Concerning the impact of relations of power, see Catherine Clinton and Michele Gillespie, eds., *The Devil's Lane: Sex and Race in the Early South* (New York: Oxford University Press, 1997); Fischer, *Suspect Relations*; Tiya Miles, *Ties That Bind: The Story of an Afro-Cherokee Family in Slavery and Freedom* (Berkeley: University of California Press, 2005); Theda Perdue, "Race and Culture: Writing the Ethnohistory of the Early South," *Ethnohistory* 51 (2004): 701–23; Susan Sleeper-Smith, *Indian Women and French Men: Rethinking Cultural Encounter in the Western Great Lakes* (Amherst: University of Massachusetts Press, 2001); Stoler, *Carnal Knowledge and Imperial Power*.

12. Eve Sedgwick, *Between Men: English Literature and Male Homosocial Desire* (New York: Columbia University Press, 1985), 25.

13. I expand Sedgwick's triangle model of homosocial bonds, which occur between two men through women as an object, the conduit of exchange, to colonial intimacies, a triangle-plus formation of Lewis and Clark/Corps (American male whiteness) + Expedition Manifest Destiny through Blackness (+York and institution of slavery) and "savage" Indianness (+Sacajawea).

14. Lowry, *Venereal Disease*, xiii.

15. See, for example, W. Raymond Wood and Thomas D. Thiessen, eds., *Early Fur Trade on the Northern Plains: Canadian Traders among the Mandan and Hidatsa Indians, 1738–1818* (Norman: University of Oklahoma Press, 1985).

16. See Ellwood Parry, *The Image of the Indian and the Black Man in American Art, 1590–1900* (New York: George Braziller, 1974).

17. Lowry, *Venereal Disease*, xv.

18. The Journals of the Lewis and Clark Expedition, http://tinyurl.com/hmgxza2 (accessed January 21, 2016).

19. Lowry, *Venereal Disease*, xv. Lowry also speculates that Sacajawea exhibited symptoms of venereal disease. Some epidemiologists and medical historians have put forth this diagnosis linking Lewis's decline within three years after the expedition to advanced stages of syphilis. See Reimert Thorolf Ravenholt, "Self Destruction on the Natchez Trace," *Magazine of Northwest History* (1999): 3–6.

20. This is where the captains met and hired Charbonneau. Sacajawea was included in his hire due to her knowledge of Shoshone language. Pregnant at the time with Charbonneau's child, Sacajawea gave birth to a son, Jean Baptiste, on February 11, 1805, and left with the Corps on April 7, 1805, carrying two-month-old Baptiste.

21. The Journals of the Lewis and Clark Expedition, http://tinyurl.com/h93cyte (accessed January 21, 2016).

22. The Journals of the Lewis and Clark Expedition, http://tinyurl.com/jhsxsz7 (accessed January 21, 2016).

23. Ambrose, *Undaunted Courage*, 195.

24. Ambrose, *Undaunted Courage*, 195.

25. Stephen Ambrose interview, http://www.pbs.org/lewisandclark/archive/ambrose.html (accessed January 21, 2016).

26. This website provides the most comprehensive online access to all the journals of the expedition, utilizing Moulton's 1999 editions. The site is supported by the University of Nebraska–Lincoln's Center for Great Plains Studies and the National Endowment for the Humanities.

27. The Journals of the Lewis and Clark Expedition, http://tinyurl.com/jpuyrwf (accessed January 21, 2016).

28. The Journals of the Lewis and Clark Expedition, http://tinyurl.com/ho8fvnv (accessed January 21, 2016).

29. The Journals of the Lewis and Clark Expedition, http://tinyurl.com/jylexdh (accessed January 21, 2016).

30. The Journals of the Lewis and Clark Expedition, http://tinyurl.com/zxutjxl (accessed January 21, 2016).

31. Stephen Ambrose interview.

32. Lowry, *Venereal Disease*, xv.

33. Although several notations about "visits" with Native women could be read as if Clark and/or Lewis participated, one December 1805 entry by Clark's noting his and Lewis refusal of "a woman each" during a trading visit has been used to generalize the captains' abstinence throughout the twenty-six-month expedition.

34. Thomas P. Slaughter, *Exploring Lewis and Clark: Reflections on Men and Wilderness* (New York: Alfred A. Knopf, 2003), 106.

35. Stephen Ambrose, *An Epic American Exploration: The Friendship of Lewis and Clark* (Minneapolis: University of Minnesota Press, 1998), 5. See also Dayton Duncan, *Out West: American Journey along the Lewis and Clark Trail* (New York: Penguin Press, 1988).

36. Ambrose, *Epic American Exploration*, 22.

37. Ambrose, *Epic American Exploration*, 23.

38. Sedgwick, *Between Men*, 3.

39. Slaughter, *Exploring Lewis and Clark*, 115.

40. Betts, *In Search of York*.

41. The Journals of the Lewis and Clark Expedition, http://tinyurl.com/z27pnmk (accessed January 21, 2016).

42. The Journals of the Lewis and Clark Expedition, http://tinyurl.com/h95fb04 (accessed January 21, 2016).

43. The Journals of the Lewis and Clark Expedition, http://tinyurl.com/jswjpn3 (accessed January 21, 2016).

44. The Journals of the Lewis and Clark Expedition, http://tinyurl.com/zejyxyw (accessed January 21, 2016).

45. The Journals of the Lewis and Clark Expedition, http://tinyurl.com/zc5bahc (accessed January 21, 2016).

46. The Journals of the Lewis and Clark Expedition, http://tinyurl.com/gp66dwj (accessed January 21, 2016).

47. Millner argues that York is portrayed through either "Sambo" or "superhero" traditions. See Darrell M. Millner, "York of the Corps of Discovery: Interpretations of York's Character and His Role in the Lewis and Clark Expedition," *Oregon Historical Quarterly* 104, no. 3 (Fall 2003): 318.

48. Slaughter, *Exploring Lewis and Clark*, 119.

49. "What Was Life Like for York, Clark's Black Slave, during the Expedition?," http://www.pbs.org/lewisandclark/living/idx_5.html (accessed January 21, 2016).

50. The Journals of the Lewis and Clark Expedition, http://tinyurl.com/zj8wfoy (accessed January 21, 2016).

51. Stephenie Ambrose Tubbs, *The Lewis and Clark Companion: An Encyclopedic Guide to the Voyage of Discovery* (New York: Henry Holt, 2003), 323.

52. The Journals of the Lewis and Clark Expedition, http://tinyurl.com/j789whp (accessed January 21, 2016).

53. Stephen Ambrose interview.

54. The Journals of the Lewis and Clark Expedition, http://tinyurl.com/hsjmu4t (accessed January 21, 2016).

55. The Journals of the Lewis and Clark Expedition, http://tinyurl.com/js7grwk (accessed January 21, 2016); Lowry, *Venereal Disease*, 61.

56. Eldon G. Chuinard, *Only One Man Died: The Medical Aspects of the Lewis and Clark Expedition* (Glendale, Calif.: Arthur H. Clark, 1979), 259.

57. Pamela Scully, "Malintzin, Pocahontas, and Krotoa: Indigenous Women and Myth Models of the Atlantic World," *Journal of Colonialism and Colonial History* 6, no. 3 (2005), http://muse.jhu.edu/ (accessed October 6, 2014).

58. Tubbo, *Lewis and Clark Companion*, 326.

59. "What Was Life Like for York?"

60. Slaughter, *Exploring Lewis and Clark*, 121.

61. James J. Holmberg, "I Wish You to See and Know All: The Recently Discovered Letters of William Clark to Jonathan Clark," *We Proceeded On* 18, no. 4 (1992): 4–12.

62. Clara Sue Kidwell, "Indian Women as Cultural Mediators," *Ethnohistory* 39, no. 2 (Spring 1992): 97–107; Joane Nagel, *Race, Ethnicity, and Sexuality: Intimate Intersections, Forbidden Frontiers* (New York: Oxford University Press, 2003).

63. Juliana Barr, *Peace Came in the Form of a Woman: Indians and Spaniards in the Texas Borderlands* (Chapel Hill: University of North Carolina Press, 2007); Gunlog Fur, "'Some Women Are Wiser than Some Men': Gender and Native American History," in *Clearing a Path*, ed. Nancy Shoemaker (New York: Routledge, 2002), 75–106; Sylvia van Kirk, *Many Tender Ties: Women in Fur Trade Society 1670–1870* (1980; Norman: University of Oklahoma Press, 1983); Theda Perdue, *Sifters: Native American Women's Lives* (New York: Oxford University Press, 2001); Theda Perdue, *Cherokee Women: Gender and Culture Change, 1700–1835* (Lincoln: University of Nebraska Press, 1999); Nancy Shoemaker, *Negotiators of Change: Historical Perspectives on Native American Women* (New York: Routledge Press, 1995); Sleeper-Smith, *Indian Women and French Men*.

64. Fischer, *Suspect Relations*, 56.

65. Fischer, *Suspect Relations*, 61.

66. Gunlog Fur, "Reading Margins: Colonial Encounters in Sapmi and Lenapehoking in the Seventeenth and Eighteenth Centuries," *Feminist Studies* 32, no. 3 (2006): 492.

67. Jennifer M. Spear, "'They Need Wives': Matissage and the Regulation of Sexuality in French Louisiana," in *Sex, Love, Race: Crossing Boundaries in North American History*, ed. Martha Hodes (New York: New York University Press, 1999), 43.

68. See Kessler, *Making of Sacagawea*; Pillow, "Searching for Sacajawea."

69. Pillow, "Searching for Sacajawea."

70. Dayton Duncan interview, http://www.pbs.org/lewisandclark/archive/duncan.html (accessed January 21, 2016).

71. Ambrose, *Epic American Exploration*, 32.

72. As noted above, in these narratives Sacajawea is "whitened" but never equal to the white woman (see Pillow, "Searching for Sacajawea"). Present-day characterizations of Sacajawea baring her breast to feed her child, while sitting with the men around the campfire, remind the reader to equate her with the simple, primitive Native woman, who possesses no modesty. These narratives at the same time employ a sexual gaze at the brown female body.

73. See Dye, *Conquest*; Hebard, *Sacajawea*; Hunsaker, *Sacagawea Speaks*.

74. Stephen Ambrose interview.

75. See Hunsaker, *Sacagawea Speaks*.

76. This theme was developed by Dye, *Conquest,* 1904. For further discussion, see Pillow, "Searching for Sacajawea."

77. By 1811, Baptiste was residing with Clark. Later Baptiste boarded at the school. Sacajawea and Charbonneau reportedly lived on and off in St. Louis from 1807 to 1811.

78. Plummer, *Telling Sexual Stories,* 167; Hartman, *Scenes of Subjection,* 11.

79. Gerald Vizenor, *Manifest Manners: Postindian Warriors of Survivance* (Middletown, Conn.: Wesleyan Press, 1994), 1.

CHAPTER 10

If We Got That Freedom

"Integration" and the Sexual Politics
of Southern College Women, 1940–1960

SUSAN K. CAHN

In the early years of the post–World War II period, white college students at the University of North Carolina's Woman's College (hereafter WC) abandoned a time-worn tradition. They allowed the annual ritual marriage ceremony between the freshman and junior classes to fade quietly away. A ceremony in which selected students from each class performed the roles of groom, bride, bridesmaids, and presiding minister in full drag—tuxes, gowns, veils, with gendered hair styles to match—the ritual had symbolized the importance of homosocial relationships to a culture in which women's education, careers, and peer relations took a far more prominent place in campus life than did dating, courtship, and marriage.[1] By 1950, however, college women at WC and elsewhere in the South stated a clear preference for marriage, the legally binding kind, to men.

This change had been prefigured during the war, when women at black and white southern colleges eagerly took advantage of USO dances and other supervised opportunities to mix with soldiers stationed nearby. Immediately after the war, the GI Bill changed the look of campuses recently dominated by women but now flooded with returning veterans attending college with government aid. The 1947 yearbook of Atlanta's Agnes Scott College, an elite college for white women, featured a photo layout heralding the "real 'co-ed' appearance" of campus during the weekends, leading one student to exult, "*This* was more like the college life we'd heard about, lo these many years!"[2] At Livingstone College, an African American school in Salisbury, North Carolina, women pointedly stated their interest in mixed-gender activities. A 1949 survey queried female students on whether too much socializing occurred on campus. A majority answered no, with claims ranging from, "This is a co-ed school, and boys and girls should have social contact with each other," to a more vociferous, "Definitely not! Socializing is one of the requirements of a well-rounded education."[3] "Socializing," to Livingstone women, meant interacting with their male peers.

These students were not alone in expressing the belief that heterosexual relations formed one—if not *the*—essential element of college life. In the 1950s, a kind of marriage mania spread to campuses around the country. Student newspapers ran columns reporting on who had come back from summer, winter, or spring vacations with engagement or wedding rings, who had gotten pinned (a pre-engagement commitment) over the weekend, and rumors of new couples and future "wedding belles." The student newspaper at Agnes Scott College announced the summer plans of graduates with the tongue-in-cheek "estimate" that "approximately 29.27% of the Class of 1953 [would] receive the MRS [marriage or Mrs.] degree shortly after carrying their AB scrolls away from Gaines chapel." College administrators facilitated the process, holding classes on marriage and bringing in guest speakers to instruct women on "How to Become Marriageable."[4]

To dramatize their own heterosexual enthusiasm, male college students of the early 1950s created a unique ritual of aggressive sexual pursuit. The "panty raid," in which male students stormed women's dormitories and demanded women's undergarments, demonstrated a brazen, nationwide "crazy for sex" attitude along with a male presumption of sex rights to women's intimate apparel and, presumably, their sexualized bodies.[5] The storied panty raids and women's marriage "mania" mesh with a standard understanding of 1950s sexuality as conservative in both its heterosexual imperative and its male dominance. Yet, as I researched women's experiences in southern colleges as part of a larger project on southern adolescent girls, I discovered evidence that shifted my point of view, leading me to see the South of the late 1940s and 1950s as a period of new sexual and gender possibilities, animated in a number of cases by a progressive consciousness about race.[6]

Links between new forms of sexual and racial subjectivity are evident in a set of distinct yet interrelated forms of protest prevalent in the postwar South. While not specific to the region, campus protests at southern colleges had a unique set of political valences. Not only did a majority of African Americans still live in the South and an even greater majority of college-bound black youth attend historically black colleges located in the South, but it would soon be southern black students who took center stage as the student sit-in movement ignited the mass civil rights movement of the 1960s. In February 1960, four male students from North Carolina Agricultural and Technical College, a state-supported college for African American students (primarily male), engaged in the first widely recognized "sit-in," the opening salvo of what became a mass protest movement of student-led sit-ins against segregated facilities in the South.[7] Students from nearby colleges quickly joined the effort, including those from Shaw University, Woman's College, and Bennett College for African American women. Curiously, the first organizational meeting at Shaw, a black college in Raleigh, was open to men only, not because women students lacked interest but because campus rules forbade women from leaving the dorms to socialize with male students in the evening. Consequently, male students served as the initial organizers in Raleigh, with women classmates joining in the daytime sit-ins.[8]

Only six years earlier, in May 1954, the students at Shaw had engaged in a different kind of protest. They staged a six-day boycott of classes to protest a number of conditions that angered them: poor food quality, dilapidated dorms, and, most immediately, the expulsion of four women who had violated campus restrictions on female students. At Shaw and other colleges, typical regulations ranged from early evening curfews and prohibited areas of campus for women to strict sign-out systems when leaving campus for dates or other social activities. Similar protests occurred on other black campuses, which had a tradition of student protest against paternalistic administrations.[9] Mississippi activist Anne Moody led a strike at a small women's college in Natchez in the late 1950s to protest the school's poor food quality and health conditions, a prelude to her entrance into the black civil rights movement.[10] Along with these dramatic moments of protest, African American and white female students began to level a steadily increasing barrage of criticism against the many rules and regulations—called parietals—restricting their physical movement and social freedom.

At first glance, there is seemingly little connection between personal concerns about boyfriends, marriage, and heterosexual freedom and the more obviously political concerns of civil rights and racial integration. But a focus on the myriad experiences of women, black and white, at southern colleges reveals new connections. Beginning in the 1940s, college women grew increasingly politicized around issues of democracy and equality, with a subset of these students—mostly African American but some white—focusing on issues of racial integration through the YWCA, the NAACP, and various interracial student congresses.[11] At the same time an entirely different rhetoric of "integration" emerged from the therapeutic culture of midcentury America. Rooted in the psychological and sociological concepts of personality development and social adjustment, therapeutic prescriptions emphasized a "well-integrated personality" signaled, in part, by women's ability to "mix" well with men and pursue heterosexual relations. The rhetoric of democratic equality in combination with heightened attention to heterosexual involvement generated mounting dissatisfaction with the extensive rules and regulations governing the behavior of female students at black, white, co-ed, and single-sex colleges.

This essay argues that during the postwar years a cohort of southern youth found the rhetoric of democracy and equality well suited to a growing awareness of their "rights" as female students; they used their sense of entitlement to challenge inequalities of gender, sexuality, and sometimes race.[12] Sexual and racial changes in the South were thus integrally related, part and parcel of a small but significant movement on college campuses that began challenging *both* racial and gender segregation in the late 1940s and 1950s. In the context of Cold War liberalism, a select group of young southern women began to rethink their worlds while even larger numbers pushed for greater sexual freedom. The lip service college administrators paid to "democratic communities" of mature, "well-integrated" adults was appropriated by students, who developed a piercing critique of adult hypocrisy. They seemed especially attuned to the ways gender restrictions limited not only their right to pursue heterosexual relationships but their freedom to participate equally in social and political activities of all sorts. Across race, women students used the terms of debate over segregation versus integration to make their own case for greater gender integration on campuses and in their surrounding environs.

Seeing these connections between race and sex offers new answers to a critical question: What conditions and discourses enable social movements to come together, articulate grievances, and enter into controversial protests against the political and social "common sense" of their time? While the four male North Carolina AT&T students who launched the sit-in movement in 1960 often seem to emerge out of nowhere, southern students had already commenced a steady stream of protest demanding greater campus democracy and social freedom, invigorating a discourse of equality and integration. In doing so, they planted experiential and ideological seeds for the mass student protests of the 1960s, from the student-led civil rights movement to feminist and sexual liberation movements. Thus these lesser-known midcentury protests for both racial and sexual "integration" establish an important connection between movements usually treated as developing along separate trajectories. By examining the intersections between, first, politicized and therapeutic concepts of integration and, second, organized protest for civil rights and sexual rights, we can reevaluate our understanding of both the timing and the content of postwar social movements.[13]

Many college students in the postwar era, it is important to note, did not see their lives in political terms and even among the politically active, few saw midcentury American politics as their main concern. Typically, college women thought about issues much closer to home—classes, grades, social life, personal happiness or unhappiness, and the immediate future. Beyond such personal concerns, both administrators and students exhibited an unremitting preoccupation with maintaining standards of ideal womanhood, expressed through terms such as a "Spelman Woman," a "WC girl," and a "true lady." Yet standards of feminine behavior and ideal womanhood did not remain static. The period from the 1930s through the 1950s saw a redefinition of womanhood among college students from an ideal predicated on selflessness and community service to a new concept of womanhood centrally concerned with personal happiness, attained through the related achievement of heterosexual "success" in dating and marriage. Integral to this transformation were psychologically based concepts of "personality" and "integration" formulated within the campus culture of the 1940s and 1950s.

Black and white colleges held overlapping ideals of the female college student and graduate. Traditionally, black colleges like Shaw, Livingstone, Bennett, and Spelman (the latter two, women's colleges) and the white-only North Carolina Woman's College defined womanhood in terms of female respectability and community service. In 1928 educator and activist Mary McCleod Bethune urged Spelman students to keep the "spirit of unselfishness burning fervently in their hearts."[14] In Greensboro, while Bennett College urged black women to develop "a consciousness of oneness with their community," Woman's College also embraced an ideal of respectable middle-class womanhood engaged in service to the white community, especially through teaching.[15]

Ideals of womanhood differed in important respects, however. Students at black colleges supported a notion of womanhood designed to upend white supremacy by establishing the superior credentials of the "best" African Americans. In contrast, white colleges upheld a feminine ideal that purposefully raised white women above black. Yet both groups agreed on a definition of womanhood rooted in middle-class ideals of propriety, manners, and refinement thought to prime young women for their duty to—and secure their high status within—a larger community.

By 1940, newer definitions of womanhood began to depart from a doctrine of propriety and service. Throughout the 1930s, students used their college newspapers to debate among themselves the accepted range of behaviors for a respectable southern woman. They squabbled over mandatory chapel attendance, proper dining hall manners, whether smoking was uncouth, and the appropriate standards of dress and behavior on and off campus. Repetitive, belabored editorials against talking during chapel, cutting class, or wearing hair rollers around campus continued into the 1940s and 1950s. Based on the frequency and stridency of criticism, a good portion of students seemed to hold the established standards of respectability in some measure of contempt.

The debate over proper manners and morals suggested an underlying question: if all agreed that college represented a transitional period from adolescence toward mature womanhood, what *kind* of woman was college preparing students to become? Students and administrators alike increasingly framed the question as one of popularity and personality. What type of personality defined the most popular—and thus presumably well-adjusted—women? Through the 1930s, the entwined concepts of personality and popularity remained linked to notions of female respectability and a cultivated manner. A student who learned to "strangle selfishness" and do precisely the "right thing at the proper time" would place herself "on the road to success and happiness as well."[16] Only through selflessness and propriety would the college woman achieve a happy, successful life.

By the 1940s, a newer notion of "personality" prevailed, one that prized an outgoing sociability geared toward achieving individual success and personal happiness. The *Shaw University Journal* ran a piece called "My View of Personality," which linked good personality not to selflessness but to social success. Inquiring, "What can this factor be that even our success depends totally upon it?" the author answered, "Why of course, Personality."[17] A subsequent advice column counseled students that "a pleasing personality makes a person complete" and "sure to make a success."[18] The reference to becoming a "complete" person points toward a subtle shift in the very concept of personality.

As more liberal political students of the late 1930s and 1940s grabbed onto the political goal of racial integration, a coinciding language of personality began to incorporate notions of psychological and social integration. In 1939, the *Campus Mirror* advised Spelman students that a young woman could develop a more "pleasing personality" by cultivating a variety of attributes "weighted and carefully blended, so as to become whole."[19] One year later a guest speaker described "living itself" as a "process of continuous integration." He explained that as Spelman women integrated into college life and the community, different parts of the self would achieve "oneness" followed by integration into the wider world.[20] On the opposite side of Atlanta, Agnes Scott students received similar guidance, learning that "a pleasing personality so vital to harmony with other forces in our world today is developed . . . in the form of poise, charm, originality, and varied interest in one's surrounding."[21] Personality traits long associated with individual popularity were now a means of harmonizing with world forces that extended far beyond the individual.

While integration in the 1940s stood as a measure of psychosocial development, it also emerged as a political goal in small campus-based movements for racial justice that originated in student responses to the Depression and the threat of world war. Students in the late 1930s participated in Citizenship Training Schools, labor strikes, peace demonstrations, and early efforts by southern college students to form interracial organizations to discuss regional race relations.[22] A single issue of the *Shaw University Journal* from 1938 informed students about antilynching legislation, international peace campaigns, the NAACP student organization, and legal challenges to the "separate but equal" doctrine.[23] Black college students focused far more intently on racial justice, but students across the region used campus organizations and college curricula to engage a similar range of issues. A study by the Conference on Education and Race Relations reported that by 1940 southern colleges and universities had instituted seventy-seven new courses "dealing with the interracial situation in America."[24]

Political interest escalated in the 1940s as the United States entered into a war against fascism, also framed as a "war for democracy."[25] Students picked up on this language to assert their own interests. One irate student at Hampton Institute, a prestigious black college in Virginia, criticized a *New York Times* columnist who had spoken on campus. To the speaker's admonition that "Rome was not built in a day," the author rejoined, "We are inclined to counter . . . with another old adage, namely, 'Time and tide wait for no man.'"[26] Consistent with a nationwide African American "Double V" campaign demanding a victory for democracy abroad and at home, students turned the language of democracy toward race relations in the South.

Among white collegians, Woman's College students participated in a variety of campus forums on race relations as well as groups such as the Intercollegiate Interracial Commission. Invited speakers advocated active opposition to segregation, while terms like "race tolerance" and "the race problem" appeared with regularity in the student press.[27] With more timidity, Agnes Scott students participated in an intercampus Methodist Student Conference organized around the theme "Know Thy Neighbor" in which students would learn about "various countries and minority groups of the world."[28] Even more activity occurred on black campuses. By the late 1940s, students at Shaw and Livingstone could pick up almost any issue of their student newspapers and read about the Fair Employment Practices Commission, the United Nations, relationships between organized labor and African Americans, and numerous accounts of both black student activism and interracial efforts to end segregation.[29]

Interest in democracy did not end with the Allied victory in 1945. Rather, the growing numbers of middle-class black students became intensely conscious of their exclusion from the "American Dream" on the basis of race alone, since economically and academically they resembled other middle-class youth. Spurred by the gap between expectations and reality, African American students formulated a powerful critique of racism focused initially on segregation, the most starkly visible evidence of racial division and inequality. Escalating activism, led by impatient black students and a small core of committed white students, developed in tandem with a growing confidence in "youth" as a political force. When delegates at the 1952 North Carolina Student Legislature Day passed a bill for the desegregation of public schools, students at Shaw concluded that "the sponsors of this project [had] hit upon the answer to much of the present unrest, that is, youth must lead the way."[30] New mass media—movies, magazines, television, and popular music—aimed directly at teenagers assisted in forging a common youth culture and identity.[31] Organizations like the National Student Association and the National Student Federation of America, each with chapters in southern women's and co-ed colleges, spurred politically oriented youth to demand liberal reform in international, national, and campus governance. Through their defense of civil liberties, activists shifted student discourse from its earlier framework of *privileges*, earned by good behavior, to youth's entitlement to a set of *rights*, irrespective of behavior.[32]

Ideas about student rights and responsibilities incorporated the notion of "integration" as both a personal and political concept necessary to student progress. In 1940 Dr. Roswell C. Long spoke to Agnes Scott students on developing an "Integrated Christian Personality." The headline in the *Agnes Scott News* read: "Dr. Long Discusses Negro Problem: Speaker Condemns Antagonism in Integrated Christian Personality." Long instructed students that an "integrated Christian personality" could not withstand internalized racial antagonism. Absent racial animosity, the "integrated" mind would then lead one to a more sympathetic stance toward "the Negro problem" and possibly a favorable stance toward racial integration.[33] Long was not unique in his views. Daryl Michael Scott argues that postwar cultural pluralism addressed racism as a matter of "prejudice," to be combated by better "human relations" or "intergroup relations." Liberal philanthropists poured money into academic research on these topics. Social scientists, very much influenced by the therapeutic ethos that permeated postwar culture, then passed their findings on to new race relations professionals and liberal activists who established "interracial human relations organizations" in the South and the North.[34]

The link between psychological integration and social justice did not sit as well with Hampton Institute administrators. Responding to a petition drive to improve building conditions and replace the school's autocratic leadership with more democratic governance, college president Ralph Bridgman specified that the objective of Hampton should not be "to train young people to fight for their rights but to live integrated lives." Bridgman thus posed a standard of individual integration *against* concepts of democratic action and social integration. Students angrily replied: "How can a group of people even entertain the thought of an integrated life until they have first obtained those rights and privileges inherent in the ideology of the nation in which they exist?" Again employing psychological terminology to address issues of social justice, protesters argued that the president's opinions were "repressive to the future Hampton students" and that as Negro college youth, they "must begin now to assume mature positions against existing injustices."[35] The multiple valences of the word *integration* reverberated through the psychological and political discourses of campus life, applied in different ways either to encourage or thwart student activism but always holding out the possibility of linked meanings. Whether students took the rhetoric about "personality integration" to heart remains unclear. But this is less important than their exposure to a concept of integration that was both personal and political—concerning individual development, social adaptation, and social justice.

The language of integration made immediate sense in a college environment that saw two critical changes during the 1940s and 1950s. Concepts of an integrated personality and individual integration with the broader society reflected the rapidly growing impact of professional psychology on college campuses. Many postwar psychologists turned the authority gained from their role in wartime Selective Service testing into positions on college campuses, where they taught courses, offered counseling, and conducted a variety of tests ranging from IQ tests to personality inventories.[36] Coinciding with this shift, student life became increasingly oriented around heterosexual interaction as the measure of a "successful"—or integrated—personality.

Students of the Depression era had already demonstrated an increased focus on heterosexual interaction, but not to the point of sacrificing female independence. By the 1940s, personal independence paled before concerns about marriageability. Student newspapers issued a steady stream of advice on how to attract a man and the importance of dating and marriage. A sample of articles from the *Carolinian* illustrates the heterosexual intensification at Woman's College. Readers were informed that "'He' Is Major Event of College Weekend" and "Dr. Lydia G. Shivers Talks on Marriage: Sociology Department Member Gives Career Girls Good Chance of Marrying."[37]

Colleges hired marriage experts to give lectures, teach classes, and consult with students. Spelman twice brought in Grace Sloan Overton, a white marriage expert who advised students on dating, sexuality, and marriage.[38] A student at Agnes Scott College recognized this as a historic shift. In "Happily Ever After," she compared earlier "militant" woman's rights crusaders to her own generation's wish to reverse declining birth rates and strengthen family bonds. "Hussies that we are," she averred, "we wish to understand the problems that we will meet in marriage." Answers could be found, she rejoiced, in the college's "numerous clinics, seminars, and courses—in marriage!" Her use of the term "hussies" indicates that sexual interest and satisfaction would be key to her generation's happiness.[39]

In less explicit terms, freshmen at Bennett College took a required course on "The Art of Living," which included sex education and guest lectures on marriage. The broader African American press translated the covert message for anyone who missed it, reporting, "Girls at Bennett College received instruction on 'how to catch a boyfriend.'"[40] Students made it clear that most wanted more than boyfriends; they wanted husbands. Articles with titles like "WC's Dream Husbands" described the fortunate women who had returned to campus in the fall married and content.[41] For those unlucky women still awaiting marriage proposals, the *Carolinian* issued regular advice on fashions that attracted men, informational articles on what men like in "a girl," and reassuring statistics on marriage rates among college women.[42]

However, an underlying anxiety persisted through the 1950s that college might, in the end, squander one's chance to marry. While high school girls saw dating and going steady as preparation for future marriage, college women received a confusing message that marriage lay just beyond graduation and that the time for marriage was *now*—leading some to fear that in postponing marriage for education, they might miss their chance. The WC *Carolinian* reported with relief that marriage expert Mrs. Ethel M. Nash "gave us some hope on the 'man getting' situation," explaining that "there should be no difficulty in obtaining a mate—provided we go somewhere where there are some men." Nash apprized her audience that wherever she traveled, girls asked the same question: "'How do I get a man?'"[43] The solution apparently did not require the same degree of sexual restraint as in the past. A humorous 1951 story from the *Agnes Scott News* portrayed a dormitory housemother trying to keep up with her socially active charges. "While I can't speak from experience about their kisses," she said coyly, "I have an idea they weren't exactly (you should pardon the expression) frigid."[44] The story illustrates both the expectation of "hotter" sexual pursuit on the part of women and the incorporation of psychiatric terminology—which defined frigidity as a woman's inability to reach orgasm—into everyday, if not exactly accurate, vocabulary.

On black campuses, students were equally bold in expressing their sexual interests. At Shaw, an article titled "College Girls" announced: "She likes men in tails. She likes men in tweeds. She likes men in anything. She likes men." About love, the author indicated similarly catholic tastes: "She believes in new love . . . in old love . . . in true love . . . in free love."[45] Female students' forthright interest in men found expression in regular advice columns that coached women on fashion and dating etiquette, urging them to tread the middle ground between reticence and "being an eager beaver."[46] Spelman students evidenced similar interests, as administrators and student groups arranged regular dances and a regulated dating system between Spelman and students from Morehouse, the neighboring men's college, as well as men from Clark, Morris Brown, and Atlanta University—also part of the cluster of black colleges that dotted Atlanta's west side.[47]

The issue of heterosocial relations necessarily raised questions and complaints about the freedom of female students under a system of in loco parentis, in which college administrators agreed to stand in as parents for girls not yet accorded status as independent adults. A 1941 campus forum, called to discuss various problems in student life, included one session on "Methods of Socializing" and another on "Bisexual Social Expression at Shaw University." Reportedly, "Most students voice a desire for a more liberal, broader and more inclusive view of bisexual [both genders present] social expression on this campus."[48] A Hampton student took a more daring stance, directly criticizing administrators for failing to provide the necessary opportunities to learn how to "fit properly" into social circles that students would inhabit after college.[49]

In questioning the fairness of postwar gender and sexual arrangements, young southern women pushed the boundaries of what John D'Emilio and Estelle Freedman have called "sexual liberalism," the set of sexual arrangements that emerged in the early twentieth century and by midcentury stood firmly in place of the previous century's Victorian paradigm. Sexual liberalism consisted of a set of beliefs and corresponding practices that recognized female sexual desire as positive (if still secondary to men's), included a notion of sexual romance and intimacy within marriage, and represented a "long-term shift toward sexual pleasure as a critical aspect of personal happiness."[50] Within sexual liberalism, a double standard that permitted sexual activity among unmarried men and demanded virginity in unmarried women still prevailed. However, by midcentury the gap between stated beliefs and actual behavior had grown to enormous proportions. Teenagers got married at record rates, many of them refusing to wait until marriage to engage in sexual intercourse.[51] College women did not want to be left behind.

Faced with a barrage of complaints, college administrations negotiated with student leaders over their demand for greater social freedom. While some school officials adopted a rigid stance, others sought a middle path between the more liberal policies requested by students and the wishes of parents to have their children's safety and reputation closely guarded while away at school. The *Livingstone College Catalogue* announced that the college would permit "the greatest possible individual liberty of action and . . . adopt few rules of conduct" while fostering "sane and healthy social contacts between men and women."[52] Guide books for Woman's College staff from the early 1940s stated a goal of "democratic community living" linked to a principle of "responsible freedom." The manuals went on to say, however, that not all students could live up to such responsibilities, especially those "immature students [who] make mountains out of mole hills." One of those "mole hills" consisted of many "incidental regulations which to a degree [could not] be ignored."[53] As students continually questioned the "degree" of regulation necessary to ensure proper comportment, administrators did not cede ground easily, especially given their belief that local residents closely scrutinized student "outsiders" for behaviors that violated community norms. Promises of liberty and freedom went largely unrealized as extensive regulations continued to restrict the movement and behavior of women students on and off college campuses.

Students and college officials at Agnes Scott reached a unique compromise. By the 1950s, the college had specified a special day allowing students to engage in otherwise banned behaviors. Called "Repressed Desires Day," like Halloween it represented a planned day of turning the tables, permitting a kind of wildness prohibited every other day of the school year. Without any apparent irony, the school paper faithfully reported: "The following desires have been approved by the Faculty." They included ringing the fire bell; screaming or sleeping in the library; wearing blue jeans, peddle pushers, or shorts to class; leaving shirt tails untucked; singing in the dining hall; riding the faculty elevator; talking during chapel; and calling faculty by their first names.[54] Notably, none of the repressed desires involved sexual expression of any sort. Sexual freedom was a point of serious contention, not one the administration felt comfortable addressing through humor. Moreover, its omission from Repressed Desires Day conveniently skirted the issue of whether students did indeed repress their sexual desires.

Heterosexuality as a primary orientation of student life eventually won administrative acceptance, whether due to student pressure or college officials' own recognition of changing times.[55] A Hampton handbook encouraged women in the first two years to "generalize" in their dating, giving the student "a chance to know many men—and incidentally [give] the men a chance to know many women." It assured the student that this would help as she narrowed the field in her last two years, almost guaranteeing she would "make a happier choice for a 'steady' in [her] senior year."[56] Older policies that required women to leave college if they married grew more permissive, accepting on-campus residence in some cases, off-campus in others. Just as gossip and advice columns about dating and marriage became a prominent feature of student discourse, marriage courses, clinics, and advice sessions became part of the formal curriculum and extracurricular programs provided by college administrators.

The liberalization of college policies regulating women's activities and heterosexual interaction failed to diminish conflict between students and administration, perhaps even exacerbating the very dissension that new, less restrictive rules intended to curb. The articulation of "rights," rather than privileges, received an infusion from the democratic discourse of WWII and the mounting campaign against racial segregation waged in the 1950s. The ideal of democracy moved from its status as a lofty aspiration—the *Carolinian* masthead read "Woman's College—'Distinguished for Its Democracy'"—to an issue of active struggle in the 1940s and 1950s. Livingstone and Shaw students focused their attention initially on poor food service on campus. One angry student complained about meals so small that "one [could] hardly imagine where a reluctant vitamin might hide." The only solution, the author proclaimed, "is for the students to continue their agitation."[57]

And agitate they did. Protests against paltry, poorly prepared meals and dilapidated, unsanitary facilities often merged with gender-related complaints.

Throughout the war and the postwar era, the most persistent student challenges concerned college regulations for women. A Hampton student issued a typical complaint in a 1944 editorial titled "The Plight of Freshman Women." Inquiring, "What is happening to democracy with respect to the freshman women and democratic ideals at Hampton?" the author complained of "very drastic and rather alarming reverses" in campus democracy. After coming to college fully expecting broadened horizons and recognition as adults, "disillusionment and frustration [had] met the attempts of freshmen women to develop adult attitudes" when rules required them to remain on campus after the lowering of the flag and prohibited them from evening use of the library. The disgruntled student announced that her female classmates' discontent was "reflected throughout the entire student body," suggesting ominously that student unrest would worsen unless authorities met with women students to "thrash out their problems concerning their . . . rights."[58] Increasingly, students saw their *plight* as a matter of *rights*.

Making emphatic use of concepts of democracy and equality, students regularly took administrators to task. In a 1946 editorial titled "Democracy in Christian Colleges," a male student at Shaw utilized the wartime discourse of democracy versus fascism to criticize the school's administration. "The college should be the promoter of the democratic spirit, not the gestapo," he argued. "How can one imagine that the student will come out a democrat while he has always been living in fear of democracy?" He then leveled the ultimate accusatory question: "What is the difference between the time of slavery and the present?"[59] The succeeding page featured a letter to the editor criticizing the school for expelling two female students who had violated what many students believed were excessively restrictive rules governing women's behavior.[60] Thirteen years later students still called for administrative accountability on the same grounds. Responding to the University of North Carolina chancellor's 1959 veto of student legislation to end the lights-out policy for freshman and to extend the general student curfew to 1:00 a.m., an irate student vented, "[A] college administration should be respected, but not feared." Only when students lost that fear could "they begin to approach the fulfillment of the role which is inherently theirs—functioning as full and equal members of the college community."[61]

Issues of democracy, civil rights, heterosexual relations, and gender politics circulated simultaneously and in relation to one another. In January 1948, the *Living Stone* reported on a recent visit to campus by Paul Robeson in which he called for a freedom fight in both Africa and the United States to win "your rights and mine."[62] A linked editorial condemned the hypocrisy of advocating for world peace when, within the United States, African Americans continued to face segregation, lynching, and injustice. On the very same page, two letters to the editor accused Livingstone administrators of unreasonable restrictions on female students and

heterosocial interaction. One complained that the college had reneged on its promise to use its brand-new gymnasium for social as well as athletic events. A second
letter, signed by "The Freshman Girls," fervidly denounced a policy forbidding them
from attending the annual football game between freshmen boys and upperclass-
men. The authors decried: "Could we, the freshman girls, go? NO!! WHY?? . . . We
do not feel that we are being given EQUAL RIGHTS when the upperclass girls can
go and cheer for their team, and the freshman girls can't even make a showing. We
Livingstonians often use the term SEGREGATION—the freshman class has never
seen a better example than the one we experienced on Saturday, December 6."[63] By
adopting the political language of equality, rights, and integration, these freshmen
ably defended their own concept of social and sexual rights.

Students deftly turned a rhetoric of campus democracy through "responsible
living" into powerful political critiques of failed democracy, off campus and on. In
March 1948, the *Living Stone* reported on an interracial meeting of the Students for
Wallace Campaign and recent legal challenges to racial segregation in southern
graduate schools. Another article proposed a change from strict administrative
policing to a student honor system. Fannie Hauser framed the issue as one of
freedom, defiantly asserting, "We continually yell for freedom from day to day; if
we got that freedom what would be the result? . . . We feel that we are not trusted
and that we are being spied upon from time to time."[64] Three issues later a male
student demanded that the school Discipline Committee "recognize students as
more than mere puppets to be cast aside at will without trial or argument. We speak
of a Civil Rights Bill: yet here, where life actually begins . . . we cannot defend nor
represent ourselves."[65] The tone intensified yet again in 1949 in letters to the editor
likening women students to prisoners policed by the FBI. Comparing Livingstone
with Sing-Sing, one student asked, "Has Goler Hall [the women's dormitory] been
named the Prison Camp for Girls? Is it necessary to have a chaperon from here
to Trent Gymnasium? We are not going to run away."[66] With this convergence
of antiracist politics and a stronger orientation toward heterosexuality, students
demonstrated a bold willingness to attack "undemocratic" gender and sexual restrictions standard on campuses everywhere.

At more restrictive colleges like Agnes Scott and Spelman, students often soft-
pedaled their criticisms but found their freedom of speech squelched nonetheless.
In 1946 the editors of the *Agnes Scott News* issued a formal apology to fellow students
for submitting to administrative pressure, having discovered that "there is no such
thing as complete freedom of the press." Claiming that under these circumstances
the *News* served as a publicity organ and not a real newspaper, the rankled staff
announced that in "this ultimate test, the *News* [stood] censored." The suppression
apparently occurred over the issue of administrative surveillance. In succeeding
issues of the paper, students complained bitterly that despite having an honor

code, in which students promised to self-report breaches of school rules, they "were constantly watched and checked" by suspicious authorities.[67]

In response to similar complaints on many campuses, committees composed of students, faculty, and administrators hashed out new guidelines. Year after year student leaders attempted to extend evening curfews and "lights-out" times (sometimes by as little as fifteen-minute increments); curtail sweeping restrictions on student use of alcohol; demand more dances and other social opportunities; and revise official student handbooks to simplify and reduce what had become an extremely detailed and elaborate code of conduct by the 1950s.[68] Reforms also included new forms of student governance. At Hampton, for instance, a student court system originally proposed in 1949 won final approval in 1955 and went into effect the following year with a Women's Senate established to deal with issues specific to female students.[69] Similar changes in student governance occurred at Woman's College.[70]

In many ways such reforms suited the interests of administrators and students equally. Students won the "right" to govern themselves, with students now serving as "judges" responsible for penalizing others accused of violating school policies. At the same time, administrators created a buffer between themselves and students, relieved of their long-standing role of the "heavy" in monitoring and punishing the misbehavior of students, who now took that role upon themselves.[71] Some students redirected their resentment at student governance, berating it for enforcing rules that they personally found ridiculous and not worthy of compliance. The tensions over women's freedom of movement and association thus remained unresolved. And conflicts of gender and generation continued to reverberate with issues of racial and campus democracy.

The tone and coverage of student newspapers became less manifestly political in the late 1950s, reducing coverage of national and international politics and providing scant attention to school integration battles raging throughout the South. As southern racial politics heated up, campus press coverage fell silent even as some students and faculty took action to support the *Brown v. Board of Education* Supreme Court decision of 1954. As the rise of massive resistance made it riskier for liberal white students to take public stances against segregation, efforts to liberalize campus restrictions on women may have become tainted with the same "integrationist" or left-wing brush. For black students, this quiet before the storm probably reflects a heightened awareness of the stakes involved in a fierce battle against an increasingly organized opposition.[72] Not only did college administrations routinely expel women who violated campus gender restrictions; many also took similar action against students involved in protests for racial integration. Students feared not only expulsion but that arrests or disciplinary actions permanently imprinted on school records would later haunt them when applying for jobs or graduate education.[73]

Yet black students did not remain completely inactive but joined NAACP youth chapters and other local organizations. A cluster of sit-ins in the late 1950s predated the storied 1960 Greensboro sit-in, occurring in scattered locations in North and South Carolina, Virginia, and the outer edges of the South in Oklahoma and Kansas.[74] In Virginia, where massive white resistance resulted in the closing of public schools, Hampton students briefly spoke louder than students elsewhere. Inspired by a speech delivered on campus in 1956 by Martin Luther King titled "On Integration," student editors condemned white resistance to integrated schools and encouraged fellow students to boycott segregated movie theaters, department stores with separate restrooms, and drugstores that refused food service to black customers.[75] Yet at least until 1960 the activist core of Hampton students constituted a minority. They voiced their displeasure in frequent articles and editorials accusing fellow students of general apathy, snobbery toward African Americans in surrounding towns, obsequious behavior toward faculty and administrators, and a myopic focus on their own social activities, Greek life, or personal careers when less-privileged black locals risked their jobs and lives to participate in civil rights activities springing up throughout Virginia. Such criticisms fell on deaf ears, however, as the preponderance of campus news consisted of announcements or descriptions of social affairs, annual elections of "Hampton Beauties," football games, and the dating scene.[76] Similarly, at Fisk College a student editorial diagnosed the student body as suffering from an "irresponsible, indolent, anti-intellectual attitude" and "an overdose of apathy."[77]

White campuses remained even quieter, at least in terms of official action or press coverage. At Woman's College, a strange juxtaposition of administrative action and official silence occurred. In the fall of 1956, the first two African American women enrolled at Woman's College after the government of North Carolina lost its appeal against a state Supreme Court decision requiring that some plan for desegregating public schools be implemented. The previous year, students and faculty sent a petition to the state in support of integration at WC, and no organized opposition of any large scale occurred when Joanne Smart and Betty Tilman moved onto campus to begin their freshman year. They shared a room in their own segregated dormitory wing, left otherwise empty so that black and white students would remain separately housed although officially "integrated." Over the next several years, additional black students enrolled but only three or four per year, ensuring that their experience at WC would be an isolated one with few African American classmates and no black faculty or administrators to turn to for support. Despite the college's official approval of desegregation and the affirmation of this move by faculty and students who publicly expressed their wish to comply, the student newspaper gave virtually no coverage to this monumental change.[78]

The silence in all probability represents an effort to suppress controversy and keep the spotlight off both the students and the administration, whose compliance went against the sentiments of the larger white public; businesses and public facilities in the town of Greensboro, for example, remained completely segregated until 1960. Yet white students also did not remain completely silent. The National Student Association created a Southern Advisory Committee in 1956. Members of this group secured grant money from the Marshall Field Foundation to establish a Southern Student Human Relations Seminar in 1958, bringing students from black and white campuses together to study and work toward racial integration. Called the Southern Project, along with its annual workshops the group hired a full-time program coordinator in Atlanta in 1959.[79] The same year, 450 out of a possible 650 students at the white-only Georgia State College for Women signed a petition favoring school desegregation over the politically popular choice to close all public schools rather than comply with court-ordered integration.[80]

Even if temporarily less vocal on racial issues, students continued to protest sex and gender restrictions in the name of a more democratic living community. For more than a decade, both black and white women (and men as well) embraced the language of democracy and integration to break down long-standing restrictions against women's freedom on campus and, in some cases, to work for racial justice and other progressive movements. Yet even with a shared discourse of rights, democracy, and integration, there are important variations to consider. Both the stakes and the meaning of political agitation on college campuses differed for white and black women, even those employing a similar rhetoric.

Given that women students in the South came from the general population, even if a possibly more educated, liberal sector, we can presume that the percentage of white versus black students supporting desegregation differed significantly. Although pro-segregationist sentiment rarely appears in the WC *Carolinian*, students' silence on integrating their own campus signals a willingness to refrain from rocking the boat. White students from WC did join the 1960 sit-in movement in Greensboro, but these activists formed a minority of the student body. At Agnes Scott College students voiced both pro and con views on school desegregation in the *Script*. One pro-integration editorialist chastised the vast majority of students for their apathetic refusal to take a stand on the issue, implying a general acceptance of the status quo. Another editorial criticized campus conformity but from the opposite perspective. The author mentioned specifically students who, knowing their teachers' views *against* segregation, wrote papers from that angle "even though we secretly are glad segregation exists."[81]

Beyond this, racial symbolism used in everyday language and social events indicates either a conscious or unconscious racism on the part of students in protected white enclaves like Agnes Scott. An article dating back to 1945 speaks to the acceptance of the racial status quo, with all the stereotypes and antipathies this stance entailed. Headlined "Dixie Manor to Replace Junior Joint," the article informed students that the annual junior class dance, called "The Junior Joint," was being "revolutionized" by its transformation to "Jazz-mine Manor" with a Deep South motif of Spanish moss, a butler ushering "belles" inside, and "ol' black mammies" appearing during the evening.[82] References to Dixie, belles, mammies, and butlers harken back to an idealized memory of "the Old South," a nostalgic term for the antebellum slave South. Six years later another article informed ASC students of a parade in downtown Atlanta celebrating the "Faded Glories of Old South," encouraging students to remember the "greatness of the dream" represented by the now-distant southern past.[83] One wonders at the reaction to this parade at nearby Spelman, whose students surely remembered the "Old South" without this romantic patina.

Social events and everyday language at white women's colleges reflected the commonplace nature of racism among students. The most striking example was the regular use of the term "Hottentot" at Agnes Scott as a somewhat affectionate moniker for bad-mannered students, especially those unable to rein in their sexual enthusiasm. Historically the term came from the early nineteenth century, when European physicians looked to Africa for evidence of racial differences in sexual physiology. European scientists transported Saarjite Baartman, a Khoisan or "Hottentot" woman from South Africa, to England and France in order to display her genitalia and buttocks to popular audiences. Renamed "Hottentot Venus," Baartman faced terrible exploitation in both life and death. After being displayed "live" in London and Paris, her death at age twenty-six enabled scientists to exhibit her postmortem sexual anatomy in the British Museum as evidence of the new "science" of race.[84]

Agnes Scott students may or may not have been aware of this history, but they did respond to the sexual connotation of the word *Hottentot*. In 1952 the *Agnes Scott News* ran the headline, "Hottentots Head Techward; Rushing Ends with Bang."[85] The headline referred to ASC students "rushing" to the all-male Georgia Tech University, presumably during rush week at Tech, where activities would include women from surrounding colleges, especially from Agnes Scott, which did not allow sorority life. Whether or not "Ends with Bang" reflects conscious sexual innuendo, the use of the term *Hottentot* in this context is evidence of the word's symbolic meaning, signifying sexual enthusiasm and lack of restraint. Its recurring comic use over several decades suggests that white students' slang employed racial imagery to signal the difference between "good" and "bad" girls, or sexual propriety and behavior on the borderline of respectability. In a similar vein, on at least one occasion Woman's College performers utilized blackface minstrelsy as a humorous way to signal gender difference to appreciative audiences.[86] In contrast to such joking use of racialized language, black students seeking greater sexual freedom had to work *against* these very racist images and practices, simultaneously demanding both expanded sexual boundaries and a sexual respect denied them in the dominant culture.

Similar events or beliefs would have carried very different meanings for liberal white and black activist students. A white woman's daring decision to step outside the "Land of Epidermis" to challenge common taboos against socializing, sharing a meal, or rooming with an African American peer during an interracial conference demonstrated substantial courage in thought and action.[87] Yet she risked little in terms of existing privileges. By contrast, a black student's participation in an interracial forum or political event was not a trial run for adult citizenship. Rather it flew in the face of existing restrictions on citizenship by trying to win rights that their parents and other black adults did not have. In acting on their convictions, they risked their personal futures, facing possible retaliation by white vigilantes or expulsion by campus administrators. Participating in off-campus boycotts and protests, students risked arrest, jail time, and the possibility of sexual or physical violence. This may explain why, generally speaking, vocal grievances at black schools seem to have been slower to brew, and students often initially took a very tentative tone when making demands on the administration. Yet by the end of the 1950s, the momentum of protest, the vociferous language, and the degree of student defiance on black campuses surpassed that occurring on white southern campuses.

Acknowledging these differences, it remains the case that at both black and white southern colleges a discourse of rights and equality had found a home in student protests against the more immediate injustices of campus life. At Shaw a steady stream of student dissatisfaction erupted in March 1954, when the entire student body carried out a six-day strike over "an accumulation of injustices over the previous years," immediately precipitated by the dismissal of four senior women accused of breaking university regulations. The strike ended when administrators upheld the expulsions but agreed to form a joint committee of students, faculty, administrators, and trustees to negotiate other student grievances.[88] Discontent did not end here, however. The *Shaw University Journal* of April 1955 featured an editorial heralding the Supreme Court's 1954 *Brown v. Board of Education* decision next to another one criticizing the campus's "almost unbelievable" sanitation facilities as well as other serious problems in living conditions and academic programs.[89] In the same issue, students proclaimed that women would play a stronger role in student government if their credibility had not been continuously undermined by "the existing regulations governing young women which restrict[ed] the extent of their off-campus activities." Another featured article reported that the Student Council had initiated an investigation of regulations governing the behavior and activities of women students who had "shown great concern over what they term[ed], 'the absence or loss of privileges.'"[90]

Student protest, which consistently challenged administrative authority in the late 1940s and 1950s, burst from its restrained beginnings in 1960 when African American college students from North Carolina shook the world by launching the sit-in movement in Greensboro, quickly followed by similar actions in Raleigh involving Shaw students. Significantly, within two years Shaw students once again turned their focus to restrictive and authoritarian campus policies, initiating a two-week protest in May 1962 that included the burning in effigy of the university's president Strassner. Now skilled in protest techniques from their involvement in off-campus racial politics, the students achieved success when the Board of Trustees dismissed Strassner within a few weeks of their dramatic action.[91]

The lessons to be learned from this story are not only historical but also historiographical. Historians have long viewed the 1950s as the quiescent period before the storm of the 1960s. For example in *The Sixties*, Terry Anderson describes the preceding decade as a time when the record number of students attending college "intended to obey the rules, study, cheer their team, and they hoped, participate in panty raids." He characterizes the end of the 1950s as a time of "social calm and economic prosperity" when "life was good, and it was simple, during happy days." Anderson contrasts this with the watershed year 1960, when just one month into the new year, "four young black college students in the South ended what *Life* labeled 'the calm of the late '50s.' They sat down at a lunch counter and began the sixties, the Decade of Tumult and Change."[92] The dynamic student-led civil rights movement seemed to come out of the blue.[93]

Similarly, some women's historians have maintained an unambiguous contrast between the sexual and gender politics of the "conservative 1950s" and the "radical 1960s." Alice Echols describes the 1960s as a time of pitched battle against "the ultradomesticity of that aberrant decade, the 1950s."[94] Women joined civil rights and left-wing student movements, in Echols's view, to fight against "a campus cultural milieu characterized by sororities and fraternities, husband and wife hunting, sports, and careerism, and the powerlessness they felt as college students without a voice in campus governance or curriculum."[95] Echols is not wrong in her view that the sixties provided an overtly radical critique of societal and campus injustices, nor that college campuses in the previous decade had been heterosexual hunting grounds dominated by sororities and fraternities. Yet the claim that the 1950s is "aberrant" may be better phrased as "paradoxical." For what seems odd about the 1950s is not the night-and-day difference between that decade and the sixties, but that the years from 1945 to 1960 served as a long, slow incubating period in which campuses dominated by conservative culture and politics could at the same time support a growing critique of inequalities based on race, gender, and sexual injustices.

This interpretation builds on revisionist studies of the civil rights and feminist movements that dispel the view of 1950s America as politically quiescent. Jacquelyn Hall, among others, has articulated a view of a "long" civil rights movement by arguing that the black freedom movement both pre- and postdates the "classic" civil rights movement of 1954–68.[96] Women's historians have also come to treat the 1950s as much more contradictory than an earlier view of the decade as singularly repressive.[97] Initiated largely by Joanne Meyerowitz and her influential collection *Not June Cleaver: Women and Gender in Postwar America, 1945–1960*, historians have found that women were quite active in both liberal and conservative politics and more willing to challenge the oppressive aspects of domesticity—what Betty Friedan called "the feminine mystique"—than previously assumed.[98] More recently, Daniel Horowitz and others have pulled apart the "wave" metaphor of feminism by identifying roots of the "second wave" in left and labor activism in the immediate post–World War II era.[99] Scholars of African American women have identified beauty shops, public housing, and women's civic organizations as sites of antiracist activism that pushed forward a distinctly woman-centered agenda that, in particular, insisted on addressing sexual violence against black women as a civil rights issue.[100]

The activism of collegians during the postwar years adds another layer of complexity to this revisionist argument. Although I would not call the gender and sexual politics at southern colleges a "social movement," they nevertheless bear studying for the significant and presaging linkages to a student activism that blended gender, racial, and sexual concerns. Where others have highlighted the midcentury ties of the women's and civil rights movements to radical social movements, I argue that the roots of dissension also emerge from within the framework of postwar liberalism and a therapeutic culture that legitimated calls to end "prejudices" of various sorts. This view builds on the work of Beth Bailey, who in her study of the "sexual revolution" in Kansas argues persuasively for a new chronology of sexual transformation rooted in changes and challenges, though not necessarily radical ones, of the 1940s and 1950s.[101] Southern collegiate women were not the gender and social rebels who founded the women's liberation movement of the late 1960s and 1970s. Very few rejected the notion of fundamental differences between "the sexes" or a commitment to sexual respectability, and only a minority (and many fewer white than black women) joined either the interracial student organizations or the campaigns against racial segregation that preceded the student-led civil rights movement of the 1960s. But they did begin to take the premises of liberalism—equality, democracy, and individual rights—and apply them to their own situation, forging an early analogy between racial and gender "segregation" to express their sexual grievances. To varying degrees, students across the political spectrum developed a critique of the contradictions inherent in Cold War liberalism. They found support from progressive organizations that often became the targets of Cold War persecutions. But they also found support in mainstream social science discourses that linked good mental health and sexual "adjustment" to integrated personalities cleansed of corrosive prejudices.[102]

This story of southern college students demanding more sexual freedom, fewer gender restrictions, and racial justice expands our understanding of the tangled skein of connections between gender and racial hierarchies. During the 1930s, middle-class black and white students remained wedded to a tradition of sexual respectability, although for different purposes. By midcentury, however, the tenor had changed. As an era of sexual liberalism reached its apogee in the frenzied actions of adolescents dancing to rock 'n' roll, "petting" with abandon, and marrying in their teens, some students turned from cultural pursuits to political activism, demanding greater racial and gender integration.

Based on their own self-commentary, the majority of midcentury college students in the South appear to have remained socially moderate and politically conservative or inactive. But even among those less politically inclined, commitment to new heterosexual norms led some students toward a critique of gender hierarchy; recall the impassioned cries of freshman women against their banned attendance at an important football game. Getting pinned and obtaining the famed MRS degree hardly count as "revolutionary" sexual behavior. In fact, we can legitimately see it as the opposite, as part of a blanketing heterosexual normativity that made it that much harder to exist as a gay, lesbian, or bisexual person. Yet even as the intensification of heterosexuality on college campuses limited opportunities for living outside the norms, it also created an awareness of sexual rights that inspired college students to attack highly restrictive campus regulations.

As women pressed for more-permissive rules on dating and heterosexual sociability, they developed a critique of the omnipresent policy of in loco parentis.[103] In their protestations, students embraced a vocabulary of democracy, integration, and political rights. This constellation of ideas spawned gender-based protest on black and white campuses, single-sex and co-ed. While some students focused only on overhauling restrictive campus policies, in its most radical manifestation the new student politics fused a critique of campus paternalism with the fight for racial justice—a two-pronged attack that developed far greater strength on black campuses but also informed the thinking of progressive white women.

A vanguard of black and white students at southern colleges thus reworked ideas about democracy, racial equality, heterosexual desire, and paternalism into surprising new configurations. An idealistic belief in youth as a self-conscious political entity fueled postwar campus activism for world peace, racial and sexual justice, and an end to dictatorial and paternalistic campus governance. This activism occurred well before the first sit-ins of the 1960s. Not surprisingly, when the sit-in movement did take off, students protested racial segregation in places relevant to their own social lives.[104] Protesters occupied the very drugstores, restaurants, and movie theaters that formed the focal point of teenage consumption, locations they frequented in co-ed groups of friends, on dates, or with their "steady" partner or future spouse.[105]

By protesting from within the dominant social and political rhetoric of their time, students shone a bright light on the failures as well as the promises of post-war democracy. In this way an empowered demographic of "youth" first critiqued a democratic society replete with racial, gender, and sexual double standards. As they demanded a single standard of "equal rights"—civil and sexual—a reputedly conservative generation of college students struck a first blow against social and political inequalities. They thus sowed seeds of discontent that would blossom among a much more populous and radical cohort of college students in the 1960s. The latter forged a far deeper critique of American society, one still unimaginable to young southern women of the 1940s and 1950s who, nevertheless, began to imagine a more egalitarian future, asking, "If we got that freedom, what would be the result?"[106]

Notes

1. Annual coverage of this event appeared in the WC newspaper, the *Carolinian*, from the early decades of the twentieth century through the 1930s, then occurred less frequently in the 1940s, and ended by the 1950s, making it hard to pinpoint the exact year the ritual ceased.

2. Agnes Scott College *Silhouette*, 1947. On similar trends nationwide, see John D'Emilio and Estelle Freedman, *Intimate Matters: A History of Sexuality in America* (New York: Harper and Row, 1988), 260–65, 273–74.

3. *Living Stone* (hereinafter *LS*), June 1949, 3.

4. *Agnes Scott News*, June 8, 1953, 2; January 11, 1956, 1.

5. Beth Bailey, "From Panty Raids to Revolution: Youth and Authority, 1950–1970," in *Generations of Youth: Youth Cultures and History in Twentieth-Century America*, ed. Joe Austin and Michael Nevin (New York: New York University Press, 1998), 187–204. See also Bailey, *Sex in the Heartland* (Cambridge, Mass.: Harvard University Press, 1999), 45–48.

6. For the larger project, see Susan K. Cahn, *Sexual Reckonings: Southern Girls in a Troubling Age* (Cambridge, Mass.: Harvard University Press, 2007).

7. On the Greensboro movement, see William Chafe, *Civilities and Civil Rights: Greensboro, North Carolina, and the Black Struggle for Freedom* (New York: Oxford University Press, 1980).

8. Allen W. Nelson, "We Shall Not Retreat: The Shaw University Experience in Social Activism, 1960–1962" (senior honors thesis, Duke University, 1986).

9. Raymond Wolters, *The New Negro on Campus: Black College Rebellions of the 1920s* (Princeton, N.J.: Princeton University Press, 1975).

10. Anne Moody, *Coming of Age in Mississippi* (New York: Dell, 1968), 233–37. Alice Walker's novel *Meridian* also recounts the oppositional rumblings of students frustrated with the conservative administration of an African American women's college, a fictionalized representation of Atlanta's Spelman College. Alice Walker, *Meridian* (New York: Pocket Books, 1976).

11. For other work on student involvement in YWCA and NAACP interracial campaigns, see Abigail Sara Lewis, "The Young Women's Christian Association's Multiracial Activism in the Immediate Postwar Era," in *Freedom Rights: New Perspectives on the Civil Rights Movement*, ed. Danielle L. McGuire and John Dittmer (Lexington: University of Kentucky Press, 2011), 71–110; Thomas L. Bynum, *NAACP Youth and the Fight for Black Freedom, 1936–1965* (Knoxville: University of Tennessee Press, 2013); Peter F. Lau, *Democracy Rising: South Carolina and the Fight for Black Equality since 1865* (Lexington: University of Kentucky, 2006); Rebecca de Schweinitz, *If We Could Change the World: Young People and America's Long Struggle for Racial Equality* (Chapel Hill: University of North Carolina Press, 2009).

12. Historians have recently begun to attend to issues of sexual violence as relevant to the civil rights movement but have not framed the issues in terms of sexual rights. On sexual violence and its relation to the civil rights movement, see Danielle L. McGuire, "'It Was like All of Us Had Been Raped': Sexual Violence, Community Mobilization, and the African American Freedom Struggle," *Journal of American History* 91 (December 2004): 906–31; Danielle L. McGuire, *At the Dark End of the Street: Black Women, Rape, and Resistance—a New History of the Civil Rights Movement from Rosa Parks to the Rise of Black Power* (New York: Vintage, 2011).

13. In the context of this essay, I use the adjectives "gender" and "sexual" interchangeably. Typically, historians would see gender as the cultural elaborations of femininity and masculinity linked to biologically based notions of female and male persons. Sexuality would be the emotions, behaviors, and identities linked to erotic experience. However, in the context of this essay, women's activism challenged strict rules that limited them as a gender. Known as "parietals," these rules governed visiting privileges and limited women's activities outside dormitory residences by time and location. Because these rules were designed to regulate female sexuality and assure sexual respectability, protests against rules that limited women students as a gender were simultaneously protests pushing for greater sexual freedom.

14. *Spelman Campus Mirror* (hereinafter *CM*) April 15, 1928.

15. "David Jones Outlines Plan for Educating Negro Girls," *Greensboro Sunday Record*, May 29, 1927, in papers of the General Education Board, box 117, folder 1061, Rockefeller Archive Center. On Woman's College, see WC *Bulletins* and *Handbooks* from the 1920s and 1930s, Special Collections, Jackson Library, University of North Carolina–Greensboro. See also Ava De Almeida, "Lifting the Veil of Sisterhood: Women's Culture and Student Activism at a Southern College, 1920–1940" (MA thesis in history, University of North Carolina Chapel Hill, 1989).

16. *CM* (March 1939).

17. *Shaw University Journal* (hereinafter *SUJ*), December 19, 1947, 2.

18. *SUJ*, May 21, 1948.

19. *CM*, March 1939.

20. *CM*, November 1940.

21. Agnes Scott Year Book, *The Silhouette*, 1943.

22. See weekly issues of the *Carolinian* for WC political activities during the 1930s; on the Student Strike for Peace, see especially the March 19, 1937, issue. At Spelman, see *CM*, February 15, 1934. On African American youth activism nationally, see de Schweinitz, *If We Could Change the World*, and Bynum, *NAACP Youth and the Fight for Black Freedom*.

23. *SUJ*, February 4, 1938.

24. *College Courses in Race Relations: An Effort to Meet the Challenge of the Southern Situation* (Atlanta: Conference on Education and Race Relations, 1939), quoted in de Schweinitz, *If We Could Change the World*, 200.

25. Patricia Sullivan, *Days of Hope: Race and Democracy in the New Deal Era* (Chapel Hill: University of North Carolina Press, 1996), 193–220.

26. *Hampton Script*, November 11, 1944, 2.

27. See late 1940s issues of the *Carolinian,* specifically the November 5, 1948, issue.

28. *Agnes Scott News*, October 24, 1944, 1.

29. See *SUJ* and the *LS* from this period.

30. *SUJ*, December 5, 1952, 1.

31. Grace Palladino, *Teenagers: An American History* (New York: Basic Books, 1996), 97–135; James B. Gilbert, *A Cycle of Outrage: America's Reaction to the Juvenile Delinquent in the 1950s* (New York: Oxford University, 1986); William Graebner, *Coming of Age in Buffalo: Youth and Authority in the Postwar Era* (Philadelphia: Temple University Press, 1990); Susan J. Douglas, *Where the Girls Are: Growing Up Female with the Mass Media* (New York: Times Books, 1994).

32. The NSA and SDA had chapters in southern women's and co-ed colleges. At WC especially these organizations received regular coverage in the student newspaper. In 1953 the paper reported on a student bill of rights proposed by the Students for a Democratic America. See *Carolinian*, December 11, 1953.

33. *Agnes Scott News*, February 14, 1940, 1.

34. Daryl Michael Scott, "Postwar Pluralism, *Brown v. Board of Education*, and the Origins of Multicultural Education" *Journal of American History* 91 (June 2004): 73–76.

35. *Hampton Script*, December 16, 1944, 1.

36. Bailey, *Sex in the Heartland*, 45–74. On the postwar expansion of psychology, see Ellen Herman, *The Romance of American Psychology: Political Culture in the Ages of Experts* (Berkeley: University of California Press, 1995).

37. *Carolinian*, March 5, 1937; March 18, 1938; December 2, 1938.

38. *CM*, February 1939; *Spelman Messenger*, February 1950.

39. *Agnes Scott Agonistic*, March 30, 1938, 4. On the national trend of increased heterosexual interest and resulting marriage advice for college women, see Lynn Peril, *College Girls: Bluestockings, Sex Kittens, and Coeds, Then and Now* (New York: W.W. Norton, 2006), 277–317.

40. "'How To Get Boy-Friends' Told Bennett Freshmen," *Norfolk Journal and Guide*, May 3, 1941, 6.

41. *Carolinian*, February 12, 1943; October 13, 1944. Agnes Scott's newspaper followed the same pattern, announcing scheduled summer weddings of 1945 graduates under the headline "Seniors Tarry Not—Wedding Bells Ring!" *Agnes Scott News*, June 4, 1945, 4.

42. "Woman's Collegians Follow National Trend; 65% Marry," *Carolinian*, February 13, 1953.

43. *Carolinian*, March 17, 1950, 2–3.

44. *Agnes Scott News*, November 15, 1950, 2.

45. *SUJ*, February 21, 1942, 3.

46. *SUJ*, November 26, 1947, 3.

47. For details, see *Campus Mirror* and the *Spelman Messenger* from the period.

48. *SUJ*, April 11, 1941, 1.

49. Alfred Talbot, "A Social Criticism," *Hampton Script*, March 9, 1940, 2. Male writers and editors dominated the student newspaper, and in general male students appear to have felt freer than their female counterparts to speak critically of school policies. This suggests both the male-dominated atmosphere of Hampton (despite a female majority in the student body) and possibly a more prohibitive atmosphere around assertive actions of any kind by women students.

50. D'Emilio and Freedman, *Intimate Matters*, xviii, 239–300.

51. Such challenges to sexual liberalism do not contradict the reputation of the 1950s as sexually repressive and intensely homophobic. In fact, the McCarthy era's persecution of homosexual individuals and organizations may have unintentionally opened the door to more heterosexual experimentation and activity among teens and young unmarried couples.

52. Livingstone College Catalogues, 1937–38 (and after), Livingstone College, Salisbury, North Carolina.

53. Woman's College "Counselor's Guide Book, 1940–41," pp.10, 24, Special Collections, Jackson Library, University of North Carolina–Greensboro.

54. *Agnes Scott News*, January 11, 1956, 1.

55. Beth Bailey discusses the mid–twentieth century as a period of sexual *evolution*, not *revolution*. Focusing on the University of Kansas, Bailey argues persuasively for a new chronology of sexual transformation rooted in changes and challenges, though not necessarily radical ones, of the 1940s and 1950s. Bailey, *Sex in the Heartland*.

56. "The Hampton Woman," no date (likely from the 1940s based on language and handbook rules), 5.

57. *SUJ*, December 21, 1942, 2. Still protesting ten years later, another student objected to a menu that "never change[d] from week to week." *SUJ*, April 11, 1952, 2. For similar protests at Livingstone College, see *LS*, March 1947, 2.

58. "The Plight of Freshman Women," *Hampton Script*, November 25, 1944, 2.

59. *SUJ*, March 1946, 5.

60. *SUJ*, March 1946, 6.

61. *Carolinian*, February 11, 1959.

62. *LS*, January 1948, 1.

63. *LS*, January 1948, 1.

64. *LS*, March 1948, 4.

65. *LS*, June 1948, 2.

66. *LS*, April 1949, 2. Using a similar reference to prison-like conditions, Anne Moody wrote of her college experience at Natchez College in 1959–60: "I had never in my entire life felt so much like a prisoner, not even when I worked for white Klan members at home." Moody, *Coming of Age in Mississippi*, 224.

67. *Agnes Scott News*, February 20, 1946, 2; February 27, 1946, 2.

68. For example, WC students voted in 1958 to alter the college's honor policy by separating "social offenses" from academic violations like cheating and also eliminating the requirement that students report others for violation. *Carolinian*, November 12, 1958, 1.

69. See the *Hampton Script* from the late 1940s through the mid-1950s, especially January 20, 1956, 1; February 17, 1956, 3.

70. See the *Carolinian* from the late 1940s through the 1950s for details.

71. School officials lost little in the bargain as they reserved the right to disapprove of any "suggested" changes voted on by student governments and alter outright any student court decisions they found unacceptable.

72. A study of the civil rights movement in the Deep South found a similar reduction of visible, vocal organizing in the late 1950s, speculating that after the Montgomery bus boycott victory, the standoff at Little Rock over school desegregation, and the "massive resistance" movement led by leading southern politicians, the costs of organizing temporarily exceeded the resources available to be effective. Charles Payne, *I've Got the Light of Freedom: The Organizing Tradition and the Mississippi Freedom Struggle* (Berkeley: University of California Press, 1996), 42–43, 55–56. Similarly, Jeffrey A. Turner argues that the combination of McCarthyism throughout the 1950s and the rise of massive white resistance to desegregation after 1955 made it more difficult for students to actively support desegregation. Turner, *Sitting In and Speaking Out: Student Movements in the American South, 1960–1970* (Athens: University of Georgia Press, 2010), 32–42.

73. Turner, *Sitting In and Speaking Out*, 36; de Schweinitz, *If We Could Change the World*, 224.

74. Aldon Morris, "Black Southern Student Sit-In Movement: An Analysis of Internal Organization," *American Sociological Review* 46 (December 1981): 744–67. See also Morris, *The Origins of the Civil Rights Movement: Black Communities Organizing for Change* (New York: Free Press, 1984). On South Carolina, see Lau, *Democracy Rising*, 216–17.

75. *Hampton Script*, October 19, 1956.

76. See, for example, *Hampton Script*, October–November, 1956; October–December, 1958.

77. *Fisk Forum*, January 29, 1957, 2, quoted in Turner, *Sitting In and Speaking Out*, 24.

78. Peter Wallenstein, "Color, Courts, and Coeds: The Desegregation of the Woman's College of North Carolina," paper delivered at the Conference of the Southern Association of Women's Historians, Richmond, Va., June 17, 2000.

79. Constance Curry, "Wild Geese to the Past," in Curry et al., *Deep in Our Hearts: Nine White Women in the Freedom Movement* (Athens: University of Georgia Press, 2000), 12–14. For Texas student involvement in the Southern Project and racial integration, see Dorothy Dawson Burlage, "Truths of the Heart," and Casey Hayden, "Fields of Blue," in *Deep in Our Hearts*, 87–130, 335–75.

80. Joan C. Browning, "Shiloh Witness," in Curry et al., *Deep in Our Hearts*, 56–57.

81. *Agnes Scott News*, March 2, 1955, 2; November 16, 1955, 2.

82. *Agnes Scott News*, February 7, 1945, 1.

83. *Agnes Scott News*, April 25, 1951, 2.

84. See Sander Gilman, "Black Bodies, White Bodies: Toward an Iconography of Female Sexuality in Late Nineteenth-Century Art, Medicine, and Literature," *Critical Inquiry* 12 (Autumn, 1985): 204–42; Clifton Crais and Pamela Scully, *Sara Baartman and the Hottentot Venus: A Ghost Story and a Biography* (Princeton, N.J.: Princeton University Press, 2009); Rachel Holmes, *African Queen: The Real Life of the Hottentot Venus* (New York: Random House, 2007).

85. *Agnes Scott News*, October 8, 1952, 3.

86. "Junior Show," in Class of 1952 Scrapbook, Jackson Library, Special Collections, University of North Carolina–Greensboro.

87. Lillian Smith, *Killers of the Dream* (New York: W. W. Norton, 1949), 85.

88. *SUJ*, March 1954, 1–2, quote on 2.

89. *SUJ*, April 1955, 2.

90. *SUJ*, April 1955, 1.

91. Nelson, "We Shall Not Retreat," 102–3.

92. Terry H. Anderson, *The Sixties,* 2nd ed. (New York: Pearson/Longman, 2004), 18.

93. For other works on social movements of the 1960s that pose a stark contrast with the 1950s, see Todd Gitlin, *The Sixties: Years of Hope, Days of Rage* (New York: Random House, 1987); William Chafe, *Unfinished Journey: America since World War II*, 3rd ed. (New York: Oxford University Press, 1995); David Steigerwald, *The Sixties and the End of Modern America* (New York: St. Martin's Press, 1995); Douglas T. Miller, *On Our Own: Americans in the Sixties* (Lexington, Mass.: D. C. Heath, 1996); Irwin Unger and Debi Unger, *America in the 1960s* (St. James, N.Y.: Brandywine Press, 1988); Maurice Isserman and Michael Kazin, *America Divided: The Civil War of the 1960s* (New York: Oxford University Press, 2000); Allan M. Winkler, "Overview: The 1960s and 1970s," in *Encyclopedia of American Cultural and Intellectual History*, vol. 2, ed. Mary C. Kupiec and Peter W. Williams (New York: Charles Scribner's Sons, 2001), 113–21; Fred Pfiel, "Countercultural Visions," in Kupiec and Williams, *Encyclopedia*, 133–41.

94. Alice Echols, "Nothing Distant about It: Women's Liberation and Sixties Radicalism," in *The Sixties: From Memory to History*, ed. David Farber (Chapel Hill: University of North Carolina Press, 1994), 152.

95. Echols, "Nothing Distant about It," 163.

96. Jacquelyn Dowd Hall, "The Long Civil Rights Movement and the Political Uses of the Past," *Journal of American History* 91 (March 2005): 1233–63. See also Glenda Elizabeth Gilmore, *Defying Dixie: The Radical Roots of Civil Rights, 1919–1950* (New York: Norton, 2008).

97. On conservative gender ideology in the postwar era, see Elaine Tyler May, *Homeward Bound: American Families in the Cold War Era* (New York: Basic Books, 1988); May, *Barren in the Promised Land: Childless Americans and the Pursuit of Happiness* (Cambridge, Mass.: Harvard University Press, 1995).

98. Joanne Meyerowitz, "Introduction" and "Beyond the Feminine Mystique: A Reassessment of Postwar Mass Culture, 1946–1961," in Meyerowitz, ed., *Not June Cleaver:*

Women and Gender in Postwar America, 1945–1960 (Philadelphia: Temple University Press, 1994), 1–16, 229–62.

99. Daniel Horowitz, *Betty Friedan and the Making of "The Feminine Mystique": The American Left, the Cold War, and Modern Feminism* (Amherst, Mass.: University of Massachusetts Press, 2000). See also Kathleen A. Laughlin and Jacqueline L. Castledine, eds., *Breaking the Wave: Women, Their Organizations, and Feminism, 1945–1985* (New York: Routledge, 2011); Nancy Hewett, ed., *No Permanent Waves: Recasting Histories of U.S. Feminism* (New Brunswick, N.J.: Rutgers University Press, 2010).

100. Tiffany M. Gill, *Beauty Shop Politics: African American Women's Activism in the Beauty Industry* (Urbana: University of Illinois Press, 2010); Christina Greene, *Our Separate Ways: Women and the Black Freedom Movement in Durham North Carolina* (Chapel Hill: University of North Carolina Press, 2005); Danielle L. McGuire, *At the Dark End of the Street: Black Women, Rape, and Resistance—a New History of the Civil Rights Movement from Rosa Parks to the Rise of Black Power* (New York: Vintage, 2011). For an overview of this literature, see Cornelia H. Dayton and Lisa Levenstein, "The Big Tent of U.S. Women's and Gender History: A State of the Field," *Journal of American History* 99 (December 2012): 793–817, 805–8.

101. Beth Bailey, *Sex in the Heartland* .

102. For more on the links between social science theories of race and sexuality, see Joanne Meyerowitz , "'How Common Culture Shapes the Separate Lives': Sexuality, Race, and Mid-Twentieth-Century Social Constructionist Thought," *Journal of American History* 96 (March 2010): 1057–84.

103. Bailey, *Sex in the Heartland*, 75–104.

104. Chafe, *Civilities and Civil Rights*; Charles M. Payne, *I've Got the Light of Freedom*; John Ditmer, *Local People: The Struggle for Civil Rights in Mississippi* (Urbana: University of Illinois Press, 1994).

105. For more on civil rights activism focused on leisure, see Victoria W. Wolcott, *Race, Riots, and Roller Coasters: The Struggle over Segregated Recreation in America* (Philadelphia: University of Pennsylvania Press, 2012).

106. *LS*, March 1948, 4.

CHAPTER 11

Strange Love

Searching for Sexual Subjectivities
in 1950s Black Print Popular Culture

LEISA D. MEYER

Two distinct reactions to the first issue of *Tan Confessions* suggest that sexuality as rendered in the intimate stories that filled the pages of this monthly was contested terrain for African American readers.

> Myrtle Hartgrove, Atlanta, GA—Dear Editor: I just finished glancing through your first issue of Tan Confessions, and frankly I feel that you've gone to a lot of trouble to waste a lot of valuable paper. What is the point behind the whole thing? Those stories that you call "true to life," are simply impossible. No self-respecting woman with an ounce of decency would allow any of those things to happen to her that you have published as "the truth." You should be ashamed to advertise such trash on the same page with such honorable publications as *Ebony* and *Negro Digest*.

> Jane White, Los Angeles, CA—Dear Editor: Thanks a lot for coming out with your new magazine, *Tan Confessions*. I am a long time buyer of romantic magazines and while I know that they are trash I would much rather spend my money for "colored trash" then "white trash."[1]

I seek in this essay to analyze the ongoing negotiations among individuals and within groups that appear—are written and crafted and responded to—in the pages of black print popular culture magazines during the period immediately following World War II. Through this interrogation, at moments we can see the complex and diverse sexual subjectivities (or potential subjectivities) of African American women—as these subjectivities are articulated, debated, weighed, explored, reconfigured, and at times rejected. What becomes clear through this material is that while there is an explicit and often direct engagement with racialist white normative cultural presumptions (stereotypes) concerning African American sexuality, alternative sexual subjectivities are also explicitly suggested, discussed, and debated within these pages.

One of the most vexing questions in studying the history of sexuality is how to research sexual subjectivity. Certainly oral histories and anthropological participant-observer methods offer routes to such inquiries as does Elaine Tyler Mays's use of the Kelly Longitudinal Study data to engage the lives and subjectivities of white, middle-class couples after World War II.[2] Even John D'Emilio and Estelle Freedman's meticulous synthesis of sexualities through three hundred years of U.S. history engages this question.[3] Yet, for the most part such studies have not made women of color central to the narrative—as the group from whom the narrative emerges or on whom the main historical narrative is based. By foregrounding and reading through African American popular cultural textual sources, African American subjects, cultural formations, and contestations not only become visible but also become the foundation from which queries and conclusions can be produced.

To some extent whenever scholars engage the question of normative cultural forms, they (we) are forced to speak to how such forms influence or are engaged by nondominant/subordinate groups or individuals who do not share the race (white), class (middle class/elite), sexual (heterosexual) markers that place them as default "normative" members of the hegemony. We need to proceed cautiously, or we sometimes get trapped by this often often-subtextual (even unspoken) presence.

Through publications such as *Ebony, Jet,* and *Tan Confessions*, African Americans responded explicitly to the presumption of a normative white, middle-class sexuality in the post–World War II era. These "public" discussions of sexuality within black print popular culture always occurred with the understanding that the "gaze" or "surveillance" of whites was never completely absent. Thus some of the ways in which sexuality was articulated in the pages of these popular cultural publications responded to and intervened in the hegemonic normative sexual system and the raced, gendered, and classed relations of power it contained. Such a reading of black print popular culture has been offered by some scholars who have characterized the black press during the twentieth century as both celebrating the accomplishments of African American people and defending African American individuals and communities in the context of racist social structures and discourses. Other historians have conceptualized elements of the black press as both "performance and commodity."[4] African American popular print culture/periodicals have also played (and continue to play) key roles in the configuration of standards of "appropriate behavior" to which African Americans should adhere.[5]

As significantly, these same pages provide some glimpses of the intraracial negotiations of sexual norms, behaviors, meanings, and knowledges within black communities themselves. In other words, the work of norm construction was always also internally contested with a variety of often-contradictory "rules" suggested by authors.[6] In his formulation of black popular culture as a "contradictory space" and a "site of strategic contestation," Stuart Hall calls for the necessity of moving beyond the binary oppositions ("us" versus "them," "heteronormative" versus "nonheteronormative," or "opposition versus homogenization") that we have used (and continue to employ) to map sexuality, race, and gender. The elements of African American print popular culture examined here are engaged in what Hall terms "struggles over hegemony," and I am suggesting that we analyze such interventions as dialogic, not simply as restoring one pole of a newly constituted binary. Thus various systems of normativity (subcultural and hegemonic) are at moments interrupted in some editorials and letters that suggest a much more fluid understanding of sexual practices, behaviors, and identities.[7]

The periodicals I examine in this essay were all published in Chicago and under the auspices of what became John Johnson's publishing empire. *Ebony* began publication in 1945 and was intended by Johnson to be a "full-service news, information, and entertainment periodical."[8] By 1951 *Ebony* had a circulation of five hundred thousand, becoming the first "mass circulation" black magazine, and was joined that year with the premier issue of its companion periodical, *Jet*.[9] In contrast to *Ebony*'s monthly issue, *Jet* was a weekly. Johnson designed *Jet* not to replace or compete with any other weekly periodical but rather to meet the need for a "convenient-sized magazine that [would] summarize the week's biggest Negro news in a well-organized, easy-to-read format."[10] In fact, while *Ebony* was ostensibly intended to mirror *Life* and *Look* magazines published in the white mainstream press, and targeted the black middle class for its readership, *Jet* was a "small-scale gossip publication" that Fath Davis Ruffin argues "appealed to Johnson's ethnic core clientele. . . . This was the place to read about the dirt on black celebrities that would not appear in *Ebony* until it had first appeared in court." *Jet* pushed the envelope especially on definitions of sexual respectability throughout the 1950s as evidenced by the editorial decision to include a centerfold of an African American woman in a bathing suit in every issue. Ruffin characterizes this decision as an "important marketing tool" that Johnson continued throughout the period despite some criticism from "various quarters of the black community."[11] In fact, historian James Hall suggests that Johnson's goal for *Ebony* was to "mobilize and maximize class desire" to create a black consumer whose aspirations could be met by purchasing these magazines and the wares advertised therein.[12] The third periodical, *Tan Confessions*, was, according to its publisher, "a unique new venture in the magazine field." This "romantic" monthly was aimed at women and intended to publish "true-to-life" stories on the topics of "love and romance, marriage and family," which Johnson described as "vital concerns of every colored man and woman, no matter what their status in life." In *Tan* Johnson "hope[d] to be able to reflect a side of Negro life that is virtually ignored in most publications today," the "bewildering problems" of "men and women in love" and "how they were able to achieve happiness."[13] Debuting in November 1950, *Tan* had a circulation of three hundred thousand one year later. While I also use particular editorials and articles from the *Chicago Defender*, the magazines I have described here form the core of my evidence.[14]

The fluidity apparent in some elements of black print popular culture suggests that this media created a space where sexuality and sexual subjectivities could be discussed and debated. As Todd Vogel comments, "A periodical analyzed as a cultural production creates an ideal stage for examining society."[15] We can interpret the articles within these periodicals as representing and reflecting "verbal exchanges between community members over crucial questions. . . . Writing, here, becomes a social act."[16]

Contesting Normativity

The domain of sexual knowledge consists in part of what we know and how we know it, what we are told we "should" know and by whom, and what we believe are the consequences of this knowledge. Interrogations of sexual knowledges make visible the politics or power relations that compete to construct sexual discourses and normalize certain sexualities.[17] Social hierarchies of race, gender, and class filter different types of sexual knowledges. These filters or modes of mediating sexual discourses demand attention to the question asked by those who see their oppression—their "deviant" status—articulated through dominant sexual discourse, namely, what do "they" think they know about "us," a question that speaks to the means by which patterns of social relations are constituted and maintained. As such, the sexual norms, presumptions, and racialized sexual discourses articulated, contested, and reconfigured in black print popular culture were part of the broader struggle against Jim Crow and other legal and cultural structures of white supremacy during the 1950s.

In the wake of a "war for democracy" and the "double V" campaign conducted by African American leaders during that war—articulating a "fight against fascism" abroad and against "racism" at home—toppling the de jure and de facto Jim Crow system of racial segregation in most of the country became a key goal of African American leaders, organizers, and activists. From Harry Truman's executive order desegregating the military in 1948, through *Brown v. the Board of Education* in 1954 and the successful Montgomery bus boycott of 1955, to the integration of Little Rock Central High School in 1957, part of the focus was challenging the stereotypes and white racist presumptions that often lay at the heart of (or were foundational to) this system of apartheid. At a moment when "science" was increasingly granted authority, many African Americans looked to emerging scientific discourses and findings to validate and give evidence to legitimate these challenges to dominant white presumptions about African American people, their behavior, folkways, and lives. Alfred Kinsey's studies of sexuality in the human male (1948) and sexuality in the human female (1953) were thus eagerly anticipated by African American leaders as offering "scientific" evidence to undercut and contest racist stereotypes of African American women and men's "natures," sexualities, and sexual subjectivities.

During the 1950s, the vast majority of the articles addressing sexuality in *Ebony*, *Tan Confessions*, *Jet*, and the *Chicago Defender* referenced Kinsey's studies in some way. Kinsey's volumes were alternately vilified and acclaimed by the popular media, religious and state leaders, and the millions of Americans who discussed his findings during the course of their daily lives. Whether it was deemed horrifying or titillating, Kinsey's work was a subject of intense conversation among friends, coworkers, and relatives for months after it was formally published. Despite the fact that most of Kinsey's subjects seemed to have led fairly conventional sexual lives, the focus of attention and debate was the varied and fluid sexual experiences recounted by the minority. This glimpse of, by dominant standards, deviant sexual expressions was profoundly unsettling to many Americans and equally affirming to others. While Kinsey's survey did not begin such conversations, it gave sexuality public legitimacy as a topic of discussion between individuals and in popular media forums. Sexuality, always intertwined with personal identity, became a means to claim liberation and simultaneously a barometer of a nation's morality.[18] Kinsey's findings—whether critiqued or accepted—became a benchmark for discussions of sexuality and a point of departure for those seeking to interrupt the racialized sexual stereotypes that inhered in what Eve Sedgwick has termed the "discursive and institutional 'common sense'" that constitutes one aspect of the terrain of sexual knowledge.[19] The invocation of Kinsey's study as well as the frequent use of medical and therapeutic discourses to address sexuality also reflected the growing national focus on the power of science to explain and effect change in the human condition.[20]

In anticipation of the release of Kinsey's study of female sexual behavior, African American periodicals such as *Jet* magazine explicitly engaged and disputed normative racialized presumptions of the "sexual nature" of "American Negroes." In one fairly typical article, a 1951 piece titled "Sex Habits of Negro Women," the unnamed author outlines the "opinions of white persons" on the subject, noting that they tended to characterize African American women as "extraordinarily sensual." In contrast to this "white" presumption, the article quotes Kinsey as finding "'little difference at all between the sexual activity of colored and white women in the same social levels'" in his preliminary research. The author goes on to conclude that "the super-sexuality of the Negro woman is just another fiction. . . . Her sex life is likely to be as civilized as that of the white society whose standards she has accepted."[21] While clearly disputing white "myths" of African American women's sexuality the author also makes "white society" the "norm" for comparison and implies, however indirectly, that "accepting" and maintaining such sexual "standards" is required for African American women to be understood as "civilized" and therefore "respectable" within both white and black culture.

Evelyn Brooks Higginbotham coined the term "politics of respectability" to describe African American women's promotion of restrained behavior, especially in terms of sexuality, as a "strategy of reform" during the early twentieth century. She suggests that this "politics of respectability" constituted a "deliberate and highly self-conscious concession to hegemonic values" that enabled African American women, through the appropriation of the discourse of "respectability," to "define themselves outside the parameters of prevailing racist discourses."[22] Thus, according to Higginbotham, African American women used the hegemonic ideals of white society to both assert respectability for themselves and interrupt dominant cultural racist presumptions. Historian Paisley Harris has further clarified this strategy and its consequences in her characterization of the "gatekeeping function" of the politics of respectability that she claims established a "behavioral entrance fee" for membership in African American communities. While this "entrance fee" offered some challenge to hegemonic cultural views of African Americans, it also constructed and maintained status distinctions within African American communities.[23]

Despite the expectations that Kinsey's work would quash white stereotypes of African American women's sexuality, when his report was finally released in 1953 black women were not included in his research sample nor in his overall findings. In response, elements of the black press accused Kinsey of accepting the presumption "so common to Americans" that "Negroes" were vastly different from "other Americans."[24] A series of editorials in *Ebony* specifically examined the question in an article titled "Why Negro Women Are Not in the Kinsey Report." These editors reached three conclusions. First, that Kinsey was not able to get a sufficient number of "Negro women" to respond to questions, noting that according to Kinsey, "Too few college educated colored women would talk . . . although those with grade and high school educations were very cooperative."[25] Second, the reason for the "tight-lipped silence" of college-educated African American women was perhaps their "reaction to the stereotypes which are so common about Negroes—such as being sexually loose." Several articles included interviews with Chicago "sex experts," including one with a child psychologist who described "upper class Negroes" as more "race conscious. . . . Their reputations have been besmirched so often that they are suspicious of almost anyone who wants to put their sex lives under a microscope."[26] Offering a similar view, a Chinese American sociologist argued that some of the women "may simply have been 'tired of being studied, fearful of being misquoted or misunderstood, afraid that erroneous generalizations would be made about them.'"[27] Finally, several agreed with Kinsey's own statements that there were generally more similarities than differences "between the sex habits of Negroes and whites on the same cultural and economic planes."[28] These reactions clarified the potential stakes in both the inclusion and exclusion of black women from the Kinsey report. The concern of possibly confirming what "others" might or did think they knew about African American women, or worse not confirming these myths but having them believed anyway, highlights the continuing fractures along lines of class or educational status found in the ongoing rationale for racial uplift—all are judged by the behavior/lives of the "lowest"—and the persistent belief that the legitimating authority of a scientific study might set things right.

Sex surveys such as Kinsey's are intriguing and give us information about how some individuals might have understood (or understand) their own sexuality and sexual norms. As useful, if not more so, however, as is clear from the responses presented above, is what came after these surveys. In other words, most fascinating are the reactions and responses to these surveys—especially because Kinsey's effort was the first to be so widely publicized.[29] The African American press and print culture response to Kinsey demonstrate how broad public discussion of information about sex that was previously sequestered in the care of "experts" enabled or made visible potential ruptures in systems of power relations—in this case raced relations of power mediated through sexual discourse. Sexual discourses are produced and contested but are often hidden by the stereotypes, presumptions, and "common sense" that are hallmarks of normalizing regimes.[30] More concretely, the normative assumption that the editorialist respondents are unmasking—that African Americans are less sexually respectable than white Americans—was challenged. In the discussion that follows, it will become clear that within the realm of African American print popular culture, sexual passion and sexual respectability were not understood as mutually exclusive for black women.

Constructing Sexual Norms or Transmitting
Appropriate Sexual Knowledges

Despite Kinsey's failure to see or address black women's sexual subjectivity, African American sexual subjectivity was articulated in black periodicals.[31] This articulation was by no means simple or straightforward, but rather a layered, multivalent discussion, at times heavy-handed and explicitly prescriptive, at other moments providing a glimpse of alternatives and possibilities.[32] Prescriptive articles both engaged the white "gaze" and refuted the hegemonic white mythography of African American sexuality. They simultaneously laid down guidelines for the "respectable" and "appropriate" exercise of sexuality for African American men and women. Evelyn Brooks Higginbotham comments on this "cognizance of the gaze of white America, which in panoptic fashion focused perpetually upon each and every black person and recorded his or her transgressions in an overall accounting of black inferiority."[33] While this "gaze of white America" continued to be a factor in constructions of African American sexual subjectivities in popular print culture, it was not the only factor as competing black voices debated the most appropriate forms of sexuality within the pages of periodical literature.

One type of "prescriptive" article took the form of advice offered to African American populations by recognized African American "celebrities." Mrs. Lucius Harper's 1953 *Tan Confessions* piece, in which she speaks to her daughter and other young women, was one such example. Textually framed with a title line that references her status as the "wife of late Executive Editor of the *Chicago Defender*" and photos with captions "advising her daughter Jeanne on getting along with men," Harper presents her credentials as knowledgeable and respectable. She then proceeds to offer counsel on dating, "feminine" appearance, and strategies for marriage. The differences between her own and her daughter's generation, Harper explains, is that "the girl or woman, who thinks that being virtuous and virginal is quite enough and that her Prince Charming will some day ride by on his white charger and sweep her off her feet hasn't a chance. . . . When men claim on questionnaires or on radio quiz shows that they may admire the pretty face but always marry the old-fashioned girls, they are lying."[34] The "freedom" to express themselves sexually that she sees as characteristic of her daughter's generation is mediated by the goal of heterosexual marriage as the "only" choice for young women. She then specifies the tactics for "getting Babykins eventually . . . trapped into walking down that aisle." These "tactics" involve careful and constant "work" for young women to look, smell, and act their best in order to both "attract" men of "good character" and keep such men "proud of" them. Mrs. Lucius Harper begins and ends her article with admonitions to young women about the various ways they must be "all" to "catch and hold" men, "As one gentleman I know sums it up: there are three kinds of women—the fine looking thing they like to be seen with; the companionable woman they like to stay home with; and the sex mate they can't live without. When he finds all of these qualities in one woman . . . he will marry her and stay married for a long time."[35]

Harper moves from presenting specific tips on clothing styles, cosmetics colors, hairstyles, and perfume as key elements of drawing the male gaze to strategies not directly related to appearance. In this section Harper focuses on ways women can ensure that the man they "get" is the one they "want." Male appearance might be the barometer of initial attraction, but the more critical assessment involved ascertaining a potential suitor's "education and interests." Noting that men "frankly study women at every opportunity," Harper suggests that women need to return the favor and study men right back. This female gaze, she argues, will enable young women to determine the eligibility of potential suitors before they go too far in any heterosexual relationship.

> On the first date, a wise woman can gather enough information about a man to fill out a Dun & Bradstreet report. From the time he makes her acquaintance to the goodbye at her doorstep, his every word and action is an index to his character. . . . The first few casual remarks reveal his education and interests. When he calls to see her, if he rings the bell and comes up the steps, he is off to an even start. If she is reasonably near ready, there is hope, too, for her. If he flops down on the davenport and sprawls out in complete repose, he also has a couch at home with greasy upholstery and busted springs. If his idea of a big night out is a western at the corner movie before the prices change and cokes when the show is over, he will no doubt want his 79 cents back in kisses before the evening is spent. For youngsters with limited funds, the coke and cut-rate show routine is acceptable, but if a grown man asks his lady fair what she would like to do (and he should show her that courtesy), she should set the pace for future dates by naming the best show and dining in a first-class place.[36]

What they should "know about men," in other words, was their class status and ability and willingness to financially provide.[37]

Harper's focus on class as a marker of "character" and sexual respectability was also key to another celebrity's advice, this time targeting African American men. In "The Truth about White Women," musician and guest reporter Cab Calloway explores the topic of interracial sexual relations for an issue of *Tan Confessions.* Calloway speaks specifically to what he sees as the association held by African American men between dating white women and increased status within the black community. He chastises African American men for their "mistaken" belief that "having and holding a white woman is more to be desired than precious gems . . . and that whiteness in women means the same as beauty and worth."[38] Juxtaposing the respectability and character of black women with their white counterparts' lack thereof, Calloway calls on African American men not to assume beauty was defined by skin color. Calloway also notes that if "Negro men" are attracted to "light skinned" women,

> there are any number of Negro women . . . throughout the country, who are actually white in color. That is one reason that I can't understand why some Negro men

who like white women only for their color, have to go outside their race to find a mate. My first wife was thought to be white by many people because she was so fair. My present wife, Nuffie, is often mistaken for a white woman. It just so happens, however, that I didn't marry either one of my wives for their color. I am not color-struck and never have been. If I'm in any way prejudiced, I guess I'm prejudiced in favor of Negro women and maybe that's because the most wonderful woman I've known—my wife, Nuffie—is one.[39]

Calloway highlights the class status and questionable respectability of white women as a contrast to black women's "beauty, talent, and intelligence."[40] He contends that this focus on skin color in selecting romantic and sexual partners has often led black men to join with white women who were not their equals in terms of education and "quality." In this piece Calloway inverts the white middle-class system of racial power relations by positioning African American women as more sexually respectable and of better character than white women and affirming the normative linkage between lower-class status and sexual deviance. By doing so, he ironically upholds the normative white middle-class presumption that only lower-class white women would associate sexually with African American men. Further, by underlining the relevance of "color" for some African American men's sexual choices, Calloway provides one example of the ways in which "color" functioned to construct status in African American communities. That he ultimately supports dating and marrying African American women who "look white" or can pass reinforces the presumption of beauty tied to white features. Historian Fath Davis Ruffin argues that the African American magazines founded in the 1940s and 1950s promoted a "kind of class hierarchy based on skin color." And that "although Black magazines served their communities by making Black news front page, they portrayed a narrow vision of ideal attractiveness with class implications."[41]

Appearing the following year (1953), the commentary "Are Negroes More Amorous Than Whites?" explicitly engages the questions of African American masculinity and color that Calloway took on in his editorial. This commentary questions the "myth" of African American men's "legendary prowess." The piece begins with the story of a "well-educated white woman" who falls in love with a "Negro man who had never graduated from public school and barely earned enough to support himself."[42] Although the two do not get along, and she loses both friends and family over the relationship, she "refuses to leave him, telling her friends that she found him more amorous than any other man she had known." The author characterizes the depiction as "part of the stereotype concerning . . . Negro males," who are by "some quirk of nature . . . gifted with qualities that make them more amorous." The author asserts instead that "Negro women . . . contradict this longtime notion" and hold in "conversations" that "Negro men are lousy lovers." The article also points to the findings of "sociologists" that there is little difference in the "relative amorous abilities of white and Negro men." It is white women, the writer asserts, who are "seeking outlets in doing 'something different,'... and see Negro mates as something 'exotic,'" thereby "demonstrating a form of discrimination in reverse."[43]

"Are Negroes More Amorous Than Whites?" uses sexuality as a site through which to address racist ideologies and laws. Interrogating the stereotypes that form the "evidence" for dominant white commonsensical understandings, it elucidates the meanings of race differences and the legal structures and practices—"white men's laws and customs"—that support and maintain such myths. In doing so, the article suggests the ways in which race and sexuality were interwoven channels for constructing norms and deviance. In other words, negotiations of the meanings of "whiteness," "blackness," and race difference both shaped and were shaped by contemporaneous shifts in constructions of sexual norms and deviance.[44]

The "unspeakable" subtext that is not explicitly discussed but which is invoked in this editorial is the myth of the black male rapist. By challenging white middle-class normative depictions of African American male sexuality (and simultaneously casting doubt on the sexual respectability of white women), the author contests and reconstructs dominant sexualized racial hierarchies. Such an inversion evokes the resistant speech of Ida B. Wells. As African American feminist scholars such as Paula Giddings and Darlene Clark Hine have demonstrated, Wells disputed the late-nineteenth- and early-twentieth-century racist presumptions of rape that rationalized the white lynching of black men, and simultaneously questioned the "passionless purity" of white southern women.[45]

Yet, while the piece makes this particular myth visible and critiques whites (especially white women) for believing it and aiding its proliferation, the author also ends somewhat paradoxically by suggesting that "Negro men" are likely to agree with some aspects of this mythic depiction of their sexuality, especially that which defines their "status" as "genuine heartbreakers" compared to white men.[46] As such, the author's "resistant cultural work" seems to retain what cultural critic Clyde Taylor has termed the "fragmentary, tell-tale presence from the myth it seeks to dispel." Thus the author also seems to affirm some aspects of the myth that might suggest African American men's possession of a masculinity—as defined by virility—superior to that of their white counterparts.[47]

While celebrity advice literature was one form of offering guidance on sexual matters, the most obviously authoritative articles (often also authored by celebrities) were those framed by the rubric of "sex education." In a 1951 piece in the *Chicago Defender*, for instance, poet Langston Hughes weighed in on the dangers of sexual ignorance (which he held led to teen pregnancy and venereal disease) and the importance of transmitting basic sexual knowledges to young men and women. Hughes began by holding parents accountable for teenage girls' pregnancies and teenage boys' acquiring of venereal diseases, arguing that parents who did not adequately educate their children on sexual matters were "to blame" for these problems. Recognizing the necessity of not feeding into white stereotypes of African American sexuality, he then notes, "Many white people believe that all Negroes are sexually uninhibited. On the contrary, I am inclined to think that many Negro parents are probably more puritanical than most whites." In other words, it was not African American teens' greater sexual knowledge but rather their lack of sexual knowledge that led to sexual "delinquencies." He argues that parents bore the most responsibility for educating their children on sexual matters and suggests that if they could not bring themselves to speak about sexuality with their children, then they should give their "growing sons" Evelyn Millis Duval's *The Facts of Life and Love for Teenagers*, published by the national YMCA.[48] Hughes's recommendation of Duval's book, with chapters such as "Where Babies Come From," "Dating Know-How," and "Petting," both parallels and plugs into the increasingly visible move for sex education under way nationally in the United States by the early 1950s.[49]

Hughes's call is echoed in another type of "educational" narrative—the "cautionary" first-person tale. One such *Tan Confessions* article was the "story of a young woman who had a great education" for being "successful in the social and business worlds" but who had to "learn about love from friends and other students—not from teachers or parents." The narrator explains that no one ever spoke with her about sex, though her mother "promises her a 'long talk' sometime . . . when [she] grow[s] up." Without parental guidance, the young woman relies on "picking up a distorted fact here, gathering an utterly false and dangerous notion there"; she admits, "By the time I got to high school I thought I knew everything there was to know."[50] This lack of sexual knowledge resulted in a wedding night during which she stops her husband when she starts to feel "emotional" (sexual passion) because this was what she had always done in these situations and did not understand how to respond differently. She implies in the story that her husband continued anyway, "but she wasn't ready." She does not blame her husband for his actions but rather faults the lack of information available to her.[51]

The greater sexual knowledges that commentators like Hughes argued were necessary for young men and women, however, should not lead to greater sexual experimentation. The narrator in "Is the Chaste Girl Chased?" suggests that the "lesser sexual inhibitions" of young women were a symbol not of greater "freedom" to be embraced but rather of the "lower morals" that pervaded contemporary society and as such a trend that should be resisted. The substance of this "tale" focuses on the "problem" of young men's presumptions of female sexual availability and details the narrator's negotiations over sex with one boyfriend, Frank. Over the course of their relationship, Frank has made a series of arguments for sexual intercourse. Invoking a psychological model, Frank draws analogies between sexual intercourse and other basic "human needs," asking, "Would a girl deny herself food if she was hungry?" and pointing to the potential "damage" to her mental health that "suppress(ing)" her sexual needs might cause. He ends by insisting that "experiment(ing) with sex" would put her in a "better position to select a future husband" and warns that if she "wanted to get married," she "must know that men no longer tolerate women who hold out." In response to Frank's logic, the author engages in her own research by consulting the works of "people who had made a study of the subject," including "social workers, psychiatrists, educators, marriage counselors, and religious leaders." Choosing to "educate" herself, she finds ammunition in these texts to refute Frank's assertions and, employing her own therapeutic framework, comes to the conclusion that while "love-making is a natural and perfectly normal function . . . it will cause unhappiness if it does not have the approval of society."[52]

The "chaste girl's" argument on this count parallels that of "Primer for Petting," published in *Jet* two years later. Starting with the questions, "Is petting a sin? Can a girl refuse to pet and still be popular?" the author notes that the "real score" on petting "according to experts handling problems of young people, weighs heavily against the teenager who indulges in petting and necking." Similar to Hughes's focus, this piece targets teen pregnancy as one of the primary "dangers" for young women and links this danger to the "lack of information" available to young women on "the facts of life." [53] The piece is framed by photos of kissing couples underlined with captions "Clinches can be catastrophic" and "Petting is particularly dangerous because it arouses emotions couples cannot always control." Offering advice on how young women can avoid difficulties, the author recommends that teenage girls double date and refrain from drinking, "parking," or kissing boys good night, and ends with the simple warning, "Nice boys don't date promiscuous petters."[54]

Despite the contradictory messages offered to young women and men in these examples, one consistent theme in most of the advice literature in these periodicals was an acknowledgment of the presence of sexual desire and passion in *both* women and men. As even the "chaste girl" notes in her tale, "There have been times when I've had my doubts, when the hunger within me cried out for complete fulfillment and when I could have easily slipped into the sex pattern of what many call the 'modern girl.'"[55] Although this narrator describes her resistance to this "hunger," its existence is never in question.

The "fact" of female sexual desire was also the subject of another type of article in the mid-1950s querying the "morals" of "bachelor girls." One typical commentary pointed to the "dangers" posed by "bachelor girls" to married women, their husbands, and the institution of marriage. The author defines these "bachelor girls" or "gimmie women" as those who "could have married but said 'no' too many times; those who wanted to marry but never received an attractive proposition; those who were widowed in early womanhood; and those who were married and divorced." Not contained within a normative heterosexual family structure, these young women are apt to "relax their morals in the face of decreasing marriage opportunities" according to "sociologists." Referencing "Name the Sponsor" as the "newest parlor game since canasta," the author notes that some "bachelor girls are undoubtedly 'sponsored' by well-heeled, variety loving men (who provide apartments, minks, cars in exchange for 'companionship')."[56] In conclusion, perhaps seeking to place female sexual agency within familiar parameters, the author invokes Kinsey's research as indicating that "the sexual morality of women still curve(s) around the enduring phenomenon—the male wolf—who in all ages has stormed the trenches of the unwary and the unwise, be she married or single."[57] Reclaiming male prerogative as of singular importance, the author thus restores conventional gender hierarchy.

Contested Constructions of Non-Normative Sexualities

Gender inversions became a primary mode of constructing sexual deviances within African American print popular cultural publications. These inversions were represented not only by depictions of "feminine" characteristics in men and "masculine" traits and attributes in women but also in the "problem" of women taking on male prerogatives including by having extramarital sexual affairs (heterosexual and same-sex) or by exhibiting sexual initiative or by making claims to "male" economic power. In other words, the instantiated male power over women inherent in a patriarchal system is also a key aspect of heteronormativity as defined and contested in African American print popular culture during this period.

Gender deviance as a signifier of sexual deviance was also prominent in discussions of male and female same-sex sexualities within black print popular culture. These discussions ranged from straightforward and occasionally sympathetic reporting to moral condemnation of "homosexuals."

The language used in editorials addressing same-sex sexualities generally was alternatively contemptuous and sympathetic. In a 1952 piece in *Jet*, for instance, "Is There Hope For Homosexuals?," gay men are depicted as presenting America with the "biggest psychological sexual problem of modern times." The author goes on to characterize gay men as "like persons afflicted with a dread disease, [who] bloat their number each year by the planned seduction of innocents" and concludes with a somewhat desperate call for more "scientific research and laws into this issue."[58] In a similar 1951 essay in *Ebony* authored by Rev. Adam Clayton Powell III, Powell defines the "cause" of "homosexuality" as "biological or psychological inclination" but also suggests that the fault for "unnatural relationships" could be equally assigned to inadequate information—because young men and women "did not, at an early age receive the proper sex education."[59] In "decrying homosexual tendencies," Powell offers a list of characteristics/attributes by which to identify such people: "The boys with the swish and the girls with the swagger are getting daily more numerous and more bold and it is highly necessary that we start doing something to help our youngsters from becoming members of the horrible no-man's-land of sex. But it is also necessary that we start doing something to help those haunted people who are touched with such degeneracy. . . . Any one who walks the streets of Chicago and New York and unfortunately attends some of the churches will notice the trend of parading homosexuals, a trend which is increasing alarmingly."[60] Powell's characterizations of the "swishing" boys and "swaggering" girls as exemplary of the "homosexual" highlighted gender inversion as a means of identifying potentially deviant sexualities.

The question remains, however, what is the relationship between knowledge and speaking of "homosexuality"? Does knowledge lead to a greater acceptance of sexual diversity? In another article in *Jet* two years later, "Are Homosexuals Becoming Respectable," the "casual acceptance" of gay men by the public is noted, and the author concludes, "People are willing to treat members of the 'third sex' as victims of an illness that needs treatment rather than criminals who should be punished."[61] Invoking Kinsey's statistics on the "prevalence" of homosexuals within the general population and giving specific examples of "prominent Negroes" who were gay, including noted civil rights activist Bayard Rustin, the article suggests that homosexuality, while an affliction, was not something to be greatly feared.[62] The shift in perspective of these reports, explicitly articulated as a move from crime to illness, is apparent through the 1950s in both white and black print popular culture.[63]

Throughout the 1950s, *Jet* also offered abundant coverage of female impersonators. These editorials, in somewhat humorous fashion, describe "night club[s] where swishing, clean-shaven men dress in women's clothes and entertain cash customers." They depict venues in which the "shapely chorus girl is as out of place as a hand crank on a Cadillac because the female impersonators have taken over."[64] In a 1953 *Jet* article covering the "annual Thanksgiving ball" in New York City, the author describes "the queenly dressed men" as "provid[ing] a good show for hundreds of on-lookers who crowded the sidewalks as policemen kept order and 'winked' at the law prohibiting men from dressing as women."[65] In these pieces, drag ball entertainments seem to be generally accepted as a part of the cultural landscape within urban African America, at least through the late 1950s.[66]

African American periodicals, like white mainstream offerings, also exhibited a fascination with the possibilities of "changing one's sex." A series of four editorials in *Jet* in 1953 presented very sympathetic reports on the former female impersonator Charles Robert Brown's attempts to obtain a sex-change operation in Europe that would enable him to marry his Army sergeant childhood sweetheart. Over a period of three months, *Jet* followed the progress of Brown toward his goal, describing him giving up his U.S. citizenship and his plans to leave America in August. The second article in this series quotes Brown as noting this overseas move as the only option for him "because of the Christine Jorgenson [*sic*] 'affair' after which the U.S. refuse[d] to give an American citizen permission to alter his sex." Far from condemning Brown's efforts, the writer goes on to breezily describe Brown as "like most women anticipating marriage" who go "shopping for a wedding gown in downtown Boston." The series went on to document Brown's imprisonment a month later for "masquerading in female attire." Although the author references the Boston laws prohibiting men from wearing female attire, the report focuses more on the "woman's coat-suit ensemble" that Brown was wearing when arrested. According to the *Jet* reporter, Brown's journey ended when he decided to "postpone" his trip to Denmark in order to have a "$500 face-lifting operation." This concluding article also describes Brown as still planning to have his "sex changed" but also "keep[ing] his ties to female impersonators" as he feels that "female impersonators are being denied their right of life, liberty and the pursuit of happiness when they are arrested for wearing female clothes."[67]

In its reporting on Charles Brown's efforts, *Jet* joined other American popular cultural media in what Joanne Meyerowitz terms the "frenzy" of attention to such procedures following American and former-G.I. Christine Jorgensen's sex-change operation in Denmark in 1952. In Charles Brown's case, the *Jet* coverage seemed to support (or at least be sympathetic to) medical intervention for the sex-change operation that would allow him to transform his non-normative lifestyle into one more consistent with the norms of heterosexuality. Yet to characterize this example as indicating the triumph of heteronormativity would be to oversimplify the multiple possibilities it suggests. *Jet's* coverage of Brown's case marks an engagement in what Meyerowitz characterizes as "the debate on the visibility and mutability of sex," enabled by the popular cultural media focus on Christine Jorgensen's story.[68] This engagement, when considered along with other sympathetic coverage of female impersonators, seems to suggest a more fluid understanding of sexuality and gender.

In contrast to the sometimes-sympathetic approach to gender inversion related to men, discussions of gender inversion related to women were often more critical. Articles highlighting "passing women" were the most explicit in laying out the "dangers" of lesbians. These pieces focused on "passing women's" "contempt" for all things feminine and their competition, like heterosexual "working wives," with men for jobs, thus invoking their violation of gendered relations of power as a main threat to the community. These essays were joined by others that focused on the "dangers" posed to heterosexual homes of "bad" or "evil" wives, most often defined by their "irritability," "shrewishness," and "uncontrollable strong sex drives." In line with the growing belief in the power of medicine and science to effect cures for various maladies, several articles described the "possibilities" offered by medicine for those suffering such "maladjustments."[69]

In "Women Who Fall for Lesbians," the author suggests that "masculine looking" lesbians "prey" on vulnerable women. Once again Kinsey's report is invoked—this time as evidence of the large number of "female sex deviates" ("as many as one in five women") and as a warning to "impressionable young" women who might otherwise be unable to "escape." Having consulted a health researcher on the topic, the author quotes the "expert" as warning that "the lesbian . . . who stalks a married home is to be considered a dangerous person."[70] The predatory "nature" of lesbians highlighted in this article offers a particular threat to heteronormativity as defined by "innocent" women, the institution of marriage, and the respectability it signifies.

The "predatory" lesbian parallels the "dangers" posed to "married homes" by the "bachelor girl" and the "working wife" in accounts linking women's work outside their homes and lifestyles that did not include marriage with "questionable" sexual behavior. All represented various types of gender inversion as defining nonnormative sexualities but also explicitly invoked the structural norms and gender and sexual hierarchies of marital heterosexuality as the "ideal" form that would and could contain such transgressions. In one example, the 1954 *Jet* article "Are Working Wives Less Moral?" offers numerous illustrations of the possible sexual pitfalls of "women's decision to chuck the double standard in favor of *invading* the work-a-day world of their husbands and boyfriends" (my emphasis). While the author in the end seeks to debunk presumptions that "working wives" might also have "office boy friends" once they "set out to help bring home the family bacon," the substance of the article is dedicated to elaborating specific instances that affirm this presumption.[71] Others feared the "housewife's" presumed leisure at home. Offering a commentary on the "innocent" women who might become "prey," one "husband of a working wife . . . cracked" that "he would rather have his spouse busy 'eight hours a day on some production line' than have her spending too many 'idle' hours at home where she might be 'easy prey'"—presumably to either lesbians or male wolves.[72]

On a more sinister note were several articles that enthusiastically recommended radical procedures as "cures" for non-normative female sexuality. In "Can Surgery Cure Evil Women," a 1953 *Jet* editorial responds to the question with a vehement, "YES!" offering several examples of women for whom surgical interventions "restored" their "femininity" and "happier" home lives. The recommended medical procedures covered in the article range from a prefrontal lobotomy performed on a "thirtyish Baltimore woman" to cure her "uncontrollable sex drive which her husband could not satisfy" to that of a clitoridectomy performed on a "young Chicago girl whose compulsive sexual drive was causing embarrassment to her family. With a few deft turns of the scalpel he [the doctor] changed her into a *normal* young woman, [and] enabled her to marry and find perfect connubial life" (my emphasis). After "weighing" the pros and cons of surgical intervention, the author concludes that while these procedures are "costly . . . and sometimes fatal, it means in many instances a happy family life."[73]

Other essays focused on the power of psychiatry and hormones to return "mannish" lesbians to the "straight and narrow." In "Women Who PASS For Men," the editorialist notes, "Problems posed by man-like women are so deep that the public has hardly begun to understand them. Doctors and psychiatrists are co-ordinating their work in the light of new psycho-sexual findings. Their research indicates that operations and psychiatric treatment can free many women of maleness caused by an imbalance of female and male hormones." The piece ends with a testimonial from singer Gladys Bentley, who proclaims that "injections of female sex hormones three times a week hastened her return to womanhood." Offering advice to others like herself based on her experiences in the "twilight of sex," Bentley, described in the article as "happily married to a West Coast cook," says, "I want the world to know that those of us who have taken the unusual paths to love are not hopeless."[74] It should be noted that, unlike Charles Brown's case, in which a procedure to change his sex from male to female was discussed sympathetically during this period, there was little support for "scientific" attempts to similarly alter women's sex from female to male. In fact, the medical interventions called for in African American popular periodicals focused on "restoring" women to a "proper" femininity, defined in part by heterosexuality and having a "sexual drive" that could be met by their husbands.[75]

Another potential "cure" for lesbians suggested by several editorials was heterosexual marriage. In "Why Lesbians Marry," the author reports this remedy is "far easier" for lesbians than "male perverts" because "the woman's sexual role demands merely that she be compliant, but a man has to be capable of being aroused if he is to play his part."[76] In this case, normative presumptions of the distinct "sexual natures" of men and women were affirmed, although the author remarks that for exceptionally "mannish" women this route was frequently unsuccessful, presumably because they could not "comply" with the prescription of female passivity. The author goes on to hold that for those lesbians for whom heterosexual marriages were "impossible," many "after trying this solution moved back into their former girlfriend's home, there to live in apparent happiness ever after."[77]

Rather than a simple tale of "victimization" suggested by much of the literature addressing the "threat" of lesbians or the "hypersexuality" of some heterosexual women, the concerns with non-normative female sexualities articulated above also offer alternative visions of African American women's sexual subjectivity.

One alternative vision is explicitly expressed in the first-person narrative "Strange Love," appearing in *Tan Confessions* in 1950. The heterosexually married narrator, Yvonne, explains her attraction to another woman, Willa, as "something intangible that attracted [her] to [Willa], something . . . at once compelling." Knowing from the beginning that she was "flirting with danger," Yvonne does not "blame Willa for what happened to [them]. She explains, "I alone was responsible for that. She couldn't help feeling the way she was . . . and I probably could have stopped things before they went as far as they did." Yvonne describes their first meeting as confusing and fascinating: "What was this fascination? Was it the way her eyes locked into mine when she played the piano? Was it the way she tossed her head as she nimbly ran her fingers over the keyboard in one of Chopin's suggestive nocturnes? How could I know?" She proceeds to have a yearlong friendship with Willa defined by lunches, shopping trips, "light embraces," and "kisses exchanged on the cheeks" when they said good-bye. She does not speak to her husband, Claude, about Willa, though when Claude finally does meet Willa, he dislikes her. "He never questioned me about what we did or where we had been, but there was always a little different something in our discussions of her which told me he was displeased, but that he wouldn't interfere if this was part of my pleasure which he was so seldom able to provide."[78] When Yvonne's husband gets caught up in a last-minute big case at work and cannot join them as planned, she and Willa end up alone for the weekend at a "guest cottage . . . near Cape Cod." Although Yvonne is upset that Claude will not be joining them, she feels more relaxed after having several drinks with Willa. Then, Willa joins her by the window and links arms with her. Yvonne recalls, "Gently her fingers reached for my hand . . . Neither of us said a word. She stood looking at me in that strange compelling way she had done when we first met and I knew then, without her saying, what it was she wanted of me." After the consummation of the affair, she and Willa "see each other less and less." Yvonne states, "For her I had been a conquest." Yvonne eventually tells her husband about the affair, and after many weeks of "deep hurt" they agree to "pick up the pieces and start off together all over again." The tale concludes with Yvonne describing it as "fate" that brought Willa into their lives: "Without her we might not have ever found the true happiness we both now know. We might never have known the real love that is ours."[79]

In Yvonne's tale, her attraction to Willa is "unwise" but not necessarily "deviant." While Willa's construction is consistent with the "lesbian predator" image alluded to earlier, Yvonne nonetheless defines her sexual desire for another woman in some ways as a reasonable response to a "compelling," "fascinating," and immensely attractive person. Similarly, the negative depiction of lesbians offered initially in "Women Who Fall for Lesbians" is qualified later in the piece. The article goes on to give an example of a "spinster . . . schoolteacher" who became "prey" to a lesbian in Missouri because she was "getting on in years without the comfort and companionship of a man." The two lived together for the rest of their lives, and "when the lesbian finally died of a heart attack, the then-retired teacher, grief-stricken, soon followed her in death."[80] Readers are left unclear about whether they should pity this woman for "falling prey" to a lesbian or envy her happiness in the latter years of her life. If some gay men found possibilities for acceptance or at least toleration within black print popular culture through the figure of the drag queen, some lesbians might have found such possibilities in the perceived similarity of the *form* of their relationships to those of heterosexually married couples and the nonsexual comforts and "companionship" such relations ideally contained.

Literary scholar Matt Richardson speaks to the problems with locating the "queer" in African American history: "The tradition of representing Black people as decent and moral historical agents has meant the erasure of the broad array of Black sexuality and gendered being in favor of a static heterosexual narrative. Far from being totally invisible, the 'queer' is present in Black history as a threat to Black respectability. Black women's sexuality has been discussed as the 'unspeakable thing unspoken' of Black life."[81] Richardson goes on to argue that "variant sexualities and genders are the things always present in Black history by virtue of their constant disavowal."[82] I would suggest that rather than only the "disavowal" of which Richardson speaks, black print popular culture also offered several possibilities for "avowing" same-sex sexual attraction and frameworks within which such relationships might be tolerated, even accepted.

During the 1950s, some elements of black print popular culture explicitly engaged sexuality and served notice of their intent to contest the hegemonic white presumptions, myths, and stereotypes that formed the foundation of contemporary sexual knowledge. In doing so, they suggested a new discursive common sense within which African American sexual norms were offered—sometimes consistent with, at other times quite distinct from those of the white middle-class normative system. They continued to take on white racist presumptions, offering in support Kinsey's statements that the "sexual habits" of "whites and Negroes" were more similar than different from each other. And in the end, this claim to legitimacy through sexual respectability rested in part on the foundation of uninterrogated and thus affirmed presumptions of the relation between class status, gender inversion, and deviant sexuality. Lower-status/lower-level whites and blacks alike were more likely to be sexually deviant, and gender inversion was perhaps the most deviant frame for expressing sexual desire. There were also moments, however, located in the contradictions within articles or between articulated stances that suggested a much more fluid understanding of sexually normative practices, behaviors, and identities, especially articles addressing African American female sexual subjectivity.

Much of this evidence for African American female sexual subjectivity comes from *Jet* and *Tan Confessions*. *Ebony*'s target audience, the "respectable," black middle class, may have precluded similarly explicit discussions of sexuality or reflected a distinct sexual culture closer to that described by white middle-class norms. Yet, as historian Nan Enstad argues for the early twentieth century, white working-class women, in their many ethnic variations, while appropriating signifiers of the white middle class, did not necessarily replicate white middle-class norms but rather found in popular culture (specifically dime novels) possibilities for alternative subjectivities.[83]

The question begged by this essay is whether "speaking sexuality" can be a political act—a mode of protest and a means of negotiating, subverting, and recasting dominant cultural norms. Or can "speaking sexuality" be unpacked as a mode of appropriation, at some moments marking accommodation and simultaneous reconfiguration of conventional normative regimes, and at other moments calling our attention to vectors of resistance to such regimes (constructed within both hegemonic and subcultural sexual systems). What might we discover should we turn our attention to the ways in which sexuality is articulated within print popular cultural forms? In this essay I suggest that we might find myriad and competing female sexual subjectivities that taken together carved out a new discursive common sense within which the right of women to speak sexual desire was both a currency of legitimacy and a basis for claims to power.

Notes

This essay originally appeared in *Feminist Studies* 38, no. 3 (Fall 2012). I am indebted to Elizabeth Lapovsky Kennedy, Kimberly Springer, Grey Gundaker, and Arthur Knight for their generosity and willingness to read and comment on earlier versions of this essay and offer my gratitude to participants and organizers of the "Connexions: Race and Sex in North America" working papers conference for their advice and suggestions. I also thank my research assistant, Amanda Howard, for her help in locating many of the articles that form the basis for this essay. Last, I want to thank Maureen Fitzgerald for her willingness to read and offer comments on multiple versions of this piece and for her unwavering support throughout this process.

1. Letters to the editor, *Tan Confessions*, December 1950, 6.

2. Elizabeth Lapovsky Kennedy and Madeline Davis, *Boots of Leather, Slippers of Gold: The History of a Lesbian Community* (New York: Penguin Books, 1994); Elaine Tyler May, *Homeward Bound: American Families in the Cold War Era* (New York: Basic Books, 1990).

3. John D'Emilio and Estelle Freedman, *Intimate Matters: A History of Sexuality in America*, 2nd ed. (Chicago: University of Chicago Press, 1998).

4. Todd Vogel, ed., *The Black Press: New Literary and Historical Essays* (New Brunswick, N.J.: Rutgers University Press, 2002), 2.

5. Abby Arthur Johnson and Ronald Mayberry, *Propaganda and Aesthetics: The Literary Politics of Afro-American Magazines in the Twentieth Century* (Amherst, Mass.: University of Massachusetts Press, 1979); Frances Smith Foster, "A Narrative of the Interesting Origins

and (Somewhat) Surprising Developments of African-American Print Culture," *American Literary History* 17, no. 4 (Winter 2005): 714–40. Also according to historian Walter Daniel, after World War II "black magazines replaced black national newspapers" in terms of both readership and influence, Walter C. Daniel, *Black Journals of the United States* (Westport, Conn.: Greenwood Press, 1982), 159.

6. As Stuart Hall suggests, "Black popular culture has enabled the surfacing, inside the mixed and contradictory modes even of some mainstream popular culture, of elements of a discourse that is different—other forms of life, other traditions of representation." Stuart Hall, "What Is This 'Black' in Black Popular Culture? (Rethinking Race)?," *Social Justice*, 20, no. 1–2 (1993): 111.

7. Hall, "What Is This 'Black'?," 104–15.

8. Fath Davis Ruffin, "Reflecting on Ethnic Imagery in the Landscape of Commerce, 1945–1975," *Advertising and Society Review* 1, no, 1 (2003): 36–37. I examined every *Ebony* issue from 1945–59 and used forty-two specific editorials, articles, and letters to the editor for this essay.

9. James Hall, "On Sale at Your Favorite Newsstand: *Negro Digest/Black World* and the 1960s," in Vogel, *Black Press*, 189.

10. Daniel, *Black Journals*, 213. For *Jet* I examined every issue from its founding in 1951 through 1959 and used fifty-two specific pieces for this essay. For *Tan Confessions* I examined every issue from its founding, in October 1950, to 1956, when it ceased publication. I used forty-five particular pieces for this essay.

11. Ruffin, "Reflecting on Ethnic Imagery," 37. Ruffin notes that "according to a 1996 Yankelovich survey, *Ebony* and *Jet* remain the two primary sources of news information for Afro-Americans, followed in close order by other, younger Afro-American publications such as *Essence* and *Emerge*, a testament to the staying power of these niche publications." The Yankelovich survey was published in a double issue of the *New Yorker*, "Black in America" (April 29 and May 6, 1996)]. On the issue of middle-class readership of *Ebony*, see Sarah S. Lochlann Jain, "'Come Up to the Kool Taste': African America Upward Mobility and the Semiotics of Smoking Menthols," *Public Culture* 15, no. 2 (2003): 307–8.

12. J. Hall, "On Sale," 194.

13. *Tan Confessions*, November 1950, 1. Opening Statement from editor John H. Johnson in premier issue.

14. I examined every issue of the *Chicago Defender* from 1945 to1959 and drew on forty-five particular articles for this sample.

15. Vogel, *Black Press*, 2–3.

16. Vogel, *Black Press*, 4.

17. My ideas here are informed by Michel Foucault, *Power/Knowledge: Selected Interviews and Other Writings, 1972–77*, trans. Colin Gordon et al., ed. Colin Gordon (New York: Pantheon Books, 1980), 159; Michel Foucault, *Discipline and Punish: The Birth of the Prison*, trans. Alan Sheridan (New York: Vintage Books, 1979), esp. 27–28; and M. M. Slaughter, "The Legal Construction of 'Mother,'" in *Mothers-in-Law: Feminist Theory and the Legal Regulation of Motherhood*, ed. Martha Fineman and Isabel Karpin (Oxford: Oxford University Press, 1995), 73–102.

18. See Julia A. Erickson with Sally A. Steffen, *Kiss and Tell: Surveying Sex in the Twentieth Century* (Cambridge, Mass.: Harvard University Press, 1999), 7, 9, 51–54.

19. Eve Kosofsky Sedgwick, *Epistemology of the Closet* (Berkeley: University of California Press, 1990), 1.

20. For an analysis of the increasing faith Americans put in science and medical technologies in the postwar period and the links between these beliefs and the "politics of conformity" during the 1950s, see David Serlin, *Replaceable You: Engineering the Body in Postwar America* (Chicago: University of Chicago Press, 2004).

21. "Sex Habits of Negro Women," *Jet*, January 10, 1952, 18–21.

22. For a discussion of the "politics of respectability" and its operation among African American women and in black communities, see Evelyn Brooks Higginbotham, *Righteous Discontent: The Women's Movement in the Black Baptist Church, 1880–1920* (Chicago: University of Chicago Press, 1997): 187, 191–92; and Higginbotham, "African American Women and the Metalanguage of Race," *Signs* 17 (1992): 254–74.

23. Paisley Harris, "Gatekeeping and Remaking: The Politics of Respectability in African American Women's History and Black Feminism," *Journal of Women's History* 15, no.1 (2003): 213.

24. "Our Opinions—The Kinsey Report," *Chicago Defender*, August 29, 1953.

25. "Why Negro Women Are Not in the Kinsey Report," *Ebony*, September 1953, 109.

26. "Why Negro Women Are Not in the Kinsey Report," 110.

27. "Sociologist Says Minorities Get 'Tired of Being Studied,'" *Ebony*, September, 1953, 112.

28. "Kinsey Sees Little Change in Sex Behavior since 1920," *Ebony*, September, 1953, 114. Darlene Clark Hine argues that middle-class African American women intentionally did not speak about sex as a means of protecting themselves from white stereotypes and sexual violence. See Darlene Clark Hine, "Rape and the Inner Lives of Black Women in the Middle West: Preliminary Thoughts on the Culture of Dissemblance," *Signs* 14, no. 4 (1989): 912–20.

29. See Erickson and Steffen, *Kiss and Tell*, 7, 9, 51–54.

30. Michel Foucault, *The History of Sexuality*, vol. 1, *An Introduction* (New York: Random House, 1980). See also Eve Sedgwick, *Epistemology of the Closet*.

31. My "reading" of popular print culture here is influenced by historian Joanne Meyerowitz's formulations in her examination of post–World War II mass culture and specifically her interpretation of mass culture as a forum for multiple and competing voices that worked to both confirm and subvert normative sexualities. See Joanne Meyerowitz, "Beyond the Feminine Mystique," in *Not June Cleaver: Women and Gender in Postwar America, 1945–1960*, ed. Joanne Meyerowitz (Philadelphia: Temple University Press, 1994), 231n7. However, while Meyerowitz focuses in her study on the textual "topics" or "intents" of the articles in her sample, I seek to demonstrate that reading "between the lines" or exploring the subtext of specific articles can give glimpses into the alternate possibilities raised by the authors.

32. I have been influenced in my interpretation of the possibilities of popular print culture by the work of literary scholar Sonja Laden, "'Making the Paper Speak Well,' or, the Pace of Change in Consumer Magazines for Black South Africans," *Poetics Today* 22,

no. 2 (2001): 515–48. Laden argues that the "sociosemiotic work of magazines" includes their function as "'cultural tools' through which specifically urban, middle-class repertoires are confirmed, codified, disseminated, and transformed" (515). She also holds that magazines are "both concrete, material objects and embodiments or carriers of meanings and social relations, both commodities in themselves and vehicles for dissemination of a range of other cultural commodities, practices, and beliefs" (517).

33. Higgenbotham, *Righteous Discontent*, 196.

34. Mrs. Lucius Harper, "What Every Girl Should Know about Men," *Tan Confessions*, January 1953, 23.

35. Harper, "What Every Girl Should Know," 23, 77, 78.

36. Harper, "What Every Girl Should Know," 77.

37. Mrs. Harper's approach to "catching" and "keeping" a man is quite different from that offered by most white mainstream advice literature during the 1950s. See Meyerowitz, "Beyond the Feminine Mystique," 22–24.

38. Cab Calloway, "The Truth about White Women," *Tan Confessions*, March, 1952, 27.

39. Calloway, "The Truth about White Women," 29, 50.

40. Calloway, "The Truth about White Women," 27.

41. Ruffin also notes, "The continuing controversy about skin color highlights how difficult it can be to interpret the meaning of images ethnic communities generate about themselves" ("Reflecting on Ethnic Imagery," 41). On the question of "colorism" in African American communities, see also Margaret L. Hunter, "'If You're Light You're Alright': Light Skin Color as Social Capital for Women of Color," *Gender and Society* 16, no. 2 (2002): 175–93; Uzo Esonwanne, "'Race' and Hermeneutics: Paradigm Shift— From Scientific to Hermeneutic Understanding of Race," *African American Review* 26, no. 4 (1992): 565- 83. In contrast to Cab Calloway's suggestion, historian Leila Hadarali argues that "photographic magazines" like *Ebony* sought to overturn "racist stereotyping of African American women as dark-skinned, unattractive mammies, maids, and laundresses" by highlighting the "Brownskin" woman as the model for "sexual attractiveness and heterosexual fulfillment." For Hadarali, it is the "Brownskin" woman, not the dark-skinned or light-skinned African American woman, who was the "center" of a "different public racial reality" and "visual discourse" in the immediate post–World War II period. This different reality positioned African American women in the concomitant roles of the "feminized worker and the domestic, heterosexual homemaker" thus reconstituting a heteronormative system defined not simply by opposite-sex attraction, intimacy, and marital relations but also by conventional gendered relations of power. Leila Haidarali, "Polishing Brown Diamonds: African American Women, Popular Magazines, and the Advent of Modeling in Early Postwar America," *Journal of Women's History* 17, no. 1 (2005): 12, 13, 15.

42. "Are Negroes More Amorous Than Whites?," *Jet,* May 14, 1953, 20.

43. "Are Negroes More Amorous Than Whites?," 20–22.

44. Siobhan Somerville, *Queering the Color Line: Race and the Invention of Homosexuality in American Culture* (Durham, N.C.: Duke University Press, 2000), 3, 5. Somerville argues in particular that "questions of race—in particular the formation of notions of 'whiteness' and 'blackness'—must be understood as a crucial part of the history and representation

of sexual formations" and that "negotiations of the color line shaped and were shaped by the emergence of notions of sexual identity."

45. For a discussion of Ida B. Wells antilynching activism and resistant speech in relation to the Clarence Thomas–Anita Hill hearings, see Paula Giddings, "The Last Taboo," in *Race-ing Justice, En-gendering Power: Essays on Anita Hill, Clarence Thomas and the Construction of Social Reality*, ed. Toni Morrison (New York: Pantheon Books, 1992), 441–63.

46. "Are Negroes More Amorous Than Whites?," 44.

47. Clyde Taylor, *The Mask of Art: Breaking the Aesthetic Contract—Film and Literature* (Bloomington: Indiana University Press, 1998), 266. See also Stuart Hall, who notes, "The ideologies of racism remain contradictory structures, which can function both as the vehicles for the imposition of dominant ideologies, and as the elementary forms for the cultures of resistance." Stuart Hall, "Race, Articulation, and Societies Structured in Dominance," in *Sociological Theories: Race and Colonialism* (Paris: UNESCO, 1980), 342, cited in Somerville, *Queering the Color Line*, 11.

48. Langston Hughes, "An Excellent New Book for Teen-Agers, about the Facts of Love and Life," *Chicago Defender*, July 14, 1951, 6.

49. See in particular a series of American Social Hygiene Association authored and sponsored articles titled "Parent and Child" that were published each month in 1950 in the *New York Times Magazine*. Sex Instruction Booklets, 1950–1970, 7638, Human Sexuality Collection, Cornell University, Ithaca, New York. See also "Sex on the Campus—Many Negro Colleges Now Offering Courses That Teach 'Facts of Life'—Teachers Gratified by Class Results," *Ebony*, April 1951, 86–93.

50. "Should Love Be Taught in School?," *Tan Confessions*, April 1953, 11, 79.

51. "Should Love Be Taught in School?," 79, 81–82.

52. "Is the Chaste Girl Chased?," *Tan Confessions*, November 1950, 6–7, 50.

53. "Primer for Petting," *Jet*, August 14, 1952, 28–30.

54. "Primer for Petting," 28–30.

55. "Is the Chaste Girl Chased?," 7.

56. "Are Bachelor Girls Less Moral?," *Jet*, June 10, 1954, 24–27.

57. "Are Bachelor Girls Less Moral?," 24–27. See also "Are Working Wives Less Moral?" *Jet*, February 3, 1955, 26.

58. "Is There Hope for Homosexuals," *Jet*, August 7, 1952, 26.

59. "Is There Hope for Homosexuals?," 34.

60. Rev. Adam Clayton Powell Jr. "Sex in the Church," *Ebony*, November 1951, 27–28, 34.

61. "Are Homosexuals Becoming Respectable?," *Jet*, April 15, 1954, 28.

62. "Are Homosexuals Becoming Respectable?," 26–28.

63. See, for instance, Allan Berube, *Coming Out under Fire: Gay Men and Women in the Military during World War II* (New York: Free Press, 1990).

64. "The Truth about Female Impersonators," *Jet*, October 2, 1952, 27. See also "Strange Love," *Tan Confessions*, November 1950, 17, 63–65.

65. "Impersonators Frolic at Annual Ball in New York," *Jet*, December 1, 1953, 16–17.

66. Historian Tim Retzloff, citing the work of Marybeth Hamilton, argues that "central to this homosexual world and to presentations of the 'public face of gay life in early twentieth century black America' was the 'freakish man,' . . . a flamboyant, sissified en-

tertainer in African American vaudeville—(who) both destabilized sexual norms and defused sexual tensions among African American men and women. . . . 'The very effeminacy that made him "freakish" made him simply more saleable to whites. While on one level it made him an insidious trickster, at another it left him a sissified Sambo, an updated version of the feminized buffoon of blackface comedy.'" Tim Retzloff, "'Seer or Queer?' Postwar Fascination with Detroit's Prophet Jones," *GLQ: A Journal of Lesbian and Gay Studies* 8, no. 3 (2002): 287–88. See also Marybeth Hamilton, "Sexual Politics and African-American Music; or, Placing Little Richard in History," *History Workshop Journal* 46 (1998): 160–76, from Retzloff, "'Seer or Queer?,'" n. 67. Retzloff also argues that drag revues fell "out of fashion" by the late 1950s (287).

67. See "Male Shake Dancer Plans to Change Sex. Wed GI in Europe," *Jet*, June 25, 1953, 24–25; "Male Dancer Becomes Danish Citizen to Change His Sex," *Jet*, June 25, 1953, 26–27; "Jail Male Shake Dancer for Posing as a Woman in Boston," *Jet*, July 9, 1953, 20–21; "Shake Dancer Postpones Sex Change for Face Lifting," *Jet*, August 5, 1953, 19.

68. Joanne Meyerowitz, *How Sex Changed: A History of Transsexuality in the United States* (Cambridge, Mass.: Harvard University Press, 2002): 1–5.

69. See Serlin, *Replaceable You.*

70. "Women Who Fall for Lesbians," *Jet*, February 25, 1954, 20–22.

71. "Are Working Wives Less Moral?," 25.

72. "Are Working Wives Less Moral?," 26.

73. "Can Surgery Cure Evil Women?," *Jet*, August 20, 1953, 25–27. See also "Can a Woman Have Too Much Sex Appeal?," *Jet*, August 25, 1954, 24–26.

74. "Women Who PASS for Men," *Jet*, January 28, 1954, 22–24. See also "I Am a Woman Again," *Ebony*, October 1952. For a discussion of Gladys Bentley's life trajectory in relation to her sexuality, see Serlin, *Replaceable You*, 111–57. Serlin argues that Bentley's "identity" was fluid and that while she might have understood herself as a lesbian in the early twentieth century, she clearly wanted to be understood as a normative heterosexual woman during the 1950s. We can ponder her motives but must show her respect as a subject in terms of how she is speaking her desires.

75. Joanne Meyerowitz argues that through the 1950s and 1960s most doctors believed that male-to-female (MTF) transsexuals far outnumbered female-to-male (FTM), and the press published only "brief reports" on FTMs. See Meyerowitz, *How Sex Changed*, 87–88, 148–52.

76. "Why Lesbians Marry," *Jet*, November 1, 1953, 21.

77. "Why Lesbians Marry," 22.

78. "Strange Love," *Tan Confessions*, November 1950, 63–64.

79. "Strange Love," 65

80. "Women Who Fall for Lesbians," *Jet*, February 25, 1954, 22.

81. Mattie Udora Richardson, "No More Secrets, No More Lies: African American History and Compulsory Heterosexuality," *Journal of Women's History* 15 (Autumn 2003): 64.

82. Richardson, "No More Secrets, 64.

83. Nan Enstad, *Ladies of Labor, Girls of Adventure: Working Women, Popular Culture, and Labor Politics at the Turn of the Twentieth Century* (New York: Columbia University Press, 1999), 50–51.

CHAPTER 12

Out and on the Outs

The 1990s Mass Marches and the Black and LGBT Communities

DEBORAH GRAY WHITE

"It's really something to be somewhere where you can be yourself," said forty-one-year-old Alice Dilbeck at the 2000 LGBT Millennium March on the Washington Mall. Her girlfriend, forty-eight-year-old Betsey Applegate, piped in, "And where you can be in the majority." The couple had come from Huntsville, Alabama, and for them it was an understatement to say that the experience was both liberating and exhilarating. "Aaaah," Applegate sighed. "It's like breathing."[1] Fifteen-year-old Troy Curtis had had a similar experience at the 1995 Million Man March. Half black and half white, Curtis never knew his white grandparents because they disowned his mother when she married his father. Having been ostracized by both blacks and whites who claimed he was not one of them, he found peace on the Washington Mall on October 16. "I felt the kind of love I have never felt in my life," he exclaimed. "It felt so good to belong for once to the majority, to look around and see a sea of black faces."[2] Separated by circumstances and generations, Charlene Ryan, a great-grandmother from Wilkes-Barre, Pennsylvania, felt the same kind of love in Philadelphia at the 1997 Million Woman March. "I feel connected," she said. "I feel like I'm meeting with family."[3]

These marchers' feelings were not atypical. The 1990s found many Americans who felt so alienated from their own country and neighborhood that they traveled to a Promise Keeper gathering, the Million Man or Woman March, an LGBT March, or the Million Mom march to express their dissatisfaction with a culture that left them unfulfilled. Despite the economic boom that left individuals and the government wealthier than ever; despite record low unemployment rates and the expansion of homeownership, the democratization of computer use and internet access; despite a decade that found no American troops extensively deployed in overseas warfare, many Americans of all walks of life were unhappy enough in the 1990s to go to a mass march to seek connection with people with whom they felt safe enough to start a group or individual process of renewal.

This was the case with many black LGBTs. They went to the Million Man (1995) and Woman (1997) Marches and the 1993 and 2000 LGBT marches searching for inclusion and renewal. They were searching for the peace that Curtis found, the connection that Ryan found, the freedom that Dilbeck and Applegate found. They wanted to be part of the LGBT community and the black community, and like W. E. B. Du Bois, who spoke of his twoness almost a century earlier, they did not want to forsake either part of themselves. They were vocal about their needs and desires and what they brought to both communities. Some found the community they were looking for, but others did not. Almost always the "community" they found was problematic. The reality, sadly enough, was that even though black LGBTs were "out" and vocal at the African American and LGBT marches, they remained on the outs in both communities.

Being Out

"Black gay men and lesbians really do exist," states Earnest E. Hite Jr. in an article titled "Lift the Ban on Gay Men and Lesbians in the Black Community. "We are invisible and that invisibility promotes a psycho-emotional diarrhea among our community and a profile cycle of shame and fear restricting the healthy development of Black gay men and lesbians."[4] Hite, a Chicago recipient of the Stonewall Award for his work with HIV/AIDS patients, joined the chorus of voices in the 1990s protesting black homophobia. When it came to the 1995 Million Man March, the chorus amped up the volume. "Our presence as openly gay men and lesbians will counter the assumption that we do not exist or do not contribute to our community. Staying home or marching incognito colludes with those who wish to keep us invisible," was the message of the National Black Gay and Lesbian Leadership Forum.[5] For Darren Hutchinson, there were several reasons why black gays and lesbians had to speak up about the march. It not only fed into the hands of those who felt that homosexuality was inherently abnormal, undesirable, and unblack, but it also allowed racist acts against black gays to go unrecognized and unpunished, which weakened the whole project of antiracist political activism. Hutchinson also felt that "the romantic embrace of patriarchal familial structures and intimate relationships . . . necessarily marginalizes lesbian (and gay) families and relationships because the latter do not directly perpetuate male domination over women."[6] Others, like Dennis Holmes of the Leadership Forum, felt that marches offer a "unique opportunity to empower black gay men and lesbians and black gay youth," by providing "positive images of open, courageous, proud and diverse black gay people."[7] Always on target, cultural critic Barbara Smith, joined the chorus of black LGBTs who cautioned black America not to blame gays for the perceived destruction of the black family: "Homosexuality is not what's breaking up the black family," she wrote. "Homophobia is."[8]

Black gays criticized LGBTs as much as they criticized black America. When Thom Bean reflected on the 1993 San Francisco Pride Parade, he described his experience as akin to being a "raisin in a sea of sour cream." Even though he had lived in San Francisco for over fifteen years, for the one and one-half hours that he stood watching the parade, he saw no familiar face. White gays, he concluded, were "willing to accept black invisibility," second-class black citizenship, the racism of gay skinheads, the National Socialist Gay League, and gay white Republicans.[9] Lesbian feminist Barbara Smith accused the leadership of the 2000 Millennium March of being "undemocratic, racist, corporate and assimilationist." "Wealthy gay white men and those white lesbians with sufficient class privilege and lack of feminist politics. . . . don't care about racism, police brutality, poverty, homelessness, or violence against women," she argued.[10] Others pointed to the privilege of those white gays whose economic wherewithal allowed them to gentrify black neighborhoods and displace poor African Americans. When white gays touted the diversity of the committees that organized the 1993 and 2000 Washington Mall marches, the fact that they were multicultural and purposely designed to represent African Americans, blacks like Don Thomas, editor of *BLK*, a national news magazine for black gays and lesbians, retorted that blacks were made visible at national high-profile political events but few were involved in running the day-to-day operations of the thousands of large and small lesbian and gay organizations across the country. "There are still gross inequities in the racial make-up within the mainstream," he said.[11] Black gays also faulted white LGBTs for their glib equation of black and gay civil rights. Whereas white LGBTs were more likely to see black and gay oppression as the same, black LGBTs emphasized similarities in the means of social control while pointing to the subtle and glaring differences between black and gay oppression.[12] Black LGBTs urged black gays to participate in the white marches if only for this reason: to make sure that white LGBTs understood the difference that race made. "For too long," argued Michael Crawford, who marched in the 1993 and 2000 marches, "the gay organizations that are predominantly white have not adequately addressed people of color issues. With the Millennium March we have the opportunity to be present and make sure that all colors of the rainbow are visible."[13] The Reverend Irene Monroe felt similarly. About the Millennium March, she said she could "condemn the march or attend it." She chose "to be in it and to make sure [there was] some sort of change that [took] place" and to make sure that the board and the movement address "a multitude of oppressions."[14]

In sum, black gays and lesbians were earnest in their desire to be one with the LGBT and black communities. Most understood that they themselves were not a monolithic group, but they also realized that it was not enough to be uncloseted, indeed, that being "out" posed hazards in both the gay and the black worlds, hazards unique only to them. They understood that they straddled both worlds and that to be comfortable in each they had to be accepted by both. At heart, black LGBTs wanted to gather for the same reasons all marchers gathered: to be at one with people who were like them, to be at peace among a majority. They felt like Monique, of Illinois, who said she went to the Million Woman March to find "the energy . . . the warmth . . . the hugs, and the tears." "I knew," she said, "that deep down inside I wanted . . . connection with other Black women in the name of sisterhood."[15]

Out at the Marches

Among the marches held on the Washington Mall in the 1990s were four that attracted black LGBTs: the LGB March on April 25, 1993; the Million Man March on October 16, 1995; the Million Woman March on October 25, 1997; and the (LGBT) Millennium March on April 30, 2000. Although each had a political agenda (more or less), the marchers' political concerns did not exist independent of their emotional need to live more comfortable and satisfying lives.[16] That is why they searched for a renewed sense of belonging among people whom they felt they could work with to have their emotional and political needs addressed. In other words, the very personal and emotional was political.

It was no different for black sexual minorities; they wanted to be comfortable in both the LGBT and the black world. How they experienced the marches, and what happened there, reflected their present circumstances and future possibilities. In both worlds they wanted to be physically and emotionally safe, and they needed to feel that safety from the speakers on the podium and the marchers around them. Though it is difficult to generalize about the experience of black LGBTs, it is fair to say, first, that the status quo prevailed; that is, even though they were out and vocal, neither community significantly changed its response to them; and, second, that some individuals went home more fulfilled than others. That said, what happened is not insignificant but very instructive.

Take, for example, the issue of physical safety. The potential for violence against all LGBTs existed at both the 1993 and 2000 march. Before the 1993 March, for example, Nadine Smith, one of the African American march co-chairs, reported that threatening calls against gays and lesbians had increased. In 1992 the National Gay and Lesbian Task Force reported that violence against gays and lesbians had increased 172 percent since the 1987 national march.[17] Because the potential for violence against black sexual minorities existed in both communities, there was reason for participants to be nervous about physical assault at all the marches.[18] As Thom Bean noted, gay skinheads and Nazi types were tolerated by white gays, whose white privilege allowed them to ignore the issue of black safety.[19] In fact, a few months after the 1993 march, Marlon Riggs, director of *Tongues Untied*, the biographical documentary about black gay men, was insulted by the white gay male who was assigned to drive him in the San Francisco Gay Pride Parade. Riggs, the appointed grand marshal, expected to be shown the respect the honor warranted but instead was greeted with intimidating hostility and rebuke.[20]

Potential for violence existed in black America as well. In Chicago, the Ad Hoc Committee of Proud Black Lesbians and Gays was at first denied a permit to march in the 1993 annual African American Bud Billiken Parade, because, as the publisher of the *Chicago Defender* argued, they "would insight [sic] negative and confrontational behavior from the general public."[21] After much wrangling, they did march in the August parade, but they were probably mindful of the report issued by the Chicago Horizons Community Services Anti-Violence Project, which reported that violence against LGBTs was up 20 percent in 1992, with much of the increase coming on the predominantly black South Side.[22] In Harlem, when fifteen black men and women bearing an LGBT banner marched up Adam Clayton Powell Jr. Boulevard in the 2000 African American Day Parade, police were alerted because the group was being followed by bottle-wielding homophobes shouting antigay epithets.[23]

The issue of violence did not raise its head at the Million Woman March as it did at the Million Man March, but at the latter, black-on-black male violence was a concern of *every* attendee, not just LGBTs. In fact, black-on-black male assault had reached such alarming proportions that ending the violence in black America was a reason for holding the march in the first place. Cleo Manago, founder of Black Men's Xchange, an advocacy group for same-gender-loving (SGL) men, wrote that everyone was full of "whisper, wonder and worry about the safety of a million Black men in D. C."[24] Manago was heartened when he came across a group of SGL men, "donned with pink triangles, gay pride placards and gay-rainbow flag cut-outs of the African continent," who were treated respectfully by the black men around them. Manago reported that even though there was plenty of gawking at two SGLs who were locked in what Manago called a more than "brotherly love" embrace, no harm came to this contingent, whose flag (the gay rainbow and pink triangles from Nazi Germany) was carried by a white gay. To his delight, "not a harsh word was exchanged."[25]

While there was no violence at any of the marches, it cannot be said that black LGBT psyches were spared abuse. Freelance writer Eric Washington, for example, was alienated by the insensitivity of some of the white gays he saw at the 1993 LGB march. Their bare backs displayed palettes of white skin lined with raised pink welts, and they were accompanied by a tall, leather-clad "master" wielding a twenty-foot bullwhip. For Washington, it was another sign of the "pressure on black lesbians and gays to conform to the white folkways of the gay community."[26] It is likely that many black LGBTs had at least been partially inoculated against such shows of thoughtlessness. As often happens when African Americans know they will be minorities at majority events, they hold events of their own to counteract feelings of isolation. This happened at both the 1993 and 2000 LGBT marches. Separate social and political black gatherings were held both before and after each march.[27]

A comparison of the gay and lesbian marches with the black marches reveals that the leaders and speakers at the gay and lesbian marches were far more sensitive to issues of diversity than those at the black marches. This is not to say that the gay marches were unproblematic. The 2000 Millennium march was especially contentious as the diversity on the podium masked the movement's turn to conservative assimilationist values that made racial diversity and antiracism secondary to issues of gay marriage, child adoption, and equality in the military. Indeed, by the Millennium March diversity and leftist politics were more fetishistic than mainstream.[28] Still, at the 1993 and 2000 marches, black sexual minorities spoke from the podium about both parts of their identity; they reminded listeners that racists and homophobes were cut from the same cloth; they announced that there was strength in diversity; they sang songs lifted directly from the black civil rights movement and spoke of the oppression of gays and lesbians in the same vein as they spoke of Rodney King, James Byrd Jr., and the Haitian immigrants who in 1993 were being detained at Guantanamo.[29]

In contrast, at the black marches no out LGBTs were allowed to speak. Cleo Manago was supposed to address Million Man marchers and had prepared his speech about black diversity but was pulled from the program at the last minute.[30] And at the Million Woman March, intolerance from the podium was pervasive enough for Sheila Alexander-Reid, executive director of the nonprofit association Women in the Life to be fearful. Instead of instilling sisterhood "across shades and tones, attitudes and beliefs, sexuality and humanity," said Alexander-Reid, the unchecked intolerance "was scary to those of us considered outside of the mainstream." She thought it counterproductive to debate, as podium speakers seemed to be doing, "who was and was not a real African woman." Daunted, she wasn't sure which was more upsetting, "the statements or the cheers that followed them."[31]

Neither march even tried to reach out to black LGBTs. Controversy arose early at the Million Woman March when word circulated that Angie and Debbie Winans, the youngest members of the popular gospel singing family, were going to sing their new song "It's Not Natural." A patently homophobic response to Ellen DeGeneres's coming out, the song preached that homosexuality was against God's principles. When an interviewer from the *Philadelphia Inquirer* asked Paula S. Peebles, the program committee chairwoman, about the controversy surrounding the group and the song, Peebles replied that the march was an interdenominational event with no single religious perspective. She said that all women of African American descent were welcome but flatly added, with no intended irony, that the march was "not dealing" with issues relating to sexual orientation.[32] To Peebles's credit, the song was not sung, but there was a general silence on issues of homosexuality at the Million Woman March.

The same was true two years earlier at the Million Man March. Given Louis Farrakhan's well-known homophobia, black LGBTs did not expect him to be welcoming or to acknowledge this aspect of black diversity. Yet they probably expected more from Jesse Jackson, Benjamin Chavis, and Joseph Lowry, all of whom supported the 1993 LGB march. In 1984 Jesse Jackson had welcomed gays and lesbians into his Rainbow Coalition, and in 1993 he acknowledged that LGBTs were "African American, Latino and white," and that they were of all religions and found in all socioeconomic strata. He noted that homophobes and racists were cut from the same cloth; that HIV/AIDS was ravishing African Americans and LGBTs; and that it was a moral imperative and politically necessary for blacks and gays to fight for gay and black rights together.[33] From the 1993 podium Benjamin Chavis, the recently elected president of the NAACP, promised LGBTs that the oldest civil rights organization in the country would stand with them against all forms of discrimination and injustice and asked them to stand with blacks in their struggle against racism, South African apartheid, and the fight for economic justice. In February of that year, the Board of Directors of the NAACP had issued a resolution supporting the right of gay people to live free of discrimination and the elimination of the ban on homosexuals in the military.[34] The Reverend Joseph Lowery supported the 1993 LGB march as well.[35]

But at the Million Man March neither Jackson, nor Chavis, nor Lowry, nor anyone else acknowledged even the existence of homosexuality, let alone black LGBTs. They talked about black manhood, the black family, violence in African America, and about unity, but not black sexual diversity. The Nation of Islam's minister of health, Alim Muhammad, spoke of HIV/AIDS without so much as a mention of homosexuality.[36] Perhaps Lowry was referencing LGBTs when he noted that black people had to free themselves from "the abuse of our sexuality," but his oblique reference was sandwiched between his call for freedom from addiction and freedom from economic impoverishment, so it was unclear what he was talking about.[37] Interestingly enough, Jesse Jackson seemed conscious of the omission. His *published* four-page speech did contain *one* line wherein he directed black America to fight against "racism, sexism, anti-Semitism, anti-Arabism, Asian bashing, homophobia and xenophobia."[38] Yet, standing before the men gathered on the Washington Mall on October 16, he dropped the word *homophobia* and said only that black America had to stand against racism, sexism, anti-Semitism, anti-Arabism, and anti-immigrationism.[39] In sum, there was no homophobia at the Million Man March, as some black LGBTs had feared, but there was also no acknowledgment of them, period. The silence was truly deafening.

On the Outs, or Majority Rules

In conclusion, a few general observations about black LGBTs and the marches are in order. First, what Donald Suggs, of the Gay and Lesbian Alliance against Defamation, said about blacks and gays held true at the marches, especially the black marches: "When the black community addresses the gay community they address the white gay community. Conversely, the white gay community addresses the black community as straight."[40] This is one way to explain the bifurcation exhibited by Chavis, Jackson, and Lowry, and the utter insensitivity of the Winans sisters and Peebles. Had any of these speakers seen black LGBTs as integral to the community they were addressing, their remarks and actions might have been more inclusive. On the other hand, there are the politics of expediency. Most probably, Chavis, Jackson, Lowry, and Peebles did a cost analysis and, consciously or not, figured that they would gain little and lose a lot by being inclusive.

Second, even though white gays seemed more sensitive to black LGBT issues, the assimilationist tendencies of both white gays and black straights almost guaranteed black LGBT exclusion. The black marches were, in part, about showing America just how "normal" African Americans were. The Million Man and Woman Marches proclaimed the majority of blacks to be good fathers and mothers who valued patriarchal households. Blacks were, they declared, hardworking, law-abiding citizens who deplored violence and who were truly committed to social, economic, and political uplift. LGBTs were saying much the same thing, especially at the Millennium March. They pronounced themselves upstanding citizens who could be and were devoted partners, good parents, and could be counted on to defend America if granted equality in the military. They were "normal" Americans. Like white suffragists and labor unionists at the turn of the twentieth century, many white LGBTs felt that the issue of racism was detrimental to the cause of their own freedom. To the extent that "normal" in black America meant being straight, and "normal" in homosexual America meant being white, by definition black LGBTs could not be "normal" and thus could never be counted among the majority in either community.

And if these two communities tried to come together in any sort of coalition, as they tried to do in the 1990s, the Christian Right was standing there to make sure that they stayed as far apart as possible. Beginning in the early 1990s, especially in 1993, the Christian Right devised a strategic plan to use black churches in their fight against LGBTs.[41]

Finally, all the marches were about unity. Marchers and podium speakers called for unity in voting, unity for social cohesion, and unity for economic progress, physical safety, and political power. The problem with unity, of course, is that it requires, as Audre Lorde once wrote, mutual stretching, for seldom does unity allow for difference. Indeed, there is something inherently contradictory in calling for solidarity and celebrating difference at the same time. Black LGBTs went to both of their communities and laid claim to their difference. It should come as no surprise that the majorities in these communities had not yet stretched enough to make common cause. They had not yet imbibed the wisdom of Audre Lorde's teaching that "unity does not require that we be identical. . . . We do not have to become each other in order to work together"[42]

Notes

1. Phuong Ly, "Making a Public Declaration," *Washington Post*, April 30, 2000, Sunday final ed., Metro C1.

2. Lizabeth Hall, "The March Hits Home: Event Topic at Rockville High," *Hartford (Conn.) Courant*, October 30, 1994, Town News, B.1.

3. "Word of Mouth Draws Throngs to March," *Christian Science Monitor*, October 27, 1997, United States, 3.

4. Earnest E. Hite Jr., "Lift the Ban on Gay Men and Lesbians in the Black Community," *Outlines* 7, no. 3 (August 1993): 26, Randy Shilts Papers (GLC 43), Series 3, Gay Research Files, James C. Hormel Gay and Lesbian Center, San Francisco Public Library, San Francisco (hereinafter Shilts Papers, Series 3, SFPL).

5. Quoted in Darren Lenard Hutchinson, "'Claiming' and 'Speaking' Who We Are: Black Gays and Lesbians, Racial Politics and the Million Man March," in *Black Men on Race, Gender, and Sexuality: A Critical Reader*, ed. Devon W. Carbado (New York: New York University Press, 1999), 38.

6. Hutchinson, "'Claiming' and 'Speaking' Who We Are," 34–35, 36.

7. Quoted in Hutchinson, "'Claiming' and 'Speaking' Who We Are," 28.

8. Barbara Smith, unpublished pamphlet, GLC-VF/Subjects/ March on Washington 1993, folder 1, GLBT Historical Society, Archives and Research Center, San Francisco.

9. Thom Bean, "Queer Monoculture on Parade," *Outlines* 7, no. 3 (August 1993): 4, Shilts Papers, Series 3, SFPL.

10. Kim Diehl, "Here's the Movement, Let's Start Building: An Interview with Barbara Smith," http://colorlines.com/archives/2000/11/heres_the_movement_lets_start_building.html (accessed March 17, 2014).

11. Don Thomas, "Liberty and Justice for All," *Advocate*, October 5, 1993, 8, acc. no. 4511-001, box 3, folder 1, Religious Right and Blacks and Gays, University of Washington Suzzallo and Allen Libraries, Gay and Lesbian Issues Collection, Seattle.

12. See, for example, Keith Boykin "A Poem for the Millennium March," *Angel Herald*, June 2000, 13 (10), GMAD, Schomburg BLGA. Sources from the Schomburg BLGA were accessed before the collection was processed. Therefore, there are no folders or box numbers attached to these citations.

13. Michael Crawford, "To Be Young, Black, Gay and Marching," *Wazzup Magazine*, March 2004, 16, Schomburg BLGA, New York.

14. Ann Scales, "Weekend Gay Rights March Doesn't Sit Well with Some Grassroots Activists," *Boston Globe*, April 29, 2000, 3rd ed., National/Foreign, A3.

15. "Million Woman March Poll," *Women in the Life*, November 1997, Schomburg BLGA.

16. The political agendas of these marches were contested. Most critics of the marches complained that the political agendas were weak or nonexistent. The issue is complex and would take us far afield of the subject of this particular essay.

17. David O'Connor, "MOW Organizers Get Hate Calls from Supremacists," *Bay Area Reporter*, March 18, 1993, 18, Periodical Collection, folder: vols. 23, nos. 8–29, February 25, 1993–July 22, 1993, GLBT Historical Society, Archives and Research Center, San Francisco.

18. Statistics on black LGBT victims of assault were, and still are, difficult to access. In 1990 Congress passed the Hate Crime Statistics Act, which required the FBI to collect data on crimes committed because of the victim's race, religion, disability, sexual orientation, or ethnicity. Given the high rate of black-on-black male crime and the fact that data did not reflect disaggregation of crimes committed on black LGBTs from black-on-black crime rates in general, it is very difficult to discern the actual rate of black-on-black LGBT crime. Similarly, there is no disaggregation of crimes committed on black LGBTs by category of hate (whether they are victims because of their race or sexuality).

19. Bean, "Queer Monoculture on Parade," 4.

20. Bean, "Queer Monoculture on Parade," 4.

21. Tracy Balm, "Activists Denied Right to March in African-American Parade," *Outlines* 7, no. 3:19, Shilts Papers, Series 3, SFPL.

22. Salim Muwakkil, "Fear of a Gay Planet," *In These Times*, August 23, 1993, 8, acc. no: 4511-001, box 3, folder 1, Religious Right and Blacks and Gays, University of Washington Suzzallo and Allen Libraries, Gay and Lesbian Issues Collection.

23. Gary English, Kim Ford, Nguru Karugu, and Kevin McGruder, "Why We March," *Angel Herald*, 14, no. 1: 3, Reprinted from the September 28–October 4 *Amsterdam News*, GMAD Schomburg, BGLA.

24. Cleo Manago, "Over a Million Men Came," *Alternatives* 4, no. 7 (November/December, n.d., circa 1995): 24–25, Schomburg BGLA.

25. Manago, "Over a Million Men Came." Manago and others addressed the issues of "white" symbols by, for example, establishing the Bawawa symbol. The term *SGL* has been adopted by some black gays to distinguish themselves from white gays.

26. Eric Washington, "Freedom Rings: The Alliance between Blacks and Gays Is Threatened by Mutual Inscrutability," *Village Voice*, June 29, 1993, acc. no. 4511-001, box 5, University of Washington Suzzallo and Allen Libraries, Gay and Lesbian Issues Collection.

27. See, for example, Mark F. Johnson, "D.C. Doings," *SBC* 2, no. 3 (June–July 1993). In his review of the black events, Johnson sardonically notes, "If you looked closely enough, you could almost see the outlines of a CLOSE-KNIT BLACK GAY AND LESBIAN COMMUNITY! Could it be possible." Johnson sarcasm is evidence that black LGBTs hardly spoke with one voice. Similarly in an article in *SBC*, Keith Fabre wrote of the absence of a black gay community. See *SBC* 2, no. 3 (June–July 1993): 17.

28. This essay focuses primarily on the 1993 march with the understanding that by the 2000 Millennium March all the issues and divisions were heightened and exacerbated as the black/gay, queer/normal, and radical/assimilationist divisions deepened.

29. The observations are based on viewing C-Span coverage of the marches. See http://www.c-span.org/video/?40062-1/gay-lesbian-march-washington (accessed March 5, 2013, link no longer active); http://www.c-span.org/video/?156814-1/millennium-march-equality (accessed March 5, 2013, link no longer active); http://www.c-span.org/video/?67630-1/million-man-march (accessed March 5, 2013, link no longer active). C-Span did not publish a tape of the Million Woman March, and national news networks hardly covered the event, a subject that is taken up in Anna Everett, "Double Click: The Million Woman March on Television and Internet" in *Television after TV: Essays on a Medium in Transition*, ed. Lynn Spigel and Jan Olson (Durham, N.C.: Duke University Press, 2004), 224–48.

30. Manago, "Over a Million Men Came," 24.

31. Sheila Alexander-Reid and Straight from L.A., "Marching to the Beat of a Different Drummer," *Women in the Life* 5, no. 9 (November 1997): 10, Schomburg BGLA.

32. "Anti-Gay Gospel Song Sparks Debate," *Outlook Magazine: The Voice of Waterloo Regions Gay and Lesbian Community*, November 1997, 8–9.

33. Jesse Jackson, "What Do Gay Rights Have to Do with Civil Rights?," *Advocate*, February 12, 1991, acc. no. 4511-001, box 3, Gay and Lesbian Politics folder, University of Washington Suzzallo and Allen Libraries, Gay and Lesbian Issues Collections. Jackson spoke at the 1993 march but before C-Span picked up coverage.

34. "Resolution Passed Unanimously by the Board of Directors of the NAACP," *NAACP News*, acc. no. 4511-001, box 3, folder 1, Religious Right and Blacks and Gays, University of Washington Suzzallo and Allen Libraries, Gay and Lesbian Issues Collection.

35. "1993 March on Washington Draws Record Support from Black Leaders," *Bay Area Reporter*, April 1, 1993, Periodical Collection, vol. 23, no. 29, February 25, 1993–July 22, 1993, GLBT Historical Society, Archives and Research Center, San Francisco.

36. See C-Span, http://www.c-span.org/video/?67630-1/million-man-march (accessed March 5, 2013, link no longer active) at the 2:44 mark.

37. See C-Span, http://www.c-span.org/video/?67630-1/million-man-march (accessed March 5, 2013, link no longer active) at the 4:50 mark.

38. Haki R. Madhubuti and Maulana Karenga, eds., *Million Man March/Day of Absence: A Commemorative Anthology, Speeches, Commentary, Photography, Poetry, Illustrations, Documents*, (Chicago: Third World Press, 1996), 32–36, esp. 35.

39. See C-Span coverage of the march: http://www.c-span.org/video/?67630-1/million-man-march (accessed March 5, 2013, link no longer active). Jackson speaks at the 5:00 mark.

40. Eric Washington, "Freedom Rings: The Alliance between Blacks and Gays Is

Threatened by Mutual Inscrutability," *Village Voice*, June 29, 1993, acc. no. 4511-001, box 5, University of Washington Suzzallo and Allen Libraries, Gay and Lesbian Issues Collection.

41. See, for example, Sara Diamond "Racial Reconciliation: New Buzz Word of Christian Right," *Oakland Tribune*, December 11, 1993; "Watch on the Right," *Humanist*, January/February 1994, 34–36; Ralph Z. Hallow, "Christian Coalition to Court Minorities," *Washington Times*, September 10, 1993, all from acc. no. 4511-001, box 3, folder 1 Religious Right and Blacks and Gays, University of Washington Suzzallo and Allen Libraries, Gay and Lesbian Issues Collections.

42. Audre Lorde, "I Am Your Sister: Black Women Organizing across Sexualities," in *Breakthrough* 17, no. 1: 40–44, box 5, Magazines, University of Washington Suzzallo and Allen Libraries, Gay and Lesbian Issues Collection.

About the Contributors

SHARON BLOCK is a professor at the University of California, Irvine. Her published work includes *Rape and Sexual Power in Early America* (University of North Carolina Press, 2006) and the fifth edition of *Major Problems in American Women's History* (Cengage Learning, 2013), which she coedited with Ruth Alexander and Mary Beth Norton. Block was one of the first scholars to bring topic modeling to the humanities in her studies of eighteenth-century newspapers as well as half a million modern historical abstracts. Her essay in the present volume is an outgrowth of *Colonial Complexions: Race and Bodies in Eighteenth-Century America*, forthcoming from the University of Pennsylvania Press.

JENNIFER BRIER directs the Program in Gender and Women's Studies at the University of Illinois at Chicago, where she is also an associate professor of gender and women's studies and history. Her research and teaching are largely focused on exploring the historical intersections of gender, race, and sexuality. Her book, *Infectious Ideas: U.S. Political Response to the AIDS Crisis*, was published by the University of North Carolina Press in 2009. In addition to curating the award-winning exhibition *Out in Chicago* at the Chicago History Museum, she leads History Moves, a public history project that engages audiences in curating untold aspects of urban history.

SUSAN K. CAHN is a professor of history at the University of Buffalo. She earned her BA from the University of California, Santa Cruz, and her PhD from the University of Minnesota. Her books include *Sexual Reckonings: Southern Girls in a Troubling Age*

(Harvard University Press, 2007); *Coming on Strong: Gender and Sexuality in Twentieth-Century Women's Sport* (Free Press, 1994; Harvard University Press, 1995; 2nd edition, University of Illinois Press, 2015); and *Women and Sports in the United States: A Documentary Reader,* coedited with Jean O'Reilly (Northeastern University Press, 2007). She has published articles in *Feminist Studies* and the *Journal of American History*, among other journals.

STEPHANIE M. H. CAMP was the Donald W. Logan Family Endowed Chair in American History at the University of Washington, Seattle. She is the author of *Closer to Freedom: Enslaved Women and Everyday Resistance in the Plantation South*, which was published in 2004 by the University of North Carolina Press as part of its Gender and American Culture series. Upon its publication in 2004, *Closer to Freedom* won the Lillian Smith Book Prize for New Voices in Non-Fiction; it was also awarded an Honorable Mention by the John Hope Franklin Prize and was short-listed for the Washington State Book Award. After completing *Closer to Freedom*, she worked with Edward E. Baptist (Cornell University) on the anthology *New Studies in the History of American Slavery* (University of Georgia Press, 2006).

JULIAN B. CARTER is an associate professor of critical studies at the California College of the Arts. He is a critical historian and performance theorist whose work focuses on normativity, embodiment, and the construction of identity. He is the author of *The Heart of Whiteness: Normal Sexuality and Race in America, 1890–1940* (Duke University Press, 2007). He sits on the editorial board of the new *Trans Studies Quarterly* and the governing board of the international Committee on LGBT History.

ERNESTO CHÁVEZ is an associate professor of history at the University of Texas at El Paso. Chávez's work intersects Chicano/Chicana, Latino/Latina, and borderlands history. In his examinations of the history of the American Southwest, he focuses on the matrix of race, class, and sexuality throughout the ethnic Mexican and Latino American past. In 2002, the University of California Press published his book *Mi Raza Primero! (My People First): Nationalism, Identity, and Insurgency in the Chicano Movement in Los Angeles, 1966–1978*. He recently completed his second book for Bedford/St. Martin's Culture and History series on the U.S.-Mexico War. Chávez's next project is the critical biography of silent-film actor Ramón Novarro tentatively titled "Contra La Corriente (Against the Current): The Life of Ramón Novarro." His work has been published in journals such as the *Journal of the History of Sexuality*.

BRIAN CONNOLLY is an associate professor of history at the University of South Florida. He completed his PhD in history at Rutgers in 2007. He is the author of *Domestic Intimacies: Incest and the Liberal Subject in the Nineteenth-Century United States*.

He is working on a book about the intersection of sovereignty, kinship, and religion in liberal, secular modernity, tentatively titled "Sacred Kin: Sovereignty, Kinship, and Religion in the Nineteenth-Century United States." He is also a founding editor of the journal *History of the Present: A Journal of Critical History*, published by the University of Illinois Press.

JIM DOWNS is an associate professor of history at Connecticut College. He earned his PhD from Columbia University. His books include *Stand by Me: The Forgotten History of Gay Liberation* (Basic Books, 2016), *Sick from Freedom: African-American Illness and Suffering during the Civil War and Reconstruction* (Oxford University Press, 2012), *Why We Write* (Routledge, 2006), and *Taking Back the Academy*, co-edited with Jennifer Manion (Routledge, 2004). He has published articles in the *Chronicle of Higher Education*, the *Huffington Post*, the *New York Times*, and *Time*.

MARISA J. FUENTES is an associate professor of women's and gender studies and history at Rutgers University–New Brunswick. She earned her PhD at the University of California, Berkeley. She is the author of *Dispossessed Lives: Enslaved Women, Violence, and the Archive* (University of Pennsylvania Press, 2016). Her current work explores the status of "refuse slaves" and the disposability of black bodies in early modern Atlantic ports. She serves on the editorial advisory board of the gender and slavery series for the University of Georgia Press.

LEISA D. MEYER is a professor of American studies and history at the College of William and Mary. She works in U.S. and American women's history, gender history, twentieth-century cultural history, and the history of sexuality. She received her PhD in American history from the University of Wisconsin–Madison in 1993. She is the author of *Creating G.I. Jane: Sexuality and Power in the Women's Army Corps during World War II* (Columbia University Press, 1996). Her current project is a book on the history of sexuality in the United States since World War II tentatively titled "Knowing Sex." She is an associate editor of the *Encyclopedia of American Lesbian, Gay, Bisexual, and Transgender History and Culture* (Scribner's, 2003), serves on the editorial advisory board for the *Journal of Women's History*, and is the history and sexuality studies editor for the journal *Feminist Studies*.

JENNIFER L. MORGAN is the author of *Laboring Women: Gender and Reproduction in the Making of New World Slavery* (University of Pennsylvania Press, 2004). Her research examines the intersections of gender and race in colonial America. She is currently working on a project that considers colonial numeracy, racism, and the rise of the transatlantic slave trade in the seventeenth-century English Atlantic, tentatively titled "Accounting for the Women in Slavery." She is a professor of history in the

Department of Social and Cultural Analysis and the Department of History at New York University and lives in New York City.

WANDA S. PILLOW is an associate professor of gender studies and education, culture, and society at the University of Utah. She is the author of *Unfit Subjects: Educational Policy and the Teen Mother* (Routledge, 2004) and the coeditor of *Working the Ruins: Feminist Poststructural Theory and Methods in Education* (Routledge, 2000). She is the author of numerous articles, which have appeared in *Cultural Studies ↔ Critical Methodologies*, *Educational Policy*, and *Power and Education*, among other publications.

MARC STEIN is the Jamie and Phyllis Pasker Professor of History at San Francisco State University. He earned his PhD from the University of Pennsylvania. His books include *Rethinking the Gay and Lesbian Movement* (Routledge, 2012), *Sexual Injustice: Supreme Court Decisions from Griswold to Roe* (University of North Carolina Press, 2010), *City of Sisterly and Brotherly Loves: Lesbian and Gay Philadelphia, 1945–1972* (University of Chicago Press, 2000; 2nd ed. with new preface, Temple University Press, 2004). He is the author of several essays and articles, which have appeared in *Law and History Review* and *Radical History Review*, among other publications.

DEBORAH GRAY WHITE is the Board of Governors Distinguished Professor of History at Rutgers University. She is the editor of *Telling Histories: Black Women Historians in the Ivory Tower* (University of North Carolina Press, 2008) and the author of *Too Heavy a Load: Black Women in Defense of Themselves, 1894–1994* (W.W. Norton, 1999), *Let My People Go: African Americans, 1800–1865* (Oxford University Press, 1999), and *Ar'n't I A Woman? Female Slaves in the Plantation South* (W. W. Norton, 1985; 2nd ed., 1999).

Acknowledgments

As is always the case with collaborative projects, we have incurred many debts bringing this collection into being. We'd like to begin by thanking Dean Richard Foley and Edward Sullivan at New York University for financial and intellectual support for the conference that began this project. Michele Mitchell was a crucial part of the original editorial/organizational team at New York University, and her vision and energy drove the first stage of the volume. Herman L. Bennett's Caribbean Epistemologies Seminar at the Graduate Center of the City University of New York provided financial and intellectual support for the second stage of collaborative meetings. We are deeply grateful to Laurie Matheson at the University of Illinois Press for her commitment to this volume since its early stages. She has been enormously patient and helpful in all stages of conceptualizing and production. Our editor Jennifer Comeau and others at UIP have been most excellent. We would like to thank Daina Ramey Berry and Ann Little for providing substantive and careful readings of the volume.

Jennifer Brier and Jennifer L. Morgan want to especially thank Michele Mitchell for getting this project started and Jim Downs for getting it finished.

Finally, we dedicate this volume to Stephanie M. H. Camp, whose vision and humor and brilliance exemplified the pleasures and importance of the kind of intervention that all the scholars in this volume strive to make. We miss her laughter and her wisdom.

Index

The University of Illinois Press
is a founding member of the
Association of American University Presses.

———————————————————————

University of Illinois Press
1325 South Oak Street
Champaign, IL 61820-6903
www.press.uillinois.edu